Introduction to Computing and Programming in Python
A Multimedia Approach

Mark Guzdial

College of Computing/GVU
Georgia Institute of Technology

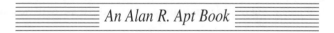

An Alan R. Apt Book

PEARSON
Prentice
Hall

Upper Saddle River, New Jersey 07458

Library of Congress Cataloging-in-Publication Data

CIP data available on file

Vice President and Editorial Director, ECS: *Marcia J. Horton*
Publisher: *Alan R. Apt*
Associate Editor: *Toni Dianne Holm*
Vice President and Director of Production and Manufacturing, ESM: *David W. Riccardi*
Executive Managing Editor: *Vince O'Brien*
Managing Editor: *Camille Trentacoste*
Production Editor: *John Keegan*
Director of Creative Services: *Paul Belfanti*
Art Director: Heather Scott
Managing Editor, AV Management and Production: *Patricia Burns*
Art Editor: *Gregory Dulles*
Director, Image Resource Center: *Melinda Reo*
Manager, Rights and Permissions: *Zina Arabia*
Manager, Visual Research: *Beth Brenzel*
Manager, Cover Visual Research and Permissions: *Karen Sanatar*
Cover Design Director: Jayne Conte
Manufacturing Manager: *Trudy Pisciotti*
Manufacturing Buyer: *Lisa McDowell*
Executive Marketing Manager: *Pamela Hersperger*
Marketing Assistant: *Barrie Reinhold*

© 2005 Pearson Education, Inc.
Pearson Prentice Hall
Pearson Education, Inc.
Upper Saddle River, NJ 07458

Pearson Prentice Hall® is a trademark of Pearson Education, Inc.

Printed in the United States of America

10 9 8 7 6 5 4 3

ISBN 0-13-117655-2

Pearson Education Ltd., *London*
Pearson Education Australia Pty. Ltd., *Sydney*
Pearson Education Singapore, Pte. Ltd.
Pearson Education North Asia Ltd., *Hong Kong*
Pearson Education Canada Inc., *Toronto*
Pearson Educación de Mexico, S.A. de C.V.
Pearson Education—Japan, *Tokyo*
Pearson Education Malaysia, Pte. Ltd.
Pearson Education, Inc., *Upper Saddle River, New Jersey*

Dedicated to my wife,
Barbara Jane Ericson

Preface

Research on computing education clearly demonstrates that one doesn't just "learn to program." One learns to program *something* [5, 20], and the motivation to do that something can make the difference between learning and not learning to program [7]. People want to communicate. We are social creatures, and the desire to communicate is one of our primal motivations. Increasingly, the computer is used as a tool for communication even more than as a tool for calculation. Virtually all published text, images, sounds, music, and movies today are prepared using computing technology.

This book is about teaching people to program in order to communicate. The book focuses on how to manipulate images, sounds, text, and movies as professionals might, but with programs written by the students. There are no illusions here. Most people will use professional-grade applications to perform these manipulations, but knowing *how* to do it with your own programs means that you *can* do it if you need to. Want to say something with your media, but you don't know how to make PhotoShop or Final Cut Pro do what you want? Knowing how to program means that you have power of expression that is not limited by the application software.

It may also be true that knowing how the algorithms in a media applications work allows you to use them better, or to move from one application to the next more easily. If your focus in an application is on what menu item does what, every application is different. But if your focus is on moving or coloring the pixels in the way you want, then maybe it's easier to get past the menu items and focus on what you want to say.

This book is not just about programming in media. Media-manipulation programs can be hard to write or may behave in unexpected ways. Natural questions arise, like "Why is the same image filter faster in Photoshop?" and "That was hard to debug—are there ways of writing programs that are *easier* to debug?" Answering questions like these is what computer scientists do. There are several chapters at the end of the book that are about *computing*, not just programming, and more generally than just media.

The computer is the most amazingly creative device that humans have ever conceived. It is completely made up of mind-stuff. The notion "Don't just dream it, be it" is really possible on a computer. If you can imagine it, you can make it "real" on the computer. Playing with programming can be and *should* be enormous fun.

To Teachers

The curricular content of this book meets the "imperative-first" approach described in the ACM/IEEE *Computing Curriculum 2001* standards document [4]. The book starts with a focus on fundamental programming constructs: assignments, sequential operations, iteration, conditionals, and defining functions. Abstractions (e.g., algorithmic complexity, program efficiency, computer organization, hierarchical decomposition, recursion, and object-oriented programming) are emphasized later, after the students have a context for understanding them.

This unusual ordering is based on the findings of research in the learning sciences. Memory is associative—we remember things based on what else we relate to them. People can learn concepts and skills on the premise that they will be useful some day, but the concepts and skills will be related only to the premises, not to everyday life. The result has been described as "brittle knowledge" [8]—the kind of knowledge that gets you through the exam, but is promptly forgotten because it doesn't relate to anything but being in that class. If we want students to gain *transferable* knowledge (knowledge that can be applied in new situations), we have to help them to relate the knowledge to more general problems, so that the memories get indexed in ways that associate with those kinds of problems [24]. Thus, we teach with concrete experiences that students can explore and relate to (e.g., iteration for removing red-eye in pictures), and later lay abstractions on top of them (e.g., achieving the same goal using recursion or functional filters and maps).

We know that starting from the abstractions doesn't really work for students. Ann Fleury has shown that novice students just don't buy what we tell them about encapsulation and reuse (e.g., [12]). Students prefer simpler code that they can trace easily, and they actually think that such code is *better*. It takes time and experience for students to realize that there is value in well-designed systems, because without experience, it's very difficult for students to learn the abstractions.

The ***media computation*** approach used in this book starts from what people use computers for: image manipulation, exploring digital music, viewing and creating Web pages, and so on. We then explain programming and computing in terms of these activities. We want students to visit Amazon (for example) and think, "Here's a catalog Web site—and I know that these are implemented with a database and a set of programs that format the database entries as Web pages." Starting from a relevant context makes transfer of knowledge and skills more likely, but it also helps with retention.

The media computation approach spends about two-thirds of the time on giving students experiences with a variety of media in contexts that they find motivating. After that two-thirds, though, they start to develop questions. "Why is that Photoshop is faster than my program?" and "Movie code is slow—how slow do programs get?" are typical. At that point, we introduce the abstractions and the valuable insights from computer science that answer *their* questions. That's what the last part of this book is about.

A different body of research in computing education explores why withdrawal or failure rates in introductory computing are so high. One common theme is that computing courses seem "irrelevant" and unnecessarily focus on "tedious details" such as efficiency [29, 1]. A communications context is perceived as relevant by students (as they tell us in surveys and interviews [14, 25]).

The relevant context is part of the explanation for the success we have had with retention in the Georgia Tech course for which this book was written.

The late entrance of abstraction isn't the only unusual ordering in this approach. We start using arrays and matrices in Chapter 3, in our first significant programs. Typically, introductory computing courses push arrays off until later, because they are obviously more complicated than variables with simple values. But a relevant context is very powerful [20]. The matrices of pixels in images occur in the students' everyday life—a magnifying glass on a computer monitor or television makes that clear.

The rate of students withdrawing from introductory computing courses or receiving a D or F grade (commonly called the *WDF rate*) is reportedly nationally in the 30–50% range, or even higher. At Georgia Tech, from 2000 to 2002, we had an average WDF rate of 28% in the introductory course required for all majors. We use this text in our course *Introduction to Media Computation*. Our first pilot offering of the course had 121 students, no computing or engineering majors, and two-thirds of the students were female. Our WDF rate was 11.5%. Spring 2004 was the first semester taught by instructors other than the author, and the WDF rate dropped to 9.5% for the 395 students who enrolled. Charles Fowler at Gainesville College in Georgia has been having similar results in his courses there.

Ways to Use This Book

This book represents what we teach at Georgia Tech in pretty much the ordering that we use. Individual teachers may skip some sections (e.g., the section on additive synthesis, MIDI, and MP3), but all of the content here has been tested with our students.

However, we can imagine using this material in many other ways.

■ A short introduction to computing could be taught with just Chapters 2 (introduction to programming) and 3 (introduction to image processing), perhaps with some material from Chapters 4 and 5. We have taught even single-day workshops on media computation using just this material.

■ Chapters 6 through 8 basically replicate the computer science concepts from Chapters 3 through 5, but in the context of sounds rather than images. We find the replication useful—some students seem to relate better to the concepts of iteration and conditionals when working with one medium than with the other. Further, it gives us the opportunity to point out that the same *algorithm* can have similar effects in different media (e.g., scaling a picture up or down and shifting a sound higher or lower in pitch are the same algorithm). But it could certainly be skipped to save time.

■ Chapter 12 (on movies) introduces no new programming or computing concepts. While motivational, movie processing could be skipped to save time.

■ We recommend getting to at least some of the chapters in the last unit, in order to lead students into thinking about computing and programming in a more abstract manner, but clearly not *all* of the chapters have to be covered.

Python and Jython

The programming language used in this book is Python. Python has been described as "executable pseudo-code." We have found that Python is learnable and usable by non-CS majors (and presumably, by computer science majors as well), and since it's actually used for communications tasks (e.g., Web site development), it's a relevant language for an introductory computing course. For example, job advertisements posted to the Python Web site (http://www.python.org) show that companies like Google and Industrial Light & Magic hire Python programmers.

The specific dialect of Python used in this book is *Jython* (http://www.jython.org). Jython *is* Python. The differences between Python (normally implemented in C) and Jython (which is implemented in Java) are akin to the differences between any two language implementations (e.g., Microsoft vs. GNU C++ implementations)–the basic language is *exactly* the same, with some library and details differences that most students will never notice.

Typographical Notations

Examples of Python code look like this: x = x + 1. Longer examples look like this:

```
def helloWorld():
   print "Hello, world!"
```

When showing something that the user types in with Python's response, it will have a similar font and style, but the user's typing will appear after a Python prompt (>>>):

```
>>> print 3 + 4
7
```

User interface components of JES (Jython Environment for Students) will be specified using a small-caps font, like SAVE menu item and the LOAD button.

There are several special kinds of sidebars that you'll find in the book.

RECIPE 1: An Example Recipe

Recipes (programs) appear like this:

```
def helloWorld():
   print "Hello, world!"
```

COMPUTER SCIENCE IDEA: An Example Idea

Key computer science concepts appear like this.

COMMON BUG: An Example Common Bug

Common things that can cause your recipe to fail appear like this.

DEBUGGING TIP: An Example Debugging Tip

If there's a good way to keep a bug from creeping into your recipes in the first place, it's highlighted here.

MAKING IT WORK TIP: An Example How to Make It Work

Best practices or techniques that really help are highlighted like this.

ACKNOWLEDGMENTS

My sincere thanks go out to the following:

■ Jason Ergle, Claire Bailey, David Raines, and Joshua Sklare, who made JES a reality with amazing quality in an amazingly short amount of time. Jason and David took JES the next steps, improving installation, debugging, and process support. Adam Wilson and Toby Ho added the wonderful support for identifying blocks, MIDI music, and a debugger. Eric Mickley improved the error messages significantly. Keith McDermott gave us MovieMaker and worked on the picture support. Adam has been the caretaker of the project and brought it to the point it is at today.

■ Adam Wilson built the MediaTools that are so useful for exploring sounds and images and processing video.

■ Andrea Forte, Mark Richman, Matt Wallace, Alisa Bandlow, Derek Chambless, Larry Olson, and David Rennie helped build course materials. Derek, Mark, and Matt created many example programs. Barbara Ericson reviewed the book as we worked on the Java version together, and made numerous suggestions and improvements.

■ There were several people who really made the effort come together at Georgia Tech. Bob McMath, Vice-Provost at Georgia Tech, and Jim Foley, Associate Dean for Education in the College of Computing, invested in this effort early on. Kurt Eiselt worked hard to make this effort real, convincing others to take it seriously. Janet Kolodner and Aaron Bobick were excited and encouraging about the idea of media computation for students new to computer science. Jeff Pierce reviewed and advised us on the design of the media functions used in the book. Aaron Lanterman gave me lots of advice on how to convey the digital material content accurately. Joan Morton, Chrissy Hendricks, David White, and all the staff of the GVU Center made sure that we had what we needed and that the details were handled to make this effort come together. Amy Bruckman and Eugene Guzdial bought me time to get the final version completed.

■ Charles Fowler was the first person outside of Georgia Tech willing to take the gamble and trial the course in his own institution (Gainesville College), for which we're very grateful.

■ The pilot course offered in Spring 2003 at Georgia Tech was very important in helping us improve the course. Andrea Forte, Rachel Fithian, and Lauren Rich did the assessment of the pilot offering of the course, which was incredibly valuable in helping us understand what worked and what didn't. The first teaching assistants (Jim Gruen, Angela Liang, Larry Olson, Matt Wallace, Adam Wilson, and Jose Zagal) did a lot to help create this approach. Blair MacIntyre, Colin Potts, and Monica Sweat helped make the materials easier for others to adopt. Jochen Rick made the CoWeb/Swiki a great place for CS1315 students to hang out.

■ Many students pointed out errors and made suggestions to improve the book. Thanks to Catherine Billiris, Jennifer Blake, Karin Bowman, Maryam Doroudi, Suzannah Gill, Baillie Homire, Jonathan Laing, Mireille Murad, Michael Shaw, Summar Shoaib, and especially Jonathan Longhitano, who has a real flair for copy-editing.

■ Most of the clip art is used with permission from the *Art Explosion* package by Nova Development.

■ Thanks to former *Media Computation* students Constantino Kombosch, Joseph Clark, and Shannon Joiner for permission to use their snapshots from class in examples.

■ The research work that led to this text was supported by grants from the National Science Foundation—from the Division of Undergraduate Education, CCLI program, and from the CISE Educational Innovations program. Thank you for the support.

■ Thanks to my publisher, Alan R. Apt, for his support and faith in the unusual curricula we have been developing at Georgia Tech, and to my production editor John Keegan.

■ Finally but most important, Barbara Ericson, and Matthew, Katherine, and Jennifer Guzdial, who allowed themselves to be photographed and recorded for Daddy's media project, and were supportive and excited about the class.

MARK GUZDIAL
Georgia Institute of Technology

Contents

APPENDICES

List of Figures

PART 1

INTRODUCTION

CHAPTER 1

Introduction to Computer Science and Media Computation

Chapter Learning Objectives

■ To explain what computer science is about and what computer scientists are concerned with.

■ To explain why we digitize media.

■ To explain why it's valuable to study computing.

■ To use the concept of an *encoding*.

■ To explain the basic components of a computer.

■ 1.1 What Is Computer Science About?

Computer science is the study of *process*: how we do things, how we specify what we do, how we specify what the stuff is that we're processing. But that's a pretty dry definition. Let's try a metaphorical one.

 COMPUTER SCIENCE IDEA: Computer science is the study of recipes

They're a special kind of recipe—one that can be executed by a computational device, but this point is only of importance to computer scientists. The important point overall is that a computer science recipe defines *exactly* what has to be done.

If you're a biologist who wants to describe how migration works or how DNA replicates, or if you're a chemist who wants to explain how an equilibrium is reached in a reaction, or if you're a factory manager who wants to define a machine-and-belt layout and even test how it works before physically moving

3

heavy things into position, then being able to write a recipe that specifies *exactly* what happens, in terms that can be completely defined and understood, is *very* useful. This exactness is part of why computers have radically changed so much of how science is done and understood.

It may sound funny to call *programs* or *algorithms* a recipe, but the analogy goes a long way. Much of what computer scientists study can be defined in terms of recipes.

■ Some computer scientists study how recipes are written: Are there better or worse ways of doing something? If you've ever had to separate whites from yolks in eggs, you know that knowing the right way to do it makes a world of difference. Computer science theoreticians worry about the fastest and shortest recipes, and the ones that take up the least amount of space (you can think about it as counter space—the analogy works). *How* a recipe works, completely apart from how it's written, is called the study of **algorithms**. Software engineers worry about how large groups can put together recipes that still work. (The recipes for some programs, like the one that keeps track of Visa/MasterCard records, have literally millions of steps!)

■ Other computer scientists study the units used in recipes. Does it matter whether a recipe uses metric or English measurements? The recipe may work in either case, but if you don't know what a pound or a cup is, the recipe is a lot less understandable to you. There are also units that make sense for some tasks and not others, but if you can fit the units to the tasks, you can explain yourself more easily and get things done faster—and avoid errors. Ever wonder why ships at sea measure their speed in *knots*? Why not use something like meters per second? Sometimes, in certain special situations—on a ship at sea, for instance—the more common terms aren't appropriate or don't work as well. The study of computer science units is referred to as **data structures**. Computer scientists who study ways of keeping track of lots of data in lots of different kinds of units are studying **databases**.

■ Can recipes be written for anything? Are there some recipes that *can't* be written? Computer scientists know that there are recipes that can't be written. For example, you can't write a recipe that can absolutely tell whether some other recipe will actually work. How about *intelligence*? Can we write a recipe such that a computer following it would actually be *thinking* (and how would you tell if you got it right)? Computer scientists in **theory**, **intelligent systems**, **artificial intelligence**, and **systems** worry about things like this.

■ There are even computer scientists who worry about whether people like what the recipes produce, like restaurant critics for a newspaper. Some of these are **human–computer interface** specialists who worry about whether people like how the recipes work ("recipes" that produce an *interface* that people use, like windows, buttons, scrollbars, and other elements of what we think about as a running program).

■ Just as some chefs specialize in certain kinds of recipes, like crepes or barbecue, computer scientists also specialize in special kinds of recipes. Computer scientists who work in *graphics* are mostly concerned with recipes that produce pictures, animations, and even movies. Computer scientists who work in *computer music* are mostly concerned with recipes that produce sounds (often melodic ones, but not always).

■ Still other computer scientists study the *emergent properties* of recipes. Think about the World Wide Web. It's really a collection of *millions* of recipes (programs) talking to one another. Why would one section of the Web get slower at some point? It's a phenomenon that emerges from these millions of programs, certainly not something that was planned. That's something that **networking** computer scientists study. What's really amazing is that these emergent properties (that things just start to happen when you have many, many recipes interacting at once) can also be used to explain non-computational things. For example, how ants forage for food or how termites make mounds can also be described as something that just happens when you have lots of little programs doing something simple and interacting.

The recipe metaphor also works on another level. Everyone knows that some things in a recipe can be changed without changing the result dramatically. You can always increase all the units by a multiplier (say, double) to make more. You can always add more garlic or oregano to the spaghetti sauce. But there are some things that you cannot change in a recipe. If the recipe calls for baking powder, you may not substitute baking soda. If you're supposed to boil the dumplings and then sauté them, the reverse order will probably not work well (Figure 1.1).

The same holds for software recipes. There are usually things you can easily change: the actual names of things (though you should change names consistently), some of the **constants** (numbers that appear as plain old numbers,

CHICKEN CACCIATORE

3 whole, boned chicken breasts
1 medium onion, chopped
1 tbsp chopped garlic
2 tbsp and later ¼ c olive oil
1 ½ c flour
¼ c Lawry's seasoning salt
1 bell pepper, chopped (optional)
  any color

1(28 oz) can chopped tomatoes
1(15 oz) can tomato sauce
1(6.5 oz) can mushrooms
1(6 oz) can tomato paste
½ of (26 oz) jar of spaghetti
  sauce*
3 tbsp Italian seasoning
1 tsp garlic powder (optional)

FIGURE 1.1: A cooking recipe—you can always double the ingredients, but throwing in an extra cup of flour won't cut it, and don't try to brown the chicken *after* adding the tomato sauce!.

Cut up the chicken into pieces about 1 inch square. Saute the onion and garlic until the onion is translucent. Mix the flour and Lawry's salt. You want about 1:4–1:5 ratio of seasoning salt to flour and enough of the whole mixture to coat the chicken. Put the cut up chicken and seasoned flour in a bag, and shake to coat. Add the coated chicken to the onion and garlic. Stir frequently until browned. You'll need to add oil to keep from sticking and burning; I sometimes add up to ¼ cup of olive oil. Add the tomatoes, sauce, mushrooms, and paste. (And the optional peppers, too.) Stir well. Add the Italian seasoning. I like garlic, so I usually add the garlic powder, too. Stir well. Because of all the flour, the sauce can get too thick. I usually cut it with the spaghetti sauce, up to ½ jar. Simmer 20–30 minutes.

not as variables), and maybe even some of the data *ranges* (sections of the data) being manipulated. But the order of the commands to the computer, however, almost always has to stay exactly as stated. As we go on, you'll learn what can be changed safely, and what can't.

Computer scientists specify their recipes with ***programming languages*** (Figure 1.2). Different programming languages are used for different purposes. Some of them are wildly popular, like Java and C++. Others are more obscure, like Squeak and T. Others are designed to make computer science ideas very easy to learn, like Scheme or Python, but the fact that they're easy to learn doesn't always make them very popular or the best choice for experts building larger or more complicated recipes. It's a hard balance in teaching computer science to pick a language that is easy to learn *and* is popular and useful enough that students are motivated to learn it.

Why don't computer scientists just use natural human languages, like English or Spanish? The problem is that natural languages evolved the way they did to enhance communications between very smart beings, humans. As we'll explain

Python/Jython

```
def hello():
  print "Hello World"
```

Java

```
class HelloWorld {
  static public void main( String args[] ) {
    System.out.println( "Hello World!" );
  }
}
```

C++

```
#include <iostream.h>

main() {
    cout << "Hello World!" << endl;
    return 0;
}
```

Scheme

```
(define helloworld
        (lambda ()
                (display "Hello World")
                (newline)))
```

FIGURE 1.2: Comparing programming languages: A common simple programming task is to print the words "Hello, World!" to the screen.

more in the next section, computers are exceptionally dumb. They need a level of specificity that natural language isn't good at. Further, what we say to one another in natural communication is not exactly what you're saying in a computational recipe. When was the last time you told someone how a videogame like Doom or Quake or Super Mario Brothers worked in such minute detail that they could actually replicate the game (say, on paper)? English isn't good for that kind of task.

There are so many different kinds of programming languages because there are so many different kinds of recipes to write. Programs written in the programming language *C* tend to be very fast and efficient, but they also tend to be hard to read, hard to write, and require units that are more about computers than about bird migrations or DNA or whatever else you want to write your recipe about. The programming language *Lisp* (and related languages like Scheme, T, and Common Lisp) is very flexible and is well suited to exploring how to write recipes that have never been written before, but Lisp *looks* so strange compared to languages like C that many people avoid it, and there are (as a natural consequence) few who know it. If you want to hire a hundred programmers to work on your project, it will be easier to find a hundred programmers who know a popular language than a less popular one—but that doesn't mean that the popular language is the best one for your task!

The programming language that we're using in this book is ***Python*** (`http://www.python.org` for more information on it). Python is a fairly popular programming language, used very often for Web and media programming. The Web search engine *Google* uses Python. The media company *Industrial Light & Magic* also uses Python. A list of companies using Python is available at `http://www.python.org/psa/Users.html`. Python is easy to learn, easy to read, very flexible, but not very efficient. The same algorithm coded in C and in Python will probably be faster in C.

The version of Python used in this book is called ***Jython*** (`http://www.jython.org`). Python is normally implemented in the programming language C. Jython is Python implemented in *Java*—this means that Jython is actually a program written in Java. Jython lets us do multimedia that will work across multiple computer platforms. Jython is a real programming language that can be used for serious work. You can download a version of Jython for your computer from the Jython Web site that will work for all kinds of purposes. We will be using Jython in this book through a special programming *environment* called ***JES*** (*Jython Environment for Students*) that has been developed to make it easier to program in Jython. But anything you can do in JES, you can also do in normal Jython—and most programs that you write in Jython will also work in Python.

Here is an explanation of some of the important terms that we'll be using in this book:

■ A ***program*** is a description in a programming language of a process that achieves some result that is useful to someone. A program can be small (like one that implements a calculator) or huge (like one your bank uses to track all of its accounts).

■ An ***algorithm*** (in contrast) is a description of a process apart from any programming language. The same algorithm may be implemented in many different languages in many different ways in many different programs—but they would all be the same ***process*** if we're talking about the same algorithm.

The term ***recipe***, as used in this book, describes programs or portions of programs that achieve some useful media-related task. A recipe may be just part of a program that's truly useful. We're going to use the term recipe to emphasize the *pieces of a program that achieve a useful **media-related** task*.

■ 1.2 What Computers Understand

Computational recipes are written to run on computers. What does a computer know how to do? What can we tell the computer to do in the recipe? The answer is "Very, very little." Computers are exceedingly stupid. They really only know about numbers.

Actually, even to say that computers *know* numbers is a myth, or more appropriately, an ***encoding***. Computers are electronic devices that react to voltages on wires. We group these wires into sets (eight of these wires are called a ***byte***, and one of them is called a ***bit***). If a wire has a voltage on it, we say that it encodes a 1. If it has no voltage on it, we say that it encodes a 0. So, from a set of eight wires (a byte), we interpret a pattern of eight 0's and 1's, e.g., 01001010. Using the ***binary*** number system, we can interpret this byte as a ***number*** (Figure 1.3). That's where we come up with the claim that a computer knows about numbers.[1]

A computer has a ***memory*** filled with bytes. Everything that a computer is working with at a given instant is stored in its memory. This means that everything a computer is working with is *encoded* in its bytes: JPEG pictures, Excel spreadsheets, Word documents, annoying Web pop-up ads, and the latest spam e-mail.

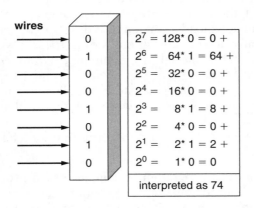

wires

0	$2^7 = 128^* \, 0 = 0 +$
1	$2^6 = 64^* \, 1 = 64 +$
0	$2^5 = 32^* \, 0 = 0 +$
0	$2^4 = 16^* \, 0 = 0 +$
1	$2^3 = 8^* \, 1 = 8 +$
0	$2^2 = 4^* \, 0 = 0 +$
1	$2^1 = 2^* \, 1 = 2 +$
0	$2^0 = 1^* \, 0 = 0$
	interpreted as 74

FIGURE 1.3: Eight wires with a pattern of voltages is a byte, which is interpreted as a pattern of eight 0's and 1's, which is interpreted as a decimal number.

---

[1] We'll talk more about this level of the computer in Chapter 13

A computer can do lots of things with numbers. It can add them, subtract them, multiply them, divide them, sort them, collect them, duplicate them, filter them (e.g., "Make a copy of these numbers, but only the even ones"), and compare them and do things based on the comparison. For example, a computer can be told in a recipe, "Compare these two numbers. If the first one is less than the second one, jump to step 5 in this recipe. Otherwise, continue on to the next step."

So far, the computer is an incredible calculator, and that's certainly why it was invented. The first use of the computer was during World War II for calculating trajectories of projectiles ("If the wind is coming from the SE at 15 MPH, and you want to hit a target 0.5 miles away at an angle of 30 degrees East of North, then incline your launcher to ..."). The computer is an amazing calculator. But what makes it useful for general recipes is the concept of *encodings*.

 COMPUTER SCIENCE IDEA: Computers can layer encodings

Computers can layer encodings to virtually any level of complexity. Numbers can be interpreted as characters, which can be interpreted in sets as Web pages, which can be interpreted to appear as multiple fonts and styles. But at the bottommost level, the computer *only* "knows" voltages, which we interpret as numbers.

If one of these bytes is interpreted as the number 65, it could simply be the number 65. Or it could be the letter *A* using a standard encoding of numbers to letters called the *American Standard Code for Information Interchange* (*ASCII*). If the 65 appears in a collection of other numbers that we're interpreting as text, and it's in a file that ends in ".html" it might be part of something that looks like this `<a href=`..., which a Web browser will interpret as the definition of a link. Down at the level of the computer, that *A* is just a pattern of voltages. Many layers of recipes up, at the level of a Web browser, it defines something that you can click on to get more information.

If the computer understands only numbers (and that's a stretch already), how does it manipulate these encodings? Sure, it knows how to compare numbers, but how does that extend to being able to alphabetize a class list? Typically, each layer of encoding is implemented as a piece or layer of software. There's software that understands how to manipulate characters. The character software knows how to do things like compare names because it has encoded that *a* comes before *b* and so on, and that the numeric comparison of the order of numbers in the encoding of the letters leads to alphabetical comparisons. The character software is used by other software that manipulates text in files. That's the layer that something like Microsoft Word or Notepad or TextEdit would use. Still another piece of software knows how to interpret *HTML* (the language of the Web), and another layer of the same software knows how to take HTML and display the right text, fonts, styles, and colors.

We can similarly create layers of encodings in the computer for our specific tasks. We can teach a computer that cells contain mitochondria and DNA, and that DNA has four kinds of nucleotides, and that factories have these kinds of presses and these kinds of stamps. Creating layers of encoding and interpretation so that the computer is working with the right units (recall back to our recipe analogy) for a given problem is the task of ***data representation*** or defining the right ***data structures***.

If this sounds like a lot of software, it is. When software is layered this way, it slows the computer down some. But the amazing thing about computers is that they're *amazingly* fast—and getting faster all the time!

 COMPUTER SCIENCE IDEA: Moore's Law

Gordon Moore, one of the founders of Intel (maker of computer processing chips for computers running Windows operating systems), claimed that the number of transistors (a key component of computers) would double at the same price every 18 months, effectively meaning that the same amount of money would buy twice as much computing power every 18 months. This means that in a year and a half, computers get as fast once again as they did in the whole time since World War II. This law has continued to hold true for decades.

Computers today can execute literally *billions* of recipe steps per second. They can hold in memory literally encyclopedias of data! They never get tired or bored. Search a million customers for an individual card holder? No problem! Find the right set of numbers to get the best value out of an equation? Piece of cake!

Process millions of picture elements or sound fragments or movie frames? That's ***media computation***.

■ 1.3 Media Computation: Why Digitize Media?

Let's consider an encoding that would be appropriate for pictures. Imagine that pictures are made up of little dots. That's not hard to imagine: Look really closely at your monitor or at a TV screen and you will see that your images are *already* made up of little dots. Each of these dots is a distinct color. You know from physics that colors can be described as the sum of *red*, *green*, and *blue*. Add the red and green to get yellow. Mix all three together to get white. Turn them all off, and you get a black dot.

What if we encoded each dot in a picture as collection of three bytes, one each for the amount of red, green, and blue at that dot on the screen? And we collect a bunch of these three-byte sets to determine all the dots of a given picture? That's a pretty reasonable way of representing pictures, and it's essentially how we're going to do it in Chapter 3.

Manipulating these dots (each referred to as a ***pixel*** or *picture element*) can take a lot of processing. There are thousands or even millions of them in a picture that you might want to work with on your computer or on the Web. But the computer doesn't get bored, and it's mighty fast.

The encoding that we will be using for sound involves 44,100 two-byte sets (called a sample) for each *second* of time. A three-minute song requires 158,760,000 bytes (twice that for stereo). Doing any processing on this takes a *lot* of operations. But at a billion operations per second, you can do lots of operations to every one of those bytes in just a few moments.

Creating encodings of this kind for media requires a change to the media. Look at the real world: It isn't made up of lots of little dots that you can see. Listen to a sound: Do you hear thousands of little bits of sound per second? The fact that you *can't* hear little bits of sound per second is what makes it possible to create these encodings. Our eyes and ears are limited: We can only perceive so much, and only things that are just so small. If you break up an image into small enough dots, your eyes can't tell that it's not a continuous flow of color. If you break up a sound into small enough pieces, your ears can't tell that the sound isn't a continuous flow of auditory energy.

The process of encoding media into little bits is called ***digitization***, sometimes referred to as "*going digital.*" *Digital* means (according to the *American Heritage Dictionary*), "Of, relating to, or resembling a digit, especially a finger." Making things digital is about turning things from continuous and uncountable, to something that we can count, as if with our fingers.

Digital media, done well, feel the same to our limited human sensory apparatus as the original. Phonograph recordings (ever seen one?) capture sound continuously, as an ***analogue*** signal. Photographs capture light as a continuous flow. Some people say that they can hear a difference between phonograph recordings and CD recordings, but to my ear and most measurements, a CD (which *is* digitized sound) sounds just the same—maybe clearer. Digital cameras at high-enough resolutions produce photograph-quality pictures.

Why would you want to digitize media? Because then the media will be easier to manipulate, to replicate exactly, to compress, and to transmit. For example, it's hard to manipulate images that are in photographs, but it's very easy when the same images are digitized. This book is about using the increasingly digital world of media and manipulating it—and learning computation in the process.

Moore's Law has made media computation feasible as an introductory topic. Media computation relies on the computer doing lots and lots of operations on lots of bytes. Modern computers can do this easily. Even with slow (but easy to understand) languages, even with inefficient (but easy to read and write) recipes, we can learn about computation by manipulating media.

■ 1.4 Computer Science for Everyone

But why should you? Why should anyone who doesn't want to be a computer scientist learn about computer science? Why should you be interested in learning about computation by manipulating media?

Most professionals today manipulate media: papers, videos, tape recordings, photographs, drawings. Increasingly, this manipulation is done with a computer. Media are very often in a digitized form today.

We use software to manipulate these media. We use Adobe Photoshop for manipulating our images, and Macromedia SoundEdit to manipulate our sounds, and perhaps Microsoft PowerPoint for assembling our media into slideshows. We use Microsoft Word for manipulating our text, and Netscape Navigator or Microsoft Internet Explorer for browsing media on the Internet.

So why should anyone who does *not* want to be a computer scientist study computer science? Why should you learn to program? Isn't it enough to learn to *use* all this great software? The following sections provide answers to these questions.

1.4.1 It's About Communication

Digital media are manipulated with software. *If you can only manipulate media with software that **someone else** made for you, you are limiting your ability to communicate.* What if you want to say something that can't be said in software from Adobe, Microsoft, Apple, and the rest, or you want to say it in a way they don't support? If you know how to program, even if it would take you *longer* to do it yourself, you have the freedom to manipulate the media your way.

What about learning these tools in the first place? In my years in computers, I've seen many types of software come and go as *the* package for drawing, painting, word-processing, video editing, and so on. You can't learn just a single tool and expect to be able to use it for your entire career. If you know *how* the tools work, you have a core understanding that can transfer from tool to tool. You can think about your media work in terms of the *algorithms*, not the *tools*.

Finally, if you're going to prepare media for the Web, for marketing, for print, for broadcast, for any use whatsoever, it's worthwhile for you to have a sense of what's possible, what can be done with media. It's even more important as a consumer of media that you know how the media can be manipulated, to know what's true and what could be just a trick. If you know the basics of media computation, you have an understanding that goes beyond what any individual tool provides.

1.4.2 It's About Process

In 1961, Alan Perlis gave a talk at MIT in which he argued that computer science, and programming explicitly, should be part of a liberal education [16]. Perlis is an important figure in the field of computer science. The highest award that a computer scientist can be honored with is the ACM Turing Award. Perlis was the first recipient of that award. He's an important figure in software engineering, and he started several of the first computer science departments in the United States.

Perlis's argument can be made in comparison with calculus. Calculus is generally considered part of a liberal education: Not *everyone* takes calculus, but if you want to be well educated, you will typically take at least a term of calculus. Calculus is the study of *rates*, which is important in many fields. Computer science, as stated earlier in this chapter, is the study of ***process***. Process is important to nearly every field, from business to science to medicine to law. Knowing process formally is important for everyone.

Problems

1.1 *Every* profession uses computers today. Use a Web browser and a search engine like Google to find sites that relate your field of study with computer science or computing or computation. For example, search for "biology computer science" or "management computing."

1.2 Find an ASCII table on the Web: a table listing every character and its corresponding numeric representation. Write down the sequence of numbers whose ASCII values make up your name.

1.3 Find a Unicode table on the Web. What's the difference between ASCII and Unicode?

1.4 Consider the representation for pictures described in Section 1.3, where each dot (pixel) in the picture is represented by three bytes, for the red, green, and blue components of the color at that dot. How many bytes does it take to represent a 640 by 480 picture, a common picture size on the Web? How many bytes does it take to represent a 1024 by 768 picture, a common screen size? (What do you think is meant now by a "three megapixel" camera?)

1.5 How many different numbers can be represented by one byte? In other words, eight bits can represent from zero to what number? What if you have two bytes? Four bytes?

*1.6 How can you represent a *floating point number* in terms of bytes? Do a search on the Web for "floating point" and see what you find.

1.7 Look up Alan Kay and the *Dynabook* on the Web. Who is he, and what does he have to do with media computation?

1.8 Look up Alan Turing on the Web. Who was he, and what does he have to do with our notion of what a computer can do and how encodings work?

1.9 Look up Kurt Goedel on the Web. Who was he, and what amazing things did he do with encodings?

To Dig Deeper

James Gleick's book *Chaos* describes more on emergent properties—how small changes can lead to dramatic effects, and the unintended impacts of designs because of difficult-to-foresee interactions.

Mitchel Resnick's book *Turtles, Termites, and Traffic Jams: Explorations in Massively Parallel Microworlds* [31] describes how ants, termites, and even traffic jams and slime molds can be described pretty accurately with hundreds or thousands of very small processes (programs) running and interacting all at once.

Exploring the Digital Domain [3] is a wonderful introductory book on computation with lots of good information about digital media.

CHAPTER 2

Introduction to Programming

2.1	Programming Is About Naming
2.2	Programming in Python
2.3	Programming in JES
2.4	Media Computation in JES
2.5	Making a Program

Chapter Learning Objectives

The media learning goals for this chapter are:

- ■ *To make and show pictures.*
- ■ *To make and play sounds.*

The computer science goals for this chapter are:

- ■ *To use JES to enter and execute programs.*
- ■ *To create and use variables to store values and objects, such as pictures and sounds.*
- ■ *To create functions.*
- ■ *To recognize different types (encodings) of data, such as integers, floating point numbers, and media objects.*
- ■ *To sequence operations in a function.*

■ 2.1 Programming Is About Naming

COMPUTER SCIENCE IDEA: Much of programming is about naming

A computer can associate names, or *symbols*, with just about anything: with a specific byte; with a collection of bytes making up a numeric variable or a bunch of letters; with a media element like a file, sound, or picture; or even with more abstract concepts, like a named recipe (a *program*) or a named encoding (a *type*). A computer scientist sees a choice of names as being high-quality in the same way that a philosopher or mathematician might: if the naming scheme (the names and what they name) should be elegant, parsimonious, and usable.

Obviously, the computer itself doesn't *care* about names. Names are for humans. If the computer were just a calculator, then remembering words and their association with values would be just a waste of the computer's memory. But for humans, this is *very* powerful. It allows us to work with the computer in a natural way, even a way that extends how we think about recipes (processes) altogether.

A ***programming language*** is really a set of names that a computer has encodings for, such that the names make the computer do expected actions and interpret our data in expected ways. Some of the programming language's names allow us to define *new* namings that allow us to create our own layers of encoding. Assigning a variable to a value is one way of defining a name for the computer. Defining a function is giving a name to a recipe.

A ***program*** is a set of names and their values, where some of these names have values of instructions to the computer ("*code*"). Our instructions will be in the Python programming language. Combining these two definitions means that the Python programming language gives us a set of useful names that have a meaning to the computer, and that our programs are then made up of Python's useful names as a way of specifying what we want the computer to do.

COMPUTER SCIENCE IDEA: Programs are for people, not computers

Remember that names are only meaningful for people, not for computers. Computers just take instructions. A good program is meaningful (understandable and useful) for humans.

There are good names and less good names. This has nothing to do with curse words, or with TLA's (three-letter acronyms). A good set of encodings and names allows us to describe recipes in a way that's natural, without having to say too much. The variety of different programming languages can be thought of as a collection of sets of namings and encodings. Some are better for some tasks than others. Some languages require you to write more to describe the same recipe than others—but sometimes that "more" leads to a much more (humanly) readable recipe that helps others to understand what you're saying.

Philosophers and mathematicians look for very similar senses of quality. They try to describe the world in a few words, seeking an elegant selection of words that cover many situations but remain understandable to their fellow philosophers and mathematicians. That's exactly what computer scientists do.

How the units and values (***data***) of a recipe can be interpreted is often also named. Remember how we said in Section 1.2 that everything is in bytes but bytes can be interpreted as numbers? In some programming languages, you can say explicitly that some value is a *byte*, and later tell the language to treat it as a number, an *integer* (or sometimes *int*). Similarly, you can tell the computer that this particular series of bytes is a collection of numbers (an ***array of integers***), or a collection of characters (a ***string***), or even as a more complex encoding of a single floating-point number (a ***float***—any number with a decimal point in it).

In Python, we will explicitly tell the computer how to interpret our values, but we will very rarely tell it that certain names are only associated with certain encodings. Languages such as Java and C++ are *strongly typed*: Their names are strongly associated with certain types or encodings.They require you to say that this name will only be associated with integers, and that one will only be a floating-point number. Python still has *types* (encodings that you can reference by name), but they're not as explicit.

2.1.1 Files and Their Names

A programming language isn't the only place where computers associate names and values. Your computer's **operating system** takes care of the files on your disk and associates names with them. Operating systems you may be familiar with or use include Windows 95, Windows 98 (Windows ME, NT, XP...), MacOS, and Linux. A **file** is a collection of values (bytes) on your **hard disk** (the part of your computer that stores things after the power is turned off). If you know the name of a file and tell it to the operating system, you will be given the values associated with the name.

You may be thinking, "I've been using the computer for years, and I've *never* given a file name to the operating system." Maybe you didn't realize that you were doing it, but when you pick a file from a file-choosing dialog in Photoshop, or double-click a file in a *directory* window (or Explorer or Finder), you are asking some software somewhere to give the name you're picking or double-clicking to the operating system, and get the values back. When you write your own recipes, though, you'll be explicitly getting file names and asking for their values.

Files are *very* important for media computation. Disks can store acres and acres of information on them. Remember our discussion of Moore's Law? Disk capacity per dollar is increasing *faster* than computer speed per dollar! Computer disks today can store whole movies, hours (days?) of sounds, and the equivalent of hundreds of film rolls of pictures.

These media are not small. Even in a *compressed* form, screen-size pictures can be over a million bytes large, and songs can be 3 million bytes or more. You need to keep them someplace where they'll last past the computer being turned off and where there's lots of space.

In contrast, your computer's **memory** is impermanent (it disappears when the power does) and relatively small. Computer memory is getting larger all the time, but it's still just a fraction of the amount of space on your disk. When you're working with media, you will load the media from the disk into memory, but you wouldn't want it to stay in memory after you're done. It's too big.

Think about your computer's memory as a dorm room. You can get to things easily in a dorm room—they're right at hand, easy to reach, easy to use. But you wouldn't want to put everything you own (or everything you hope to own) in that one dorm room. All your belongings? Your skis? Your car? Your boat? That's silly. Instead, you store large things in places designed to store large things. You know how to get them when you need them (and maybe take them back to your dorm room if you need to or can).

When you bring things into memory, you will name the value so that you can retrieve it and use it later. In that sense, programming is something like *algebra*. To write equations and functions that were generalizable (i.e., that worked for any number or value), you wrote them with *variables*, like $PV = nRT$ or $e = Mc^2$ or $f(x) = sin(x)$. Those P's, V's, R's, T's, e's, M's, c's, and x's were names for values. When you evaluated $f(30)$, you knew that the x was the name for 30 when computing f. We'll be naming media (as values) in the same way when using them in programming.

■ 2.2 Programming in Python

The programming language that we're going to be using in this book is called **Python**. It's a language invented by Guido van Rossum. He named his language for the famous British comedy troupe *Monty Python*. Python has been used for years by people without formal computer science training—it's aimed at being easy to use. The particular form of Python that we're going to be using is *Jython* because it lends itself to cross-platform multimedia.

You'll actually be programming using a tool called *JES* for "*Jython Environment for Students*." JES is a simple *editor* (tool for entering program text) and interaction tool so that you can try things out in JES and create new recipes within it. The media names (functions, variables, encodings) that we'll be talking about in this book were developed to work from within JES (i.e., they're not part of a normal Jython distribution, though the basic language we'll be using is normal Python).

If you have the CD in the back of the book, you will find a folder that you can drag onto your computer. It will install Java, Jython, and JES for you, and give you a nice icon to double-click on to start JES. If you don't have a CD or you want to get the latest version you'll need to get JES from `http://coweb.cc.gatech.edu/mediaComp-plan/MediacompSoftware`.

DEBUGGING TIP: Getting Java, if you have to

For most people, dragging the JES folder onto their hard disk is all they need to do to get started. However, if you have Java installed, and it's an older version that can't run JES, you might have trouble getting JES started. If you do have problems, get a new version from the Sun site at `http://www.java.sun.com`

■ 2.3 Programming in JES

How you start JES depends on your platform. In Linux, you'll probably cd into your Jython directory and type a command like `java -cp jes`. In Windows and Macintosh, you'll have a JES icon that you'll simply double-click. See the instructions on the CD for what will work for your computer.

COMMON BUG: JES can be slow to start

JES can take a while to load. Don't worry—you may see the splash screen for a long time, but if you see the splash screen, it will load. It will often start faster after the first use.

COMMON BUG: Making JES run faster

As we'll talk more about later, when you're running JES, you're actually running Java. Java needs memory. If you find that JES runs slowly, give it more memory. You can do this by quitting out of other applications you're running. Your e-mail program, your instant messenger, and your digital music player all take up memory (sometimes lots of it!). Quit out of those and JES will run faster.

Once you start JES, it will look something like Figure 2.1. There are two main areas in JES (the bar between them moves so that you can differentially resize the two areas).

■ The top part is the **_Program Area_**. This where you write _your_ recipes: The programs that you're creating and their names. This area is simply a text editor—think of it as Microsoft Word for your programs. The computer doesn't actually try to interpret the names that you type up in the program area until you press the LOAD button and you can't press LOAD until you've saved your program (by using the SAVE menu item, which is visible in Figure 2.1 under the FILE menu).

Don't worry if you hit LOAD before you remember to save. JES won't load the program until it's saved, so it will give you a chance to save the program then.

■ The bottom part is the **_Command Area_**. This is where you literally _command_ the computer to do something. You type your commands at the >>> prompt, and when you hit the RETURN (Apple) or ENTER (Windows) key, the computer will interpret your words (i.e., apply the meanings and encodings of the Python programming language) and do what you have told it to do. This interpretation will include whatever you typed and loaded from the program area as well.

Other features of JES are visible in Figure 2.1, but we won't be doing much with them yet. The watcher button opens up the **_watcher_** (**_a debugger_**), a window with tools for watching how the computer executes your program. The STOP button allows you to stop a running program (e.g., if you think it's been running too long, or if you realize that it's not doing what you wanted it to do).

MAKING IT WORK TIP: Get to know your Help!

An _important_ feature to start exploring is the HELP menu. There is a lot of great help for programming and for using JES available under this menu. Start exploring it now so that you have a sense of what's there when you start writing your own programs.

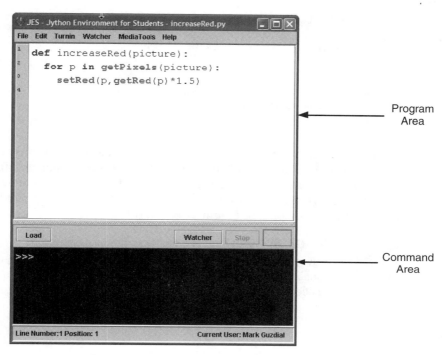

FIGURE 2.1: JES with Program and Command Areas noted.

■ 2.4 Media Computation in JES

We're going to start out by simply typing commands in the Command Area—not defining new names yet, but simply using the names that the computer already knows from within JES.

The name `print` is an important one to know. It's always used with something following it. The meaning for `print` is "Display a readable representation of whatever follows." Whatever follows can be a name that the computer knows, or an *expression* (literally, in the algebraic sense). Try typing `print 34 + 56` by clicking in the command area, typing the command, and hitting ENTER—like this:

```
>>> print 34 + 56
90
```

`34 + 56` is a numeric expression that Python understands. Obviously, it's composed of two numbers and an operation (in our sense, a *name*) that Python knows how to do, + meaning "add." Python understands other kinds of expressions, not all of them numeric.

```
>>> print 34.1/46.5
0.7333333333333334
```

```
>>> print 22 * 33
726
>>> print 14 - 15
-1
>>> print "Hello"
Hello
>>> print "Hello" + "Mark"
HelloMark
```

Python understands quite a few standard math operations. It also knows how to recognize different kinds of numbers, both integer and floating point. It also knows how to recognize *strings* (lists of characters) that are started and ended with " (quote) marks. It even knows what it means to "add" two strings together: It simply puts one right after the other.

COMMON BUG: Python's types can produce odd results

Python takes types seriously. If it sees you using integers, it thinks you want an integer result from your expressions. If it sees you use floating-point numbers, it thinks you want a floating-point result. Sounds reasonable, no? But how about:

```
>>> print 1.0/2.0
0.5
>>> print 1/2
0
```

1/2 is 0? Well, sure! I and 2 are integers. There is no integer equal to 1/2, so the answer must be 0! Adding ".0" to an integer convinces Python that we're talking about floating-point numbers, so the result is in floating-point form.

Python also understands about *functions*. Remember functions from algebra? They're a "box" into which you put one value, and out comes another. One of the functions that Python knows takes a character as the *input* value (the value that goes into the box) and returns or outputs (the value that comes out of the box) the number that is the ASCII mapping for that character. The name of this function is ord (for *ordinal*), and you can use print to display the value that the function ord returns:

```
>>> print ord("A")
65
```

Another function that's built into Python is named abs—it's the absolute value function. It returns the absolute value of the input value.

```
>>> print abs(1)
1
>>> print abs(-1)
1
```

DEBUGGING TIP: Common typos

If you type something that Python can't understand at all, you'll get a syntax error.

```
>>> pint "Hello"
Your code contains at least one syntax
error, meaning it is not legal jython.
```

If you try to access a word that Python doesn't know, Python will say that it doesn't know that name.

```
>>> print a
A local or global name could not be found.
```

A *local name* is a name defined inside a function, and a *global name* is a name available to all functions (such as `pickAFile`).

Another function that JES knows is one that allows you to pick a file from your disk.[1] It takes no input, as `ord` did, but it does return a string which is the name of the file on your disk. The name of the function is `pickAFile`. Python is very picky about capitalization—neither `pickafile` nor `Pickafile` will work! Try it like this: `print pickAFile()`. When you do, you will get something that looks like Figure 2.2.

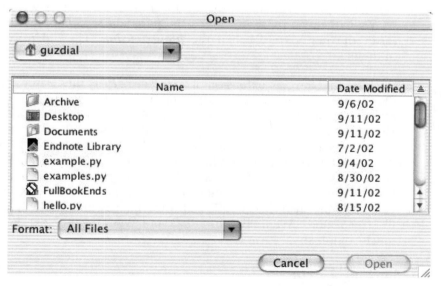

FIGURE 2.2: The file picker.

---

[1] You may notice that I have switched from saying "Python knows" to "JES knows". `print` is something that all Python implementations know. `pickAFile` is something that we built for JES. In general, you can ignore the difference, but if you try to use another kind of Python, it will be important to know what is common and what isn't.

You're probably already familiar with how to use a file picker or file dialog:

■ Double-click on folders/directories to open them.
■ Click to select and then click OPEN, or double-click, to select a file.

Once you select a file, what gets returned is the *file name* as a string (a sequence of characters). (If you click CANCEL, pickAFile returns the *empty string*—a string of characters, with no characters in it, e.g., "".) Try it: Do print pickAFile() and OPEN a file.

```
>>> print pickAFile()
/Users/guzdial/mediasources/barbara.jpg
```

What you get when you finally select a file will depend on your operating system. On Windows, your file name will probably start with C: and will have backslashes in it (e.g., \ ). On Linux or MacOS, it will probably look something like the above. There are really two parts to this file name:

■ The character between words (e.g., the / between "Users" and "guzdial") is called the ***path delimiter***. Everything from the beginning of the file name to the last path delimiter is called the *path* to the file. That describes exactly *where* on the hard disk (in which ***directory***) a file exists.
■ The last part of the file (e.g., "barbara.jpg") is called the ***base file name***. When you look at the file in the Finder/Explorer/Directory window (depending on your operating system), that's the part you see. The last three characters (after the period) are called the ***file extension***. They identify the encoding of the file.

Files that have an extension of ".jpg" are ***JPEG*** files. They contain pictures. (To be more literal, they contain data that can be *interpreted* to be a *representation* of a picture—but that's close enough to say "they contain pictures.") JPEG is a standard *encoding* (representation) for any kind of image. The other media files that we'll be using frequently are ".wav" files (Figure 2.3). The ".wav" extension means that these are ***WAV*** files. They contain sounds. WAV is a standard encoding for sounds. There are many other kinds of extensions for files, and there are even many other kinds of media extensions. For example, there are also GIF (".gif") files for images and AIFF (".aif" or ".aiff") files for sounds. We'll stick to JPEG and WAV in this text, just to avoid too much complexity.

2.4.1 Showing a Picture

So now we know how to get a complete file name: path and base name. This *doesn't* mean that we have the file itself loaded into memory. To get the file into memory, we have to tell JES how to interpret it. *We* know that JPEG files are pictures, but we have to tell JES explicitly to read the file and make a picture from it. There is a function for that, too, named makePicture.

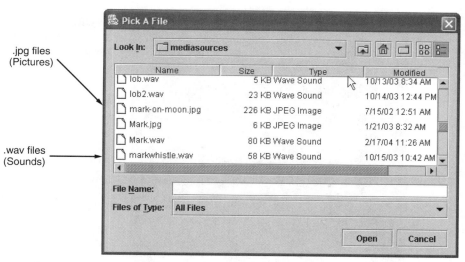

FIGURE 2.3:   File picker with media types identified.

makePicture *does* require an ***argument***—some input to the function. Just like ord, the input is specified inside parentheses. It takes a file name. Lucky us—we know how to get one of those.

```
>>> print makePicture(pickAFile())
Picture, filename /Users/guzdial/mediasources/barbara.jpg
height 294 width 222
```

The result from print suggests that we did in fact make a picture, from a given filename and a given height and width. Success! Oh, you wanted to actually *see* the picture? We'll need another function! (Did I mention somewhere that computers are stupid?) The function to show the picture is named show. show *also* takes an argument—a Picture. We can now pick a file, make a picture, and show it in a couple of different ways.

■ We can do it all at once because each function can just be input to the next one: show(makePicture(pickAFile())). That's what we see in Figure 2.4.

■ The second way is to *name* each of the pieces by using =. We can name the file (with the name file) that we get from pickAFile, then the picture that we get from file using makePicture, then show that. That's what we see in Figure 2.5. We'll see more on this way in the next section.

If you try print show..., you'll notice that the output from show is None. Functions in Python don't *have* to return a value, unlike real mathematical functions. If a function *does* something (like opening up a picture in a window), it can be useful without also needing to return a value. Computer scientists use the term ***side-effect*** for when a function does computation other than through

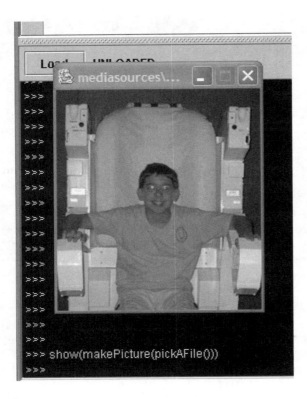

FIGURE 2.4: Picking, making, and showing a picture, using each function as input to the next.

FIGURE 2.5: Picking, making, and showing a picture, naming the pieces.

its input-to-return value computation. Displaying windows and making sounds is often side-effect computation.

2.4.2 Playing a Sound

We can replicate this entire process with sounds.

- We still use `pickAFile` to find the file we want and get its file name.
- We now use `makeSound` to make a sound. `makeSound`, as you might imagine, takes a file name as input.
- We will use `play` to play the sound. `play` takes a sound as input, but returns None.

Here are the same steps we saw previously with pictures:

```
>>> print pickAFile()
/Users/guzdial/mediasources/hello.wav
>>> print makeSound(pickAFile())

Sound of length 54757
>>> print play(makeSound(pickAFile()))
None
```

(We'll explain what the length of the sound means in the next chapter.) Please try this on your own, using JPEG files and WAV files that are on your own computer, that you make yourself, or that came on your CD. (We will talk more about where to get the media and how to create it in future chapters.)

Congratulations! You've just worked your first media computation!

2.4.3 Naming Your Media (and Other Values)

`print play(makeSound(pickAFile()))` looks awfully complicated and long to type. You may be wondering if there are ways to simplify it. There are. We can actually simplify it just the way that mathematicians have simplified things for centuries: We name the pieces! The results from functions can be named, and these names can be used in the inputs to other functions.

Since we have already mentioned naming so often, it probably won't come as any surprise that you can create your own names. Later, we'll show you how to name your own functions. Right now, let's name our data. We call our names for data *variables*.

We name data using =. We can check our namings using `print`, just as we have been doing.

```
>>> myvariable=12
>>> print myvariable
12
>>> anothervariable=34.5
>>> print anothervariable
34.5
```

```
>>> myname="Mark"
>>> print myname
Mark
```

Don't read = as "equals." That's what it means in mathematics, but that's not at all what we're doing here. Read = as "becomes a name for." myvariable=12 thus means "myvariable becomes a name for 12." The reverse (putting the *expression* on the left and the name on the right) thus makes no sense: 12=myvariable would then mean "12 becomes a name for myvariable."

```
>>> x = 2 * 8
>>> print x
16
>>> 2 * 8 = x
Your code contains at least one syntax error, meaning it is
not legal jython.
```

We can easily reuse names.

```
>>> print myvariable
12
>>> myvariable="Hello"
>>> print myvariable
Hello
```

The *binding* between the name and the data only exists until (a) the name gets assigned to something else or (b) you quit JES. The relationship between names and data (or even names and functions) only exists during a session of JES.

Remember that data have encodings or types. How data act in expressions depends in part on their types. Note how the *integer* 12 and the *string* "12" act differently for multiplication below. Both are doing something reasonable for their type, but they are very different actions.

```
>>> myvariable=12
>>> print myvariable*4
48
>>> myothervariable="12"
>>> print myothervariable*4
12121212
```

We can assign names to the *results* of functions. If we name the result from pickAFile, we will get the same result each time we print the name. We don't rerun pickAFile. Naming code in order to re-execute it is what we're doing when we define functions, which comes up in just a few pages.

```
>>> file = pickAFile()
>>> print file
C:\mediasources\640x480.jpg
>>> print file
C:\mediasources\640x480.jpg
```

In the following example, we assign names to the file name and the picture.

```
>>> myfilename = pickAFile()
>>> print myfilename
/Users/guzdial/mediasources/barbara.jpg
>>> mypicture = makePicture(myfilename)
>>> print mypicture
Picture, filename /Users/guzdial/mediasources/barbara.jpg
height 294 width 222
```

Note that the algebraic notions of *substitution* and *evaluation* work here as well. mypicture = makePicture(myfilename) causes the exact same picture to be created as if we had executed makePicture(pickAFile()),[2] because we set myfilename to be equal to the result of pickAFile(). The values are substituted for the names when the expression is evaluated. makePicture(myfilename) is an expression that is expanded, at evaluation time, into makePicture("/Users/guzdial/mediasources/barbara.jpg") because "/Users/guzdial/mediasources/barbara.jpg" is the name of the file that was picked when pickAFile() was evaluated and the returned value was named myfilename.

We can also replace the function *invocations* (or *calls*) with the *value* returned. pickAFile() returns a *string*—a bunch of characters enclosed inside quotes. We can make the last example work like this, too.

```
>>> myfilename = "/Users/guzdial/mediasources/barbara.jpg"
>>> print myfilename
/Users/guzdial/mediasources/barbara.jpg
>>> mypicture = makePicture(myfilename)
>>> print mypicture
Picture, filename /Users/guzdial/mediasources/barbara.jpg
height 294 width 222
```

Or even substitute for the name.

```
>>> mypicture = makePicture("/Users/guzdial/mediasources/
barbara.jpg")
>>> print mypicture
Picture, filename /Users/guzdial/mediasources/barbara.jpg
height 294 width 222
```

COMPUTER SCIENCE IDEA: We can substitute names, values, and functions

We can substitute a value, a name assigned to that value, and the function returning the same value *interchangeably*. The computer cares about the value, not whether it comes from a string, a name, or a function call. The key is that the computer is *evaluating* the value, the name, and the function. As long as these *expressions* evaluate to the same thing, they can be used interchangeably.

---

[2] Assuming, of course, that you picked the same file.

We actually don't need to use print every time we ask the computer to do something. If we want to call a function that doesn't return anything (and so is pretty useless to print), we can just call the function by typing its name and its input (if any) and hitting return.

```
>>> show(mypicture)
```

We tend to call these statements to the computer that are telling it to do things *commands*. print mypicture is a command. So is myfilename = pickAFile(), and show(mypicture). These are more than expressions: They're telling the computer to *do* something.

■ 2.5 Making a Program

We have now used names to stand for values. The values are substituted for the names when the expression is evaluated. We can do the same for programs. We can name a series of commands and then just use the name whenever we want the commands to be executed. In Python, the name we define will be a *function*. A *program* in Python, then, is a collection of one or more functions that together perform a useful task. We're going to use the term *recipe* to describe programs (or portions of programs) that perform a useful media operation, even if whatever is covered by the term is not enough to make a useful program in itself.

Remember when we said earlier that just about anything can be named in computers? We've seen naming values. Now we'll see naming recipes.

 MAKING IT WORK TIP: Try *every* recipe!
To really understand what's going on, type in, load, and execute *every* recipe in the book. *EVERY* one. None of them are long, and the practice will go a long way to convincing you that the programs work, developing your programming skill, and helping you understand *why* they work.

The name that Python understands as *defining* the name of new recipes is def. def isn't a function—it's a command like print. def is used to *define* new functions. There are certain things that have to come after the word def, though. The structure of what goes on the line with the def command is referred to as the *syntax* of the command—the words and characters that have to be there for Python to understand what's going on, and the order of those things.

def needs three things to follow it on the same line:

■ The name of the recipe you're defining, like showMyPicture.

■ Whatever *inputs* this recipe will take. The recipe can be a function that takes inputs, like abs or makePicture. The inputs are named and placed between parentheses separated by commas. If your recipe takes no inputs, you simply enter () to indicate no inputs.

■ The line ends with a colon, :.

What comes after this are the commands to be executed, one after the other, whenever the recipe is told to execute. We create a collection of commands by defining a ***block***. The block of commands that follow a def command (or *statement*) are the ones associated with the name of the function.

Most real programs that do useful things, especially those that create user interfaces, require the definition of more than one function. Imagine that you have several def commands in the program area. How do you think Python will figure out that one function has ended and a new one has begun? (Especially because it *is* possible to define functions *inside of* other functions.) Python needs some way of figuring out where the *function body* ends—which statements are part of this function, and which are part of the next.

The answer is ***indentation***. All the statements that are part of the definition are slightly indented after the def statement. I recommend using exactly two spaces—it's enough to see, it's easy to remember, and it's simple. (In JES, you could also use one *tab*—a single press of the tab key.) You enter the function in the program area like this (where ⊔ indicates a single space, a single press of the spacebar):

```
def hello():
⊔⊔print "Hello"
```

We can now define our first recipe. You type this into the program area of JES. When you're done, save the file: Use the extension ".py" to indicate a Python file. (I saved mine as pickAndShow.py.)

RECIPE 1: Pick and show a picture

```
def pickAndShow():
  myfile = pickAFile()
  mypict = makePicture(myfile)
  show(mypict)
```

You'll notice a thin blue box around the body of the function while you're typing. The blue box indicates the blocks in your program (Figure 2.6). All the commands in the same block as the statement containing the cursor (the vertical bar where you're typing) are enclosed in the same blue box. You know that you have the indentation right when all the commands you *expect* to be in the block *are* in the box.

FIGURE 2.6: Visualizing the blocks in JES.

Once you've typed in your recipe and saved it, you can load it. Click the LOAD button.

DEBUGGING TIP: Don't forget to LOAD!

The most common mistake that I make with JES is typing in the function, saving it, and then trying the function in the command area. You have to click the LOAD button to get it available in the command area.

Now you can execute your recipe. Click in the command area. Since you aren't taking any input and aren't returning any value (i.e., this isn't a strict mathematical function), simply type the name of your recipe as a command:

```
>>> pickAndShow()
>>>
```

You'll be prompted for a file, and then the picture will appear (Figure 2.7). We can similarly define our second recipe to pick and play a sound.

RECIPE 2: Pick and play a sound

```
def pickAndPlay():
    myfile = pickAFile()
    mysound = makeSound(myfile)
    play(mysound)
```

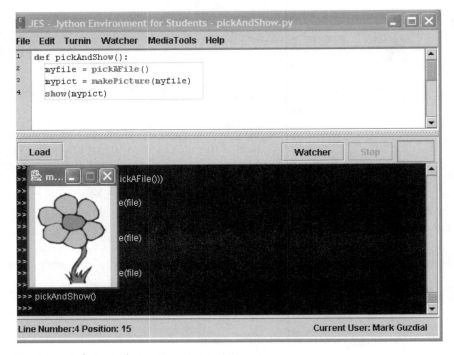

FIGURE 2.7: Defining and executing pickAndShow.

MAKING IT WORK TIP: Name the names you like

In the last section, we used the names `myfilename` and `mypicture`. In this recipe, I used `myfile` and `mypict`. Does it matter? It doesn't matter to the computer at all. We could call all our pictures `myglyph` or even `mything`. The computer doesn't care what names you use—they're entirely for your benefit. Pick names that (a) are meaningful to you (so that you can read and understand your program), (b) are meaningful to others (so that anyone you show your program to can understand it), and (c) are easy to type. Names with 25 characters, like `myPictureThatIAmGoingToOpenAfterThis` are meaningful and easy to read, but are a pain to type.

These recipes probably aren't really useful as programs. Needing to pick the file over and over again is annoying if you want the same picture to appear, for example. But now that we have the power to define recipes, we can define new ones to perform whatever tasks we want. Let's define one that will open a specific picture we want, and another that opens a specific sound we want.

Use `pickAFile` to get the file name of the sound or picture you want. We're going to need the name in defining the recipe to play that specific sound or show that specific picture. We'll just set the value of `myfile` *directly*, instead of as a result of `pickAFile`, by putting the string between quotes directly in the recipe.

RECIPE 3: Show a specific picture

Be sure to replace **FILENAME** below with the complete path to your own picture file; for example,
"/Users/guzdial/mediasources/barbara.jpg"

```
def showPicture():
  myfile = "FILENAME"
  mypict = makePicture(myfile)
  show(mypict)
```

How it works: The variable `myfile` takes on the value of the filename—the same one that the function `pickAFile` would return if it were to pick that file. We then make a picture from the file and name it `mypict`. Finally, we show the picture in `mypict`.

RECIPE 4: Play a specific sound

Be sure to replace **FILENAME** below with the complete path to your own sound file; for example,
"/Users/guzdial/mediasources/hello.wav".

```
def playSound():
  myfile = "FILENAME"
  mysound = makeSound(myfile)
  play(mysound)
```

COMMON BUG: Windows filenames and backslashes

Windows uses backslashes as file delimiters. Python gives special meanings to certain backslash-and-character combinations, as we'll talk more about later. For example, '\n' means the same thing as the ENTER or RETURN key. These combinations can occur naturally in Windows filenames. To avoid having Python misinterpret these characters, you have to type your filenames with an "r" in front, like this:

```
>>> myfile = r"C:\mediasources\barbara.jpg"
>>> print myfile
C:\mediasources\barbara.jpg
```

MAKING IT WORK TIP: Copying and pasting

Text can be copied and pasted between the program and command areas. You can use `print pickAFile()` to print a filename, then select it and COPY it (from the EDIT menu), then click in the command area and PASTE it. Similarly, you can copy whole commands from the command area up to the program area. That's an easy way to test the individual commands and then put them all in a recipe once you have the order right and they're working. You can also copy text within the command area. Instead of retyping a command, select it, COPY it, PASTE it into the bottom line (make sure the cursor is at the end of the line!), and hit ENTER to execute it.

2.5.1 Variable Recipes: Real Math-like Functions That Take Input

How do we create a real function, like a function in mathematics, that takes inputs, such as ord or makePicture? Why would you *want* to?

An important reason for using a variable to specify input to the recipe is to make a program more *general*. Consider Recipe 3, showPicture. That's for a specific file name. Would it be useful to have a function that could take *any* file name, then make and show the picture? That kind of function handles the *general* case of making and showing pictures. We call that kind of generalization **abstraction**. Abstraction leads to general solutions that work in lots of situations.

Defining a recipe that takes input is very easy. It continues to be a matter of *substitution* and *evaluation*. We'll put a name inside those parentheses on the def line. That name is sometimes called the **parameter** or **input variable**.

When you evaluate the function by specifying its name with an **input value** (also called the **argument**) inside parentheses (like makepicture(myfilename) or show(mypicture)), the input value is *assigned* to the input variable. We say that the input variable *takes on* the input value. During the execution of the function (recipe), the input value will be *substituted* for the value.

Here's what a recipe would look like that takes the file name as an input variable:

RECIPE 5: Show the picture file whose file name is input

```
def showNamed(myfile):
    mypict = makePicture(myfile)
    show(mypict)
```

When I type

```
showNamed("/Users/guzdial/mediasources/barbara.jpg")
```

and hit enter, the variable `myfile` takes on the value

```
"/Users/guzdial/mediasources/barbara.jpg".
```

`myPict` will then be assigned to the picture resulting from reading and interpreting the file at

```
"/Users/guzdial/mediasources/barbara.jpg"
```

Then the picture is shown.

We can do a sound in the same way.

RECIPE 6: Play the sound file whose file name is input

```
def playNamed(myfile):
    mysound = makeSound(myfile)
    play(mysound)
```

We can also write recipes that take pictures or sounds in as the input values. Here's a recipe that shows a picture but takes the picture object as the input value instead of the filename.

RECIPE 7: Show the picture provided as input

```
def showPicture(mypict):
    show(mypict)
```

Now, what is the difference between the function `showPicture` and the built-in JES function `show`? Nothing at all. We can certainly create a function that provides a new name to another function. If that makes your code easier for you to understand, than it's a great idea.

What is the *right* input value for a function? Is it better to input a filename or a picture? And what does "better" mean here, anyway? You'll read more about all of these issues later, but here's a short answer: Write the function that is most useful to you. If defining `showPicture` is more readable for you than `show`, then that's useful. If what you really want is a function that takes care of making the picture and showing it to you, then you might find the `showNamed` function the most useful.

Programming Summary

In this chapter, we talk about several kinds of encodings of data (or objects).

Integers (e.g., 3)	Numbers without a decimal point—they can't represent fractions.
Floating-point numbers (e.g., 3.0, 3.01)	Numbers with a fractional piece to them.
Strings (e.g., "Hello!")	A sequence of characters (including spaces, punctuation, etc.) delimited on either end with a quote character.
File name	A string whose characters represent a path, path delimiters, and a base file name.
Pictures	Encodings of images, typically coming from a JPEG file.
Sounds	Encodings of sounds, typically coming from a WAV file.

Here are the program pieces introduced in this chapter:

`print`	Displays an expression (variable, value, formula, whatever) in its text form.
`def`	Defines a function and its input variables (if any).
`ord`	Returns the equivalent numeric value (from the ASCII standard) for the input character.
`abs`	Inputs a number and returns the absolute value of it.
`pickAFile`	Lets the user pick a file and returns the complete path name as a string. No input.
`makePicture`	Takes a filename as input, reads the file, and creates a picture from it. Returns the picture.
`show`	Shows a picture provided as input. No return value.
`makeSound`	Takes a filename as input, reads the file, and creates a sound from it. Returns the sound.
`play`	Plays a sound provided as input. No return value.

Problems

2.1 Some computer science concept questions:
- What is an algorithm?
- What is hierarchical decomposition? What is it good for?
- Why would you want to put comments in a program?

- What is an encoding?
- What is Moore's Law?

2.2 Test your understanding of Python:
- What does def mean? What does the statement def someFunction(x,y): do?
- What does print mean? What does the statement print a do?
- What does show(p) do? (Hint: There's more than one answer to this question.)

2.3 Try some other operations with strings in JES. What happens if you multiply a number by a string, like 3 * "Hello"? What happens if you try to multiply a string by a string, "a" * "b"?

2.4 You can combine the sound-playing and picture-showing commands in the same recipe. You can have many statements in the same function.
- Trying playing a sound and then showing a picture while the sound is playing.
- Try playing a sound and opening several pictures while the sound is still playing.

2.5 We evaluated the expression pickAFile() when we wanted to execute the function named pickAFile. But what is the name pickAFile anyway? What do you get if you print pickAFile? How about print makePicture? What prints, and what do you think it means?

To Dig Deeper

The best (deepest, most material, most elegant) computer science textbook is *Structure and Interpretation of Computer Programs,* by Abelson, Sussman, and Sussman [2]. It's a challenging book to get through, but definitely worth the effort. A newer book more aimed at the programming novice but in the same spirit is *How to Design Programs* [11].

Neither of these books is really aimed at students who want to program because it's fun or because they have something small they want to do. They're aimed at future professional software developers. The best books for the student exploring computing are by Brian Harvey. His *Simply Scheme* uses the same programming language as the Abelson et al. book, but is more approachable. My favorite of this class of books, though, is Brian's three-volume set *Computer Science Logo Style* [21], which combines good computer science with creative and fun projects.

PART 2

PICTURES

CHAPTER 3

Modifying Pictures Using Loops

Chapter Learning Objectives

The media learning goals for this chapter are:

- *To understand how images are digitized by taking advantage of limits in human vision.*

- *To identify different models for color, including RGB, the most common one for computers.*

- *To manipulate color values in pictures, like increasing or decreasing red values, or lightening or darkening the colors.*

- *To convert a color picture to grayscale, using more than one method.*

- *To convert a color picture to its negative representation.*

The computer science goals for this chapter are:

- *To use a matrix representation in finding pixels in a picture.*

- *To use the objects pictures and pixels.*

- *To use iteration (with a **for** loop) for changing the color values of pixels in a picture.*

- *To nest blocks of code within one another.*

■ *To choose between having a function* return *a value and just providing* side effects.

■ *To determine the* scope *of a variable name.*

■ 3.1 How Pictures Are Encoded

Pictures (images, graphics) are an important part of any media communication. In this chapter, we discuss how pictures are represented on a computer (mostly as *bitmap* images—each dot or *pixel* is represented separately) and how they can be manipulated. The chapters that follow this one will introduce alternative image representations, such as *vector* images.

Pictures are two-dimensional arrays of *pixels*. Each of these terms will be described in this section.

For our purposes, a picture is an image stored in a JPEG file. ***JPEG*** is an international standard for how to store images with high quality but in little space. JPEG is a ***lossy compression*** format. That means that it is *compressed*, made smaller, but not with 100% of the quality of the original format. Typically, though, what gets thrown away is stuff that you don't see or don't notice anyway. For most purposes, a JPEG image works fine.

A two-dimensional array is a ***matrix***. An *array* is a sequence of elements, each with an index number associated with it. A matrix is a collection of elements arranged in both a horizontal and a vertical sequence. Instead of talking about an element at index j, that is *array$_j$*, we're now talking about an element at column i and row j, that is, *matrix$_{i,j}$*.

In Figure 3.1, you see an example matrix (or part of one, the upper-left-hand corner of one). At *coordinates* $(1, 2)$ (horizontal, vertical), you'll find the matrix element whose value is 9. $(1, 1)$ is 15, $(2, 1)$ is 12, and $(3, 1)$ is 13. We will often refer to these coordinates as (x, y) ((*horizontal*, *vertical*)).

What's stored at each element in the picture is a ***pixel***. The word "pixel" is short for "picture element." It's literally a dot, and the overall picture is made up of lots of these dots. Have you ever taken a magnifying glass to the pictures

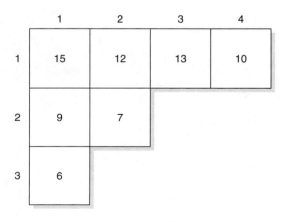

FIGURE 3.1: An example matrix.

in a newspaper or magazine, or to a television or even your own monitor? (Figure 3.2 was generated by taking an Intel microscope and pointing it at the screen at 60*x* magnification.) It's made up of many, many dots. When you look at the picture in the magazine or on the television, it doesn't look like it's broken up into millions of discrete spots, but it is.

You can get a similar view of individual pixels using the JES MediaTools picture tool, which is discussed later in this chapter. The picture tool allows you to zoom a picture up to 500% where each individual pixel is visible (Figure 3.3).

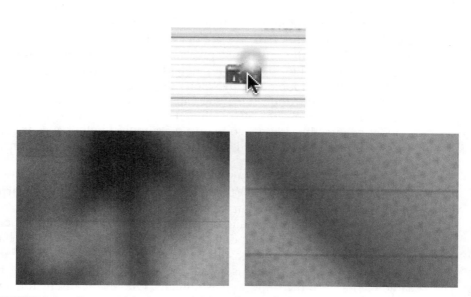

FIGURE 3.2:   Cursor and icon at regular magnification on top, and close-up views of the cursor (*left*) and the line below the cursor (*right*).

FIGURE 3.3:   Image shown in JES MediaTools picture tool: 100% image on left and 500% on right.

Our human sensory apparatus can't distinguish (without magnification or other special equipment) the small bits in the whole. Humans have low visual *acuity*—we don't see as much detail as, say, an eagle. We actually have more than one kind of vision system in use in our brain and our eyes. Our system for processing color is different from our system for processing black-and-white (or **luminance**). We use luminance to detect motion and sizes of objects, for example. We actually pick up luminance detail better with the sides of our eyes than from the center of our eye. That's an evolutionary advantage, since it allows you to pick out the sabertooth tiger sneaking up on your right in those bushes over there.

The lack of resolution in human vision is what makes it possible to digitize pictures. Animals that perceive greater detail than humans (e.g., eagles or cats) may actually see the individual pixels. We break up the picture into smaller elements (pixels), but there are enough of them and they are small enough that the picture doesn't look choppy when one looks at it overall. If you *can* see the effects of the digitization (e.g., you can see little rectangles in some spots), we call that *pixelization*—the effect when the digitization process becomes obvious.

Picture encoding is more complex than sound encoding. A sound is inherently linear—it progresses forward in time. A picture has two dimensions, width and height.

Visible light is continuous—visible light is any wavelength between 370 and 730 nanometers (0.00000037 and 0.00000073 meters). But our perception of light is limited by how our color sensors work. Our eyes have sensors that trigger (peak) around 425 nanometers (blue), 550 nanometers (green), and 560 nanometers (red). Our brain determines what a particular color is based on the feedback from these three sensors in our eyes. There are some animals with only two kinds of sensors, like dogs. These animals still perceive color, but not the same colors or in the same way as humans. One of the interesting implications of our limited visual sensory apparatus is that we actually perceive two kinds of orange. There is a *spectral* orange—a particular wavelength that is natural orange. There is also a mixture of red and yellow that hits our color sensors just right so that we perceive it as the same orange.

Based on how we perceive color, as long as we encode what hits our three kinds of color sensors, we're recording our human perception of color. Thus, we will encode each pixel as a triplet of numbers. The first number represents the amount of red in the pixel. The second is the amount of green, and the third is the amount of blue. We can make up any human-visible color by combining red, green, and blue light (Figure 3.4) (replicated in color insert Figure I.1). Combining all three gives us pure white. Turning off all three gives us black. We call this the **RGB color model**.

There are other models for defining and encoding colors besides the RGB color model. There's the *HSV color model* which encodes Hue, Saturation, and Value (sometimes also called the *HSB* color model for Hue, Saturation, and Brightness). The nice thing about the HSV model is that some notions, like making a color "lighter" or "darker," map cleanly to it—for example, you simply change the saturation (Figure 3.5). Another model is the *CMYK*

FIGURE 3.4: Merging red, green, and blue to make new colors.

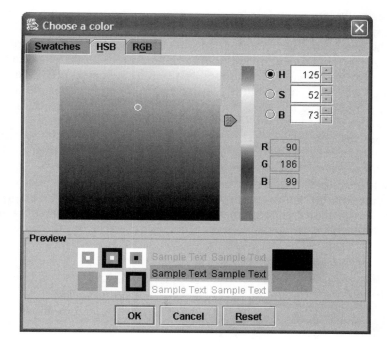

FIGURE 3.5: Picking colors using the HSB color model.

color model, which encodes Cyan, Magenta, Yellow, and black ("B" could be confused with blue). The CMYK model is what printers use—those are the inks they combine to make colors. However, with four elements there is more to encode on a computer, so the model is less popular for media computation. RGB is the most popular model on computers.

Each color component (sometimes called a ***channel***) in a pixel is typically represented with a single byte, eight bits. Eight bits can represent 256 patterns (2^8): 0000000, 00000001, up through 11111111. We typically use these patterns to represent the values 0 to 255. Each pixel, then, uses 24 bits to represent colors. There are 2^{24} possible patterns of 0's and 1's in those 24 bits, which means that the standard encoding for color using the RGB model can represent 16,777,216 colors. We can actually perceive more than 16 million colors, but it turns out that it just doesn't matter. There is no technology that comes even close to being able to replicate the whole color space that we can see. We do have devices that can represent 16 million distinct colors, but those 16 million colors don't cover the entire space of color (or luminance) that we can perceive. So the 24-bit RGB model is adequate until technology advances.

There are computer models that use more bits per pixel. For example, there are 32-bit models that use the extra eight bits to represent *transparency*—how much of the color "below" the given image should be blended with this color. These additional eight bits are sometimes called the ***alpha channel***. There are other models that use more than eight bits for the red, green, and blue channels, but they are uncommon.

We actually perceive borders of objects, motion, and depth through a *separate* vision system. We perceive color through one system, and *luminance* (how light/dark things are) through another system. Luminance is not actually the *amount* of light, but our *perception* of the amount of light. We can measure the amount of light (e.g., the number of photons reflected off the color) and show that a red spot and a blue spot are each reflecting the same amount of light, but we perceive the blue as darker. Our sense of luminance is based on comparisons with the surroundings—the optical illusion in Figure 3.6 highlights how we perceive gray levels. The two end quarters are actually the same level of gray, but because the two mid-quarters end in a sharp contrast of lightness and darkness, we perceive one end as darker than the other.

Most tools for allowing users to pick out colors let the users specify the color as RGB components. The Macintosh offers RGB sliders in its basic color picker (Figure 3.7). The color chooser in JES (which is the standard Java Swing color chooser) offers a similar set of sliders (Figure 3.8).

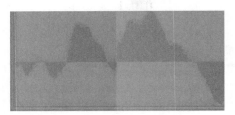

FIGURE 3.6: The ends of this figure are the same colors of gray, but the middle two quarters contrast sharply, so the left looks darker than the right.

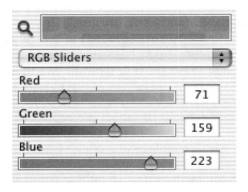

FIGURE 3.7: The Macintosh OS X RGB color picker.

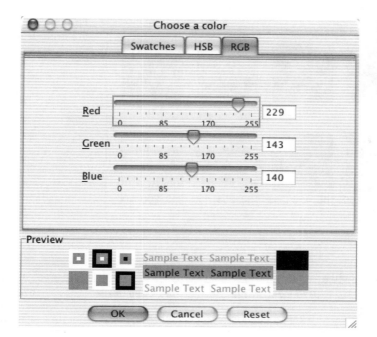

FIGURE 3.8: Picking a color using RGB sliders from JES.

As mentioned, a triplet of $(0, 0, 0)$ (red, green, blue components) is black, and $(255, 255, 255)$ is white. $(255, 0, 0)$ is pure red, but $(100, 0, 0)$ is red too—just less intense. $(0, 100, 0)$ is a light green, and $(0, 0, 100)$ is light blue. When the red component is the same as the green and as the blue, the resultant color is gray. $(50, 50, 50)$ would be a fairly dark gray, and $(100, 100, 100)$ is lighter.

Figure 3.9 (replicated by Figure I.2 in the color insert) is a representation of pixel RGB triplets in a matrix representation. Thus, the pixel at $(2, 1)$ has color $(30, 30, 255)$, which means that it has a red value of 30, a green value of 30, and a blue value of 255—it's a mostly blue color, but not pure blue. Pixel at $(3, 2)$ has pure green but also more red and blue $((150, 255, 150))$, so it's a fairly light green.

Images on disk and even in computer memory are usually stored in *compressed* form. The amount of memory needed to represent every pixel of even small images is pretty large (Table 3.1). A fairly small image of 320 pixels across by 240 pixels wide, with 24 bits per pixel, takes up 230,400 bytes—that's roughly 230 *kilobytes* (1000 bytes) or 1/4 *megabyte* (million bytes). A computer monitor with 1024 pixels across and 768 pixels vertically with 32 bits per pixel takes up three megabytes just to represent the screen.

■ 3.2 Manipulating Pictures

We manipulate pictures in JES by making a picture object out of a JPEG file, then changing the pixels in the picture. To change the pixels we change the colors associated with them by manipulating the red, green, and blue

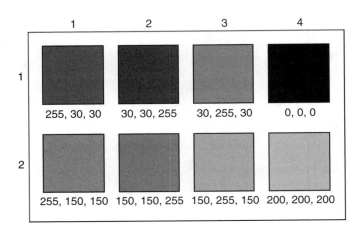

FIGURE 3.9: RGB triplets in a matrix representation.

TABLE 3.1 Number of bytes needed to store pixels at various sizes and formats

	320 x 240 image	**640 x 480 image**	**1024 x 768 image**
24-bit color	230,400 bytes	921,600 bytes	2,359,296 bytes
32-bit color	307,200 bytes	1,228,800 bytes	3,145,728 bytes

components. Manipulating pictures, thus, is pretty similar to manipulating samples in a sound, but a little more complex, since it's in two dimensions rather than one.

We make pictures using makePicture. We make the picture appear with show.

```
>>> file=pickAFile()
>>> print file
/Users/guzdial/mediasources/barbara.jpg
>>> picture=makePicture(file)
>>> show(picture)
>>> print picture
Picture, filename /Users/guzdial/mediasources/barbara.jpg
height 294 width 222
```

What makePicture does is to scoop up all the bytes at the input filename, bring them into memory, reformat them slightly, and place a sign on them announcing "This is a picture!" When you execute mypicture = makePicture(filename), you are saying, "The name for that picture object (note the sign on it) is now mypicture."

Pictures know their width and their height. You can query them with getWidth and getHeight.

```
>>> print getWidth(picture)
222
>>> print getHeight(picture)
294
```

We can get any particular pixel from a picture using getPixel with the picture, and the coordinates of the pixel desired. We can also get all the pixels with getPixels.

```
>>> pixel=getPixel(picture,1,1)
>>> print pixel
Pixel, color=color r=168 g=131 b=105
>>> pixels=getPixels(picture)
>>> print pixels[0]
Pixel, color=color r=168 g=131 b=105
```

 COMMON BUG: Don't try printing the pixels: *Way* too big!

getPixels literally returns an array of all the pixels (as opposed to a samples object, like getSamples returns). If you try to print the return value from getPixels, you'll get the printout of each pixel, as you see above. How many pixels are there? Well, the small sample picture "barbara.jpg" has a width of 222 and a height of 294. How many lines would print? 222 * 294 = 65,268! A printout of 65,000 lines is very big. You probably don't want to wait for it to finish. If you do this accidentally, just quit JES and restart it.

Pixels know where they come from. You can ask them their *x* and *y* coordinates with getX and getY.

```
>>> print getX(pixel)
1
>>> print getY(pixel)
1
```

Each pixel knows how to getRed and setRed. (Green and blue work similarly.)

```
>>> print getRed(pixel)
168
>>> setRed(pixel,255)
>>> print getRed(pixel)
255
```

You can also ask a pixel for its color with getColor, and you can also set the color with setColor. Color objects know their red, green, and blue components. You can make new colors with makeColor.

```
>>> color=getColor(pixel)
>>> print color
color r=255 g=131 b=105
>>> setColor(pixel,color)
```

```
>>> newColor=makeColor(0,100,0)
>>> print newColor
color r=0 g=100 b=0
>>> setColor(pixel,newColor)
>>> print getColor(pixel)
color r=0 g=100 b=0
```

If you change the color of a pixel, the picture to which the pixel belongs is also changed.

```
>>> print getPixel(picture,1,1)
Pixel, color=color r=0 g=100 b=0
```

COMMON BUG: Seeing changes in the picture

If you show your picture, and then change the pixels, you may wonder where the changes are. Picture displays don't automatically update. If you execute `repaint` with the picture, e.g., `repaint(picture)`, the picture will update.

One of the important things that you can do with colors is to compare them. Some recipes for manipulating pictures will do *different* things with pixels depending on the color of the pixel. There are several ways of comparing pictures.

One way to compare colors is the same as how one would compare numbers. We can subtract one color from the other. If we do that, we get a new color whose red, green, and blue components are the differences of each. So if $color_1$ has red, green, and blue components (r_1, g_1, b_1), and $color_2$ has (r_2, g_2, b_2), then $color_1 - color_2$ creates a new color ($r_1 - r_2, g_1 - g_2, b_1 - b_2$). We can also use == (test for equality) to compare colors.

```
>>> print c1
color r=10 g=10 b=10
>>> print c2
color r=20 g=20 b=20
>>> print c2-c1
color r=10 g=10 b=10
```

Another method of comparing pictures is with a notion of color `distance`. You often won't care about an *exact* match of colors—two shades of blue might be *close enough* for your purposes. `distance` lets you measure close enough.

```
>>> print color
color r=81 g=63 b=51
>>> print newcolor
color r=255 g=51 b=51
>>> print distance(color,newcolor)
174.41330224498358
```

The distance between two colors is the Cartesian distance between the colors as points in a three-dimensional space where red, green, and blue are the three dimensions. Recall that the distance between two points (x_1, y_1) and (x_2, y_2) is:

$$\sqrt{(x_1 - x_2)^2 + (y_1 - y_2)^2}$$

The similar measure for two colors $(red_1, green_1, blue_1)$ and $(red_2, green_2, blue_2)$ is:

$$\sqrt{(red_1 - red_2)^2 + (green_1 - green_2)^2 + (blue_1 - blue_2)^2}$$

You can automatically get the darker or lighter versions of colors with makeDarker or makeLighter. (Remember that this was easy in HSV, but not so easy in RGB. These functions do it for you.)

```
>>> print color
color r=168 g=131 b=105
>>> print makeDarker(color)
color r=117 g=91 b=73
>>> print color
color r=117 g=91 b=73
```

You can also make colors from pickAColor, which gives you several ways to pick a color.

```
>>> newcolor=pickAColor()
>>> print newcolor
color r=255 g=51 b=51
```

Once you have a color, you can get it in lighter or darker versions with makeLighter and makeDarker.

```
>>> print c
color r=10 g=100 b=200
>>> makeLighter(c)
>>> print c
color r=14 g=142 b=255
>>> makeDarker(c)
>>> print c
color r=9 g=99 b=178
```

When you have finished manipulating a picture, you can write it out with writePictureTo.

```
>>> writePictureTo(picture,"/Users/guzdial/newpicture.jpg")
```

COMMON BUG: End with .jpg

Be sure to end your filename with ".jpg" in order to get your operating system to recognize it as a JPEG file.

COMMON BUG: Saving a file quickly—and how to find it again!
What if you don't know the whole path to a directory of your choosing? You don't have to specify anything more than the base name.

```
>>> writePictureTo(picture,"newpicture.jpg")
```

The problem is finding the file again. In what directory was it saved? This is a pretty simple bug to resolve. The default directory (the one you get if you don't specify a path) is wherever JES is. If you have used `pickAFile()` recently, the default directory will be whatever directory you picked the file from. If you have a standard media folder (e.g., MEDIASOURCES) where you keep your media and pick files from, that's where your files will be saved if you don't specify a complete path.

We don't have to write new functions to manipulate pictures. We can do it from the Command Area using the functions just described.

```
>>> file="/Users/guzdial/mediasources/katie.jpg"
>>> pict=makePicture(file)
>>> show(pict)
>>> setColor(getPixel(pict,10,100),yellow)
>>> setColor(getPixel(pict,10,101),yellow)
>>> setColor(getPixel(pict,10,102),yellow)
>>> setColor(getPixel(pict,10,103),yellow)
>>> setColor(getPixel(pict,10,104),yellow)
>>> setColor(getPixel(pict,10,105),yellow)
>>> repaint(pict)
```

The result, showing a small yellow line on the left side (to the left of the foot), appears in Figure 3.10. This is 10 pixels across, and the pixels 101, 102, 103, 104, and 105 down.

FIGURE 3.10: Directly modifying the pixel colors via commands: Note the small yellow line on the left.

MAKING IT WORK TIP: Use JES Help!

JES has a wonderful help system. Forget what function you need? Just choose an item from the JES Help menu (Figure 3.11—it's all hyperlinked, so hunt around for what you need). Forget what a function you're already using does? Select it and choose Explain from the Help menu and get an explanation of what you have selected (Figure 3.12).

3.2.1 Exploring Pictures

On your CD, you will find the MediaTools application with documentation for how to get it started. You will also find a MediaTools menu in JES. Both kinds of MediaTools have a set of image exploration tools that are really useful for studying a picture. You saw the JES ones in Figure 3.3. The MediaTools application one appears in Figure 3.14.

The JES MediaTools picture tool works from picture objects that you have defined *and named* in the Command Area. If you don't have the picture named, you can't view it with the JES MediaTools. p = makePicture(pickAFile()) will allow you to define a picture and name it p. You can then choose Picture tool... from the MediaTools menu, which will give you a pop-up menu of the available picture objects (by their variable names) and the opportunity to choose one of them by clicking OK (Figure 3.13).

The JES picture tool allows you to zoom at various levels of magnification by choosing a level in the Zoom menu. As you move your cursor around in the picture, press down with the mouse button. You'll be shown the (x, y)

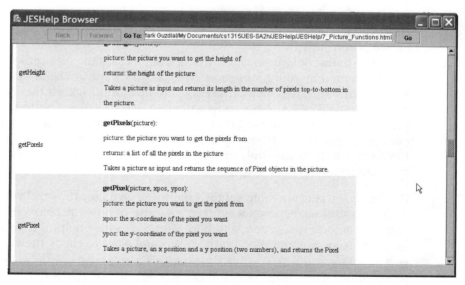

FIGURE 3.11: An example JES Help entry.

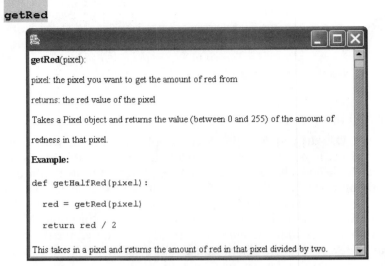

FIGURE 3.12: An example JES Explain entry.

FIGURE 3.13: Opening a picture in the JES MediaTools picture tool.

(horizontal, vertical) coordinates and the RGB values of the pixel your mouse cursor is currently over.

The MediaTools application works from files on the disk rather than picture objects named in your Command Area. If you want to check out a file before loading into JES, use the MediaTools *application.* Click on the PICTURE TOOLS box in MediaTools, and the tools will open. Use the OPEN button to bring up a file selection box—you click on directories you want to explore on the left, and on images you want on the right, then click OK. When the image appears, you have several different tools available. Move your cursor over the picture and press down with the mouse button.

■ The red, green, and blue values will be displayed for the pixel you're pointing at. This is useful when you want to get a sense of how the colors in your picture map to numeric red, green, and blue values. It's also helpful if you're going to be doing some computation on the pixels and want to check the values.

■ The *x* and *y* positions will be displayed for the pixel you're pointing at. This is useful when you want to figure out regions of the screen (e.g., if you want to process only part of the picture). If you know the range of *x* and *y* coordinates

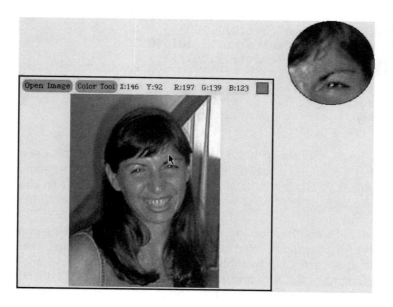

FIGURE 3.14: Using the MediaTools image exploration tools.

where you want to process, you can tune your for loop to reach just those sections.

■ Finally, a magnifier is available to let you see the pixels blown up. (The magnifier can be clicked and dragged around.)

■ 3.3 Changing Color Values

The easiest thing to do with pictures is to change the color values of their pixels by changing the red, green, and blue components. You can get radically different effects by simply tweaking these values. Some of Adobe Photoshop's *filters* do just what we're going to be doing in this section.

The way we're going to manipulate colors is by computing a *percentage* of the original color. If we want 50% of the amount of red in the picture, we're going to set the red channel to 0.50 times whatever it is right now. If we want to increase the red by 25%, we're going to set the red to 1.25 times whatever it is right now. Recall that the asterisk (*) is the operator for multiplication in Python.

3.3.1 Using Loops in Pictures

What we could do is to get each pixel in the picture and set it to a new value of red or green or blue. Let's say that we want to decrease the red by 50%. We can always write code like this:

```
>>> file="/Users/guzdial/mediasources/barbara.jpg"
>>> pict=makePicture(file)
>>> show(pict)
```

```
>>> setRed(getPixel(pict,11,100),0.50
* getRed(getPixel(pict,11,100)))
>>> setRed(getPixel(pict,11,101),0.50
* getRed(getPixel(pict,11,101)))
>>> setRed(getPixel(pict,11,102),0.50
* getRed(getPixel(pict,11,102)))
>>> setRed(getPixel(pict,11,102),0.50
* getRed(getPixel(pict,11,103)))
>>> repaint(pict)
```

That's pretty tedious to write, especially for all the pixels even in a small image. What we need is a way of telling the computer to do the same thing over and over again. Well, not exactly the same thing—we want to change what's going on in a well-defined way. We want to take one step each time, or process one additional pixel.

We can do this with a for loop. A for loop executes some commands (that you specify) for a *sequence* (that you provide), where each time the commands are executed, a particular variable (that you name) will have the value of a different element of the sequence. A sequence is an ordered collection of data. getPixels returns a sequence of all the pixel objects in an input picture.

We're going to write statements that look like this:

```
for pixel in getPixels(picture):
```

Let's talk through the pieces here.

■ First comes the command name for.

■ Next comes the variable name that you want to use in your code for addressing (and manipulating) the elements of the sequence. We're using the word pixel here because we want to process each of the pixels in the picture.

■ The word in is **required**—you must type it! Typing in makes the command more readable than leaving it out, so there's a benefit to the extra four keystrokes (space-i-n-space).

■ Then you need a *sequence*. The variable pixel is going to be assigned to each element of the sequence each time through the loop: one element of the sequence, one iteration through the loop, the next element of the sequence, the next iteration through the loop. We use the function getPixels to generate a sequence for us.

■ Finally, you need a colon (":"). The colon is important—it signifies that what comes next is a *block* (you should recall reading about blocks in the last chapter).

What comes next are the commands that you want to execute for each pixel. Each time the commands are executed, the variable (in our example pixel) will be a different element from the array. The commands (called the *body*) are specified as a block. This means that they should follow the for statement, each on its own line, *and indented by two more spaces!* For example, here is the for loop that sets each pixel's red channel to its own value (a useless exercise that will get more interesting in just a few pages).

```
for pixel in getPixels(picture):
  value = getRed(pixel)
  setRed(pixel,value)
```

Let's talk through this code.

■ The first statement says that we're going to have a `for` loop that will set the variable `pixel` to each of the elements of the sequence that is output from `getPixels(picture)`.

■ The next statement is indented, so it's part of the body of the `for` loop—one of the statements that will be executed each time `pixel` has a new value (whatever the next pixel in the picture is). It says to name the value of the red component of the pixel in the variable `pixel`. The name for that red component is `value`.

■ The third statement is still indented, so it's still part of the loop body. Here we set the value of the red channel (`setRed`) of the pixel named `pixel` to the value of the variable `value`.

Note that the earlier paragraph emphasized by two *more* spaces. Remember that what comes after a function definition `def` statement is *also* a block. If you have a `for` loop inside a function, then the `for` statement is indented two spaces already, so the body of the `for` loop (the statements to be executed) must be indented *four* spaces. The `for` loop's block is inside the function's block. That's called a ***nested block***—one block is nested inside the other. Here's an example of turning our useless loop into an equally useless function:

```
def doNothing(picture):
  for pixel in getPixels(picture):
    value = getRed(pixel)
    setRed(pixel,value)
```

You don't actually have to put loops into functions to use them. You can type them into the Command Area of JES. JES is smart enough to figure out that you need to type more than one command if you're specifying a loop, so it changes the prompt from >>> to .... Of course, it can't figure out when you're done, so you'll have to just hit ENTER without typing anything else to tell JES that you're done with the body of your loop. You probably realize that we don't really need the variable `value`—we can simply replace the variable with the function holding the same value. Here's how to do it at the command line:

```
>>> for pixel in getPixels(picture):
...   setRed(pixel,getRed(pixel))
```

Now that we see how to get the computer to do thousands of commands without writing thousands of individual lines, let's do something useful with this.

3.3.2 Increasing/Decreasing Red (Green, Blue)

A common desire when working with digital pictures is to shift a picture's *redness* (or greenness or blueness—most often the redness). You can shift it higher to "warm" the picture, or reduce it to "cool" the picture or to deal with overly red digital cameras.

The recipe given below reduces the amount of color 50% in an input picture. It uses the variable p to stand for the pixel (where we used the variable `pixel` before). It doesn't matter—the names are merely our choices.

RECIPE 8: Reduce the amount of red in a picture by 50%

```
def decreaseRed(picture):
    for p in getPixels(picture):
        value=getRed(p)
        setRed(p,value*0.5)
```

Go ahead and type the preceding code into your JES Program Area. Click Load to get Python to process the function (be sure to save it, something like `decreasered.py`) and thus make the name `decreaseRed` stand for this function. Follow along the example below to get a better idea of how this all works.

This recipe takes a picture as input—the one that we'll use to get the pixels from. To get a picture, we need a filename, and then we need to make a picture from it. After we apply the function `decreaseRed` to the picture, we'll want to repaint the picture to see the effect. Therefore, the recipe can be used like this:

```
>>> file="/Users/guzdial/mediasources/Katie-smaller.jpg"
>>> picture=makePicture(file)
>>> show(picture)
>>> decreaseRed(picture)
>>> repaint(picture)
```

COMMON BUG: Patience—for loops always end

The most common bug with this kind of code is to give up and hit the stop button before it ends on its own. If you're using a **for** loop, the program will *always* stop. But it might take a full minute (or two!) for some of the manipulations we'll do—especially if your source image is large.

The original picture and its red-reduced version appear in Figure 3.15 (and in color insert Figure I.3). 50% is obviously a *lot* of red to reduce. The picture looks like it was taken through a blue filter.

FIGURE 3.15: The original picture (*left*) and red-reduced version (*right*).

Tracing the Program: How Did That Work?

COMPUTER SCIENCE IDEA: The most important skill is tracing

The most important skill that you can develop in programming is the ability to *trace* your program. (This is sometimes also called *stepping* or *walking through* your program.) To trace your program is to walk through it, line by line, and figure out what happens. Looking at a program, can you *predict* what it's going to do? You should be able to by thinking through what it does.

How it works: Let's *trace* the function to decrease red and see how it worked. We want to break in at the point where we just called decreaseRed:

```
>>> file="/Users/guzdial/mediasources/Katie-smaller.jpg"
>>> picture=makePicture(file)
>>> show(picture)
>>> decreaseRed(picture)
```

What happens now? decreaseRed really stands for the function that we saw earlier, so it begins to execute.

```
def decreaseRed(picture):
  for p in getPixels(picture):
    value=getRed(p)
    setRed(p,value*0.5)
```

The first line we execute is def decreaseRed(picture):. This says that the function should expect some input, and that the input will be named picture during the execution of the function.

COMPUTER SCIENCE IDEA: Names inside of functions are different from names outside of functions

The names inside a function (like `picture`, `p`, and `value` in the `decreaseRed` example) are *completely* different from the names in the Command Area or any other function. We say that they have a different *scope*.

Inside the computer, we can imagine what it now looks like: There is some association between the word `picture` and the picture object that we gave it as input.

picture

Now we get to the line `for p in getPixels(picture):`. This means that all the pixels from the picture are lined up (within the computer) as a sequence, and that variable p should be assigned (associated with) the first one. We can imagine that inside the computer it now looks like this:

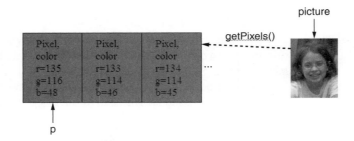

The pixel objects are all lined up, each with its own RGB values. p points at the first. Note that the variable `picture` is still there—we may not use it anymore, but it's still there.

Now we're at `value=getRed(p)`. This simply adds another name to the ones the computer is already tracking for us and gives it a simple numeric value.

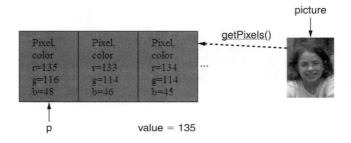

Finally, we're at the bottom of the loop. The computer executes `setRed(p,value*0.5)` which changes the red channel of the pixel p to 50% of the `value`. The value of p is odd, so the new value of the pixel rounds *down*. (Actually, the fractional part of the number is simply truncated.)

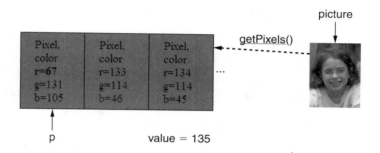

What happens next is very important: The loop starts over again! We go back to the `for` loop and take the *next* value in the sequence. The name p gets associated with that next value.

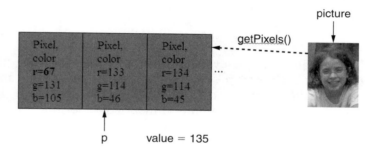

We get a new value for `value` at `value=getRed(p)`, so now `value` is 133, rather than the 135 it was from the first pixel.

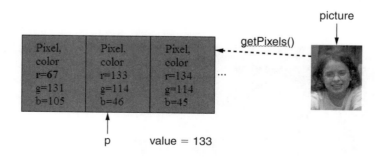

And then we change *that* pixel's red channel.

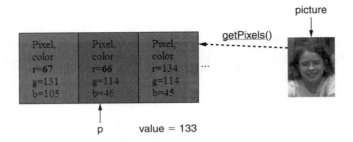

Eventually, we get Figure 3.15 (and color insert Figure I.3). We keep going through all the pixels in the sequence and changing all the red values.

3.3.3 Testing the Program: Did That Really Work?

How do we know that what we did really worked? Sure, *something* happened to the picture, but did we really decrease the red? By 50%?

MAKING IT WORK TIP: Don't just trust your own programs!

It's easy to mislead yourself into thinking that your program worked. After all, you told the computer to do something, so you shouldn't be surprised if the computer did what you wanted. But computers are really stupid—they can't figure out what you want. They only do what you tell them. It's pretty easy to get it *almost* right. Be sure to check.

We can check it several ways. One way is with the MediaTools. Create two picture objects, p = makePicture(pickAFile()) and p2 = makePicture(pickAFile()) and pick the same picture each time. Decrease the red in one of them. Open them both in the MediaTools picture tool, then check the RGB values at the same x and y coordinates (Figure 3.16).

We can also use the functions that we know in the Command Area to check the red values of individual pixels.

```
>>> file = pickAFile()
>>> pict = makePicture(file)
>>> pixel = getPixel(pict,1,1)
```

FIGURE 3.16: Using the MediaTools picture tool to convince ourselves that the red was decreased.

```
>>> print pixel
Pixel, color=color r=168 g=131 b=105
>>> decreaseRed(pict)
>>> newPixel = getPixel(pict,1,1)
>>> print newPixel
Pixel, color=color r=84 g=131 b=105
>>> print 168 * 0.5
84.0
```

3.3.4 Increasing Red

Let's increase the red in the picture now. If multiplying the red component by 0.5 reduced it, multiplying it by something over 1.0 should increase it.

RECIPE 9: Increase the red component by 20%

```
def increaseRed(picture):
    for p in getPixels(picture):
        value=getRed(p)
        setRed(p,value*1.2)
```

How it works: We would use increaseRed using the same kind of Command Area statements as we did for decreaseRed. When we type something like increaseRed(pict), the same kind of process occurs. We get all the pixels of the input picture pict (whatever that is), then assign the variable p to the first pixel in the list. We get its red value (say, 100) and name that value. We assign the red value of the pixel currently represented by the name p to 1.2 * 100 or 120. We then repeat the process for *every* pixel p in the input picture.

We can even get rid of a color component completely. The next recipe erases the blue component from a picture (in the color insert, Figure I.4).

RECIPE 10: Clear the blue component from a picture

```
def clearBlue(picture):
    for p in getPixels(picture):
        setBlue(p,0)
```

■ 3.4 Creating a Sunset

We can certainly do more than one picture manipulation at once. Once, I wanted to generate a sunset out of a beach scene. My first attempt was to increase the red, but that doesn't work. Some of the red values in a given picture are pretty high. If you go past 255 for a channel value, you *wrap-around*. If you setRed of a pixel to 256, you'll actually get *zero*. So increasing red created bright blue-green (no red) spots.

FIGURE 3.17: Original beach scene (*left*) and at (fake) sunset (*right*).

My second thought was that maybe what happens in a sunset is that there is *less* blue and green, thus *emphasizing* the red, without actually increasing it. Here is the program that I wrote for that:

RECIPE 11: Making a sunset

```
def makeSunset(picture):
    for p in getPixels(picture):
        value=getBlue(p)
        setBlue(p,value*0.7)
        value=getGreen(p)
        setGreen(p,value*0.7)
```

How it works: As in past examples, we take an input `picture` and make the variable p stand for each pixel in the input picture. We get each blue component and then set it again after multiplying its original value by 0.70. We then do the same to the green. Effectively, we're changing both the blue and green channels—reducing each by 30%. The effect works pretty well, as seen in Figure 3.17 (and in the color insert Figure I.5).

3.4.1 Making Sense of Functions

You probably have lots of questions about functions at this point. Why did we write these functions in this way? How is it that we're reusing variable names like `picture` in both the function and the Command Area? Are there other ways to write these functions? Is there such a thing as a better or worse function?

Since we're always picking a file (or typing in a filename) and *then* making a picture before calling one of our picture manipulation functions and *then* showing or repainting the picture, it's natural to ask why we don't build those in. Why doesn't *every* function have `pickAFile()` and `makePicture` in it?

We do the functions in the way that makes them more *general* and *reusable*. We want each function to do one and only one thing, so that we can use the function again in a new context where we need that one thing done. An example may make this clearer. Consider the recipe to make a sunset (Recipe 11). It works by reducing the green and blue, each by 30%. What if we rewrote this function so that it calls two *smaller* functions that just do the two pieces of the manipulation? We'd end up with something like Recipe 12.

RECIPE 12: Making a sunset as three functions

```
def makeSunset(picture):
  reduceBlue(picture)
  reduceGreen(picture)

def reduceBlue(picture):
  for p in getPixels(picture):
    value=getBlue(p)
    setBlue(p,value*0.7)

def reduceGreen(picture):
  for p in getPixels(picture):
    value=getGreen(p)
    setGreen(p,value*0.7)
```

How it works: The first thing to realize is that this actually does work. make-Sunset does the same thing here as in the previous recipe. The function makeSunset takes an input picture, then calls reduceBlue with the same input picture. reduceBlue makes p stand for each pixel in the input picture, and reduces the blue of each by 30% (by multiplying it by 0.7). reduceBlue then ends, and the *flow of control* (i.e., which statement executes next) returns to makeSunset and the *next* statement is executed. That is the call to the function reduceGreen with the same input picture. As before, reduceGreen walks each of the pixels and reduces the green value by 30%.

It's perfectly okay to have multiple functions in one Program Area, saved in one file. It's perfectly okay to have one function (makeSunset in this case) use other functions written by the programmer in the same file (reduceBlue and reduceGreen). You use makeSunset just as you did before. It's the same recipe (it tells the computer to do the same thing), but with different functions. The earlier recipe did everything in one function, and this one does it in three. In fact, you can also use reduceBlue and reduceGreen—make a picture in the Command Area and pass it as input to either of them. They work just like decreaseRed.

What's different is that the function makeSunset is somewhat simpler to read. It states pretty clearly, "To make a sunset means to reduce blue and reduce green." Being simple to read *is* important.

COMPUTER SCIENCE IDEA: Programs are for people.

Computers couldn't care less what a program looks like. Programs are written to communicate with *people*. Making programs easy to read and understand means that they are more easily changed and reused, and they more effectively communicate process to other humans.

What if we had written reduceBlue and reduceGreen with pickAFile and show and repaint in it? We would be asked for the picture twice—once in each function. Because we wrote these functions to *only* reduce the blue and reduce the green ("one and only one thing"), we can use them in new functions like makeSunset.[1]

Now let's say that we put pickAFile and makePicture into the makeSunset. The functions reduceBlue and reduceGreen are completely flexible and reusable again. But makeSunset is now less flexible and reusable. Is that a big deal? No, not if you only care about having the function to give a sunset look to a single frame. But what if you later want to build a movie with a few hundred frames, to each of which you want to add a sunset look? Do you really want to pick out each of those few hundred frames? Or would you rather make a loop to go through the frames (which we'll learn how to do in a few chapters) and send each of them as input to the *more general* form of makeSunset? That's why we make functions general and reusable—you never know when you're going to want to use a function again, in a larger context.

MAKING IT WORK TIP: Don't start by trying to write applications

New programmers often want to write complete applications that a non-technical user can use. You may want to write a makeSunset application that goes out and fetches a picture for a user and generates a sunset. Building good user interfaces that anyone can use is hard work. Start out more slowly. It's hard enough to make a function that takes a picture as input. You can work on user interfaces later.

We could also write these functions with explicit filenames by saying at the beginning of one of the programs:

```
file="/Users/guzdial/mediasources/katie.jpg"
```

That way, we wouldn't be prompted for a file each time. But then the functions only work for the one file, and if we want them to work for some other file, we have to modify them. Do you really want to change the function each time you use it? It's easier to leave the function alone, and change the picture that you hand to it.

Of course, we could change any of our functions to be handed a filename rather than a picture. For example, we could write:

```
def makeSunset(filename):
    reduceBlue(filename)
    reduceGreen(filename)

def reduceBlue(filename):
    filename = makePicture(filename)
    for p in getPixels(picture):
```

---

[1] The new makeSunset will take twice as long to finish as the original one because every pixel is changed twice. We address this in Chapter 13. The important issue is still to write the code readably *first*, and worry about efficiency later.

```
      value=getBlue(p)
      setBlue(p,value*0.7)

  def reduceGreen(filename):
    picture=makePicture(filename)
    for p in getPixels(picture):
      value=getGreen(p)
      setGreen(p,value*0.7)
```

Is this better or worse than the code we saw before? At some level, it doesn't matter—we can work with pictures or filenames, whichever makes more sense to us. The filename-as-input version does have several disadvantages, though. For one, it doesn't work! The picture is made in each of reduceGreen and reduceBlue, but then it isn't saved, so it gets lost at the end of the function. The earlier version of makeSunset (and its *subfunctions*, the functions it calls) works by *side effects*—the function doesn't return anything, but it changes the input object directly.

We could fix the loss-of-the-picture by saving the file to disk after we're done with each function, but then the functions are doing more than "one and only one thing." There's also the inefficiency of making the picture twice, and if we were to add in the saving, saving the picture twice. Again, the best functions do "one and only one thing."

Even larger functions, like makeSunset, do "one and only one thing." makeSunset makes a sunset-looking picture. It does so *by* reducing green and reducing blue. It calls two other functions to do that. What we end up with is a *hierarchy* of goals—the "one and only one thing" that is being done. makeSunset does its one thing by asking two other functions to do their one thing. We call this **hierarchical decomposition** (breaking down a problem into smaller parts, and then breaking down the smaller parts until you get something that you can easily program), and it's very powerful for creating complex programs out of pieces that you understand.

Names in functions are *completely* separate from names in the Command Area. The *only* way to get any data (pictures, sounds, filenames, numbers) from the Command Area into a function is by passing it in as input to the function. Within the function, you can use any names you want. Names that you first define within the function (like picture in the last example) and names that you use to stand for the input data (like filename) *only* exist while the function is running. When the function is done, variable names literally do not exist anymore.

This is really an advantage. Earlier, we said that naming is very important to computer scientists: We name everything, from data to functions. But if each name could mean one and only one thing *forever*, we'd run out of names. In natural language, words mean different things in different contexts (e.g., "What do you mean?" and "You are being mean!"). A function is a different context—names can mean something different than they do outside of that function.

Sometimes you will compute something inside a function that you want to return to the Command Area or to a calling function. We've already seen functions that output a value, like `pickAFile`, which outputs a filename. If you did a `makePicture` inside a function, you might want to output the picture that you created inside the function. You can do this by using `return`, which we'll talk more about later.

The name you give to a function's input can be thought of as a *placeholder*. Whenever the placeholder appears, imagine the input data appearing instead. So in a function like:

```
def decreaseRed(picture):
  for p in getPixels(picture):
    value=getRed(p)
    setRed(p,value*0.5)
```

We are going to call `decreaseRed` with a statement like `decreaseRed(myPicture)`. Whatever picture is in `myPicture` *becomes known as* `picture` while `decreaseRed` is running. For those few seconds, `picture` in `decreaseRed` and `myPicture` in the Command Area *refer to the same picture*. Changing the pixels in one changes the pixels in the other.

We've now talked about different ways of writing the same function—some better, some worse. There are other ways that are pretty much equivalent, and some that are much better. Let's consider a few more ways that we can write functions.

We can pass in more than one input at a time. Consider this version of decreaseRed:

```
def decreaseRed(picture, amount):
  for p in getPixels(picture):
    value=getRed(p)
    setRed(p,value*amount)
```

We would use this one by saying something like `decreaseRed(mypicture,0.25)`. This use would reduce the red by 75%. We could say `decreaseRed(mypicture,1.25)` and *increase* red by 25%. Perhaps this function should be better named `changeRed`, because that's what it is now—a general way of changing the whole amount of red in a picture. That's a pretty useful and powerful function.

Recall seeing this code in Recipe 10:

```
def clearBlue(picture):
  for p in getPixels(picture):
    setBlue(p,0)
```

We could also write the same recipe like this:

```
def clearBlue(picture):
  for p in getPixels(picture):
    value = getBlue(p)
    setBlue(p,value*0)
```

It's important to note that this function achieves the *exact same* thing as the earlier recipe did. Both set the blue channel of all pixels to zero. An advantage of the latter function is that it is the same *form* as all the other color-changing functions we've seen. This may make it more understandable, which is useful. It is somewhat less efficient—it's not really necessary to *get* the blue value before setting it to zero, nor is it necessary to multiply by zero when we just want the value of zero. The function is really doing more than it needs to do—it's not doing "one and only one thing."

■ 3.5 Lightening and Darkening

To lighten or darken a picture is pretty simple. It's the same pattern we saw previously, but instead of changing a color component, you change the overall color. Here are lightening and then darkening as recipes. Figure 3.18 (color insert Figure I.6) shows the lighter and darker versions of the original picture seen earlier.

RECIPE 13: Lighten the picture

```
def lighten(picture):
    for px in getPixels(picture):
        color = getColor(px)
        makeLighter(color)
        setColor(px,color)
```

How it works: The variable px is used to represent each of the pixels in the input picture. (Not p! Does it matter? Not to the computer—if p means "pixel" to you, then use it, but feel free to use px or px1 or even pixel!) color takes on the color of the pixel px. The function makeLighter changes the input color as a *side effect*—makeLighter doesn't return anything, but directly changes the input color. We then set the color of the pixel px to the newly lightened color, and move on to the next pixel.

RECIPE 14: Darken the picture

```
def darken(picture):
    for px in getPixels(picture):
        color = getColor(px)
        makeDarker(color)
        setColor(px,color)
```

■ 3.6 Creating a Negative

Creating a *negative image* of a picture is much easier than you might at first imagine. Let's think it through. What we want is the opposite of each of the current values for red, green, and blue. It's easiest to understand at the extremes. If we have a red component of 0, we want 255 instead. If we have 255, we want the negative to have a zero.

FIGURE 3.18: Lightening (*left below*) and darkening (*right below*) of original picture (*at top*).

Now let's consider the middle ground. If the red component is slightly red (say, 50), we want something that is almost completely red—where the "almost" is the same amount of redness in the original picture. We want the maximum red (255), but 50 less than that. We want a red component of 255 − 50 = 205. In general, the negative should be 255 − *original*. We need to compute the negative of each of the red, green, and blue components, then create a new negative color, and set the pixel to the negative color.

Here's the recipe that does it, and you can see that it really does work (Figure 3.19 and color insert Figure I.7).

RECIPE 15: Create the negative of the original picture

```
def negative(picture):
    for px in getPixels(picture):
        red=getRed(px)
        green=getGreen(px)
        blue=getBlue(px)
        negColor=makeColor( 255-red, 255-green, 255-blue)
        setColor(px,negColor)
```

How it works: We use px to represent each of the pixels in the input picture. For each pixel px, we use the variables red, green, and blue to name the red, green, and blue components of the pixel's color. We make a *new* color with makeColor whose red component is 255-red, the green is 255-green, and the blue is 255-blue. This means that the new color is the *opposite* of the

FIGURE 3.19: Negative of the image.

original color. Finally, we set the color of the pixel px to the new negative color (negColor), and move on to the next pixel.

■ 3.7 Converting to Grayscale

Converting to grayscale is a fun recipe. It's short, not hard to understand, and yet has such a nice visual effect. It's a really nice example of what one can do easily yet powerfully by manipulating pixel color values.

Recall that the resultant color is gray whenever the red component, green component, and blue component have the same value. This means that our RGB encoding supports 256 levels of gray, from $(0, 0, 0)$ (black) to $(1, 1, 1)$ through $(100, 100, 100)$ and finally $(255, 255, 255)$ (white). The tricky part is figuring out what the replicated value should be.

What we want is a sense of the *intensity* of the color, called the *luminance*. It turns out that there is a pretty easy way to compute it: We average the three component colors. Since there are three components, the formula we're going to use for intensity is:

$$\frac{(red\ +\ green\ +\ blue)}{3}$$

This leads us to the following simple recipe and Figure 3.20 (and color insert Figure I.8).

RECIPE 16: Convert to grayscale

```
def grayScale(picture):
    for p in getPixels(picture):
        intensity = (getRed(p)+getGreen(p)+getBlue(p))/3
        setColor(p,makeColor(intensity,intensity,intensity))
```

FIGURE 3.20: Color picture converted to grayscale.

This is actually an overly simple notion of grayscale. Below is a recipe that takes into account how the human eye perceives *luminance*. Remember that we consider blue to be darker than red, even if there's the same amount of light reflected off. So we *weight* blue lower, and red more, when computing the average.

RECIPE 17: Convert to grayscale with weights

```
def grayScaleNew(picture):
    for px in getPixels(picture):
        newRed = getRed(px) * 0.299
        newGreen = getGreen(px) * 0.587
        newBlue = getBlue(px) * 0.114
        luminance = newRed+newGreen+newBlue
        setColor(px,makeColor(luminance,luminance,luminance))
```

How it works: We make px stand for each pixel in the picture. We then *weight* the redness, greenness, and blueness based on what empirical research shows about how we perceive the luminance of each of these colors. Note that 0.299 + 0.587 + 0.114 is 1.0. We're still going to end up with a value between 0 and 255, but we're going to make *more* of the luminance value come from the green part, less from the red, and still less from blue (which, we have already established, is perceived to be darkest). We then add these three weighted values together to get our new luminance. We make the color and set the color of the pixel px to the new color we have made.

Programming Summary

In this chapter, we talk about several kinds of encodings of data (or objects).

Pictures	Encodings of images, typically coming from a JPEG file.
Pixels	Sequences of Pixel objects. They *flatten* the two-dimensional nature of the pixels in a picture and give you instead an array-like sequence of pixels. `pixels[1]` returns the leftmost pixel in a picture.
Pixel	A dot in the picture. It has a color and an (x, y) position associated with it. It remembers its own picture so that a change to the pixel changes the real dot in the picture.
Color	A mixture of red, green, and blue values, each between 0 and 255.

Picture program pieces

`getPixels`	Takes a picture as input and returns the sequence of pixel objects in the picture.
`getPixel`	Takes a picture, an *x* position, and a *y* position (two numbers), and returns the pixel object at that point in the picture.
`getWidth`	Takes a picture as input and returns its width in the number of pixels across the picture.
`getHeight`	Takes a picture as input and returns its length in the number of pixels top-to-bottom in the picture.
`writePictureTo`	Takes a picture and a file name (string) as input, then writes the picture to the file as a JPEG. (Be sure to end the filename in ".jpg" for the operating system to understand it properly.)

Pixel program pieces

`getRed, getGreen, getBlue`	Each of these functions takes a pixel object and returns the value (between 0 and 255) of the amount of redness, greenness, and blueness (respectively) in that pixel.
`setRed, setGreen, setBlue`	Each of these functions takes a pixel object and a value (between 0 and 244) and sets the redness, greenness, or blueness (respectively) of that pixel to the given value.
`getColor`	Takes a pixel and returns the color object at that pixel.
`setColor`	Takes a pixel object and a color object and sets the color for that pixel.
`getX, getY`	Takes a pixel object and returns the *x* or *y* position (respectively) of where that pixel is at in the picture.

Color program pieces

makeColor	Takes three inputs for the red, green, and blue components (in order), then returns a color object.
pickAColor	Takes no input but puts up a color picker. Find the color you want, and the function will return the color object of what you picked.
distance	Takes two color objects and returns a single number representing the distance between the colors. The red, green, and blue values of the colors are taken as a point in (x, y, z) space, and the Cartesian distance is computed.
makeDarker, makeLighter	Each takes a color and returns a slightly darker or lighter version (respectively) of the color.

There are a bunch of ***constants*** that are useful in this chapter. These are variables with predefined values. These values are colors: black, white, blue, red, green, gray, darkGray, lightGray, yellow, orange, pink, magenta, cyan.

Problems

3.1   Some picture concepts questions:
- Why don't we see red, green, and blue spots at each position in our picture?
- What is luminance?
- Why is the maximum value of any color channel 255?
- The color encoding we're using is RGB. What does this mean, in terms of the amount of memory required to represent color? Is there a limit to the number of colors that we can represent? Are there *enough* colors representable in RGB?

3.2
```
def testme(p,q,r):
    if q > 50:
        print r
    value = 10
    for i in range(1,p):
        print "Hello"
        value = value - 1
    print value
    print r
```
If we execute testme(5,51,"Hello back to you!"), what will print?

3.3   Recipe 8 is obviously too much color reduction. Write a version that only reduces the red by 10%, then one by 20%. Can you find pictures where each is most useful? Note that you can always repeatedly reduce the redness in a picture, but you don't want to have to do it *too* many times.

3.4   Write the blue and green versions of the reduce red function—Recipe 8.

3.5   Each of the following is equivalent to the increase red function—Recipe 9. Test them and convince yourself that they work. Which do you prefer and why?

```
def increaseRed2(picture):
  for p in getPixels(picture):
    setRed(p,getRed(p)*1.2)

def increaseRed3(picture):
  for p in getPixels(picture):
    redComponent = getRed(p)
    greenComponent = getGreen(p)
    blueComponent = getBlue(p)
    newRed=int(redComponent*1.2)
    newColor = makeColor(newRed,greenComponent,
  blueComponent)
    setColor(p,newColor)
```

3.6 If you keep increasing the red, eventually some pixels become *bright* green and blue. If you check those pixels with the MediaTools, you'll find that the values of red are very *low*. What do you think is going on? How did they get so small?

3.7 Rewrite clear blue (Recipe 10) to clear red and green. For each of these, which would be the most useful in actual practice? How about combinations of them?

3.8 Rewrite clear blue Recipe 10 to *maximize* blue (i.e., set it to 255) instead of clearing it. Is this useful? Would the red or green versions of the maximize function be useful? Under what conditions?

3.9 Write a new version of the function increaseRed and decreaseRed (and blue and green) called changeColor that takes as input a picture *and* an amount to increase or decrease a color by *and* a number 1 (for red), 2 (for green), or 3 (for blue). The amount will be a number between −.99 and .99.

- changeColor(pict,-.10,1) should decrease the amount of red in the picture by 10%.
- changeColor(pict,.30,2) should increase the amount of green in the picture by 30%.
- changeRed(pict,0,3) should do nothing at all to the amount of blue (or red or green) in the picture.

3.10 As we have seen, there is more than one way to compute the right grayscale value for a color value. The simple recipe that we use in Recipe 16 may not be what your grayscale printer uses when printing a color picture. Compare the color (relatively unconverted by the printer) grayscale image using our simple algorithm in color insert Figure I.8 with the original color picture that the printer has converted to grayscale (left of Figure 3.15). How do the two pictures differ?

To Dig Deeper

A wonderful new book on how vision works, and how artists have learned to manipulate it, is *Vision and Art: The Biology of Seeing* by Margaret Livingstone [26].

CHAPTER 4

Modifying Pixels in a Range

4.1 Copying Pixels

4.2 Mirroring a Picture

4.3 Copying and Transforming Pictures

4.4 Replacing Colors: Red-Eye, Sepia Tones, and Posterizing

4.5 Combining Pixels: Blurring

4.6 Comparing Pixels: Edge Detection

Chapter Learning Objectives

The media learning goals for this chapter are:

- *To mirror pictures horizontally or vertically.*

- *To compose pictures into one another and create collages.*

- *To rotate pictures by flipping them on the diagonal.*

- *To scale pictures smaller and larger, and use blurring to smooth degradation.*

- *To implement controlled color changes, like red-eye removal, sepia tones, and posterizing.*

The computer science goals for this chapter are:

- *To use a* **for** *loop to generate indices.*

- *To use nested loops for addressing elements of a matrix.*

- *To use conditionals to create differentiated processes.*

- *To develop some debugging strategies—specifically, to use* **print** *statements to explore executing code.*

■ 4.1 Copying Pixels

We can only get so far in our image processing with `getPixels` before we need to know *where* a pixel is. For example, if we want to process only some of the pixels in a picture (say, just the red in someone's eyes, but not the red in her dress), we need to control which pixels we're manipulating. To do that, we'll need to start building our own `for` loops using `range`. Once we start doing this, we have more control over the exact *x* and *y* coordinates that we're processing, so we can start moving pixels where we want them. This is a very powerful feature.

Remember that a `for` loop makes an index variable take on each value in turn from a sequence. We've used sequences generated from `getPixels`, but it turns out that we can easily generate sequences of numbers using the function `range`. The function `range` takes two inputs: an integer starting point, and an integer ending point *which is not included in the sequence.*[1]

```
>>> print range(1,3)
[1, 2]
>>> print range(1,10)
[1, 2, 3, 4, 5, 6, 7, 8, 9]
```

Optionally, `range` can take a third input: how much to increment between elements of the sequence.

```
>>> print range(1,10,3)
[1, 4, 7]
>>> print range(1,10,2)
[1, 3, 5, 7, 9]
```

4.1.1 Looping Across the Pixels with range

Unlike sounds and samples (as we'll see later), we can't use just a single `for` loop if we want to address every pixel. We have to use *two* `for` loops—one to move horizontally across the pixels, and the other to move vertically to get every pixel. The function `getPixels` did this inside itself, to make it easier to write simple picture manipulations. But if you want to access each individual pixel, you'll need to use two loops, one for each dimension of the picture. The inner loop will be *nested* inside the outer loop, literally inside its block. At this point, you're going to have to be careful in how you space your code to make sure that your blocks line up right.

Your loops will look something like this:

```
for x in range(1,getWidth(picture)):
  for y in range(1,getHeight(picture)):
    pixel=getPixel(picture,x,y)
```

For example, here's Recipe 13, but using explicit pixel references.

---

[1] This can be unexpected but is part of the definition of Python, so it's not something up for change if you want to learn how Python really works.

RECIPE 18: Lighten the picture using nested loops

```
def lighten(picture):
    for x in range(1,getWidth(picture)):
        for y in range(1,getHeight(picture)):
            px = getPixel(picture,x,y)
            color = getColor(px)
            makeLighter(color)
            setColor(px,color)
```

How it works: Let's walk through (trace) how it would work. Imagine that we have just executed `lighten(myPicture)`.

1. `def lighten(picture):` The variable `picture` becomes the new name for the picture in `myPicture`.

2. `for x in range(1,getWidth(picture)):` Variable x takes on the value 1.

3. `for y in range(1,getHeight(picture)):` Variable y takes on the value 1.

4. `px = getPixel(picture,x,y)`. Variable px takes on the value of the pixel object at location $(1, 1)$.

5. `...setColor(px,color)`. We set the pixel at $(1, 1)$ to be the new lighter color.

6. `for y in range(1,getHeight(picture)):` Variable y now becomes 2. In other words, we're slowly moving down the first column of pixels, the column where x is 1.

7. `px = getPixel(picture,x,y)` px becomes the pixel at position $(1, 2)$.

8. We lighten that color.

9. `for y in range(1,getHeight(picture)):` Variable y now becomes 3. And so on, until y becomes one less than the height of the picture.

10. `for x in range(1,getWidth(picture)):` Variable x takes on the value 2.

11. Now y becomes 1 again, and we start down the next column.

12. And so on until all the colors of all the pixels are lightened.

■ 4.2 Mirroring a Picture

Let's start out with an interesting effect that is only occasionally useful, but is fun. Let's mirror a picture along its vertical axis. In other words, imagine that you have a mirror, and you place it on a picture so that the left side of the picture shows up in the mirror. That's the effect we're going to implement. We'll do it in a couple of different ways.

First, let's think through what we're going to do. We'll pick a horizontal `mirrorpoint`—halfway across the picture, `getWidth(picture)/2`. We'll have the xOffset value move from 1 to the `mirrorpoint`. At each value of xOffset, we want to copy the color at the pixel xOffset pixels to the *left* of the mirrorpoint to the pixel xOffset pixels to the *right* of the mirrorpoint. The left would be `mirrorpoint-xOffset`, and the right

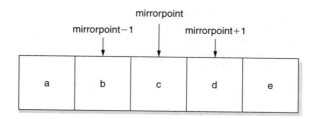

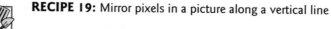

FIGURE 4.1: Once we pick a **mirrorpoint**, we can just walk xOffset halfway and subtract/add to **mirrorpoint**.

would be `mirrorpoint+xOffset`. Take a look at Figure 4.1 to convince yourself that we'll actually reach every pixel using this scheme. Here's the actual recipe.

RECIPE 19: Mirror pixels in a picture along a vertical line

```
def mirrorVertical(source):
    mirrorpoint = getWidth(source)/2
    for y in range(1,getHeight(source)):
        for xOffset in range(1,mirrorpoint):
            pright = getPixel(source, xOffset+mirrorpoint,y)
            pleft = getPixel(source, mirrorpoint-xOffset,y)
            c = getColor(pleft)
            setColor(pright,c)
```

How it works: `mirrorVertical` takes a source picture as input. We're using a vertical mirror halfway across the picture, so the `mirrorpoint` is the width of the picture divided by 2. We do the entire height of the picture, so the loop for y goes from 1 to the height of the picture. The `xOffset` goes from 1 to `mirrorPoint`, so that each reference to `xOffset+mirrorpoint,y` will be to a pixel on the right and `xOffset+mirrorPoint,y` will be a pixel on the left. Each time through the `xOffset` loop, we copy another column of pixels farther away from the `mirrorPoint` than the preceding iteration. We then get the color of the left pixel and set the right pixel to it.

We'd use it like this, and the result appears in Figure 4.2.

```
>>> file="/Users/guzdial/mediasources/santa.jpg"
>>> print file
/Users/guzdial/mediasources/santa.jpg
>>> picture=makePicture(file)
>>> mirrorVertical(picture)
>>> show(picture)
```

Can we mirror horizontally? Sure!

RECIPE 20: Mirror pixels horizontally, top to bottom

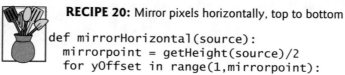

```
def mirrorHorizontal(source):
    mirrorpoint = getHeight(source)/2
    for yOffset in range(1,mirrorpoint):
```

```
        for x in range(1,getWidth(source)):
            pbottom = getPixel(source,x,yOffset+mirrorpoint)
            ptop = getPixel(source,x,mirrorpoint-yOffset)
            setColor(pbottom,getColor(ptop))
```

Now this last recipe copies from the top of the picture onto the bottom (see Figure 4.3). You can see that we're getting the color from p2, which is from `mirrorpoint-y`—which will always be *above* `mirrorpoint` because smaller values of y are nearer the top of the picture. To copy from the bottom up, simply swap `ptop` and `pbottom` (Figure 4.3).

RECIPE 21: Mirror pixels horizontally, bottom to top

```
def mirrorHorizontal(source):
    mirrorpoint = getHeight(source)/2
    for yOffset in range(1,mirrorpoint):
        for x in range(1,getWidth(source)):
            pbottom = getPixel(source,x,yOffset+mirrorpoint)
            ptop = getPixel(source,x,mirrorpoint-yOffset)
            setColor(ptop,getColor(pbottom))
```

Mirroring Usefully

While mirroring is mostly used for interesting effects, occasionally it has some more serious (but still fun) purposes. I took a picture of the Temple of Hephaestus in the ancient agora in Athens, Greece, when traveling to a conference (Figure 4.4). By sheer luck, I got the pediment dead horizontal. The pediment of the Temple of Hephaestus is damaged. I wondered if I could "fix" it by mirroring the good part onto the broken part.

FIGURE 4.2: Original picture (*left*) and mirrored along the vertical axis (*right*).

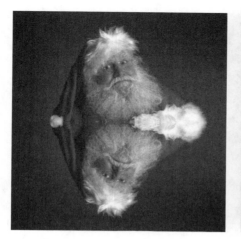
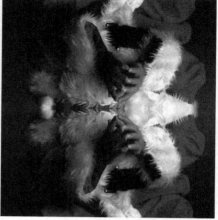

FIGURE 4.3:   Santa mirrored horizontally, bottom to top (*left*) and top to bottom (*right*).

FIGURE 4.4: Temple of Hephaestus from the ancient agora in Athens.

FIGURE 4.5: Coordinates where we need to do the mirroring.

I used MediaTools to figure out the range of values where I would need to do the mirroring and the point where I should mirror (Figure 4.5). The function I wrote to do the repair is below, and the final picture is in (Figure 4.6)—it worked pretty well! Of course, it is possible to tell that it was digitally manipulated. For example, if you check the shadows, you can see that the sun must have been on the left and the right at the same time.

FIGURE 4.6: The manipulated temple.

RECIPE 22: Mirror the Temple of Hephaestus

```
def mirrorTemple():
    source = makePicture(getMediaPath("temple.jpg"))
    mirrorpoint = 277
    lengthToCopy = mirrorpoint - 14
    for xOffset in range(1,lengthToCopy):
        for y in range(28,98):
            pleft = getPixel(source,mirrorpoint-xOffset,y)
            pright = getPixel(source,mirrorpoint+xOffset,y)
            setColor(pright,getColor(pleft))
    show(source)
    return source
```

How it works: We know that the mirrorPoint has to be at 277, from use of MediaTools. We don't really have to copy from 1 to 277, because the edge of the temple is at x column 14. We really only have to copy 263 (277-14) pixels. So xOffset takes that range, from 1 (copying the columns right next to the mirrorPoint to 263 (copying the pixels at the farthest edges of the temple).

In this recipe, we're using getMediaPath. The function getMediaPath is a shorthand. If you keep your media in one place, and you'd like to refer to it just by its base name, you can use getMediaPath, which actually generates a complete path for you. *However, you can only use it if you use setMediaPath first.* setMediaPath lets you specify the place (directory) where you store your media. setMediaPath tells getMediaPath how to construct the path.

This recipe is also one of the first ones we've written where we explicitly return a value. Return sets the value that the function provides as output. In mirrorTemple(), the return value is the picture object source where the repaired temple is stored. If we invoked this function with fixedTemple = mirrorTemple(), the name fixedTemple would represent the picture returned from mirrorTemple().

COMMON BUG: Return is always last

The statement **return** specifies what the return value is from the function, but it also has the effect of *ending* the function. A common bug is to try to **print** or **show** *after* a **return** statement, but that won't work. Once **return** is executed, no more statements in the function are executed.

Why do we `return` the fixed temple picture object? Why *haven't* we ever returned before? The functions we've written before this directly manipulate the input objects—this is called computation by *side effect*. We can't do it in this case—there are no inputs to `mirrorTemple()`. The rule of thumb on when to `return` is this: If you *create* the object of interest inside the function, you need to `return` it or else the object will just disappear when the function ends. Because the picture object `source` is created (using `makePicture`) inside the function `mirrorTemple()`, the object only exists within the function.

Why `return` anything at all? We do it for future use. Can you imagine *possibly* wanting to do something with the mirrored temple? Maybe composing it into a collage? Change its color? You should `return` the object so that you will have that option later.

The temple example is a good one to ask ourselves about. If you really understand it you can answer questions like "What is the *first* pixel to be mirrored in this function?" and "How many pixels get copied anyway?" You should be able to figure out the answers by thinking through the program—pretend you're the computer and execute the program in your mind.

If that's too hard, you can insert `print` statements, like this:

```
def mirrorTemple():
  source = makePicture(getMediaPath("temple.jpg"))
  mirrorpoint = 277
  lengthToCopy = mirrorpoint - 14
  for x in range(1,lengthToCopy):
    for y in range(28,98):
      print "Copying color from",mirrorpoint-x,y
      print "to",mirrorpoint+x,y
      p = getPixel(source,mirrorpoint-x,y)
      p2 = getPixel(source,mirrorpoint+x,y)
      setColor(p2,getColor(p))
  show(source)
  return source
```

When we run this version, it takes a *long* time to finish. Hit STOP after a little bit, since we only really care about the first few pixels. Here's what I got:

```
>>> p2=mirrorTemple()
Copying color from 276 28 to 278 28
Copying color from 276 29 to 278 29
Copying color from 276 30 to 278 30
```

It copies from right next to the mirror point (277), since x is 1 at first, and we copy from `mirrorpoint-x` to `mirrorpoint+x`. Thus, we copy down the column before the mirrorpoint to the column of pixels to the right of the mirrorpoint. Then we move back one column to the left, and copy one column farther to the right.

How many pixels did we process? We can have the computer figure that one out, too. Before the loops, we say that our count is zero. Each time we copy a pixel, we add one to our count.

```
def mirrorTemple():
  source = makePicture(getMediaPath("temple.jpg"))
  mirrorpoint = 277
  lengthToCopy = mirrorpoint - 14
  count = 0
  for x in range(1,lengthToCopy):
    for y in range(28,98):
      p = getPixel(source,mirrorpoint-x,y)
      p2 = getPixel(source,mirrorpoint+x,y)
      setColor(p2,getColor(p))
      count = count + 1
  show(source)
  print "We copied",count,"pixels"
  return source
```

This comes back with We copied 18340 pixels. Where did this number come from? We copy 70 rows of pixels (y goes from 28 to 98). We copy 262 columns of pixels (x goes from 1 to $(277 - 14)$ 262). $70 * 262$ is 18,340.

■ 4.3 Copying and Transforming Pictures

We can create wholly new pictures when we copy pixels *across* pictures. We're going to end up keeping track of a *source* picture that we take pixels from and a *target* picture that we're going to set pixels in. Actually, we don't copy the pixels—we simply make the pixels in the target the same color as the pixels in the source. Copying pixels requires us to keep track of multiple index variables: the (x, y) positions in the source and the (x, y) in the target.

What's exciting about copying pixels is that making some small changes in how we deal with the index variables leads not only to *copying* the image but to *transforming* it. In this section, we're going to talk about copying, cropping, rotating, and scaling pictures.

We're going to make use of the *utility function* getMediaPath to make our coding of multiple file programs. We've seen it before. It's particularly helpful when you want to deal with several pieces of media in the same directory but don't want to spell out the whole directory name. You just have to remember to use setMediaPath first. All that getMediaPath does is to prepend the path found in setMediaPath to the input filename.

```
>>> setMediaPath()
New media folder: C:\Documents and Settings\Mark Guzdial\My
Documents\mediasources\
>>> getMediaPath("barbara.jpg")
'C:\\Documents and Settings\\Mark Guzdial\\My
Documents\\mediasources\\barbara.jpg'
>>> barb=makePicture(getMediaPath("barbara.jpg"))
```

Our target will be the paper-sized JPEG file in the mediasources directory; this is 7×9.5 inches, which will fit on a 9×11.5 inch lettersize piece of paper with 1 inch margins.

```
>>> paperfile=getMediaPath("7inx95in.jpg")
>>> paperpicture=makePicture(paperfile)
>>> print getWidth(paperpicture)
504
>>> print getHeight(paperpicture)
684
```

4.3.1 Copying

To copy a picture from one object to another, we simply make sure that we increment sourceX and targetX variables (the source and target index variables for the X axis) together, and the sourceY and targetY variables together. We could use a for loop, but that only increments *one* variable. We have to make sure that we increment the *other* variable (whichever one is *not* in the for) loop using an expression at the same time (as close as we can) as when the for loop increments things. We'll do this by setting initial values *just before* the loop starts, then adding to the index variable at the *bottom* of the loop.

Here's a recipe for copying the picture of Barbara to the canvas.

RECIPE 23: Copying picture to canvas

```
def copyBarb():
  # Set up the source and target pictures
  barbf=getMediaPath("barbara.jpg")
  barb = makePicture(barbf)
  canvasf = getMediaPath("7inX95in.jpg")
  canvas = makePicture(canvasf)
  # Now, do the actual copying
  targetX = 1
  for sourceX in range(1,getWidth(barb)):
    targetY = 1
    for sourceY in range(1,getHeight(barb)):
      color = getColor(getPixel(barb,sourceX,sourceY))
      setColor(getPixel(canvas,targetX,targetY), color)
      targetY = targetY + 1
    targetX = targetX + 1
  show(barb)
  show(canvas)
  return canvas
```

COMPUTER SCIENCE IDEA: Comments are good!

You see in Recipe 23 the use of lines with "#" at the start of them. This symbol says to Python "Ignore the rest of this line." What good is that? It allows you to put messages in the program to be read by humans and not the computer—messages that explain how things work, what sections of the program do, and why you did what you did. Remember that programs are for humans, not computers. Comments make the programs better suited to humans.

How it works: This program copies the picture of Barbara to the canvas (Figure 4.7).

■ The first few lines just set up the source (barb) and target (canvas) pictures.

■ Next comes the loop for managing the X index variables, sourceX for the source picture and targetX for the target picture. Here are the key parts of the loop:

```
targetX = 1
for sourceX in range(1,getWidth(barb)):
    # Y LOOP GOES HERE
    targetX = targetX + 1
```

Because of the way these statements are arranged, from the point of view of the Y loop, targetX and sourceX are always incremented together. targetX becomes 1 just before sourceX becomes 1 in the for loop. At the end of the for loop, targetX is incremented by 1, and then the loop starts over and sourceX is also incremented by 1 through the for statement.

The statement to increment targetX may look a little strange. targetX = targetX + 1 isn't making a mathematical statement (which couldn't possibly be true). Instead it's giving directions to the computer. It says "Make the value of targetX to be (right side of =) whatever the *current* value of targetX is *plus* 1."

■ Inside the loop for the X variables is the loop for the Y variables. It has a very similar structure, since its goal is to keep targetY and sourceY in sync in exactly the same way.

```
targetY = 1
for sourceY in range(1,getHeight(barb)):
```

FIGURE 4.7: Copying a picture to a canvas.

```
    color = getColor(getPixel(barb,sourceX,sourceY))
    setColor(getPixel(canvas,targetX,targetY), color)
    targetY = targetY + 1
```

It's inside the Y loop that we actually get the color from the source and set the corresponding pixel in the target to the same color.

It turns out that we can just as easily put the target variables in the for loops and set the source variables. The recipe that follows does the same as Recipe 23.

RECIPE 24: Copying picture to canvas another way

```
def copyBarb2():
  # Set up the source and target pictures
  barbf=getMediaPath("barbara.jpg")
  barb = makePicture(barbf)
  canvasf = getMediaPath("7inX95in.jpg")
  canvas = makePicture(canvasf)
  # Now, do the actual copying
  sourceX = 1
  for targetX in range(1,getWidth(barb)):
    sourceY = 1
    for targetY in range(1,getHeight(barb)):
      color = getColor(getPixel(barb,sourceX,sourceY))
      setColor(getPixel(canvas,targetX,targetY), color)
      sourceY = sourceY + 1
    sourceX = sourceX + 1
  show(barb)
  show(canvas)
  return canvas
```

Of course, we don't have to copy from $(1, 1)$ in the source to $(1, 1)$ in the target. We can easily copy somewhere else in the canvas. All we have to do is to change where the target X and Y coordinates *start*. The rest stays exactly the same (Figure 4.8).

RECIPE 25: Copy elsewhere into the canvas

```
def copyBarbMidway():
  # Set up the source and target pictures
  barbf=getMediaPath("barbara.jpg")
  barb = makePicture(barbf)
  canvasf = getMediaPath("7inX95in.jpg")
  canvas = makePicture(canvasf)
  # Now, do the actual copying
  targetX = 100
  for sourceX in range(1,getWidth(barb)):
    targetY = 100
    for sourceY in range(1,getHeight(barb)):
      color = getColor(getPixel(barb,sourceX,sourceY))
      setColor(getPixel(canvas,targetX,targetY), color)
      targetY = targetY + 1
```

```
    targetX = targetX + 1
show(barb)
show(canvas)
return canvas
```

Similarly, we don't have to copy a *whole* picture. *Cropping* is taking only part of a picture out of the whole picture. Digitally, that's just a matter of changing your start and end coordinates. To grab just Barb's face out of the picture, we only have to figure out what the coordinates are where her face is located, then use them on the dimensions of sourceX and sourceY (Figure 4.9). The face is at $(45, 25)$ to $(200, 200)$.

RECIPE 26: Cropping a picture onto a canvas

```
def copyBarbsFace():
  # Set up the source and target pictures
  barbf=getMediaPath("barbara.jpg")
  barb = makePicture(barbf)
  canvasf = getMediaPath("7inX95in.jpg")
  canvas = makePicture(canvasf)
  # Now, do the actual copying
  targetX = 100
  for sourceX in range(45,200):
    targetY = 100
    for sourceY in range(25,200):
      color = getColor(getPixel(barb,sourceX,sourceY))
      setColor(getPixel(canvas,targetX,targetY), color)
      targetY = targetY + 1
    targetX = targetX + 1
```

FIGURE 4.8: Copying a picture midway into a canvas.

```
show(barb)
show(canvas)
return canvas
```

How it works: The only difference between this program and the previous ones is the ranges on the `source` indices. We only want the x pixels between 45 and 200, so they are the inputs to `range` for `sourceX`. We only want the y pixels between 25 and 200, so they are the inputs to `range` that we use for `sourceY`. The rest is exactly the same.

We can still swap which variables are in the `for` loop and which are incremented. Computing the range for the target is a little complicated, though. If we want to start copying to $(100, 100)$, then the length of the picture is $200 - 45$ and the height is $200 - 25$. Here's the recipe.

RECIPE 27: Cropping the face into the canvas differently

```
def copyBarbsFace2():
    # Set up the source and target pictures
    barbf=getMediaPath("barbara.jpg")
    barb = makePicture(barbf)
    canvasf = getMediaPath("7inX95in.jpg")
    canvas = makePicture(canvasf)
    # Now, do the actual copying
    sourceX = 45
    for targetX in range(100,100+(200-45)):
      sourceY = 25
      for targetY in range(100,100+(200-25)):
        color = getColor(getPixel(barb,sourceX,sourceY))
```

FIGURE 4.9: Copying part of a picture onto a canvas.

```
        setColor(getPixel(canvas,targetX,targetY), color)
        sourceY = sourceY + 1
      sourceX = sourceX + 1
  show(barb)
  show(canvas)
  return canvas
```

How it works: Let's look at a small example to see what's going on in the copying recipe. We start out with a source and a target, and copy from the source to the target, pixel by pixel.

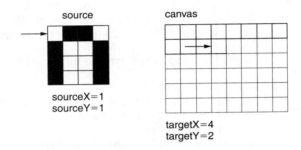

We then increment both `sourceY` and `targetY`, and copy again.

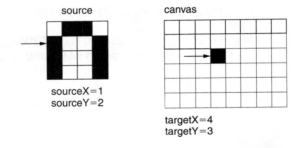

We continue down the column, incrementing both Y index variables.

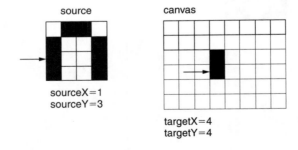

When done with that column, we increment the X index variables and move on to the next column, until we have copied every pixel.

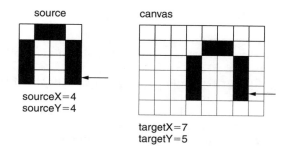

4.3.2 Creating a Collage

Here are a couple images of flowers (Figure 4.10), each 100 pixels wide. Let's make a *collage* of them, by combining several of our effects to create different flowers. We'll copy them all into the blank image 640x480.jpg. All we really have to do is to copy the pixel colors to the right places.

Here's how we run the collage (Figure 4.11):

```
>>> flowers=createCollage()
Picture, filename /Users/guzdial/mediasources/flower1.jpg
height 138 width 100 Picture, filename
/Users/guzdial/mediasources/flower2.jpg
height 227 width 100
Picture, filename /Users/guzdial/mediasources/640x480.jpg
height 480 width 640
```

FIGURE 4.10: Flowers to use in the collage.

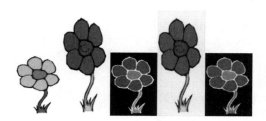

FIGURE 4.11: Collage of flowers.

RECIPE 28: Creating a collage

```
def createCollage():
  flower1=makePicture(getMediaPath("flower1.jpg"))
  print flower1
  flower2=makePicture(getMediaPath("flower2.jpg"))
  print flower2
  canvas=makePicture(getMediaPath("640x480.jpg"))
  print canvas
  #First picture, at left edge
  targetX=1
  for sourceX in range(1,getWidth(flower1)):
    targetY=getHeight(canvas)-getHeight(flower1)-5
    for sourceY in range(1,getHeight(flower1)):
      px=getPixel(flower1,sourceX,sourceY)
      cx=getPixel(canvas,targetX,targetY)
      setColor(cx,getColor(px))
      targetY=targetY + 1
    targetX=targetX + 1
  #Second picture, 100 pixels over
  targetX=100
  for sourceX in range(1,getWidth(flower2)):
    targetY=getHeight(canvas)-getHeight(flower2)-5
    for sourceY in range(1,getHeight(flower2)):
      px=getPixel(flower2,sourceX,sourceY)
      cx=getPixel(canvas,targetX,targetY)
      setColor(cx,getColor(px))
      targetY=targetY + 1
    targetX=targetX + 1
  #Third picture, flower1 negated
  negative(flower1)
  targetX=200
  for sourceX in range(1,getWidth(flower1)):
    targetY=getHeight(canvas)-getHeight(flower1)-5
    for sourceY in range(1,getHeight(flower1)):
      px=getPixel(flower1,sourceX,sourceY)
      cx=getPixel(canvas,targetX,targetY)
      setColor(cx,getColor(px))
      targetY=targetY + 1
    targetX=targetX + 1
  #Fourth picture, flower2 with no blue
  clearBlue(flower2)
  targetX=300
  for sourceX in range(1,getWidth(flower2)):
    targetY=getHeight(canvas)-getHeight(flower2)-5
    for sourceY in range(1,getHeight(flower2)):
      px=getPixel(flower2,sourceX,sourceY)
      cx=getPixel(canvas,targetX,targetY)
      setColor(cx,getColor(px))
      targetY=targetY + 1
```

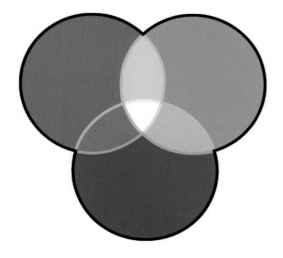

FIGURE 1.1: Merging red, green, and blue to make new colors

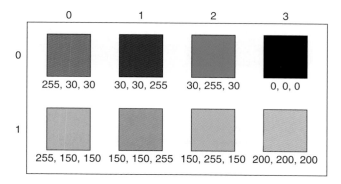

FIGURE 1.2: Color: RGB triplets in a matrix representation

FIGURE I.3: Color: The original picture (left) and red-reduced version (right)

FIGURE I.4: Color: Original (left) and blue erased (right)

FIGURE I.5: Original beach scene (left) and at (fake) sunset (right)

FIGURE I.6: Color: Lightening and darkening of original picture

FIGURE I.7: Color: Negative of the image

FIGURE I.8: Color: Color picture converted to grayscale

FIGURE 1.9:   Color: Increasing reds in the browns, within a certain range

FIGURE 1.10:   Color: Increasing reds in the browns

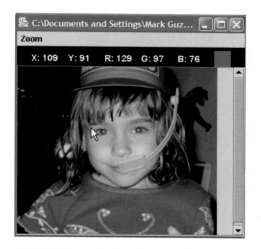
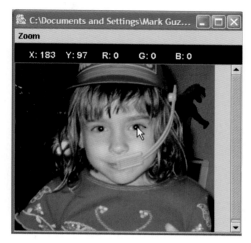

FIGURE 1.11: Finding the range of where Jenny's eyes are red, then changing them to black

FIGURE 1.12: Frames from the slow sunset movie

FIGURE 1.13: Frames from the slow fade-out movie

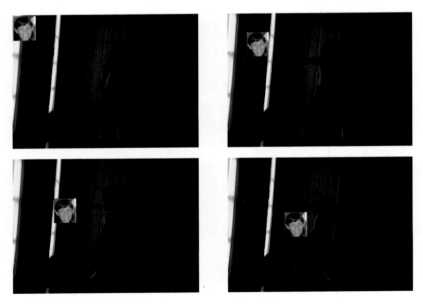

FIGURE 1.14: Frames from the Mommy watching Katie move

FIGURE 1.15: Frames from the original too dark movie

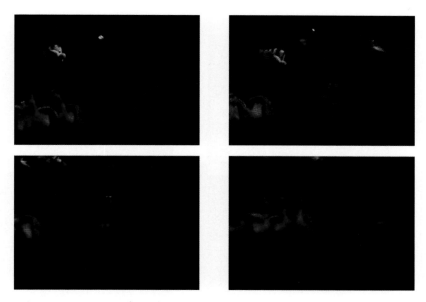

FIGURE 1.16: Frames from the modified lighter movie

FIGURE 1.17: Frames from the original movie with kids crawling in front of a blue screen

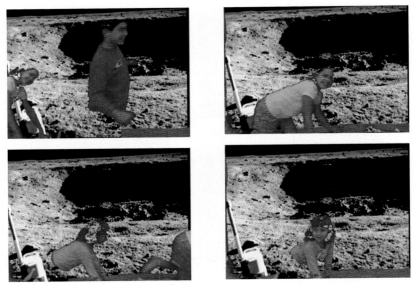

FIGURE 1.18: Frames from the kids on the moon movie

```
        targetX=targetX + 1
    #Fifth picture, flower1, negated with decreased red
    decreaseRed(flower1)
    targetX=400
    for sourceX in range(1,getWidth(flower1)):
      targetY=getHeight(canvas)-getHeight(flower1)-5
      for sourceY in range(1,getHeight(flower1)):
        px=getPixel(flower1,sourceX,sourceY)
        cx=getPixel(canvas,targetX,targetY)
        setColor(cx,getColor(px))
        targetY=targetY + 1
      targetX=targetX + 1
    show(canvas)
    return(canvas)
```

How it works: While this program looks long, it's really just the same copying loop we've seen repeatedly now, but one loop after the other.

■ First we create the flower1 and flower2 picture objects that we're copying into the canvas.

■ The first flower is just a plain copy of picture1 at the leftmost edge of the canvas. We want the bottom of the flower to be five pixels from the edge, so targetY starts at the height of the canvas (that would be the bottommost index), minus the flower's height, minus 5. As targetY gets incremented (added to), it will grow *down* toward the bottom. It will get incremented for the number of pixels in the height of the flower (see the sourceY loop), so the maximum value targetY will take is the canvas height minus 5.

■ We next copy the second picture in, starting targetX 100 pixels to the right, but the same loops really.

■ Now we negate flower1, then copy it in, moving farther to the right (targetX is now starting at 300).

■ Then we clear the blue from flower2 and copy it into the canvas even farther to the right.

■ The fifth flower decreases the red of flower1 *which is already negated* (from the third set of loops).

■ We then show the canvas and return it. We need to return the canvas because we made it inside the collage function. If we don't return it, it simply disappears when the function ends and the function's context ends.

As long as this is, it would be even longer if we actually put all the effects in the same function. Instead, I copied the functions we did earlier. My whole program area looks like this:

```
def createCollage():
  flower1=makePicture(getMediaPath("flower1.jpg"))
  print flower1
  flower2=makePicture(getMediaPath("flower2.jpg"))
```

```
print flower2
canvas=makePicture(getMediaPath("640x480.jpg"))
print canvas
#First picture, at left edge
targetX=1
for sourceX in range(1,getWidth(flower1)):
  targetY=getHeight(canvas)-getHeight(flower1)-5
  for sourceY in range(1,getHeight(flower1)):
    px=getPixel(flower1,sourceX,sourceY)
    cx=getPixel(canvas,targetX,targetY)
    setColor(cx,getColor(px))
    targetY=targetY + 1
  targetX=targetX + 1
#Second picture, 100 pixels over
targetX=100
for sourceX in range(1,getWidth(flower2)):
  targetY=getHeight(canvas)-getHeight(flower2)-5
  for sourceY in range(1,getHeight(flower2)):
    px=getPixel(flower2,sourceX,sourceY)
    cx=getPixel(canvas,targetX,targetY)
    setColor(cx,getColor(px))
    targetY=targetY + 1
  targetX=targetX + 1
#Third picture, flower1 negated
negative(flower1)
targetX=200
for sourceX in range(1,getWidth(flower1)):
  targetY=getHeight(canvas)-getHeight(flower1)-5
  for sourceY in range(1,getHeight(flower1)):
    px=getPixel(flower1,sourceX,sourceY)
    cx=getPixel(canvas,targetX,targetY)
    setColor(cx,getColor(px))
    targetY=targetY + 1
  targetX=targetX + 1
#Fourth picture, flower2 with no blue
clearBlue(flower2)
targetX=300
for sourceX in range(1,getWidth(flower2)):
  targetY=getHeight(canvas)-getHeight(flower2)-5
  for sourceY in range(1,getHeight(flower2)):
    px=getPixel(flower2,sourceX,sourceY)
    cx=getPixel(canvas,targetX,targetY)
    setColor(cx,getColor(px))
    targetY=targetY + 1
  targetX=targetX + 1
#Fifth picture, flower1, negated with decreased red
decreaseRed(flower1)
targetX=400
for sourceX in range(1,getWidth(flower1)):
  targetY=getHeight(canvas)-getHeight(flower1)-5
```

```
      for sourceY in range(1,getHeight(flower1)):
        px=getPixel(flower1,sourceX,sourceY)
        cx=getPixel(canvas,targetX,targetY)
        setColor(cx,getColor(px))
        targetY=targetY + 1
      targetX=targetX + 1
    show(canvas)
    return(canvas)

  def clearBlue(picture):
    for p in getPixels(picture):
      setBlue(p,0)

  def negative(picture):
    for px in getPixels(picture):
      red=getRed(px)
      green=getGreen(px)
      blue=getBlue(px)
      negColor=makeColor( 255-red, 255-green, 255-blue)
      setColor(px,negColor)

  def decreaseRed(picture):
    for p in getPixels(picture):
      value=getRed(p)
      setRed(p,value*0.5)
```

4.3.3 Rotation

The image can be transformed by using the index variables differently or incrementing them differently, but otherwise keeping the same copying algorithm. Let's rotate Barb 90 degrees—at least that's the way it will seem. What we'll really do is to flip the image across the diagonal. We'll do that by simply swapping the X and Y variables in the target—we increment them the exact same way, but we'll *use* them X for Y and Y for X (Figure 4.12).

RECIPE 29: Rotating (flipping) a picture

```
def copyBarbSideways():
  # Set up the source and target pictures
  barbf=getMediaPath("barbara.jpg")
  barb = makePicture(barbf)
  canvasf = getMediaPath("7inX95in.jpg")
  canvas = makePicture(canvasf)
  # Now, do the actual copying
  targetX = 1
  for sourceX in range(1,getWidth(barb)):
    targetY = 1
    for sourceY in range(1,getHeight(barb)):
```

```
        color = getColor(getPixel(barb,sourceX,sourceY))
        setColor(getPixel(canvas,targetY,targetX), color)
        targetY = targetY + 1
      targetX = targetX + 1
    show(barb)
    show(canvas)
    return canvas
```

How it works: Rotating (as flipping across the diagonal) starts with the same source and target, and even the same variable values, but since we *use* the target X and Y differently, we get a different effect.

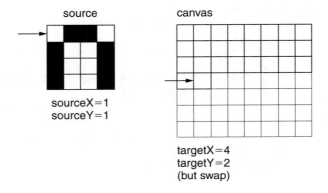

Now, as we increment the Y variables, we're moving *down* the source, but *across* the target.

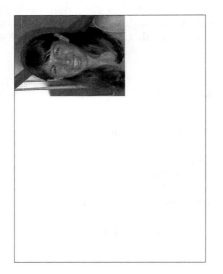

FIGURE 4.12: Copying a picture to a canvas.

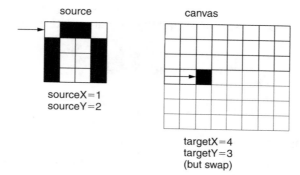

When we're done, we've done the same copy, but the result is completely different.

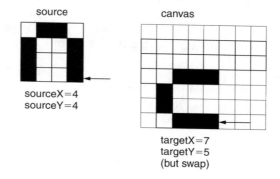

How would we *really* rotate 90 degrees? We need to think about where we want each pixel. The program below actually *does* a 90 degree rotation of the picture. The key difference is in the setColor function call. Note that we swap the x and y indices from previous examples, but we use an equation for y: width-targetX+1. Try tracing it to convince yourself that this does a real rotation.

RECIPE 30: Rotating a picture

```
def rotateBarbSideways():
    # Set up the source and target pictures
    barbf=getMediaPath("barbara.jpg")
    barb = makePicture(barbf)
    canvasf = getMediaPath("7inX95in.jpg")
    canvas = makePicture(canvasf)
    # Now, do the actual copying
    targetX = 1
    width = getWidth(barb)
    for sourceX in range(1,getWidth(barb)+1):
        targetY = 1
        for sourceY in range(1,getHeight(barb)+1):
```

```
      color = getColor(getPixel(barb,sourceX,sourceY))
      setColor(getPixel(canvas,targetY,width-targetX+1),
color)
      targetY = targetY + 1
    targetX = targetX + 1
  show(barb)
  show(canvas)
  return canvas
```

4.3.4 Scaling

A very common transformation for pictures is to scale them. Scaling up means to make them larger, and scaling down makes them smaller. It's common to scale a 1-megapixel or 3-megapixel picture down to a smaller size to make it easier to place on the Web. Smaller pictures require less disk space, and less network bandwidth, and thus are easier and faster to download.

Scaling a picture requires the use of *sampling*, which we'll also use with sounds later. To scale a picture *smaller* we are going to take *every other* pixel when copying from the source to the target. To scale a picture *larger* we are going to take *every pixel twice*.

Scaling the picture down is the easier function. Instead of incrementing the source X and Y variables by 1, we simply increment by 2. We divide the amount of space by 2, since we'll fill half as much room–our length will be $(200 - 45)/2$ and the height will be $(200 - 25)/2$, still starting at $(100, 100)$. The result is a small face in the canvas (Figure 4.13).

RECIPE 31: Scaling a picture down (smaller)

```
def copyBarbsFaceSmaller():
    # Set up the source and target pictures
```

FIGURE 4.13: Scaling the picture down.

```
barbf=getMediaPath("barbara.jpg")
barb = makePicture(barbf)
canvasf = getMediaPath("7inX95in.jpg")
canvas = makePicture(canvasf)
# Now, do the actual copying
sourceX = 45
for targetX in range(100,100+((200-45)/2)):
  sourceY = 25
  for targetY in range(100,100+((200-25)/2)):
    color = getColor(getPixel(barb,sourceX,sourceY))
    setColor(getPixel(canvas,targetX,targetY), color)
    sourceY = sourceY + 2
  sourceX = sourceX + 2
show(barb)
show(canvas)
return canvas
```

How it works:

■ We start out creating the picture objects: barb as our source, and canvas into which we'll compose Barb.

■ Barb's face is in the rectangle (45,25) to (200,200). That means that the sourceX starts at 45 and the sourceY starts at 25. We don't specify the end of the range for the source indices, because they're controlled by the for loops for the target indices.

■ We're going to start targetX and targetY at 100 each. What are the end points for the ranges? We want to get *all* of Barb's face. The width of Barb's face is 200-45 (the maximum x index minus the minimum y index). Since we want to shrink Barb's face by two, we'll be skipping every other pixel. That means that we'll have only half the width in the final composition: (200-45)/2 across. If we're starting targetX at 100, the end point for the range is 100 plus (200-45)/2. targetY works the same way.

■ Because we want to skip every other pixel in the source, we increment sourceX and sourceY by 2 each time through the loop.

 MAKING IT WORK TIP: What about that last pixel?
Remember that **range** does *not* include the last number in the range. Should we be adding 1 to the end point to get every last pixel? Probably, to be exact. But for our purposes, it doesn't really matter. You're not going to notice a single pixel. Undercounting pixels (or samples in audio) is not a big deal for our examples. Overcounting pixels can be a bigger problem. If you try to reference a pixel that's beyond the edge of the target or the source picture objects, you will get an error about the array index being out of bounds.

Scaling up the picture (making it larger) is a little trickier. We want to take every pixel twice. What we're going to do is to increment the source index variables by 0.5. Now we can't reference pixel 1.5. But if we reference

FIGURE 4.14: Scaling up a picture.

int(1.5) (integer function) we'll get 1 again, and that will work. The sequence of 1, 1.5, 2, 2.5... will become 1,1,2,2... The result is a larger form of the picture (Figure 4.14).

RECIPE 32: Scaling the picture up (larger)

```
def copyBarbsFaceLarger():
    # Set up the source and target pictures
    barbf=getMediaPath("barbara.jpg")
    barb = makePicture(barbf)
    canvasf = getMediaPath("7inX95in.jpg")
    canvas = makePicture(canvasf)
    # Now, do the actual copying
    sourceX = 45
    for targetX in range(100,100+((200-45)*2)):
        sourceY = 25
        for targetY in range(100,100+((200-25)*2)):
            color = getColor(getPixel(barb,int(sourceX),
int(sourceY)))
            setColor(getPixel(canvas,targetX,targetY), color)
            sourceY = sourceY + 0.5
        sourceX = sourceX + 0.5
    show(barb)
    show(canvas)
    return canvas
```

You might want to be able to scale a picture to a particular size instead of always using the canvas pictures. There is a function called makeEmptyPicture that creates a picture of a desired width and height (both specified in pixels). makeEmptyPicture(640,480) would create a picture object that is 640 pixels wide by 480 pixels tall—just like the canvas.

How it works: We start from the same place as the original copy.

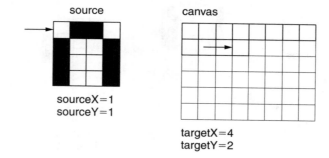

When we increment `sourceY` by 0.5, we end up referring to the same pixel in the source, but the target has moved on to the next pixel.

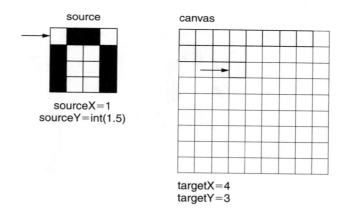

When we increment `sourceY` a second time by 0.5, we now move on to the next pixel, which we'll end up copying twice.

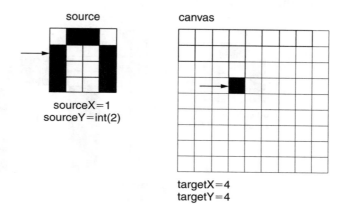

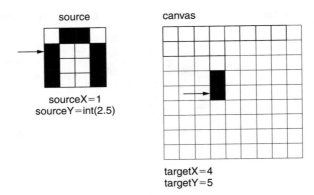

When we move to a new row in the target, we stay in the *same* row in the source. Thus, we end up copying every pixel twice, both horizontally and vertically.

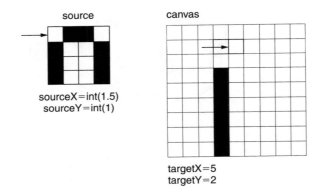

Eventually we end up doubling the picture in both directions, effectively quadrupling the area of the figure. Note that the end result is degraded a bit—it's choppier than the original.

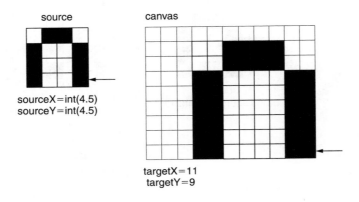

■ **4.4** Replacing Colors: Red-Eye, Sepia Tones, and Posterizing

Replacing colors with another color is pretty easy. We can do it broadly, or just within a range. This approach allows us to create some interesting overall effects or tune the effect to do something like turn someone's teeth purple.

Here's a recipe that replaces the brown color in Barbara's hair with red. I used the MediaTools pixel tools to figure out roughly what the RGB values were for Barb's brown hair, then wrote a program to look for colors close to that and increase the redness of those pixels. I played a lot with the value that I used for distance (here, 50.0) and the amount of redness increase (here, 50% increase). The result is that the wood behind her gets increased too (as shown in color insert Figure I.9).

RECIPE 33: Turn Barbara into a redhead

```
def turnRed():
    brown = makeColor(57,16,8)
    file="/Users/guzdial/mediasources/barbara.jpg"
    picture=makePicture(file)
    for px in getPixels(picture):
        color = getColor(px)
        if distance(color,brown)<50.0:
            redness=int(getRed(px)*1.5)
            blueness=getBlue(px)
            greenness=getGreen(px)
            setColor(px,makeColor(redness,blueness,greenness))
    show(picture)
    return(picture)
```

How it works: This is actually quite similar to our increase-red recipe, but uses an alternative method of setting the color.

■ We create a brown color that is what we found in Barb's hair from MediaTools.

■ We create the picture of Barb.

■ For each of the pixels px in the picture, we get the color and then compare the color to the brown color we identified earlier. We want to know if the color at pixel px is *close enough* to brown. How do we define "close enough"? We say that it's within 50.0. Where did I get that number? I tried 10.0, but very little changed. I tried 100.0, and way too much matched (like the wood behind Barb's head). I tried different numbers until I got the effect I wanted.

■ If the color is "close enough," we get the red, green, and blue components of the color at px. We increase the red by 50% by multiplying it by 1.5.

■ We then set the color at px to a new color with the adjusted red and the same blue and green components. Then move on to the next pixel.

With the MediaTools, we can also figure out the coordinates just around Barb's face, and then just do the browns near her face. The effect isn't too good, though it's clear that it worked. The line of redness is too sharp and rectangular (in color insert Figure I.10).

RECIPE 34: Color replacement in a range

```
def turnRedInRange():
  brown = makeColor(57,16,8)
  file="/Users/guzdial/mediasources/barbara.jpg"
  picture=makePicture(file)
  for x in range(70,168):
    for y in range(56,190):
      px=getPixel(picture,x,y)
      color = getColor(px)
      if distance(color,brown)<50.0:
        redness=int(getRed(px)*1.5)
        blueness=getBlue(px)
        greenness=getGreen(px)
        setColor(px,makeColor(redness,blueness,greenness))
  show(picture)
  return(picture)
```

4.4.1 Reducing Red-Eye

"Red-eye" is the effect where the flash from the camera bounces off the back of the subject's eyes. Reducing red-eye is a really simple matter. We find the pixels that are "pretty close" (a distance from red of 165 works well) to red, then insert a replacement color.

We probably don't want to change the whole picture. In Figure 4.15, Jenny is wearing a red dress—we don't want to wipe out that red. We'll fix that by only changing the *range* where Jenny's eyes are. Using the MediaTools, we find the upper left and lower right corners of her eyes. Those points were (109, 91) and (202, 107).

FIGURE 4.15: Finding the range of where Jenny's eyes are red.

RECIPE 35: Reduce red-eye

```
def removeRedEye(pic,startX,startY,endX,endY,
replacementcolor):
    red = makeColor(255,0,0)
    for x in range(startX,endX):
        for y in range(startY,endY):
            currentPixel = getPixel(pic,x,y)
            if (distance(red,getColor(currentPixel)) < 165):
                setColor(currentPixel,replacementcolor)
```

We call this function with:

```
removeRedEye(jenny, 109, 91, 202, 107, makeColor(0,0,0))
```

to replace the red with black—certainly other colors could be used for the replacement color. The result was good, and we can check that the eye really does now have all-black pixels (Figure 4.16). (See also color insert Figure I.11.)
How it works: This algorithm is really very similar to the one that we used for changing Barbara's hair to red.

■ This function was written to be useful for many different pictures, so it takes a lot of inputs (*parameters*) that the user can simply change for different programs. The function takes an input picture, then the rectangle coordinates where the color change should occur, then the color to replace red with.

■ We define red to be a pure, strong red—makeColor(255,0,0).

■ For x and y within the rectangle provided as input, we get the currentPixel.

■ We check whether the currentPixel is close enough to red. We determine "close enough" by looking for a distance within a *threshold value*. We tried different distances, and settled on 165 as the distance that caught most of the eye redness that we cared about.

■ We then swap the replacementColor for the "close enough" color at pixel currentPixel.

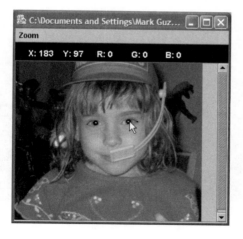

FIGURE 4.16: Finding the range of where Jenny's eyes are red.

4.4.2 Sepia-Toned and Posterized Pictures: Using Conditionals to Choose the Color

So far, we've done color subtraction by simply replacing one color with another. We can be more sophisticated in our color swapping. We can look for a range of colors by using if and choosing to replace some function of the original color or by changing to a specific color. The results are quite interesting.

For example, we might want to generate sepia-toned prints. Older prints sometimes have a yellowish tint. We could just do an overall color change, but the end result isn't aesthetically pleasing. By looking for different kinds of colors—highlights, shadows—and treating them differently, we can get a better effect (Figure 4.17).

The way we do this is to first convert everything to grayscale, both because older prints were in a grayscale, and because it makes it a little easier to work with. We then look for high and low ranges of color (really, luminance), and change them separately. (Why these particular values? Trial and error—tweaking them until we liked the effect.)

RECIPE 36: Convert a picture to sepia tones

```
def sepiaTint(picture):
  #Convert image to grayscale
  grayScaleNew(picture)

  #loop through picture to tint pixels
  for p in getPixels(picture):
    red = getRed(p)
    blue = getBlue(p)

    #tint shadows
    if (red < 63):
      red = red*1.1
      blue = blue*0.9
```

FIGURE 4.17: Original scene (*left*) and using our sepia-tone recipe (*right*).

```
#tint midtones
 if (red > 62 and red < 192):
   red = red*1.15
   blue = blue*0.85

 #tint highlights
 if (red > 191):
   red = red*1.08
   if (red > 255):
     red = 255

   blue = blue*0.93

 #set the new color values
 setBlue(p, blue)
 setRed(p, red)
```

How it works: The function starts by taking in a picture as input, then uses our grayScaleNew function to convert it to grayscale. (This means that the grayScaleNew function *must* be in the program area along with sepiaTint—we're just not seeing it here.) For each of the pixels, we grab the redness and blueness of the pixel. We know that the red and blue will be the *same* values, since the picture is now all gray, but we'll want the redness and blueness for *changing*. We look for specific ranges of colors and treat them differently. Note that with tinting the highlights (where the light is brightest) we have an if inside an if block. The idea here is that we don't want the values to wrap around—if red gets too high, we want to cap it at 255. Finally, we set the blue and red values to the new red and blue values, and move on to the next pixel.

Posterizing is a very similar process which results in converting a picture to a smaller number of colors. We're going to do that by looking for a specific range of color, then setting the color to *one* value in that range. The result is that we reduce the number of colors in the picture (Figure 4.18). For example, in the recipe below, if red is 1, 2, 3...64, we make it 31. We thus wipe a whole range of red variance, and make it one specific red value.

FIGURE 4.18: Reducing the colors (*right*) from the original (*left*).

RECIPE 37: Posterizing a picture

```
def posterize(picture):

  #loop through the pixels
  for p in getPixels(picture):
    #get the RGB values
    red = getRed(p)
    green = getGreen(p)
    blue = getBlue(p)

    #check and set red values
    if(red < 64):
      setRed(p, 31)
    if(red > 63 and red < 128):
      setRed(p, 95)
    if(red > 127 and red < 192):
      setRed(p, 159)
    if(red > 191 and red < 256):
      setRed(p, 223)

    #check and set green values
    if(green < 64):
      setGreen(p, 31)
    if(green > 63 and green < 128):
      setGreen(p, 95)
    if(green > 127 and green < 192):
      setGreen(p, 159)
    if(green > 191 and green < 256):
      setGreen(p, 223)

    #check and set blue values
    if(blue < 64):
      setBlue(p, 31)
    if(blue > 63 and blue < 128):
      setBlue(p, 95)
    if(blue > 127 and blue < 192):
      setBlue(p, 159)
    if(blue > 191 and blue < 256):
      setBlue(p, 223)
```

An interesting effect comes from using both grayscale and posterize together. We do this by computing a luminance, but then only set the pixel's color to either black or white—only two levels. The result is a picture that looks a bit like a stamped image or like a charcoal drawing (Figure 4.19).

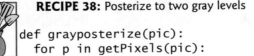

RECIPE 38: Posterize to two gray levels

```
def grayposterize(pic):
  for p in getPixels(pic):
```

FIGURE 4.19: Picture posterized to two gray levels.

```
r = getRed(p)
g = getGreen(p)
b = getBlue(p)
luminance = (r+g+b)/3
if luminance < 128:
  setColor(p,black)
if luminance >= 128:
  setColor(p,white)
```

■ 4.5 Combining Pixels: Blurring

When we make pictures larger (scaling them up), we usually get rough edges: sharp steps in lines, which we call ***pixelation***. We can reduce pixelation by *blurring* the image—purposefully making some of the hard edges "soft" (i.e., smoother and more curved).

There are *many* ways (algorithms) for blurring. We're going to use a really simple one here. What we do is set each pixel to a color which is an *average* of the colors of the pixels around it.

RECIPE 39: A simple blur

```
def blur(filename):
  source=makePicture(filename)
  target=makePicture(filename)
  for x in range(2, getWidth(source)):
    for y in range(2, getHeight(source)):
      top = getPixel(source,x,y-1)
      left = getPixel(source,x-1,y)
      bottom = getPixel(source,x,y+1)
      right = getPixel(source,x+1,y)
      center = getPixel(target,x,y)
      newRed=(getRed(top)+ getRed(left)+ getRed(bottom)+
getRed(right)+ getRed(center))/5
      newGreen=(getGreen(top)+ getGreen(left)+
getGreen(bottom)+ getGreen(right)+ getGreen(center))/5
      newBlue=(getBlue(top)+ getBlue(left)+ getBlue(bottom)+
getBlue(right)+ getBlue(center))/5
```

```
          setColor(center, makeColor(newRed, newGreen, newBlue))
    return target
```

MAKING IT WORK TIP: Don't break lines midway in Python

In examples like these, you may see lines "wrap"—lines that you would expect to be all on one line actually appear on two. That's a necessity to fit the code onto the page, but we can't really break lines that way in Python. We can't break lines by hitting ENTER until the statement or expression is completed.

Figure 4.20 shows the flower from the collage made bigger, then blurred. You can see the pixelation in the bigger version—the sharp, blocky edges. With the blur, some of the pixelation goes away. More careful blurs take regions of colors into account (so that edges between colors are kept sharp), and thus are able to reduce pixelation without removing sharpness.

How it works: We use this function with something like `newpic = blur (pickAFile())`. We then create two copies of the picture filename provided as input. We modify only the `target` so that we always average *original* colors from the `source`. We walk through the x index values from 2 to the width—here we're explicitly taking advantage of the fact that `range` won't include the end values. We do the same with the y indices. The reason is that we're going to add 1 and subtract 1 from each of x and y to compute the averages. We won't be averaging the edge pixels, then, but it'll be pretty hard to tell. For each (x, y), we get the pixel to the left $(x - 1, y)$, to the right $(x + 1, y)$, above $(x, y - 1)$, and below $(x, y + 1)$, as well as the pixel itself at the center (x, y) (from `target` because we can be sure that we haven't changed (x, y) yet). We compute the average of the reds of all five pixels, the greens, and the blues, then set color at (x, y) to the average color.

While this works surprisingly well (Figure 4.20), it's not quite as good as we might get. Some detail is lost when you simply blur like this. What if we blurred to get rid of pixelation but kept detail? How might we do that? What if we checked luminance values before we computed the average—perhaps we shouldn't blur across large luminance boundaries because that would reduce detail? That's just one idea—there are lots of good algorithms for blurring.

FIGURE 4.20: Making the flower bigger (*left*), then blurring it to reduce pixelation (*right*).

■ **4.6** Comparing Pixels: Edge Detection

Blurring is a process of computing an average across multiple pixels. *Edge detection* is a similar process where we compare pixels to determine what to put in a given pixel, but we basically only set the pixel to black or white. The idea is to try to draw lines the way an artist might sketch a drawing with lines.

It's really an amazing feature of our visual systems that we can look at a line drawing of someone and pick out a face or other features. Look at the world around you—there really aren't sharp lines defining features of the world. There are no clear lines around your nose or eyes, but any child can draw a face with a checkmark for a nose and two circles for eyes—and we will all recognize it as a face! Typically, we *see* a line where there is a difference in luminance.

We can try to model this process (Figure 4.21). In the recipe below, we compare each pixel's luminance to the pixel *below* it and to the *left* of it. If there is a suitable difference in luminance below *and* to the left, then we make the pixel black. (Experimentation found that a threshold value of only 2 worked pretty well!) Otherwise, we leave it white.

RECIPE 40: Create a simple line drawing using edge detection

```
def linedetect(filename):
    orig = makePicture(filename)
    makebw = makePicture(filename)
    for x in range(1,getWidth(orig)):
        for y in range(1,getHeight(orig)):
            here=getPixel(makebw,x,y)
            thered=getPixel(orig,x,y+1)
            therer=getPixel(orig,x+1,y)
            herel=(getRed(here)+getGreen(here)+getBlue(here))/3
            theredl=(getRed(thered)+getGreen(thered)+
getBlue(thered))/3
            thererl=(getRed(therer)+getGreen(therer)+
getBlue(therer))/3
            if abs(herel-theredl)>2 and abs(herel-thererl)>2:
                setColor(here,black)
            else:
                setColor(here,white)
    show(makebw)
    return makebw
```

FIGURE 4.21: Daisies (*left*) converted to a "line drawing" (*right*).

How it works: Like the gray-levels posterizing, the goal here is to set each pixel to either black or white, depending on whether there is a luminance difference or not.

■ We call the function with something like `bwversion = line detect (pickAFile())`. We make two copies of the picture from the input file-name—the source `orig` (original) and the target `makebw`.

■ We use indices for x and y from 1 to the width and height, but we're counting on the fact here that the `range` won't include the last value. We're going to be comparing the pixel at (x, y) to the pixels at $(x + 1, y)$ (right) and at $(x, y + 1)$ (down).

■ We get the pixel in `here`, the pixel down `thered` (there-down), and the pixel to the right `therer` (there-right).

■ We compute the luminance of all three pixels.

■ If the *absolute value* (`abs`) of the difference between the luminance in the comparison pixel (`herel`) and the luminance to the right (`thererl`–there-right-luminance) and below (`theredl`) is greater than the threshold value of 2, then we make the pixel black. We use absolute value because we only care about the *difference* between the two luminance values. We don't really care which one is larger.

■ We use an `else` clause to handle the case where we're not within the threshold value. The `else:` block executes only if the `if` test is *false*. If the difference between the luminances is *not* greater than the threshold value, then we set the pixel to white.

There are algorithms to do much better edge detection and line drawing. For example, here we're simply setting each pixel to black or white—we're not really considering the notion of a "line." We could use techniques like blurring to smooth the image and make the dots seem more like lines. We could also make pixels black only if we are going to make nearby pixels black, that is, create a line rather than simply make dots.

Programming Summary

`range`	Function that creates a sequence of numbers. Useful for creating indices to an array or matrix.
`setMediaPath`	Lets you pick a folder where you can easily access media using `getMediaPath`.
`getMediaPath`	Takes an input of a base file name, then returns the complete path to that file (assuming it's in the media folder).
`makeEmptyPicture`	Takes a height and width and returns an empty (all black) picture of the desired size.

Problems

4.1   Start with a picture of someone you know, and make some specific color changes to it:
■ Turn the teeth purple.
■ Turn the eyes red.
■ Turn the hair orange.
Of course, if your friend's teeth are already purple, or eyes red, or hair orange, choose a different target color.

4.2
```
def newFunction(a, b, c):
    print a
    list1 = range(1,5)
    value = 0
    for x in list1:
        print b
        value = value +1
    print c
    print value
```
If you call the function above by typing: newFunction("I", "you", "walrus"), what will print?

4.3   Which of the recipes below takes a picture and removes all the blue from every pixel that already has a blue value of more than 100?
1. A only
2. D only
3. B and C
4. C and D
5. None
6. All
What do the other ones do?
```
A.      def blueOneHundred(picture):
            for x in range(1,100):
                for y in range(1,100):
                    pixel = getPixel(picture,x,y)
                    setBlue(pixel,100)
B.      def removeBlue(picture):
            for p in getPixels(picture):
                if getBlue(p) > 0:
                    setBlue(p,100)
C.      def noBlue(picture):
            blue = makeColor(0,0,100)
            for p in getPixels(picture):
                color = getColor(p)
                if distance(color,blue) > 100:
                    setBlue(p,0)
D.      def byeByeBlue(picture):
            for p in getPixels(picture):
                if getBlue(p) > 100:
                    setBlue(p,0)
```

4.4 Write a program checkLuminance that will input red, green, and blue values, and compute the luminance using the weighted average (as below). But then print out a warning to the user based on the computed luminance:

- If the luminance is less than 10, "That's going to be awfully dark."
- If the luminance is between 50 and 200, "Looks like a good range."
- Over 250, "That's going to be nearly white!"

4.5 We've seen that if you increment the source picture index by 2 while incrementing the target picture index by 1 for each copied pixel, you end up with the source being scaled down onto the target. What happens if you increment the target picture index by 2 as well? What happens if you increment both by 0.5 and use int to get just the integer part?

4.6 Can you rewrite the vertical mirroring function (Recipe 19) to do horizontal mirroring? How about mirroring along the diagonal from $(1, 1)$ to $(width, height)$?

4.7 Here are some possible program outcomes:

- Mirror the input picture's leftmost 20 pixels to pixels 21 to 40.
- Copy the good part of the temple pediment to the broken part.
- Copy the broken part of the temple pediment to the working part.
- Mirror the input picture left to right
- Mirror the input picture left to right

Which of the following programs does which of the preceding outcomes?

A.
```
def mirrorTemple():
    source = makePicture(getMediaPath("temple.jpg"))
    mirrorpoint = 277
    lengthToCopy = mirrorpoint - 14
    for x in range(1,lengthToCopy):
        for y in range(28,98):
            p = getPixel(source,mirrorpoint-x,y)
            p2 = getPixel(source,mirrorpoint+x,y)
            setColor(p2,getColor(p))
    show(source)
    return source
```

B.
```
def mirrorTemple():
    source = makePicture(getMediaPath("temple.jpg"))
    mirrorpoint = 277
    lengthToCopy = mirrorpoint - 14
    for x in range(1,lengthToCopy):
        for y in range(28,98):
            p = getPixel(source,mirrorpoint-x,y)
            p2 = getPixel(source,mirrorpoint+x,y)
            setColor(p,getColor(p2))
    show(source)
    return source
```

C.
```
def mirrorVertical(source):
    mirrorpoint = int(getWidth(source)/2)
Tracing the printing
```

```
        for y in range(1,getHeight(source)):
          for xOffset in range(1,mirrorpoint):
            pright = getPixel(source, xOffset+
      mirrorpoint,y)
              pleft = getPixel(source, mirrorpoint-
      xOffset,y)
            c = getColor(pleft)
            setColor(pright,c)
D.      def mirrorVertical(source):
          mirrorpoint = int(getWidth(source)/2)
          for y in range(1,getHeight(source)):
            for xOffset in range(1,mirrorpoint):
              pright = getPixel(source, xOffset+
      mirrorpoint,y)
                pleft = getPixel(source, mirrorpoint-
      xOffset,y)
              c = getColor(pright)
              setColor(pleft,c)
E.      def mirrorVertical(source):
          mirrorpoint = 20
          for y in range(1,getHeight(source)):
            for xOffset in range(1,mirrorpoint):
              pright = getPixel(source, xOffset+
      mirrorpoint,y)
                pleft = getPixel(source, mirrorpoint-
      xOffset,y)
              c = getColor(pleft)
              setColor(pright,c)
```

4.8 Consider this program:

```
      def copyBarbsFaceScaled(factor):
        # Set up the source and target pictures
        barbf=getMediaPath("barbara.jpg")
        barb = makePicture(barbf)
        canvasf = getMediaPath("7inX95in.jpg")
        canvas = makePicture(canvasf)
        # Now, do the actual copying
        sourceX = 45
        for targetX in range(100,100+int((200-45)*factor)):
          sourceY = 25
          for targetY in range(100,100+int((200-25)
      *factor)):
            print "Copying from ",sourceX,sourceY," to ",
      targetX,targetY
            color = getColor(getPixel(barb,int(sourceX),
      int(sourceY)))
            setColor(getPixel(canvas,targetX,targetY),
      color)
            sourceY = sourceY + (1.0/factor)
```

```
            sourceX = sourceX + (1.0/factor)
        show(barb)
        show(canvas)
        return canvas
```

A. What pictures will appear when you execute copyBarbsFaceScaled(0.5)? What will be the first four lines printed?

B. What pictures will appear when you execute copyBarbsFaceScaled(2.0)? What will be the first four lines printed?

C. What pictures will appear when you execute copyBarbsFaceScaled(1.5)? What will be the first four lines printed?

4.9   Write a function named mycollage to create a collage of the same image at least four times fit onto the 7x95in.jpg blank JPEG. (You are welcome to add additional images.) One of those four copies can be the original picture. The other three should be modified forms. You can scale, crop, or rotate the image, create a negative of the image, shift or alter colors on the image, and make it darker or lighter.

After composing your image, *mirror it*. You can do this vertically or horizontally (or otherwise), in any direction—just make sure that your four base images are still visible after mirroring.

Your single function should make all of this happen—all of the effects and compositing must occur from the single function mycollage. Of course, it is perfectly okay to *use* other functions, but make it so that a tester of your program need only call setMediaPath(), put all your input pictures in a mediasources directory, and then execute mycollage() in order to see a collage generated, shown, and returned.

*4.10   Think about how the grayscale algorithm works. Basically, if you know the *luminance* of anything visual (e.g., a small image, a letter), you can replace a pixel with that visual element in a similar way to create a collage image. Try implementing this. You'll need 256 visual elements of increasing lightness, all of the same size. You can create a collage by replacing each pixel in the original image with one of these visual elements.

To Dig Deeper

The "bible" of computer graphics is *Introduction to Computer Graphics* [13]. It's highly recommended.

CHAPTER 5

Making Pictures by Combining Pieces

Chapter Learning Objectives

The media learning goals for this chapter are:

- *To use blending to combine images.*

- *To use background subtraction to separate foreground from background images, and to understand when and how it will work.*

- *To use chromakey to separate foreground from background images.*

- *To be able to add text and images to existing pictures.*

The computer science goals for this chapter are:

- *To be able to choose between using vector and bitmapped image formats.*

- *To be able to choose when one should write a program for a task versus using existing applications software.*

■ 5.1 Blending Pictures

In this chapter, we talk about techniques for creating pictures from other pieces. We'll compose pictures in new ways (e.g., pulling someone out from one background and putting them in a new setting) and create pictures from scratch without explicitly setting every pixel.

One of the ways that we can combine pictures to create new pictures is by mixing the colors of the pixels to reflect both pictures. When we create collages by copying, any overlap typically means that one picture shows *over* another. The last picture painted on is the one that appears on

FIGURE 5.1: Blending the picture of mom and daughter.

top of the other. But it doesn't have to be that way. We can *blend* pictures by multiplying their colors and adding them. This gives us the effect of *transparency*.

We know that 100% of something is the whole thing. 50% of one and 50% of another also is a whole. In the recipe below, we blend a picture of the mother and the daughter with an overlap of 70 (the width of Barbara minus 150) columns of pixels (Figure 5.1).

RECIPE 41: Blending two pictures

```
def blendPictures():
  barb = makePicture(getMediaPath("barbara.jpg"))
  katie = makePicture(getMediaPath("Katie-smaller.jpg"))
  canvas = makePicture(getMediaPath("640x480.jpg"))
  #Copy first 150 columns of Barb
  sourceX=1
  for targetX in range(1,150):
    sourceY=1
    for targetY in range(1,getHeight(barb)):
      color = getColor(getPixel(barb,sourceX,sourceY))
      setColor(getPixel(canvas,targetX,targetY),color)
      sourceY = sourceY + 1
    sourceX = sourceX + 1
  #Now, grab the rest of Barb
  # at 50% Barb and 50% Katie
  overlap = getWidth(barb)-150
  sourceX=1
  for targetX in range(150,getWidth(barb)):
    sourceY=1
    for targetY in range(1,getHeight(katie)):
      bpixel = getPixel(barb,sourceX+150,sourceY)
```

```
        kpixel = getPixel(katie,sourceX,sourceY)
        newred= 0.50*getRed(bpixel)+0.50*getRed(kpixel)
        newgreen=0.50*getGreen(bpixel)+0.50*getGreen(kpixel)
        newblue = 0.50*getBlue(bpixel)+0.50*getBlue(kpixel)
        color = makeColor(newred,newgreen,newblue)
        setColor(getPixel(canvas,targetX,targetY),color)
        sourceY = sourceY + 1
      sourceX = sourceX + 1
  # Last columns of Katie
  sourceX=overlap
  for targetX in range(150+overlap,150+getWidth(katie)):
    sourceY=1
    for targetY in range(1,getHeight(katie)):
      color = getColor(getPixel(katie,sourceX,sourceY))
      setColor(getPixel(canvas,targetX,targetY),color)
      sourceY = sourceY + 1
    sourceX = sourceX + 1
  show(canvas)
  return canvas
```

How it works: This function has three parts to it—the part where Barb is there without Katie, the part where there's some of each, and the part where there's just Katie.

■ We start out creating the picture objects for barb, katie, and the target canvas.

■ For 150 pixel columns, we simply copy pixels from barb into the canvas.

■ The next section is the actual blending. Our targetX index starts at 150, because we already have 150 columns from barb in the canvas. We're using sourceX and sourceY to index *both* barb and katie, but we have to add 150 to sourceX when indexing barb because we've already copied 150 pixels of barb. Our y index will only go up to the height of the katie picture because it's shorter than the barb picture.

■ The body of the loop is where the blending occurs. We get a pixel from barb and call it bpixel. We get one from katie and call it kpixel. We then compute the red, green, and blue for the target pixel (the one at targetX and targetY) by taking 50% of the red, green, and blue of each of the source pictures.

■ Finally, we end up copying in the rest of the katie pixels.

■ 5.2 Background Subtraction

Let's imagine that you have a picture of someone, and a picture of where they stood without them there (Figure 5.2). Could you *subtract* the background of the person (i.e., figure out where the colors are exactly the same), and then replace another background? Say, of the moon (Figure 5.3)?

FIGURE 5.2:   A picture of a child (Katie), and her background without her.

FIGURE 5.3: A new background, the moon.

RECIPE 42: Subtract the background and replace it with a new one

```
def swapbg(pic1, bg, newbg):
  for x in range(1,getWidth(pic1)):
    for y in range(1,getHeight(pic1)):
      p1px = getPixel(pic1,x,y)
      bgpx = getPixel(bg,x,y)
      if (distance(getColor(p1px),getColor(bgpx)) < 15.0):
        setColor(p1px,getColor(getPixel(newbg,x,y)))
  return pic1
```

How it works: The function swapbg (swap background) takes a picture (with both foreground and background in it), a picture of the background, and a new background. For all the pixels in the input picture, we:

■ Get the matching pixels (same coordinates) from both the picture and the background.

■ Compare the distances between the colors. We use a threshold value here of 15.0, but do try it with others.

■ If the distance is small (less than the threshold value), then assume that the pixel is part of the background. Take the color from the pixel at the same coordinates in the *new* background, and set the pixel in the input picture to the new color.

You can do this, but the effect isn't as good as you'd like (Figure 5.4). My daughter's shirt color was too close to the color of the wall, so the moon bled into her shirt. Though the light was dim, a shadow is definitely having an effect here—the shadow wasn't in the background picture, so the algorithm places the shadow as part of the foreground. This suggests that the difference in color between the background and the foreground is important for making background subtraction work, and so is having good lighting!

I tried the same thing with a picture of two students in front of a tiled wall. I used a tripod (really critical to get the pixels to line up), but unfortunately left autofocus on, so the two original pictures (Figure 5.5) weren't all

FIGURE 5.4: Katie on the moon.

FIGURE 5.5: Two people in front of a wall, and a picture of the wall.

that comparable. The background swap (again with the jungle scene) hardly did anything at all. I changed the threshold value to 50, and finally got *some* swapping (Figure 5.6).

Simply changing the threshold doesn't always improve things. It certainly makes more of the foreground get classified as background. But for problems like bleeding through of the new background into the clothing because of matching colors, the threshold value doesn't help much.

■ 5.3 Chromakey

Weatherpersons wave to show a storm front coming in across a map by standing before a background of a fixed color (usually blue or green) and then subtracting that color. This is called *chromakey*. It's easier to subtract off the known color and isn't as sensitive to lighting problems. I took my son's blue sheet, attached it to the family entertainment center, then took a picture of myself in front of it using a timer on a camera (Figure 5.7).

FIGURE 5.6: Swapping a jungle for the wall, using background subtraction, with a threshold of 50.

FIGURE 5.7: Mark in front of a blue sheet.

RECIPE 43: Chromakey: Replace all blue with the new background

```
def chromakey(source,bg):
  # source should have something in front of blue, bg is the
new background
  for x in range(1,getWidth(source)):
    for y in range(1,getHeight(source)):
      p = getPixel(source,x,y)
      # My definition of blue: If the redness + greenness <
blueness
      if (getRed(p) + getGreen(p) < getBlue(p)):
      #Then, grab the color at the same spot from the new
background
        setColor(p,getColor(getPixel(bg,x,y)))
  return source
```

How it works: Here we take in just a source (with both foreground and background in it) and a new background bg. *These must be the same size!* I used MediaTools to come up with a rule for what would be "blue" for this recipe. I didn't want to look for equality or even a distance to the color $(0, 0, 255)$ because I knew that very little of the blue would be *exactly* full-intensity blue. I found that pixels I thought of as blue tended to have smaller red and green values, and in fact, the blue values were greater than the sum of the red and the green. So that's what I looked for in this recipe. Wherever the blue was greater than the red and green, I swapped in the new background pixel's color instead.

The effect is really quite striking (Figure 5.8). Do note the "folds" in the lunar surface, though. The really cool thing is that this recipe works for any background that's the same size as the image (Figure 5.9).

There's another way of writing this code, which is shorter but does the same thing. It uses the getX and getY functions to figure out the coordinates. This leads to a somewhat messier setColor statement.

FIGURE 5.8: Mark on the moon.

FIGURE 5.9: Mark in the jungle.

FIGURE 5.10:   Student in front of a red background without the flash (*left*), and with flash on (*right*).

RECIPE 44: Chromakey, shorter

```
def chromakey2(source,bg):
    for p in pixels(source):
        if (getRed(p)+getGreen(p) < getBlue(p)):
            setColor(p,getColor(getPixel(bg,getX(p),getY(p))))
    return source
```

You don't really want to do chromakey with a common color like red—something that there's a lot of in your face. I tried it with the two pictures in Figure 5.10—one with the flash on, and one with it off. I changed the test to `if getRed(p) > (getGreen(p) + getBlue(p)):`. The one without a flash was terrible—the student's face was "jungleified." The one with the flash was better, but the flash is still visible after the swap (Figure 5.11). It's clear why moviemakers and weather people use blue or green backgrounds for chromakey—there's less overlap with common colors, like face colors.

FIGURE 5.11: Using chromakey recipe with red background, flash off (*left*) and flash on (*right*).

■ 5.4 Drawing on Images

Sometimes you want to create your *own* images from scratch. We know that this is just a matter of setting pixel values to whatever we want, but setting individual pixel values to draw a line or a circle or some letters is hard. One way of drawing on images is to simply set the pixels appropriately. Here's an example that creates a graph over the top of Santa (Figure 5.12). It works by simply setting all the pixels in a line to black. The gap between the lines is five pixels.

RECIPE 45: Draw lines by setting pixels

```
def lineExample():
    img = makePicture(pickAFile())
    new = verticalLines(img)
    new2 = horizontalLines(img)
    show(new2)
    return new2

def horizontalLines(src):
    for x in range(1,getHeight(src),5):
        for y in range(1,getWidth(src)):
            setColor(getPixel(src,y,x),black)
    return src

def verticalLines(src):
    for x in range(1,getWidth(src),5):
        for y in range(1,getHeight(src)):
            setColor(getPixel(src,x,y),black)
    return src
```

Note that this program is using the color name black. You may remember that JES predefines a bunch of colors for you: black, white, blue, red, green, gray, lightGray, darkGray, yellow, orange, pink, magenta, and cyan. You can use any of these just as you would any other function or command.

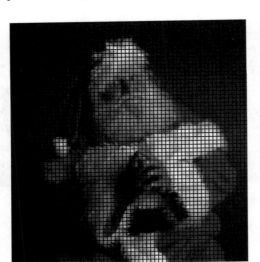

FIGURE 5.12: Santa with lines all over him.

We can imagine drawing anything we want like this, by simply setting individual pixels to whatever colors we want. We could draw rectangles or circles simply by figuring out what pixels need to be what color. We could even draw letters—by setting the appropriate pixels to the appropriate colors, we could make any letter we want. While we could do it, it would involve a lot of work to do all the math for all the different shapes and letters. That's work that lots of people need, so basic drawing tools have been built into libraries for you.

5.4.1 Drawing with Drawing Commands

Most modern programming languages with graphics libraries provide functions that enable us to draw directly a variety of different kinds of shapes onto pictures and to draw text directly onto a picture. Here are some of those functions:

■ addText(pict,x,y,string) puts the string starting at position (x, y) in the picture.

■ addLine(picture,x1,y1,x2,y2) draws a line from position $(x1, y1)$ to $(x2, y2)$.

■ addRect(pict,x1,y1,w,h) draws a rectangle with black lines with the upper-left-hand corner at $(x1, y1)$, a width of w, and a height of h.

■ addRectFilled(pict,x1,y1,w,h,color) draws a rectangle filled with the color that you pick with the upper-left-hand corner at $(x1, y1)$, a width of w, and a height of h.

We can use these commands to add things to existing pictures. What would it look like if a mysterious red box washed up on the beach? We can make that scene appear with these kinds of commands (Figure 5.13).

FIGURE 5.13: A box washed up on the shore of the beach.

RECIPE 46: Adding a box to a beach

```
def addABox():
    beach = makePicture(getMediaPath("beach-smaller.jpg"))
    addRectFilled(beach,150,150,50,50,red)
    show(beach)
    return beach
```

Below is another example of using these drawing commands (Figure 5.14).

RECIPE 47: An example of using drawing commands

```
def littlepicture():
    canvas=makePicture(getMediaPath("640x480.jpg"))
    addText(canvas,10,50,"This is not a picture")
    addLine(canvas,10,20,300,50)
    addRectFilled(canvas,0,200,300,500,yellow)
    addRect(canvas,10,210,290,490)
    return canvas
```

5.4.2 Vector and Bitmap Representations

Here's a thought: Which of these is smaller—the picture (Figure 5.14) or the recipe? The picture, on my disk, is about 15 kilobytes (a *kilobyte* is 1000 bytes). Recipe 47 is less than 100 bytes. But for many uses, they are *equivalent*. What if you just saved the program and not the pixels? That's what a **vector representation** for graphics is about.

Vector-based graphical representations are executable programs that generate the picture when desired. Vector-based representations are used in Postscript, Flash, and AutoCAD. When you make a change to an image in Flash or AutoCAD, you are actually making a change to the underlying representation—essentially, you're changing the program, like the one in Recipe 47. The program is then executed again to make the image appear. But thanks to Moore's Law, the execution and new display occurs so fast that it feels like you're changing the picture.

This is not a picture

FIGURE 5.14: A very small, drawn picture.

Font-definition languages like Postscript and TrueType actually define miniature programs (or equations) for each and every letter or symbol. When you want the letter or symbol at a particular size, the program is run to figure out which pixels should be set to what values. (Some specify more than one color to create the effect of smoother curves.) Because the programs are written to handle desired font size as an input, the letters and symbols can be generated at any size.

Bitmap graphical representations, on the other hand, store every individual pixel or a compressed representation of the pixels. Formats like BMP, GIF, and JPEG are essentially bitmap representations. GIF and JPEG are compressed representations—they don't represent each and every pixel with 24 bits. Instead, they represent the same information but with fewer bits.

What does *compression* mean? It means that various techniques have been used to make the file smaller. Some compression techniques are *lossy compression*—some detail is lost, but hopefully the least significant detail (perhaps even invisible to the human eye, or ear). Other techniques, known as *lossless compression*, lose no detail, but still scrunch the file. One lossless technique is *run length encoding* (RLE).

Imagine that you've got a long line of yellow pixels in a picture, surrounded by some blue pixels. Something like this:

B B Y Y Y Y Y Y Y Y Y B B

What if you encoded this, not as a long line of pixels, but as something like

B B 9 Y B B

In words, you encode "blue, blue, then nine yellows, then blue and blue." Since each of the yellow pixels takes 24 bits (3 bytes for red, green and blue), but recording "nine" takes just a single byte, there's a huge savings. We say that we're encoding the *length* of the *run* of yellows—thus, run length encoding. That's just one of the compression methods that is used to make pictures smaller.

There are several benefits to vector-based representations over bitmap representations. If you can represent the picture you want to send (say, over the Internet) using a vector-based representation, it's much smaller than sending all the pixels—in a sense, vector notation is already compressed. Essentially, you're sending the *instructions* for how to make the picture, rather than sending the picture itself. For very complex images, however, the instructions can be as long as the image (imagine sending all the directions on how to paint the *Mona Lisa*), so there is no benefit. But when the images are simple enough, representations like those used in Flash make for faster upload and download times than sending the same JPEG images.

The real benefit of vector-based notations come when you want to change the image. Let's say that you're working on an architectural drawing, and you extend a line in your drawing tool. If your drawing tool is only working with bitmapped images (sometimes called a ***painting tool***), then all you have are more pixels on the screen that are adjacent to the other pixels on the screen representing the line. There's nothing in the computer that says that all those pixels represent a line of any kind—they're just pixels. But if your drawing tool is working with vector-based representations (sometimes called a ***drawing tool***), then extending a line means that you're changing an underlying representation of a line.

Why is that important? The underlying representation is actually a *specification* of the drawing, and it can be used anywhere that a specification is needed. Imagine taking the drawing of a part, then actually running the cutting and stamping machines based on that drawing. This happens regularly in many shops, and it's possible because the drawing isn't just pixels—it's a specification of the lines and their relationships, which can then be scaled and used to determine the behavior of machines.

You might be wondering, "But how could we *change* the program? Can we write a program that would essentially retype the program or parts of the program?" Yes, we can, and we'll do it in the chapter on text.

■ 5.5 Programs as Specifying Drawing Process

Drawing functions like these can be used to create pictures that are exactly specified—things that might be too hard to do by hand. Take, for example, Figure 5.15.

This is my rendering of a famous optical illusion, and it's not as effective as the famous ones—but it's simple to understand how this version works. Our eyes tell us that the left half of the picture is lighter than the right half, even though the end quarters are exactly the same shade of gray. The effect is caused by the sharp boundary between the middle quarters, where one moves (left to right) from gray to white, and the other moves black to gray.

FIGURE 5.15: A programmed grayscale effect.

The image in Figure 5.15 is a carefully defined and created picture. It would be very hard to do with pencil and paper. It would be possible with something like Photoshop, but it wouldn't be easy. Using the graphics functions in this chapter, however, we can easily specify exactly what that picture should be.

RECIPE 48: Draw the gray effect

```
def grayEffect():
  file = getMediaPath("640x480.jpg")
  pic = makePicture(file)
  # First, 100 columns of 100-gray
  gray = makeColor(100,100,100)
  for x in range(1,100):
    for y in range(1,100):
      setColor(getPixel(pic,x,y),gray)
  # Second, 100 columns of increasing grayness
  grayLevel = 100
  for x in range(100,200):
    gray = makeColor(grayLevel, grayLevel, grayLevel)
    for y in range(1,100):
      setColor(getPixel(pic,x,y),gray)
    grayLevel = grayLevel + 1
  # Third, 100 columns of increasing grayness, from 0
  grayLevel = 0
  for x in range(200,300):
    gray = makeColor(grayLevel, grayLevel, grayLevel)
    for y in range(1,100):
      setColor(getPixel(pic,x,y),gray)
    grayLevel = grayLevel + 1
  # Finally, 100 columns of 100-gray
  gray = makeColor(100,100,100)
  for x in range(300,400):
    for y in range(1,100):
      setColor(getPixel(pic,x,y),gray)
  return pic
```

Graphics functions are very good at drawings that are repeated where the positions of lines and shapes and the selection of colors can be made by mathematical relationships.

RECIPE 49: Draw the picture in Figure 5.16

```
def coolpic():
  canvas=makePicture(getMediaPath("640x480.jpg"))
  for index in range(25,1,-1):
    color = makeColor(index*10,index*5,index)
    addRectFilled(canvas,0,0,index*10,index*10,color)
  show(canvas)
  return canvas
```

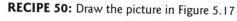

RECIPE 50: Draw the picture in Figure 5.17

```
def coolpic2():
    canvas=makePicture(getMediaPath("640x480.jpg"))
    for index in range(25,1,-1):
        addRect(canvas,index,index,index*3,index*4)
        addRect(canvas,100+index*4,100+index*3,index*8,index*10)
    show(canvas)
    return canvas
```

FIGURE 5.16: Nested colored-rectangles image.

FIGURE 5.17: Nested blank-rectangles image.

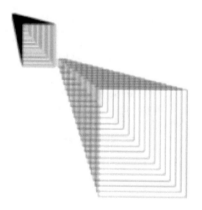

5.5.1 Why Do We Write Programs?

Why do we write programs, especially programs that draw pictures? Could we draw pictures like these in Photoshop or Visio? Certainly we can, but we'd have to know *how*, and that's not easy knowledge to come by. Could I *teach* you how to do this in Photoshop? Probably, but that may take a lot of effort—Photoshop isn't simple.

But if I *give* you these programs, you can create the picture anytime you want. What's more, by giving you the program, I'm giving you the *exact* definition that you can go and change for yourself.

 COMPUTER SCIENCE IDEA: We write programs to encapsulate and communicate process

The reason why we write programs is to exactly specify a process and communicate it to others.

Imagine that you have some process to communicate. It doesn't have to be drawing—imagine that it's a financial process (such that you could do it in a spreadsheet or in a program like Quicken) or something that you do with text (such as laying out text for a book or a brochure). If you can do something by hand, you should just do it. If you need to *teach* someone else to do it, consider writing a program to do it. If you need to explain to *lots* of people how to do it, definitely use a program. If you want lots of people to be able to do the process themselves, without someone having to teach them something first, definitely write a program and give the people the program.

Programming Summary

Here are the functions introduced in this chapter:

`addText(pict,x,y,string)`	Puts the string starting at position (x, y) in the picture.
`addLine(picture,x1,y1,x2,y2)`	Draws a line from position $(x1, y1)$ to $(x2, y2)$.
`addRect(pict,x1,y1,w,h)`	Draws a rectangle with black lines with the upper-left-hand corner at $(x1, y1)$, a width of w, and a height of h.
`addRectFilled(pict,x1,y1,w,h, color)`	Draws a rectangle filled with the `color` that you pick with the upper-left-hand corner at $(x1, y1)$, a width of w, and a height of h.

Problems

5.1 Try doing chromakey in a range—grab something out of its background where the something is only in one part of a picture. For example, put a halo around someone's head, but don't mess with the rest of the body.

5.2 Using the drawing tools presented here, draw a house—just go for the simple child's house with one door, two windows, walls, and a roof.

5.3 Put a cabana on the beach. Draw the house from the previous exercise on the beach where we put the mysterious box previously.

5.4   Now use your house to draw a town with dozens of houses at different sizes. You'll probably want to modify your house function to draw at an input coordinate, then change the coordinate where each house is drawn.

5.5   Draw a rainbow—use what you know about colors, pixels, and drawing operations to draw a rainbow. Is this easier to do with our drawing functions or by manipulating individual pixels? Why?

PART 3

SOUNDS

CHAPTER 6

Modifying Sounds Using Loops

6.1 How Sound Is Encoded
6.2 Manipulating Sounds
6.3 Changing the Volume of Sounds
6.4 Normalizing Sounds

Chapter Learning Objectives

The media learning goals for this chapter are:

- *To understand how we digitize sounds, and the limitations of human hearing that allow us to digitize sounds.*
- *To use the Nyquist theorem to determine the sampling rate necessary for digitizing a desired sound.*
- *To manipulate volume.*
- *To create (and avoid) clipping.*

The computer science goals for this chapter are:

- *To understand and use arrays as a data structure.*
- *To use the formula that n bits result in 2^n possible patterns in order to figure out the number of bits needed to save values.*
- *To use the sound object.*
- *To debug sound programs.*
- *To use iteration (in* for *loops) for manipulating sounds.*
- *To use scope to understand when a variable is available for us.*

■ 6.1 How Sound Is Encoded

There are two parts to understanding how sound is encoded and manipulated.

- ■ First, what are the physics of sound? How is it that we hear a variety of sounds?
- ■ Next, how can we then map sounds into the numbers of a computer?

135

6.1.1 The Physics of Sound

Physically, sounds are waves of air pressure. When something makes a sound, it makes ripples in the air just like stones or raindrops dropped into a pond cause ripples in the surface of the water (Figure 6.1). Each drop causes a wave of pressure to pass over the surface of the water, which causes visible rises in the water, and less visible but just as large depressions in the water. The rises are increases in pressure and the lows are decreases in pressure. Some of the ripples we see actually arise from *combinations* of ripples—some waves are the sums and interactions of other waves.

In the air, we call these increases in pressure *compressions* and decreases in pressure *rarefactions*. It's these compressions and rarefactions that lead to our hearing. The shape of the waves, their *frequency*, and their *amplitude* all impact what we perceive in the sound.

The simplest sound in the world is a **sine wave** (Figure 6.2). In a sine wave, the compressions and rarefactions arrive with equal size and regularity. In a sine wave, one compression plus one rarefaction is called a **cycle**. At some point in the cycle, there has to be a point where there is zero pressure, just between the compression and the rarefaction. The distance from the zero point to the greatest pressure (or least pressure) is called the **amplitude**.

Formally, amplitude is measured in *Newtons per meter-squared* (N/m^2). That's a rather hard unit to understand in terms of perception, but you can get a sense of the amazing range of human hearing from it. The smallest sound that humans typically hear is $0.0002 N/m^2$, and the point at which we sense the vibrations in our entire body is $200 N/m^2$. In general, amplitude is the most important factor in our perception of *volume*: If the amplitude rises, we typically perceive the sound as being louder. Other factors like air pressure also factor into our perception of increased volume. Ever noticed how sounds sound differently on very humid days as compared with very dry days?

When we perceive an increase in volume, we say that we're perceiving an increase in the *intensity* of sound. Intensity is measured in watts per

FIGURE 6.1: Raindrops causing ripples on the surface of the water, just as sound causes ripples in the air.

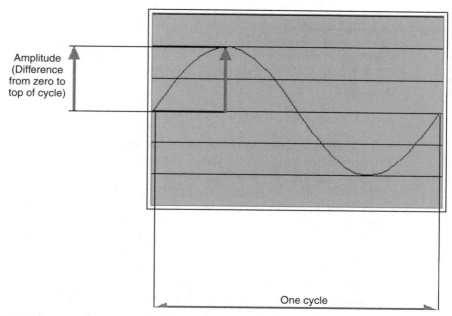

FIGURE 6.2: One cycle of the simplest sound, a sine wave.

meter-squared (W/m^2). (Yes, those are watts just like the ones you're referring to when you get a 60-watt light bulb—it's a measure of power.) The intensity is proportional to the square of the amplitude. For example, if the amplitude doubles, intensity quadruples.

Human perception of sound is not a direct mapping from the physical reality. The study of the human perception of sound is called *psychoacoustics*. One of the odd facts about psychoacoustics is that most of our perception of sound is *logarithmically* related to the actual phenomena. Intensity is an example of this. A change in intensity from $0.1 W/m^2$ to $0.01 W/m^2$ sounds the *same* to us (as in the same amount of volume change) as a change in intensity of $0.001 W/m^2$ to $0.0001 W/m^2$.

We measure the change in intensity in ***decibels*** (dB). That's probably the unit that you most often associate with volume. A decibel is a logarithmic measure, so it matches the way we perceive volume. It's always a ratio, a comparison of two values. $10 * log_{10}(I_1/I_2)$ is the change in intensity in decibels between I_1 and I_2. If two amplitudes are measured under the same conditions, we can express the same definition as amplitudes: $20 * log_{10}(A_1/A_2)$. If $A_2 = 2 * A_1$ (i.e., the amplitude doubles), the difference is roughly 6 dB.

When decibel is used as an absolute measurement, it's in reference to the threshold of audibility at *sound pressure level* (SPL): 0 dB SPL. Normal speech has an intensity about 60 dB SPL. Shouted speech is about 80 dB SPL.

FIGURE 6.3: The note A above middle C is 440 Hz.

How often a cycle occurs is called the **frequency**. If a cycle is short, then there can be lots of them per second. If a cycle is long, then there are fewer of them. As the frequency increases we perceive the **pitch** to increase. We measure frequency in *cycles per second* (cps) or *Hertz* (Hz).

All sounds are periodic—there is always some pattern of rarefaction and compression that leads to cycles, In a sine wave, the notion of a cycle is easy. In natural waves, it's not so clear where a pattern repeats. Even in the ripples in a pond, the waves aren't as regular as you might think. The time between peaks in waves isn't always the same—it varies. This means that a cycle may involve several peaks and valleys until it repeats.

Humans hear between 2 Hz and 20,000 Hz (or 20 kilohertz, abbreviated 20 kHz). Again, as with amplitudes, that's an enormous range. To give you a sense of where music fits into that spectrum, the note A above middle C is 440 Hz in traditional *equal temperament* tuning (Figure 6.3).

Like intensity, our perception of pitch is almost exactly proportional to the log of the frequency. We don't perceive absolute differences in pitch, but the *ratio* of the frequencies. If you heard a 100 Hz sound followed by a 200 Hz sound, you'd perceive the same pitch change (or *pitch interval*) as a shift from 1000 Hz to 2000 Hz. Obviously, a difference of 100 Hz is a lot smaller than a change of 1000 Hz, but we perceive it to be the same.

In standard tuning, the ratio in frequency between the same notes in adjacent octaves is 2 : 1. Frequency doubles each octave. We told you earlier that A above middle C is 440 Hz. You know, then, that the next A up the scale is 880 Hz.

How we think about music is dependent upon our cultural standards, but there are some universals. Among them are the use of pitch intervals (e.g., the ratio between notes C and D remains the same in every octave), the constant relationship between octaves, and the existence of four to seven main pitches (not considering sharps and flats here) in an octave.

What makes the experience of one sound different from another? Why does a flute playing a note sound *so* different from a trumpet or a clarinet playing the same note? We still don't understand everything about psychoacoustics and what physical properties influence our perception of sound, but here are some of the factors that lead us to perceive different sounds (especially musical instruments) as distinct.

■ Real sounds are almost never single-frequency sound waves. Most natural sounds have *several* frequencies in them, often at different amplitudes. These additional frequencies are sometimes called *overtones*. When a piano plays the note C, for example, part of the richness of the tone is that the notes E and G are *also* in the sound, but at lower amplitudes. Different instruments have different overtones in their notes. The central tone, the one we're trying to play, is called the *fundamental*.

■ Instrument sounds are not continuous with respect to amplitude and frequency. Some come slowly up to the target frequency and amplitude (like wind instruments), while others hit the frequency and amplitude very quickly and then the volume fades while the frequency remains pretty constant (like a piano).

■ Not all sound waves are well represented by sine waves. Real sounds have funny bumps and sharp edges. Our ears can pick these up, at least in the first few waves. We can do a reasonable job of synthesizing with sine waves, but synthesizers sometimes also use other kinds of wave forms to get different kinds of sounds (Figure 6.4).

6.1.2 Exploring How Sounds Look

On your CD, you will find the MediaTools application with documentation for how to get it started. The MediaTools application contains tools for sound, graphics, and video. Using the sound tools, you can actually observe sounds as they come into your computer's microphone to get a sense of what louder and softer sounds look like, and what higher- and lower-pitched sounds look like.

You will also find a MediaTools menu in JES. The JES MediaTools also allow you to inspect sounds and pictures, but you can't look at sounds in *real time*—as they hit your computer's microphone.

The basic sound editor looks like Figure 6.5. You can record sounds, open WAV files on your disk, and view the sounds in a variety of ways. (Of course, assuming that you have a microphone on your computer!)

To view sounds, click the Record Viewer button, then the RECORD button. (Hit the STOP button to stop recording.) There are three kinds of views that you can make of the sound.

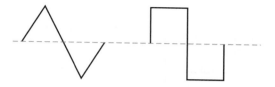

FIGURE 6.4: Some synthesizers use triangular (or *sawtooth*) or square waves.

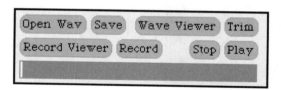

FIGURE 6.5: Sound editor main tool.

The first is the **signal view** (Figure 6.6). In the signal view, you're looking at the sound raw—each increase in air pressure results in a rise in the graph, and each decrease in sound pressure results in a drop in the graph. Note how rapidly the wave changes. Try some softer and louder sounds so that you can see how their look changes. You can always get back to the signal view from another view by clicking the SIGNAL button.

The second view is the **spectrum view** (Figure 6.7). The spectrum view is a completely different perspective on the sound. In the preceding section, you read that natural sounds are often actually composed of several different frequencies at once. The spectrum view shows these individual frequencies. This view is also called the *frequency domain*.

Frequencies increase in the spectrum view from left to right. The height of a column indicates the amount of energy (roughly, the volume) of that frequency in the sound. Natural sounds look like Figure 6.8 with more than one *spike* (rise in the graph). (The smaller rises around a spike are often seen as *noise*.)

The technical term for how a spectrum view is generated is called a **Fourier transform**. A Fourier transform takes the sound from the *time domain* (rises and falls in the sound over time) into the frequency domain (identifying which frequencies are in a sound, and the energy of those frequencies, over time). The

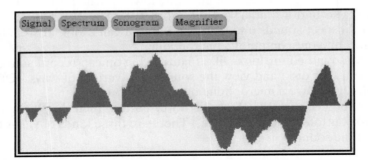

FIGURE 6.6: Viewing the sound signal as it comes in.

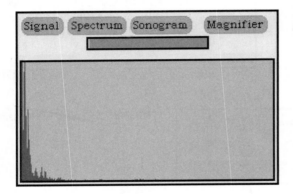

FIGURE 6.7: Viewing the sound in a spectrum view.

"Spikes"

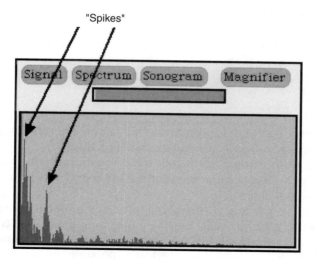

FIGURE 6.8: Viewing a sound in spectrum view with multiple spikes.

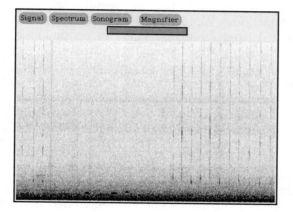

FIGURE 6.9: Viewing the sound signal in a sonogram view.

specific technique being used in the MediaTools signal view is a **Fast Fourier Transform** (or *FFT*), a very common way to do Fourier transforms quickly on a computer so that we can get a real-time view of the changing spectra.

The third view is the *sonogram view* (Figure 6.9). The sonogram view is very much like the spectrum view in that it's describing the frequency domain, but it presents these frequencies over time. Each column in the sonogram view, sometimes called a *slice* or *window (of time)*, represents all the frequencies at a given moment in time. The frequencies increase in the slice from lower (bottom) to higher (top). The *darkness* of the spot in the column indicates the amount of energy of that frequency in the input sound at the given moment. The sonogram view is great for studying how sounds change over time (e.g., how the sound of a piano key being struck changes as the note fades, or how different instruments differ in their sounds, or how different vocal sounds differ).

MAKING IT WORK TIP: Explore sounds!

You really should try these different views on real sounds. You'll get a much better understanding of sound and of what the manipulations we're doing in this chapter are doing to the sounds.

6.1.3 Encoding the Sound

You just read about how sounds work physically and how we perceive them. To manipulate sounds on a computer and play them back on a computer, we have to digitize them. To digitize sound means to take this flow of waves and turn it into numbers. We want to be able to capture a sound, perhaps manipulate it, and then play it back (through the computer's speakers) and hear what we captured as exactly as possible.

The first part of the process of digitizing sound is handled by the computer's hardware—the physical machinery of the computer. If a computer has a microphone and appropriate sound equipment (like a SoundBlaster sound card on Windows computers), then it's possible, at any moment, to measure the amount of air pressure against the microphone as a single number. Positive numbers correspond to rises in pressure, and negative numbers correspond to rarefactions. We call this an *analog-to-digital conversion (ADC)*—we've moved from an analog signal (a continuously changing sound wave) to a digital value. This means that we can get an instantaneous measure of the sound pressure, but it's only one step along the way. Sound is a continuously changing pressure wave. How do we store that in our computer?

By the way, playback systems on computers work essentially the same in reverse. Sound hardware does *digital-to-analog conversion (DAC)*, and the analog signal is then sent to the speakers. The DAC process also requires numbers representing pressure.

If you've had calculus, you've got some idea of how we might do this. You know that we can get close to measuring the area under a curve with more and more rectangles whose height matches the curve (Figure 6.10). With this idea, it's pretty clear that if we capture enough of those microphone pressure readings, we capture the wave. We call each pressure reading a *sample*—we are literally "sampling" the sound at that moment. But how many samples do we need? In integral calculus, you compute the area under the curve by (conceptually) having an infinite number of rectangles. While computer memories are growing larger and larger all the time, we can't capture an infinite number of samples per sound.

Mathematicians and physicists wondered about these kinds of questions long before there were computers, and the answer to how many samples we need was actually computed long ago. The answer depends on the highest *frequency* you want to capture. Let's say that you don't care about any sounds higher

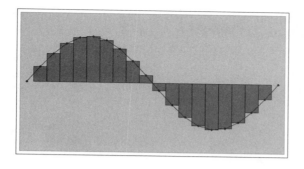

FIGURE 6.10: Area under a curve estimated with rectangles.

than 8,000 Hz. The **Nyquist theorem** says that we would need to capture 16,000 samples per second to completely capture and define a wave whose frequency is less than 8,000 cycles per second.

COMPUTER SCIENCE IDEA: Nyquist theorem

To capture a sound of at most n cycles per second, you need to capture $2n$ samples per second.

This isn't just a theoretical result. The Nyquist theorem influences applications in our daily life. It turns out that human voices don't typically get over 4,000 Hz. That's why our telephone system is designed around capturing 8,000 samples per second. That's why playing music through the telephone doesn't really work very well. The limits of (most) human hearing are around 22,000 Hz. If we were to capture 44,000 samples per second, we would be able to capture any sound that we could actually hear. CD's are created by capturing sound at 44,100 samples per second—just a little bit more than 44 kHz for technical reasons and for a fudge factor.

We call the rate at which samples are collected the *sampling rate*. Most sounds that we hear in daily life are at frequencies far below the limits of our hearing. You can capture and manipulate sounds in this class at a sampling rate of 22 kHz (22,000 samples per second), and they will sound quite reasonable. If you use too low a sampling rate to capture a high-pitched sound, you'll still hear something when you play the sound back, but the pitch will sound strange.

Typically, each of these samples are encoded in two bytes, or 16 bits. Though there are larger *sample sizes*, 16 bits works perfectly well for most applications. CD-quality sound uses 16-bit samples.

In 16 bits, the numbers that can be encoded range from $-32{,}768$ to $32{,}767$. These aren't magic numbers—they make perfect sense when you understand the encoding. These numbers are encoded in 16 bits using a technique called **two's complement notation**, but we can understand it without knowing the details of that technique. We've got 16 bits to represent positive and negative numbers. Let's set aside one of these bits (remember, it's just 0 or 1) to represent whether we're talking about a positive (0) or negative (1) number. We call this the *sign bit*. That leaves 15 bits to represent the actual value. How many different patterns of 15 bits are there? We could start counting:

```
000000000000000
000000000000001
000000000000010
000000000000011

...
111111111111110
111111111111111
```

This looks forbidding. Let's see if we can figure out a pattern. If we've got two bits, there are four patterns: 00, 01, 10, 11. If we've got three bits, there are eight patterns: 000, 001, 010, 011, 100, 101, 110, 111. It turns out that 2^2 is four, and 2^3 is eight. Play with four bits. How many patterns are there? $2^4 = 16$ It turns out that we can state this as a general principle.

 COMPUTER SCIENCE IDEA: 2^n patterns in n bits

If you have n bits, there are 2^n possible patterns in those n bits.

$2^{15} = 32{,}768$. Why is there one more value in the negative range than the positive? Zero is neither negative nor positive, but if we want to represent it as bits, we need to define some pattern as zero. We use one of the positive range values (where the sign bit is zero) to represent zero, so that it takes up one of the 32,768 patterns.

The sample size is a limitation on the amplitude of the sound that can be captured. If you have a sound that generates a pressure greater than 32,767 (or a rarefaction greater than $-32{,}768$), you'll only capture up to the limits of the 16 bits. If you were to look at the wave in the signal view, it would look like somebody had taken some scissors and *clipped* off the peaks of the waves. We call this effect *clipping* for that very reason. If you play (or generate) a sound that's clipped, it sounds bad—it sounds like your speakers are breaking.

There are other ways of digitizing sound, but this is by far the most common. The technical term for this way of encoding sound is *pulse coded modulation (PCM)*. You may encounter this term if you read further in audio or play with audio software.

What this means is that a sound in a computer is a long list of numbers, each of which is a sample in time. There is an ordering in these samples: If you played the samples out of order, you wouldn't get the same sound at all. The most efficient way to store an ordered list of data items on a computer is with an ***array***. An array is literally a sequence of bytes right next to one another in memory. We call each value in an array an ***element***.

We can easily store the samples that make up a sound into an array. Think of each two bytes as storing a single sample. The array will be large—for CD-quality sounds, there will be 44,100 elements for every second of recording. A minute-long recording will result in an array with 26,460,000 elements.

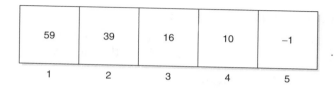

FIGURE 6.11: A depiction of the first five elements in a real sound array.

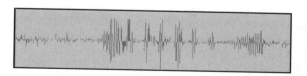

FIGURE 6.12: A sound recording graphed in MediaTools.

Each array element has a number associated with it called its ***index***. The index numbers increase sequentially. The first one is 1, the second one is 2, and so on. You can think about an array as a long line of boxes, each one holding a value and each box having an index number (Figure 6.11).

Using the MediaTools, you can graph a sound file (Figure 6.12) and get a sense of where the sound is quiet (small amplitudes), and loud (large amplitudes). This is important if you want to manipulate the sound. For example, the gaps between recorded words tend to be quiet—at least quieter than the words themselves. You can pick out where words end by looking for the gaps, as in Figure 6.12.

You will soon read about how to read a file containing a recording of a sound into a *sound object*, view the samples in the sound, and change the values of the sound array elements. By changing the values in the array, you change the sound. Manipulating a sound is simply a matter of manipulating the elements in an array.

■ 6.2 Manipulating Sounds

Now that we know how sounds are encoded, we can manipulate sounds using our Python programs. Here's what we'll need to do.

1. We'll need to get the filename of a WAV file and make a sound from it. You saw how to do that in an earlier chapter.

2. You will often get the samples of the sound. Sample objects are easy to manipulate, and they know that when you change them, they should automatically change the original sound. You'll read first about manipulating the samples to start with, then about how to manipulate the sound samples from within the sound itself.

3. Whether you get the sample objects out of a sound or just deal with the samples in the sound object, you will then want to do something to the samples.

4. You may want to write the sound back out to a new file for use elsewhere. (Most sound-editing programs know how to deal with audio.)

6.2.1 Open Sounds and Manipulating Samples

You have already seen how to find a file with `pickAFile` and then make a sound object with `makeSound`. Here's an example of doing that in JES.

```
>>> filename=pickAFile()
>>> print filename
/Users/guzdial/mediasources/preamble.wav
>>> sound=makeSound(filename)
>>> print sound
Sound of length 421109
```

What `makeSound` does is to scoop up all the bytes from the filename provided as input, dump them into memory, and place a big sign on them saying, "This is a sound!" When you execute `mysound = makeSound(myfilename)`, you are saying, "Call that sound object over there `mysound`!" When you use the sound as input to functions, you are saying "Use that sound object over there (yeah, the one I named `mysound`) as input to this function."

You can get the samples from a sound using `getSamples`. The function `getSamples` takes a sound as input and returns an array of all the samples as sample objects. When you execute this function, it may take quite a while before it finishes—longer for longer sounds, shorter for shorter sounds.

```
>>> samples=getSamples(sound)
>>> print samples
Samples, length 421109
```

The function `getSamples` is making an array of sample *objects* out of the basic sample array. An *object* is more than just a simple value like you read about earlier—for one difference, a sample object also knows what sound it came from and what its index is. You will read more about objects later, but take it at face value now that `getSamples` provides you with a bunch of sample objects that you can manipulate—and in fact makes manipulation pretty easy. You can get the value of a sample object by using `getSample` (with a sample object as input), and you set the sample value with `setSample` (with a sample object and a new value as input).

But before we get to the manipulations, let's look at some other ways to get and set samples. We can use the function `getSampleValueAt` to ask the sound to give us the values of specific samples at specific indices. The input values to `getSampleValueAt` are a sound and an index number.

```
>>> print getSampleValueAt(sound,1)
36
>>> print getSampleValueAt(sound,2)
29
```

What numbers can we use as index values? Anything between 1 and the length of the sound in samples. We get this length (the maximum index value) with `getLength`. Note the error that we get below if we try to get a sample past the end of the array.

```
>>> print getLength(sound)
43009
>>> print getSampleValueAt(sound,43010)
```
I wasn't able to do what you wanted. The error
JavaSoundException has occurred JavaSoundException: You are
trying to access the sample at index: 43010, but there are
only 43009 samples in the file!

DEBUGGING TIP: Getting more information on errors

If you're getting an error and want more information on it, go the OPTIONS item in the EDIT menu of JES and choose EXPERT instead of NORMAL (Figure 6.13). Expert mode can sometimes tell you more details—maybe more than you wanted, and probably more than once, but it can be helpful sometimes.

We can similarly change sample values by using setSampleValueAt. It also takes a sound and an index as input values, but also a new value for the sample at that index number. We can check it again with getSampleValueAt.

```
>>> print getSampleValueAt(sound,1)
36
>>> setSampleValueAt(sound,1,12)
>>> print getSampleValueAt(sound,1)
12
```

COMMON BUG: Mistyping a name

You just saw a whole bunch of function names, and some of them are pretty long. What happens if you type one of them wrong? JES will complain that it doesn't know what you mean, like this:

```
>>> writeSndTo(sound,"mysound.wav")
```
A local or global name could not be found.

It's no big deal. JES will let you copy the mistyped command, paste it into the bottommost line of the command area, then fix it. Be sure to put the cursor at the end of the line before you press the ENTER key.

What do you think would happen if we played this sound? Would it really sound different than it did before, now that we've turned the first sample from

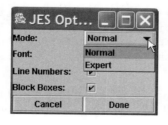

FIGURE 6.13: Turning on Expert errors mode.

the number 36 to the number 12? Not really. To explain why not, let's find out what the sampling rate is for this sound, using the function getSamplingRate, which takes a sound as its input.

```
>>> print getSamplingRate(sound)
22050.0
```

The sound that we're manipulating in this example (a recording of me reading part of the U.S. Constitution's preamble) has a sampling rate of 22,050 samples per second. Changing one sample changes 1/22,050 of the first second of the sound. If you can hear that, you have amazingly good hearing—and I will have my doubts about your truthfulness!

Obviously, to make a significant manipulation to the sound, we have to manipulate hundreds if not thousands of samples. We're certainly not going to do that by typing thousands of lines of

```
setSampleValueAt(sound,1,12)
setSampleValueAt(sound,2,24)
setSampleValueAt(sound,3,100)
setSampleValueAt(sound,4,99)
setSampleValueAt(sound,5,-1)
```

We need to take advantage of the computer executing our recipe, by telling it to go do something hundreds or thousands of times. That's the topic for the next section.

But we will end this section by talking about how to write your results back out to a file. Once you've manipulated your sound and want to save it out to use elsewhere, you use writeSoundTo, which takes a sound and a new filename as input. Be sure that your file ends with the extension ".wav" if you're saving a sound so that your operating system knows what to do with it.

```
>>> print filename
/Users/guzdial/mediasources/preamble.wav
>>> writeSoundTo(sound, "/Users/guzdial/mediasources/
new-preamble.wav")
```

COMMON BUG: Saving a file quickly—and how to find it again! What if you don't know the whole path to a directory of your choosing? You don't have to specify anything more than the base name.

```
>>> writeSoundTo(sound,"new-preamble.wav")
```

The problem is finding the file again. In what directory was it saved? This is a pretty simple bug to resolve. The default directory (the one you get if you don't specify a path) is wherever JES is. If you have a standard media folder (e.g., MEDIASOURCES) where you keep your media and pick files from, and you've used setMediaPath() to set it, that's where your files will be saved if you don't specify a complete path.

You'll probably figure out, when playing sounds a lot, that if you use play a couple of times in quick succession, you'll mix the sounds. How do you make sure that the computer plays only a single sound and then waits for it to end? You use blockingPlay. This works the same as play, but it waits for the sound to end so that no other sound can interfere while it's playing.

6.2.2 Using MediaTools for Looking at Captured Sounds

The MediaTools for manipulating sounds that you read about earlier can also be used to study sound files. Any WAV file on your computer can be opened and studied within the sound tools. There are two sets of MediaTools—the external application you saw in the last section and a set built-in to JES. They have similar capabilities.

Using the MediaTools Application

From the basic sound editor tool in the MediaTools application, click on FILE to get the option to open a WAV file (Figure 6.14). The MediaTools open file dialog will then appear. Find a WAV file by clicking on the directories on the left until you find one that contains the WAV files you want on the right (Figure 6.15), then click OK.

Your CD contains a mediasources directory on it. Most of the examples in the book use the media in this directory. You'll probably want to drag the mediasources folder onto your hard disk so that you can use it there.

You will then be shown the file in the sound editor view (Figure 6.16). The sound editor lets you explore a sound in many ways (Figure 6.17). As you scroll through the sound and change the *sound cursor* (the red/blue line in the graph) position, the INDEX changes to show you which sound array element you're currently looking at, and the VALUE shows you the value at that index. You can also fit the whole sound into the graph to get an overall view (but currently break the index/value displays). You can even "play" your recorded sound as if it were an instrument—try pressing the piano keys across the bottom of the editor. You can also set the cursor (via the scrollbar or by dragging in the graph window) and play the sound before the cursor—a good way to hear what part of the sound corresponds to what index positions. Clicking the <> button provides a menu of options that includes getting an FFT view of the sound.

Using the JES MediaTools

The JES MediaTools are available from the MEDIATOOLS menu in JES. Unlike the application MediaTools, the JES MediaTools know about the picture and

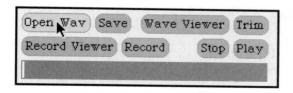

FIGURE 6.14: The sound editor open menu in MediaTools application.

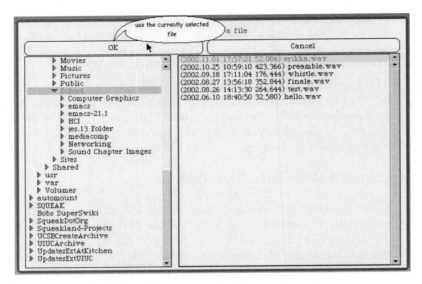

FIGURE 6.15: MediaTools application open file dialog.

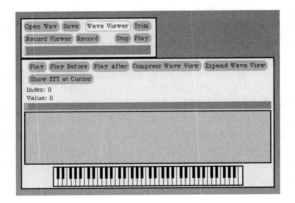

FIGURE 6.16: A sound opened in the editor in MediaTools application.

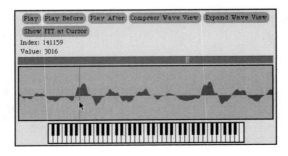

FIGURE 6.17: Exploring the sound in the editor in MediaTools application.

FIGURE 6.18: Picking a sound in JES MediaTools.

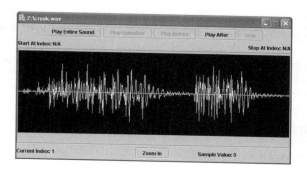

FIGURE 6.19: JES MediaTools sound tool.

sound objects that you're manipulating in JES. When you choose the picture or sound tool, you will be offered a pop-up menu of *variable* names of pictures or sounds, appropriate to whichever tool you chose (Figure 6.18). Click OK and you'll enter the JES MediaTools sound tool.

The sound tool has similar functions to the application version (Figure 6.19).

■ You can play the sound, then click anywhere in it to set a cursor point, then play it before or after the cursor.

■ You can select a region (by clicking and dragging) and then play only that region.

■ As you set a cursor, you're shown the sample index and sample value at that point.

■ You can also zoom in to the sound (Figure 6.20), which allows you to see all the detail while scrolling the length of the sound.

6.2.3 Introducing the Loop

The problem we're facing is a common one in computing: How do we get the computer to do something over and over again? We need to get the computer to *loop or iterate*. Python has commands especially for looping (or iterating). We're mostly going to use the command for. A for loop executes commands (that you

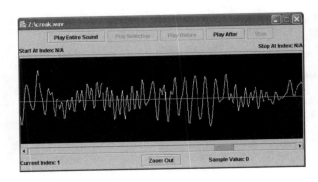

FIGURE 6.20: Zoomed in to the JES MediaTools sound tool.

specify) for sequence (that you provide), where each time the commands are executed, a particular variable (that you name) will have the value of a different element of the sequence.

We are going to use the `getSamples` function we saw earlier to provide our array. We will use a `for` loop that looks like this:

```
for sample in getSamples(sound):
```

Let's talk through the pieces here.

■ First comes the command name `for`.

■ Next comes the variable name that you want to use in your code for addressing (and manipulating) the elements of the sequence.

■ The word `in` is **required**. It makes the command more readable than leaving it out, so there's a benefit to the extra four keystrokes (space-i-n-space).

■ Then you need the sequence. We use the function `getSamples` to generate a sequence.

■ Finally, you need a colon (":"). The colon is important—it signifies that what comes next is a *block* (you should recall reading about blocks in earlier chapters).

What comes next are the commands that you want to execute for each sample. Each time the commands are executed, the variable (in our example `sample`) will be a different element from the array. The commands (called the *body*) are specified as a block. This means that they should follow the `for` statement, each on their own line, *and indented by two more spaces!* For example, here is the `for` loop that simply sets each sample to its own value (a useless exercise, but it will get more interesting in just a couple of pages).

```
for sample in getSamples(sound):
  value = getSample(sample)
  setSample(sample,value)
```

Let's talk through this code.

- The first statement says that we're going to have a `for` loop that will set the variable `sample` to each of the elements of the sequence that is output from `getSamples(sound)`.
- The next statement is indented, so it's part of the body of the `for` loop—one of the statements that will get executed each time `sample` has a new value. It says to name the value of the sample in the variable `sample`. That name is `value`.
- The third statement is still indented, so it's still part of the loop body. Here we set the value of the sample to the value of the variable `value`.

Here's the exact same code (it would work *exactly* the same), but with different variable names.

```
for s in getSamples(sound):
  v = getSample(s)
  setSample(s,v)
```

What's the difference? These variable names are slightly more confusing. `s` and `v` are not as obvious about what they are naming as `sample` and `value`. Python doesn't care which we use, and the single-character variable names are clearly easier to type. But the longer variable names make it easier to understand your code later.

Note that the earlier paragraph emphasized by adding two *more* spaces. Remember that what comes after a function definition `def` statement is *also* a block. If you have a `for` loop inside a function, then the `for` statement is indented two spaces already, so the body of the `for` loop (the statements to be executed) must be indented *four* spaces. The `for` loop's block is inside the function's block. That's called a *nested block*—one block is nested inside the other. Here's an example of turning our useless loop into an equally useless function:

```
def doNothing(sound):
  for sample in getSamples(sound):
    value = getSample(sample)
    setSample(sample,value)
```

You don't actually have to put loops into functions to use them. You can type them into the command area of JES. JES is smart enough to figure out that you need to type more than one command if you're specifying a loop, so it changes the prompt from >>> to .... Of course, it can't figure out when you're done, so you'll have to just hit ENTER without typing anything else to tell JES that you're done with the body of your loop. It looks something like this:

```
>>> for sample in getSamples(sound):
...    value = getSample(sample)
...    setSample(sample,value)
```

You probably realize that we don't need the variable `value` (or v). We can combine the two statements in the body into one. Here's how to do it at the command line:

```
>>> for sample in getSamples(sound):
...     setSample(sample,getSample(sample))
```

Now that we see how to get the computer to do thousands of commands without writing thousands of individual lines, let's do something useful with this.

COMMON BUG: Keep sounds short

Longer sounds take up more memory and will process more slowly.

COMMON BUG: Windows and WAV files

The world of WAV files isn't as compatible and smooth as one might like. WAV files created with other applications (e.g., Windows Recorder) *may* not play in JES, and JES WAV files may not play in all other applications (e.g., WinAmp 2). Apple QuickTime Player Pro (`http://www.apple.com/quicktime`) is good at reading *any* WAV file and exporting a new one that most any other application can read.

■ 6.3 Changing the Volume of Sounds

Earlier, we said that the amplitude of a sound is the main factor in the volume. This means that if we increase the amplitude, we increase the volume. Or if we decrease the amplitude, we decrease the volume.

Don't get confused here—changing the amplitude doesn't reach out and twist up the volume knob on your speakers. If your speaker's volume (or computer's volume) is turned down, the sound will never get very loud. The point is getting the sound itself louder. Have you ever watched a movie on TV where, without changing the volume on the TV, the sound becomes so low that you can hardly hear it? (Marlon Brando's dialogue in the movie *The Godfather* comes to mind.) Or have you noticed how commercials are always louder than normal TV programs? That's what we're doing here. We can make sounds *shout* or *whisper* by tweaking the amplitude.

6.3.1 Increasing Volume

Here's a function that doubles the amplitude of an input sound.

RECIPE 51: Increase an input sound's volume by doubling the amplitude

```
def increaseVolume(sound):
    for sample in getSamples(sound):
        value = getSample(sample)
        setSample(sample,value * 2)
```

Go ahead and type the above into your JES Program Area. Click LOAD to get Python to process the function and make the name increaseVolume stand for this function. Follow along the example below to get a better idea of how this all works.

To use this recipe, you have to create a sound first, then pass it in as input. In the example below, we get the filename by setting the variable f explicitly to a string that is a filename, as opposed to using pickAFile. Don't forget that you can't type this code in and have it work as-is: Your path names will be different from mine.

```
>>> f="/Users/guzdial/mediasources/gettysburg10.wav"
>>> s=makeSound(f)
>>> increaseVolume(s)
```

We then create a sound that we name s. When we evaluate increase-Volume(s), the sound that is named s is *also* named sound, but just within that function. This is a *very* important point. **Both names refer to the same sound!** The changes that take place in increaseVolume are really changing the *same* sound. You can think of each name as an *alias* for the other: They refer to the same *thing*.

There's a side point to mention here just in passing, but it becomes more important later: When the function increaseVolume ends, the name sound *has no value*. It only exists during the duration of that function's execution. We say that it only exists within the *scope* of the function increaseVolume.

We can now play the file to hear that it's louder, and write it to a new file.

```
>>> play(s)
>>> writeSoundTo(s,"/Users/guzdial/mediasources/
louder-g10.wav")
```

6.3.2 Did That Really Work?

Now, is it really louder, or does it just seem that way? We can check this in several ways. You could always make the sound even louder by evaluating increaseVolume on our sound a few more times—eventually, you'll be totally convinced that the sound is louder. But there are ways to test even more subtle effects.

If we compared graphs of the two sounds using the JES MediaTools sound tool, you'd find that the graph of the sound does have greater amplitude after increasing it using our function. Check it out in Figure 6.21.

Maybe you're unsure that you're really seeing a larger wave in the second picture. You can use the MediaTools to check the individual sample values. You can actually use the JES MediaTools as in Figure 6.21—the value at the first index (index number 1) is −30 in the original sound and −60 in the second sound. You can also use the MediaTools Application (Figure 6.22). Open up both WAV files, and open the sound editor for each. Scroll down into the middle

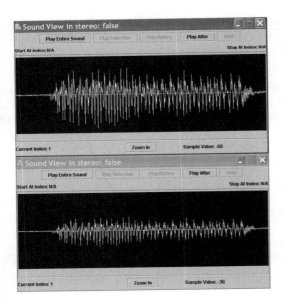

FIGURE 6.21: Comparing the graphs of the original sound (*bottom*) and the louder one (*top*).

of the sound, then drag the cursor to any value you want. Now do the same to the second one. You'll see that the louder sound really does have double the value of the same sample in the original sound.

Finally, you can always check for yourself from within JES. If you've been following along with the example,[1] then the variable s is now the louder sound. f should still be the filename of the original sound. Go ahead and make a new sound object which is the *original* sound—named below as soriginal (for *sound original*). Check any sample value that you want—it's always true that the louder sound has twice the sample values of the original sound.

```
>>> print s
Sound of length 220567
>>> print f
/Users/guzdial/mediasources/gettysburg10.wav
>>> soriginal=makeSound(f)
>>> print getSampleValueAt(s,1)
118
>>> print getSampleValueAt(soriginal,1)
59
>>> print getSampleValueAt(s,2)
78
>>> print getSampleValueAt(soriginal,2)
39
>>> print getSampleValueAt(s,1000)
-80
>>> print getSampleValueAt(soriginal,1000)
-40
```

[1] What? You haven't? You *should!* It'll make much more sense if you try it yourself.

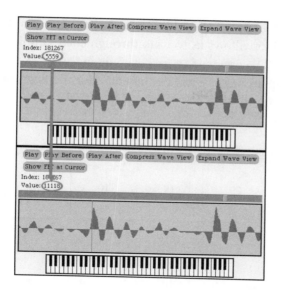

FIGURE 6.22: Comparing specific samples in the original sound (*top*) and the louder one (*bottom*).

You can see from the bottom value that even negative values become *more* negative. That's what's meant by "increasing the amplitude." The amplitude of the wave goes in *both* directions. We have to make the wave larger in both the positive and negative dimensions.

It's important to do what you just read in this chapter: *Doubt* your programs. Did that *really* do what I wanted it to do? The way you check is by *testing*. That's what this section is about. You just saw several ways to test:

- By looking at the result overall (as with the graphs),
- By checking pieces of the results (as with the MediaTools), and
- By writing additional code statements that check the results of the original program.

Figuring Out How It Worked

Let's walk through the code, slowly, and consider how this program worked.

```
def increaseVolume(sound):
  for sample in getSamples(sound):
    value = getSample(sample)
    setSample(sample,value * 2)
```

Recall our picture of how the samples in a sound array might look.

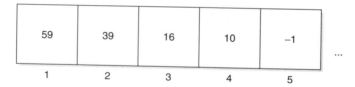

This is what `getSamples(sound)` would return: An array of sample values, each numbered. The `for` loop allows us to walk through each sample, one at a time. The name `sample` will be assigned to each sample in turn.

When the `for` loop begins, `sample` will be the name for the first sample.

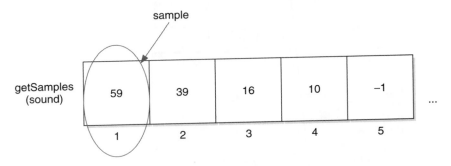

The variable `value` will take on the value of 59 when `value=getSample-(sample)` is executed. The sample that the name `sample` references will then be doubled with `setSample(sample,value*2)`.

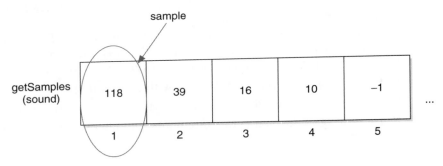

That's the end of the first pass through the body of the `for` loop. Python will then start the loop again and move `sample` on to point at the *next* element in the array.

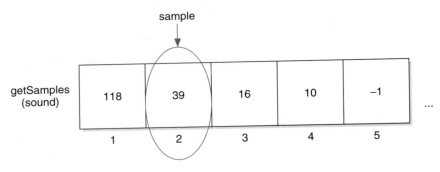

The `value` is again set to the value of the sample, then the sample will be doubled.

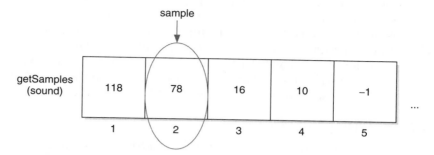

The loop again repeats through the five samples pictured.

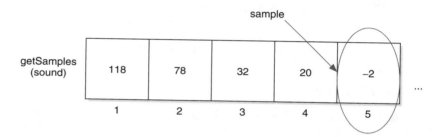

The `for` loop *keeps* going through all the samples—tens of thousands of them! Thank goodness it's the *computer* executing this recipe!

One way to think about what's happening here is that the `for` loop doesn't really *do* anything, in the sense of changing anything in the sound. Only the *body* of the loop does work. The `for` loop tells the computer *what* to do. It's a manager. What the computer actually does is something like this:

```
sample = sample #1
value = value of the sample, 59
change sample to 118
sample = sample #2
value = 39
change sample to 78
sample = sample #3
...
sample = sample #5
value = -1
change sample to -2
...
```

The `for` loop is only saying, "Do all of this for every element in the array." It's the *body* of the loop that contains the Python commands that are executed.

What you have just read in this section is called *tracing* the program. We slowly went through how each step in the program was executed. We drew pictures to describe the data in the program. We used numbers, arrows, equations, and even plain English to explain what was going on in the program. This is the single most important technique in programming. It's part of *debugging*. Your program will *not* always work. Absolutely, guaranteed, without a shadow of a doubt—you will write code that does not do what you want. But the computer *will* do *something*. How do you figure out what it *is* doing? You debug, and the most powerful way to do that is by tracing the program.

6.3.3 Decreasing Volume

Decreasing volume is the reverse of the process described above.

RECIPE 52: Decrease an input sound's volume by halving the amplitude

```
def decreaseVolume(sound):
    for sample in getSamples(sound):
        value = getSample(sample)
        setSample(sample,value * 0.5)
```

How it works:

■ Our function takes a sound object as input. Within the function decrease-Volume, the input sound will be called sound—no matter what name it has in the Command Area.

■ The variable sample will stand for each and every sample in the input sound.

■ Each time sample is assigned a new sample, we will get the *value* of the sample. We put it in the variable value.

■ We then set the sample value to 50% of its current value by multiplying value by 0.5, and setting the sample value to that.

We can use it like this.

```
>>> f=pickAFile()
>>> print f
/Users/guzdial/mediasources/louder-g10.wav
>>> sound=makeSound(f)
>>> print sound
Sound of length 220568
>>> play(sound)
>>> decreaseVolume(sound)
>>> play(sound)
```

We can even do it again, and lower the volume even further.

```
>>> decreaseVolume(sound)
>>> play(sound)
```

6.3.4 Making Sense of Functions, in Sounds

The lessons about how functions work in pictures (from Section 3.4.1) apply here in sounds as well. For example, we could put all the pickAFile and makeSound calls directly into our functions like increaseVolume and decreaseVolume, but that would mean that the functions are doing more than *one and only one thing*. If we had to increase or decrease the volume to a bunch of sounds, we'd find it annoying to have to keep picking files.

We can write functions that take multiple inputs. For example, here's a recipe to changeVolume. It accepts a factor that is multiplied by each sample value. This function can be used to increase or decrease the amplitude (and thus, volume).

RECIPE 53: Change a sound's volume by a given factor

```
def changeVolume(sound, factor):
    for sample in getSamples(sound):
        value = getSample(sample)
        setSample(sample,value * factor)
```

This recipe is clearly more flexible than increaseVolume or decrease-Volume. Does that make it better? Certainly it is for some purposes (e.g., if you were writing software to do general audio processing), but in other purposes, having separate and clearly named functions for increasing and decreasing volume is better. Remember that software is written for humans—write software that is understandable for the people who will be reading and using your software.

We are reusing the name sound a lot. We use it to name sounds that we read from disk in the Command Area, and we're using it to serve as a placeholder for inputs to functions. *That's okay.* Names can have different meanings depending on context. Inside a function is a different context than the Command Area. If you create a variable in a function context (like value in Recipe 53), then that variable won't exist when you get back out to the Command Area. We can return values from a function context back out to the Command Area (or other calling function) by using return, which we'll talk more about later.

■ 6.4 Normalizing Sounds

If you think about it, you may find it strange that the last two recipes work. We can multiply the numbers representing a sound—and the sound will seem (essentially) the same to our ears but louder. The way we experience a sound depends less on the specific numbers than on the *relationship* between them. Remember that the overall shape of the sound waveform is dependent on *many* samples. In general, if we multiply all the samples by the same multiplier, we only affect our sense of volume (intensity), not the sound itself. (We'll work to change the sound itself in future sections.)

A common operation that people want to do with sounds is to make them as **loud as possible**. This is called ***normalizing***. It's not really hard to do, but it takes more lines of Python code than we've used previously and a few more variables, but we can do it. Here's the recipe, in English, that we need to tell the computer to do.

■ We have to figure out what the largest sample in the sound is. If it's already at the maximum value (32,767), then we can't really increase the volume and still get what seems like the same sound. Remember that we have to multiply all the samples by the same multiplier.

It's an easy recipe (*algorithm*) to find the largest value—sort of a *subrecipe* within the overall normalizing recipe. Define a name (say, `largest`) and assign it a small value (0 works). Now check all the samples. If you find a sample larger than `largest`, make the larger value the new meaning for `largest`. Keep checking the samples, now comparing to the *new* largest. Eventually, the very largest value in the array will be in the variable `largest`.

To do this, we'll need a way of figuring out the maximum value of two values. Python provides a built-in function called `max` that can do this.

```
>>> print max(8,9)
9
>>> print max(3,4,5)
5
```

■ Next we need to figure out what value to multiply all the samples by. We want the largest value to become 32,767. Thus we want to figure out a *multiplier* such that

$$(multiplier)(largest) = 32767.$$

Solve for the multiplier:
$multiplier = 32767/largest$. The multiplier will need to be a floating-point number (have a decimal component), so we need to convince Python that not everything here is an integer. Turns out that that's easy—use 32,767.0. Simply stick on ".0".

■ Now loop through all the samples, as we did for `increaseVolume`, and multiply the sample by the multiplier.

Here's a recipe to normalize sounds.

RECIPE 54: Normalize the sound to a maximum amplitude

```
def normalize(sound):
    largest = 0
    for s in getSamples(sound):
        largest = max(largest,getSample(s) )
    multiplier = 32767.0 / largest
```

```
        print "Largest sample value in original sound was",
    largest
        print "Multiplier is", multiplier

        for s in getSamples(sound):
            louder =  multiplier * getSample(s)
            setSample(s,louder)
```

There are several notational items to note about this program.

■ There are blank lines in there! Python doesn't care about them. Adding blank lines can be useful to break up and improve the understandability of longer programs.

■ There are `print` statements in there! `print` statements can be *really* useful. First, they give you some feedback that the program is running—a useful thing in long-running programs. Second, they show you what it's finding, which can be interesting. Third, it's a terrific testing method and a way to debug your programs. Let's imagine that the printout showed that the multiplier was less than 1.0. We know that this kind of multiplier *decreases* volume. You should probably suspect that something went wrong.

■ Some of the statements in this recipe are pretty long, so they wrap around in the text. *Type them as a single line!* Python doesn't let you hit ENTER until the end of the statement—make sure that your print statements are all on one line.

Here's what the program looks like running.

```
>>> normalize(sound)
Largest sample in original sound was 5656
Multiplier is 5.7933168316831685
>>> play(sound)
```

Exciting, huh? Obviously, the interesting part is hearing the much louder volume, which is awfully hard to demonstrate in a book.

6.4.1 Generating Clipping

Earlier, we talked about *clipping*, the effect when the normal curves of the sound are broken by the limitations of the sample size. One way of generating clipping is to keep increasing the volume. Another way is to explicitly force clipping.

What if you *only* had the largest and smallest possible sample values? What if all the positive values were the *maximum* values and all the negative values were the minimum values? Try this recipe, particularly on sounds with words in them.

RECIPE 55: Set all samples to maximum values

```
def onlymaximize(sound):
    for sample in getSamples(sound):
        value = getSample(sample)
        if value > 0:
            setSample(sample,32767)
        if value < 0:
            setSample(sample,-32768)
```

When you play the sound back, you'll hear some awful noises. That's clipping. The really amazing thing is that you can *still* make out the words in the sounds that you manipulate with this function. Our ability to decipher words from noise is incredibly powerful.

Programming Summary

In this chapter, we talk about several kinds of encodings of data (or objects).

Sounds	Encodings of sounds, typically coming from a WAV file.
Samples	Collections of sample objects, each indexed by a number (e.g., sample #1, sample #2). `samples[1]` is the first Sample object. You can manipulate each sample in the samples like this `for s in samples:`.
Sample	A value between −32,000 and 32,000 (roughly) representing the voltage that a microphone would generate at a given instant when recording a sound. The length of the instant is typically either 1/44,100 of a second (for CD-quality sound) or 1/22,050 of a second (for good-enough sound on most computers). A sample object remembers what sound it came from, so if you change its value, it knows to go back and change the right sample in the sound.

Here are the functions used or introduced in this chapter:

int	Returns the integer part of the input value
max	Takes as many numbers as you want, and returns the largest value

Sound file functions and pieces

pickAFile	Lets the user pick a file and returns the complete path name as a string. No input
makeSound	Takes a filename as input, reads the file, and creates a sound from it. Returns the sound.

Sound object functions and pieces

play	Plays a sound provided as input. No return value.
getLength	Takes a sound as input and returns the number of samples in the sound.
getSamples	Takes a sound as input and returns the samples in the sound.
blockingPlay	Plays the sound provided as input and makes sure that no other sound plays at the exact same time. (Try two play's right after each other.)
playAtRate	Takes a sound and a rate (1.0 means normal speed, 2.0 is twice as fast, and 0.5 is half as fast), and plays the sound at that rate. The duration is always *the same* (e.g., if you play it twice as fast, the sound plays *twice* to fill the given time).
playAtRateDur	Takes a sound, a rate, and a duration as the number of samples to play.
writeSoundTo	Takes a sound and a filename (a string) and writes the sound to the file as a WAV file. (Make sure that the filename ends in ".wav" if you want the operating system to treat it right.)
getSamplingRate	Takes a sound as input and returns the number representing the number of samples in each second for the sound.
getLength	Returns the length of the sound as a number of samples

Sample-oriented functions and pieces

getSampleValueAt	Takes a sound and an index (an integer value), and returns the value of the sample (between $-32{,}000$ and $32{,}000$) for that object.
setSampleValueAt	Takes a sound, an index, and a value (should be between $-32{,}000$ and $32{,}000$), and sets the value of the sample at the given index in the given sound to the given value.
getSampleObjectAt	Takes a sound and an index (an integer value), and returns the sample object at that index.
getSample	Takes a sample object and returns its value (between $-32{,}000$ and $32{,}000$). getValue will also work.
setSample	Takes a sample object and a value, and sets the sample to the value. setValue will also work.
getSound	Takes a sample object and returns the sound that it remembers as its own.

Problems

6.1 Open up the SONOGRAM view and say some vowel sounds. Is there a distinctive pattern? Do "oh's" always sound the same? Do "ah's"? Does it matter whether you switch speakers—are the patterns the same?

6.2 Get a couple of different instruments and play the same note on them into the MediaTool application's sound editor with the sonogram view open. Are all "C's" made equal? Can you *see* some of why one sound is different from another?

6.3 Try out a variety of WAV files as instruments, using the piano keyboard in the Media-Tools application sound editor. What kinds of recordings work best as instruments?

6.4 The increase volume recipe (Recipe 51) takes a sound as input. Write a function increaseVolumeNamed that takes a file name as input, then plays the louder sound.

6.5 Rewrite increase volume (Recipe 51) so that it takes two inputs: the sound to increase in volume, and a filename where the newly louder sound should be stored. Then increase the volume, and write the sound out to the name file. You might also try rewriting it so that it takes an input filename instead of the sound, so that inputs are both filenames.

6.6 Rewrite increase volume (Recipe 51) so that it takes two inputs: a sound to increase in volume, and a *multiplier*. Use the multiplier as *how much* to increase the amplitude of the sound samples. Can we use the same function to both increase and decrease the volume? Demonstrate commands that you would execute to do each.

6.7 In Section 6.3.1, we walked through how Recipe 51 worked. Draw the pictures to show how Recipe 52 works in the same way.

6.8 What happens if you increase a volume too far? Explore this by creating a sound object, then increasing the volume once, and again, and again. Does it always keep getting louder? Or does something else happen? Can you explain why?

6.9 Try sprinkling in some specific values into your sounds. What happens if you set the value of a few hundred samples in the middle of a sound to 32,767? Or a few hundred to $-32,768$? Or a bunch of zeroes? What happens to the sound?

6.10 Instead of multiplying samples by a multiplier (like 2 or 0.5), try *adding* a value to them. What happens to a sound if you add 100 to every sample? 1,000?

To Dig Deeper

There are many wonderful books on psychoacoustics and computer music. One of my favorites for understandability is *Computer Music: Synthesis, Composition, and Performance* by Dodge and Jerse [10]. The "*bible*" of computer music is Curtis Roads' massive *The Computer Music Tutorial* [32].

CHAPTER 7

Modifying Samples in a Range

Chapter Learning Objectives

The media learning goals for this chapter are:

- *To splice sounds together to make sound compositions.*
- *To reverse sounds.*
- *To mirror sounds.*

The computer science goals for this chapter are:

- *To iterate an index variable for an array across a* range.
- *To use comments in programs, and why.*
- *To identify some algorithms that cross media boundaries.*

■ 7.1 Manipulating Different Sections of the Sound Differently

In the last chapter we described some useful things to do to sounds overall, but really interesting effects come from chopping up sounds and manipulating them differentially: some words this way, other sounds that way. How would you do that? We need to be able to loop through *portions* of the sample, without walking through the whole thing. Turns out to be an easy thing to do, but we need to manipulate samples somewhat differently (e.g., we have to use index numbers), and we have to use our for loop in a slightly different way.

Recall that each sample has a number, and that we can get each individual sample with getSampleValueAt (with a sound and an index number as input). We can set any sample with setSampleValueAt (with inputs of a sound, an index number, and a new value). That's how we can manipulate samples without using `getSamples` and sample objects. But we still don't want to have to write code like:

```
setSampleValueAt(sound,1,12)
setSampleValueAt(sound,2,28) ...
```

Not for tens of thousands of samples!

What we need is to get the computer to address each sample, in turn, by index number. We need to get the `for` loop to go from 1 to 20,000-something (or whatever the length of the sound may be). As you might expect, Python does have a way of doing this. It's called the function `range`. `range` takes two inputs and returns an array of the integers between the two numbers—including the first one, but stopping before the last one. Some examples will help to make clearer what it does.

```
>>> print range(1,3)
[1, 2]
>>> print range(3,1)
[]
>>> print range(-1,5)
[-1, 0, 1, 2, 3, 4]
>>> print range(1,100)
[1, 2, 3, 4, 5, 6, 7, 8, 9, 10, 11, 12, 13, 14, 15, 16,
17, 18, 19, 20, 21, 22, 23, 24, 25, 26, 27, 28, 29, 30,
31, 32, 33, 34, 35, 36, 37, 38, 39, 40, 41, 42, 43, 44,
45, 46, 47, 48, 49, 50, 51, 52, 53, 54, 55, 56, 57, 58,
59, 60, 61, 62, 63, 64, 65, 66, 67, 68, 69, 70, 71, 72,
73, 74, 75, 76, 77, 78, 79, 80, 81, 82, 83, 84, 85, 86,
87, 88, 89, 90, 91, 92, 93, 94, 95, 96, 97, 98, 99]
```

You might be wondering what this square bracket stuff is (e.g., [1,2] in the first example above). That's the notation for an array—it's how Python prints out a series of numbers to show that this is an array.[1] If we use `range` to generate the array for the `for` loop, our variable will walk through each of the sequential numbers we generate.

It turns out that `range` can also take *three* inputs. If a third input is provided, it's an *increment*—the amount to step between generated integers.

```
>>> print range(0,10,2)
[0, 2, 4, 6, 8]
>>> print range(1,10,2)
[1, 3, 5, 7, 9]
>>> print range(0,100,3)
[0, 3, 6, 9, 12, 15, 18, 21, 24, 27, 30, 33, 36, 39, 42,
45, 48, 51, 54, 57, 60, 63, 66, 69, 72, 75, 78, 81, 84,
87, 90, 93, 96, 99]
```

---

[1] Technically, `range` returns a *sequence*, which is a somewhat different collection of data from an array. But for our purposes we'll call it an array.

Using range, we can do everything that we were doing with getSamples, but now directly referencing the index numbers. Here's Recipe 51 written using range.

RECIPE 56: Increase an input sound's volume using range

```
def increaseVolumeByRange(sound):
    for sampleIndex in range(1,getLength(sound)+1):
        value = getSampleValueAt(sound,sampleIndex)
        setSampleValueAt(sound,sampleIndex,value * 2)
```

Try it—you'll find that it performs just like the previous one.

But now we can do some really fun things with sounds, because we can control which samples we're talking to. The next recipe *increases* the sound for the first half of the sound, then *decreases* it in the second half. See if you can trace how it's working.

RECIPE 57: Increase the volume, then decrease it

```
def increaseAndDecrease(sound):
    for sampleIndex in range(1,getLength(sound)/2):
        value = getSampleValueAt(sound,sampleIndex)
        setSampleValueAt(sound,sampleIndex,value * 2)
    for sampleIndex in range(getLength(sound)/2,
  getLength(sound)+1):
        value = getSampleValueAt(sound,sampleIndex)
        setSampleValueAt(sound,sampleIndex,value * 0.2)
```

How it works: There are two loops in increaseAndDecrease, each of which deals with one half of the sound.

■ The first loop deals with the samples from 1 to halfway through the sound. These samples all get multiplied by 2, to double their amplitude.

■ The second loop goes from halfway through to the end of the sound. Here, we multiply each sample by 0.2, thus decreasing the volume by 80%.

Another Way of Writing Array References

It's worth pointing out that in many languages square brackets ([ ]) are standard notation for manipulating arrays. It works that way in Python. For any array, array[index] returns the index-th element in the array. The number inside the square brackets is always an index variable, but it's sometimes referred to as a *subscript* because of the way that mathematicians refer to the *i*-th element of *a*, e.g., a_i.

MAKING IT WORK TIP: Indices start with zero in Python

There is one catch from what we've been doing earlier: Arrays in Python are *traditional* computer science arrays. The first index is zero. The media functions built-in to JES allow you to think in terms of starting with 1, like most normal human endeavors. But when you do the square brackets, you're dealing with raw Python.

Let's do it here with samples to demonstrate.

```
>>> samples = getSamples(sound)
>>> print samples[1]
Sample at 2 value at 696
>>> print samples[0]
Sample at 1 value at 0
>>> print samples[22000]
Sample at 22001 value at 22364
```

To demonstrate it in ways that you can trust the result (because you don't really know what's in the sound in the preceding examples), let's use range to make an array, then reference it the same way.

```
>>> myArray = range(0,100)
>>> print myArray[1]
1
>>> print myArray[0]
0
>>> print myArray[35]
35
>>> mySecondArray = range(0,100,2)
>>> print mySecondArray[35]
70
```

■ 7.2 Splicing Sounds

Splicing sounds is a term that dates back to when sounds were recorded on tape—juggling the order of things on the tape involved literally cutting the tape into segments and then gluing it back together in the right order. That's "splicing." When everything is digital, it's *much* easier.

To splice sounds, we simply have to copy elements around in the array. It's easiest to do this with two (or more) arrays, rather than copy within the same array. If you copy all the samples that represent someone saying the word "the" up to the beginning of a sound (starting at index number 1), then you make the sound start with the word "the." Splicing lets you create all kinds of sounds, speeches, nonsense, and art.

The easiest kind of splice is when the sounds are in separate files. All that you need to do is to copy each sound, in order, into a target sound. Here's a recipe that creates the start of a sentence "Guzdial is ...". (Readers are welcome to complete the sentence.)

RECIPE 58: Merging words into a single sentence

```
def merge():
  guzdialsound = makeSound(getMediaPath("guzdial.wav"))
  issound = makeSound(getMediaPath("is.wav"))
  target = makeSound(getMediaPath("sec3silence.wav"))
  index = 1
  # Copy in "Guzdial"
  for source in range(1,getLength(guzdialsound)):
    value = getSampleValueAt(guzdialsound,source)
    setSampleValueAt(target,index,value)
    index = index + 1
  # Copy in 0.1 second pause (silence) (0)
  for source in range(1,int(0.1*getSamplingRate(target))):
    setSampleValueAt(target,index,0)
    index = index + 1
  # Copy in "is"
  for source in range(1,getLength(issound)):
    value = getSampleValueAt(issound,source)
    setSampleValueAt(target,index,value)
    index = index + 1
  normalize(target)
  play(target)
  return target
```

How it works: There are three loops in this function `merge`, each of which copies one segment into the target sound—a segment being either a word or a silence between words.

■ The function starts by creating sound objects for the word "Guzdial" (`guzdialsound`), the word "is" (`issound`), and the target silence (`target`).

■ Note that we set `index` (for the target) equal to 1 before the first loop. We then increment it in every loop, but we never again set it to a specific value. That's because `index` is always the index for the *next empty sample* in the target sound. Because each loop follows the previous one, we just keep tacking samples onto the end of the target.

■ In the first loop, we copy each and every sample from `guzdialsound` into the `target`. We have the index `source` go from 1 to the length of `guzdialsound`. We get the sample value at `source` from `guzdialsound`, then set the sample value at `index` in the `target` sound to the value that we got from `guzdialsound`. We then increment `index` so that it points at the next empty sample index.

■ In the second loop, we create 0.1 seconds of silence. Since `getSampling-Rate(target)` gives us the number of samples in one second of `target`, 0.1 times tells us the number of samples in 0.1 seconds. We don't get any source value here—we simply set the `index`-th sample to 0 (for silence), then increment the `index`.

■ Finally, we copy in all the samples from issound, just like the first loop where we copied in guzdialsound.

■ We normalize the sound to make it louder. This means that the function normalize *must* be in the Program Area with merge, even though we're not showing it here. We then play and return the sound.

We return the sound because we created the sound in the function. It wasn't handed in as input to the function. In our recipes, like the one for increasing the volume, we changed the input sound as a *side effect*. If we didn't return the sound we created in merge, it would disappear with the end of the merge function context (*scope*). By returning it, we allow another function to use the resulting sound.

To use makeEmptySound in this example, simply replace the creation of the target with something like:

```
target = makeEmptySound(3)
```

The more common kind of splicing is when the words are in the middle of an existing sound, and you need to pull them out from there. The first thing to do in splicing like that is to figure out the index numbers that delimit the pieces you're interested in. Using the MediaTools, that's pretty easy to do.

■ Open your WAV file in the MediaTools sound tools.

■ Open the editor.

■ Scroll and move the cursor (by dragging in the graph) until you think that the cursor is before or after a sound of interest.

■ Check your positioning by playing the sound before and after the cursor, using the buttons in the sound editor.

Using exactly this process, I found the ending points of the first few words in preamble10.wav. (I figure that the first word starts at the index 1, but that might not be true for every sound.)

Word	Ending index
We	15730
the	17407
People	26726
of	32131
the	33413
United	40052
States	55510

Writing a loop that copies things from one array to another requires a little bit of juggling. You need to think about keeping track of two indices: where you are in the array that you're copying *from*, and where you are in the array that you're copying *to*. These are two different variables, tracking two different indexes. But they both increment in the same way.

The way that we're going to do it (another *subrecipe*) is to use one index variable to point at the right entry in the *target* array (the one we're copying *to*), use a for loop to have the second index variable move across the right entries in the *source* array (the one we're copying *from*), and (*very important!*) move the target index variable each time we do a copy. This is what keeps the two index variables synchronized.

We make the target index move by adding 1 to it. Very simply, we'll tell Python to do targetIndex = targetIndex + 1. If you're a mathematician, that probably looks nonsensical. "How can any variable equal itself plus one?" It's never true that $x = x + 1$. But remember that "=" doesn't assert that the two sides are equal—it means "Make the name on the left stand for the value on the right." Thus, targetIndex = targetIndex + 1 makes a lot of sense: Make the name targetIndex now be whatever targetIndex currently is plus one. That moves the target index. If we put this in the body of the loop where we're changing the source index, we'll get them moving in synchrony.

The general form of the subrecipe is:

```
targetIndex = Where-the-incoming-sound-should-start for
sourceIndex in range(startingPoint,endingPoint)
  setSampleValueAt(target, targetIndex, getSampleValueAt
(source, sourceIndex))
  targetIndex = targetIndex + 1
```

Below is the recipe that changes the preamble from "We the people of the United States" to "We the *united* people of the United States."

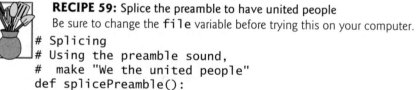

RECIPE 59: Splice the preamble to have united people
Be sure to change the file variable before trying this on your computer.

```
# Splicing
# Using the preamble sound,
#  make "We the united people"
def splicePreamble():
    file = "/Users/guzdial/mediasources/preamble10.wav"
    source = makeSound(file)
    # This will be the newly spliced sound
    target = makeSound(file)

    # targetIndex starts at just after
    # "We the" in the new sound
    targetIndex=17408
    # Where the word "United" is in the sound
    for sourceIndex in range(33414, 40052):
        value = getSampleValueAt(source, sourceIndex)
```

```
        setSampleValueAt(target, targetIndex, value)
        targetIndex = targetIndex + 1

    # Where the word "People" is in the sound
    for sourceIndex in range(17408, 26726):
        value = getSampleValueAt(source, sourceIndex)
        setSampleValueAt(target, targetIndex, value)
        targetIndex = targetIndex + 1

    #Stick some quiet space after that
    for index in range(1,1000):
        setSampleValueAt(target, targetIndex,0)
        targetIndex = targetIndex + 1

    #Let's hear and return the result
    play(target)
    return target
```

We'd use it as simply as saying:

```
>>> newSound=splicePreamble()
```

How it works: There's a lot going on in this recipe. Let's walk through it, slowly.

Note that there are lots of lines with "#" in them. The hash character signifies that what comes after that character on the line is a note to the programmer *and should be ignored by Python*. It's called a *comment*.

MAKING IT WORK TIP: Comments are good!

Comments are great ways to explain what you're doing to others—and to yourself! The reality is that it's hard to remember all the details of a program, so it's often *very* useful to leave notes about what you did in case you ever play with the program again.

The function `splice Preamble` takes no parameters. Sure, it would be great to write a single function that can do any kind of splicing we want, in the same way as we've done generalized increasing volume and normalization. But how would you do this? How do you generalize all the start and end points? It's easier, at least to start, to create single recipes that handle specific splicing tasks.

We see here three of the copying loops like we set up earlier. Actually, there are only two. The first one copies the word "united" into place. The second one copies the word "people" into place. "But wait," you might be thinking. "The word 'people' was *already* in the sound!" That's true, but when we copy "united" in, we overwrite some of the word "people," so we copy it in again.

Here's the simpler form. Try it and listen to the result:

```
def spliceSimpler():
  file = "/Users/guzdial/mediasources/preamble10.wav"
  source = makeSound(file)
  # This will be the newly spliced sound
```

```
target = makeSound(file)
# targetIndex starts at just after "We the" in the
new sound
targetIndex=17408
# Where the word "United" is in the sound
for sourceIndex in range(33414, 40052):
    value = getSampleValueAt(source, sourceIndex)
    setSampleValueAt(target, targetIndex, value)
    targetIndex = targetIndex + 1
#Let's hear and return the result
play(target)
return target
```

Let's see if we can figure out what's going on mathematically. Recall the table back on page 173. We're going to start inserting samples at sample index 17,408. The word "united" has (40,052 − 33,414) 6,638 samples. (Exercise for the reader: How long is that in seconds?) This means that we'll be writing into the target from 17,408 to (17,408 + 6,638) sample index 24,046. We know from the table that the word "people" ends at index 26726. If the word "people" is more than (26,726 − 24,046) 2,680 samples, then it will start earlier than 24,046, and our insertion of "united" is going to trample on part of it. If the word "united" is over 6,000 samples, I doubt that the word "people" is less than 2,000. That's why it sounds crunched. Why does it work with where the "of" is? The speaker must have paused in there. If you check the table again, you'll see that the word "of" ends at sample index 32,131 and the word before it ends at 26,726. The word "of" takes fewer than (32,131 − 26,726) 5,405 samples, which is why the original recipe works.

The third loop in the original Recipe 59 looks like the same kind of copy loop, but it's really only putting in a few 0's. As you might have already guessed, samples with 0's are silent. Putting a few in creates a pause that sounds better. (There's an exercise which suggests pulling them out and seeing what you hear.)

Finally, at the very end of the recipe, there's a new statement we haven't seen with sounds yet: return. We've now seen many functions in Python that return values. This is how one does it. It's important for splice to return the newly spliced sound. Because of the scope of the function splice, if the new sound wasn't created, it would simply disappear when the function ended. By returning it, it's possible to give it a name and play it (and even further manipulate it) after the function stops executing.

Figure 7.1 shows the original preamble10.wav file in the top sound editor, and the new spliced one (saved with writeSoundTo) on the bottom. The lines are drawn so that the spliced section lies between them, while the rest of the sounds are identical.

■ 7.3 Backwards Sounds

In the splicing example, we copied the samples from the words just as they were in the original sound. We don't have to always go in the same order. We can reverse the words—or make them faster, slower, louder, or softer. For an example, here's a recipe that plays a sound in a file backwards.

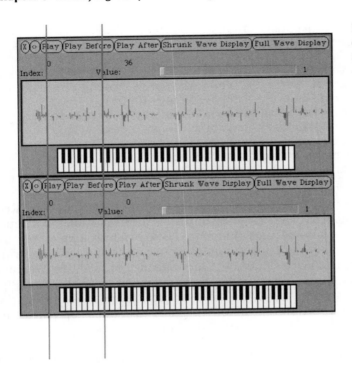

FIGURE 7.1: Comparing the original sound (*top*) to the spliced sound (*bottom*).

RECIPE 60: Play the given sound backwards

```
def backwards(filename):
    source = makeSound(filename)
    target = makeSound(filename)

    sourceIndex = getLength(source)
    for targetIndex in range(1,getLength(target)+1):
        sourceValue = getSampleValueAt(source,sourceIndex)
        setSampleValueAt(target,targetIndex,sourceValue)
        sourceIndex = sourceIndex - 1

    return target
```

How it works: This recipe uses another variant of the array element copying subrecipe that we've already seen.

■ The recipe starts the `sourceIndex` at the *end* of the array rather than the front.

■ The `targetIndex` moves from 1 to the length, during which time the recipe:

  ■ Gets the sample value in the source at the `sourceIndex`.

  ■ Copies that value into the target at the `targetIndex`.

■ *Reduces* the sourceIndex by 1, meaning that the sourceIndex moves from the end of the array back to the beginning.

Once we know how to play sounds forwards and backwards, *mirroring* a sound is the exact same process as mirroring a picture. Compare this to Recipe 19. Do you see that this is the same *algorithm* even though we're dealing with a different medium?

RECIPE 61: Mirror a sound front to back

```
def mirrorSound(sound):
   mirrorpoint=getLength(sound)/2
   for sampleOffset in range(1,mirrorpoint-1):
     samplelater = getSampleObjectAt(sound,
mirrorpoint+sampleOffset)
     samplebefore = getSampleObjectAt(sound,
mirrorpoint-sampleOffset)
       value = getSample(samplebefore)
       setSample(samplelater,value)
```

MAKING IT WORK TIP: Off by one errors

In the last two recipes, we added 1 or subtracted 1 from a **range** endpoint. In **backwards**, we added 1 to get *every* sample because **range** usually ignores the end point. In **mirrorSound**, we subtracted 1 to make sure that we didn't end up going past the end of the sound when we added **mirrorPoint** to **mirrorPoint**. In general, being off by one in our media examples isn't a big deal—we can hardly perceive a single sample or pixel. It's only an issue in trying to avoid going past the end of a sound—if we try to index beyond the end of the sound, we'll get an error.

Programming Summary

In this chapter, we talk about several kinds of encodings of data (or objects).

Sounds	Encodings of sounds, typically coming from a WAV file.
Samples	Collections of sample objects, each indexed by a number (e.g., sample #1, sample #2). samples[1] is the first sample object. You can manipulate each sample in the samples like this for s in samples:.
Sample	A value between −32,000 and 32,000 (roughly) representing the voltage that a microphone would generate at a given instant when recording a sound. The length of the instant is typically either 1/44,1000 of a second (for CD-quality sound) or 1/22,050 of a second (for good-enough sound on most computers). A sample object remembers what sound it came from, so if you change its value, it knows to go back and change the right sample in the sound.

Here are the functions used or introduced in this chapter:

range	Takes two numbers, and returns an array of all integers starting at the first number and stopping before the last number.
range	Can also take three numbers, and then returns an array of all the integers from the first, up to but not including the second, incrementing each time by the third.

Problems

7.1   In increase/decrease volume in a range (Recipe 56), we add 1 to getLength(sound) in the range function. Why did we do that?

7.2   Rewrite Recipe 57 so that two input values are provided to the function: the sound, and a *percentage* of how far into the sound to go before dropping the volume.

7.3   Rewrite Recipe 57 so that you normalize the first second of a sound, then slowly decrease the sound in steps of $1/5$ for each following second. (How many samples are in a second? getSamplingRate is the number of samples per second for the given sound.)

7.4   Try rewriting Recipe 57 so that you have a linear increase in volume to halfway through the sound, then linearly decrease the volume down to zero in the second half.

7.5   What happens if you take out the bit of silence added in to the target sound in the splicing example (Recipe 59)? Try out? Can you hear any difference?

7.6   I think that if we're going to say "We the united people" in the splice (Recipe 59), "united" should be really emphasized—really loud. Change the recipe so that the word "united" is maximally loud (normalized) in the phrase "united people."

7.7   Try using a stopwatch to time the execution of the recipes in this chapter. Time from hitting return on the command until the next prompt appears. What is the relationship between execution time and the length of the sound? Is it a linear relationship (i.e., longer sounds take longer to process and shorter sounds take less time to process)? Or is it something else? Compare the individual recipes. Does normalizing a sound take longer than raising (or lowering) the amplitude a constant amount? How much longer? Does it matter whether the sound is longer or shorter?

7.8   Make an audio collage. Make it at least five seconds long, and include at least two different sounds (e.g., they come from different files). Make a copy of one of those different sounds and modify it using any of the techniques described in this chapter (e.g., mirroring, splicing, volume manipulations). Splice together the original two sounds and the modified sound to make the complete collage

7.9   Compose a sentence that no one ever said by combining words from other sounds into a grammatically correct new sound. Write a function named audioSentence to generate a sentence out of individual words. Use at least three words in your sentence. You can use the words in the Speech folder on your CD or record your own words. Be sure to include a tenth (1/10) of a second pause between the words. (*Hint 1:* Remember that zeroes for the sample values generate silence or pause.)

(*Hint 2:* Remember that the sampling rate is the number of samples per second. From there, you should be able to figure out how many samples need to be made zero to generate a tenth of a second pause.) Be sure to access your sounds in your Media Folder using getMediaPath so that it will work for users of your program as long as they first execute setMediaPath.

7.10 Write a program called erasePart to set all the samples in the second second of "thisisatest.wav" to 0's—essentially, making the second second go silent. (*Hint:* Remember that getSamplingRate(sound) tells you the number of samples in a single second in a sound.) Play and return the partially erased sound.

7.11 We've seen a function that reverses a sound and a function that can process samples by index number.

Write a function called backhalfback that takes a filename as input, then turns backwards just the second half of the sound and returns the result. For example, if the sound said "MarkBark," the returned sound should say "MarkkraB."

To Dig Deeper

When you are using the MediaTools application, you are actually using a programming language called *Squeak*, developed initially and primarily by Alan Kay, Dan Ingalls, Ted Kaehler, John Maloney, and Scott Wallace [23]. Squeak is now open-source,[2] and is an excellent cross-platform multimedia tool. There is a book that introduces Squeak including its sound capabilities [18], and another book on Squeak [19] that includes a chapter on *Siren*, a variation of Squeak by Stephen Pope especially designed for computer music exploration and composition.

---

[2] http://www.squeak.org

CHAPTER 8

Making Sounds by Combining Pieces

Chapter Learning Objectives

The media learning goals for this chapter are:

- *To blend sounds so that one fades into another.*

- *To create echoes.*

- *To change the frequency (pitch) of a sound.*

- *To create sounds that don't exist in nature by composing more basic sounds (sine waves).*

- *To choose between sound formats such as MIDI and MP3 for different purposes.*

The computer science goals for this chapter are:

- *To use file paths to reference files at different places on the disk.*

- *To explain blending as an algorithm that crosses media boundaries.*

- *To build programs from multiple functions.*

■ 8.1 Composing Sounds Through Addition

Creating sounds digitally that didn't exist previously is lots of fun. Rather than simply move samples around or multiply them, we actually change their values—add waves together. The result are sounds that never existed until you made them.

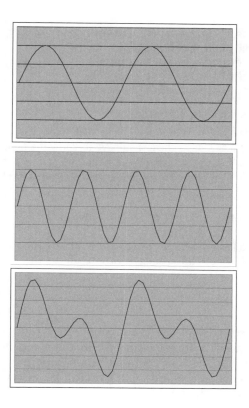

FIGURE 8.1: The top and middle waves are added together to create the bottom wave.

In physics, adding sounds involves issues of cancelling waves out and enforcing other factors. In math, it's about matrices. In computer science, it's the easiest process in the world. Let's say that you've got a sound, source, that you want to add in to the target. *Simply add the values at the same index numbers* (as in Figure 8.1). That's it!

```
for sourceIndex in range(1,getLength(source)+1):
  targetValue=getSampleValueAt(target,sourceIndex)
  sourceValue=getSampleValueAt(source,sourceIndex)
  setSampleValueAt(source,sourceIndex,sourceValue
  +targetValue)
```

To make some of our manipulations easier, we're going to be using set-MediaPath and getMediaPath. JES knows how to *set* a media folder and then reference media files within the folder. This makes it much easier to reference media files—you don't have to spell out the whole path. The functions we'll use are setMediaPath and getMediaPath. setMediaPath will put up a file picker—pick any file in your media folder. getMediaPath takes a base file name as an argument and will stick the path to the media folder in front of the base name and return a whole path to it.

```
>>> setMediaPath()
New media folder: /Users/guzdial/mediasources/
>>> print getMediaPath("barbara.jpg")
/Users/guzdial/mediasources/barbara.jpg
>>> print getMediaPath("sec1silence.wav")
/Users/guzdial/mediasources/sec1silence.wav
```

COMMON BUG: It's not a file, it's a string

Just because getMediaPath returns something that looks like a path doesn't mean that a file really exists there. You have to know the right base name, and if you do, it's easier to use in your code. But if you put in a nonexistent file, you'll get a path to a nonexistent file. getMediaPath will warn you.

```
>>> print getMediaPath("blah-blah-blah")
Note: There is no file at
/Users/guzdial/mediasources/blah-blah-blah
/Users/guzdial/mediasources/blah-blah-blah
```

■ 8.2 Blending Sounds

In this example, we take two sounds—someone saying "Aah!" and a bassoon instrument sound of C in the fourth octave—and *blend* them. To do this we copy part of the "Aah!", then add 50% of each, and then copy the C. This is very much like mixing 50% of each at a sound mixing board. It's also very much like the way we blended pictures in Recipe 41.

RECIPE 62: Blending two sounds

```
def blendSounds():
    bass = makeSound(getMediaPath("bassoon-c4.wav"))
    aah = makeSound(getMediaPath("aah.wav"))
    canvas = makeSound(getMediaPath("sec3silence.wav"))
    #Each of these is over 40K samples
    for index in range(1,20000):
      setSampleValueAt(canvas,index,getSampleValueAt(aah,index))
    for index in range(1,20000):
      aahSample = getSampleValueAt(aah,index+20000)
      bassSample=getSampleValueAt(bass,index)
      newSample = 0.5*aahSample + 0.5 * bassSample
      setSampleValueAt(canvas,index+20000,newSample)
    for index in range(20000,40000):
      setSampleValueAt(canvas,index+20000,getSampleValueAt
    (bass,index))
    play(canvas)
    return canvas
```

How it works: Like blending the picture (Recipe 41), there are loops in this function for each segment of the blended sound.

■ We start by creating the bass and aah sounds for blending, and a silent sound canvas that we're blending into. The length of these sounds is over 40,000 samples, but we're just going to use the first 40,000 as an example.

■ In the first loop, we simply get 20,000 samples from aah and copy them into canvas. Note that we're not using a separate index variable for the canvas—instead, we're using the same index variable, index, for both sounds.

■ In the next loop, we copy 20,000 samples from both aah and bass blended into canvas. We use the index variable, index, to index all three sounds—we use the basic index for accessing bass, and add 20,000 to index to access aah and canvas (since we have already copied 20,000 samples from aah into canvas). We get a sample from each of aah and bass, then multiply each by 0.5 and add the results together. The result is a sample that represents 50% of each.

■ Finally, we copy another 20,000 samples from bass. The resultant sound is returned (since it would disappear otherwise), which sounds like "Aah," a little of each, then just a bassoon note.

■ 8.3 Creating an Echo

Creating an echo effect is similar to the splicing recipe (Recipe 59) that we saw in the last chapter, but involves creating sounds that didn't exist before. We do this by *adding* wave forms. What we're doing here is adding samples from a delay number of samples away into the sound, but multiplied by 0.6 so that they're fainter.

RECIPE 63: Make a sound and a single echo of it

```
def echo(delay):
    f = pickAFile()
    s1 = makeSound(f)
    s2 = makeSound(f)
    for index in range(delay+1, getLength(s1)):
        # set delay to original value + delayed value * .6
        echoSample = 0.6*getSampleValueAt(s2, index-delay)
        setSampleValueAt(s1, index, getSampleValueAt(s1,index) +
echoSample)
    play(s1)
    return s1
```

How it works: The echo function takes as input the amount of delay between echoes, and returns the echoed sound. Try this with different amounts of delay. With low values of delay, the echo will sound more like *vibrato*. Higher values (try 10,000 or 20,000) will give you a real echo.

■ This function prompts you for a filename to echo (not a great idea if we want to use the echo-generating function for other purposes), then creates two copies of the sound. s1 is where we'll create the echoed sound. s2 is where we'll get the original, unadulterated samples for creating the echo. (You could try this with just a single sound to get some interesting layered echoes.)

■ Our `index` loop skips over the `delay` samples, then goes to the end of the sound.

■ The echoed sound is `delay` samples back, so `index-delay` is the sample we need. We multiply it by 0.6 to make it softer in volume.

■ We then add the echoed sample to the current sample at `index`.

■ At the end, we `play` the sound and `return` it.

8.3.1 Creating Multiple Echoes

This recipe lets you set the number of echoes you get. You can generate some amazing effects with it.

RECIPE 64: Creating multiple echoes

```
def echoes(sndfile, delay,num):
    # Create a new snd, that echoes the input soundfile
    # num number of echoes, each delay apart
    s1 = makeSound(sndfile)
    ends1 = getLength(s1)
    ends2 = ends1 + (delay * num)
    #ends2 is in samples -- must covert to seconds
    s2 = makeEmptySound(1+int(ends2/getSamplingRate(s1)))

    echoAmplitude = 1.0
    for echoCount in range(1,num+1):
      # 60% smaller each time
      echoAmplitude = echoAmplitude * 0.6
      for posns1 in range(1,ends1):
        posns2 = posns1+(delay*echoCount)
        values1 = getSampleValueAt(s1,posns1)*echoAmplitude
        values2 = getSampleValueAt(s2,posns2)
        setSampleValueAt(s2,posns2,values1+values2)
    play(s2)
    return s2
```

■ 8.4 How Sampling Keyboards Work

Sampling keyboards are keyboards that use recordings of sounds (e.g., pianos, harps, trumpets) to create music by playing them in the desired pitch. Modern music and sound keyboards (and synthesizers) allow musicians to record sounds in their daily lives and turn them into "instruments" by shifting their original frequencies. How do the synthesizers do this? It's not really complicated. The interesting part is that it allows you to use any sound you want as an instrument.

Sampling keyboards use huge amounts of memory to record lots of different instruments at different pitches. When you press a key on the keyboard, the recording *closest* (in pitch) to the note you pressed is selected and then is shifted to exactly the pitch you requested.

This first recipe works by creating a sound that *skips* every other sample. You read that right—after being so careful to treat all the samples the same, we're now going to skip half of them! In the `mediasources` directory, you'll find a sound named `c4.wav`. This is the note C, in the fourth octave of a piano, played for one second. It makes a good sound to experiment with, but any sound will work.

RECIPE 65: Double the frequency of a sound

```
def double(filename):
    source = makeSound(filename)
    target = makeSound(filename)

    targetIndex = 1
    for sourceIndex in range(1, getLength(source)+1, 2):
        setSampleValueAt(target, targetIndex, getSampleValueAt
(source, sourceIndex))
        targetIndex = targetIndex + 1

    #Clear out the rest of the target sound -- it's only half
full!
    for secondHalf in range(getLength(target)/2, getLength
(target)):
        setSampleValueAt(target,targetIndex,0)
        targetIndex = targetIndex + 1

    play(target)
    return target
```

Here's how I use it.

```
>>> file = pickAFile()
>>> print file
/Users/guzdial/mediasources/c4.wav
>>> c4 = makeSound(file)
>>> play(c4)
>>> c4doubled=double(file)
```

This recipe looks like it's using the array-copying subrecipe we saw earlier, but note that the `range` uses the third parameter—we're incrementing by 2. If we increment by 2, we only fill half the samples in the target, so the second loop just fills the rest with zeroes.

Try it![1] You'll see that the sound really does double in frequency.

How did that happen? It's not really all that complicated. Think of it this way: The frequency of the basic file is really the number of cycles that pass by in a certain amount of time. If you skip every other sample, the new sound has just as many cycles, but has them in half the amount of time.

Now let's try the other way. Let's take every sample twice. What happens then?

To do this, we need to use the Python function `int` to return the integer portion of the input.

```
>>> print int(0.5)
0
>>> print int(1.5)
1
```

Here's the recipe that *halves* the frequency. We're using the array-copying subrecipe again, but we're sort of reversing it. The `for` loop moves the `targetIndex` along the length of the sound. The `sourceIndex` is now being incremented—but only by 0.5. The effect is that we'll take every sample in the source twice. The `sourceIndex` will be 1, 1.5, 2, 2.5, and so on, but because we're using the `int` of that value, we'll take samples 1, 1, 2, 2, and so on.

RECIPE 66: Half the frequency

```
def half(filename):
    source = makeSound(filename)
    target = makeSound(filename)

    sourceIndex = 1
    for targetIndex in range(1, getLength(target)+1):
        value = getSampleValueAt(source, int(sourceIndex))
        setSampleValueAt(target, targetIndex, value)
        sourceIndex = sourceIndex + 0.5

    play(target)
    return target
```

How it works: `half` takes a filename as input. We create two copies of the sound `source` and `target`. We set a `sourceIndex` to 1 (that's where in the `source` we're copying into), and we have a loop for `targetIndex` from 1 to the end of the `target` sound. We get a sample value from `source` at the *integer* value (`int`) of the `sourceIndex`. We set the `target` at `targetIndex` to the sample that we got from the `source`. We then add 0.5 to the `sourceIndex`. This means that the `sourceIndex`, each time through the loop, will take on the values 1, 1.5, 2, 2.5, 3, 3.5, and so on. But the integer part of this sequence is 1, 1, 2, 2, 3, 3, and so on. The result is that we take each sample from the `source` sound *twice*.

---

[1] You are now trying this out as you read, aren't you?

Think about what we're doing here. Imagine that the number 0.5 above was actually 0.75, or 2, or 3. Would this work? The for loop would have to change, but essentially the idea is the same in all these cases. We are *sampling* the source data to create the target data. Using a *sample index* of 0.5 slows down the sound and halves the frequency. A sample index larger than 1 speeds up the sound and increases the frequency.

Let's try to generalize this sampling with the recipe that follows. (Note that this one *won't* work right.)

RECIPE 67: Shifting the frequency of a sound: BROKEN!

```
def shift(filename,factor):
    source = makeSound(filename)
    target = makeSound(filename)

    sourceIndex = 1
    for targetIndex in range(1, getLength(target)+1):
        setSampleValueAt(target, targetIndex, getSampleValueAt
(source, int(sourceIndex)))
        sourceIndex = sourceIndex + factor

    play(target)
    return target
```

Here's how we could use this:

```
>>> hello=pickAFile()
>>> print hello
/Users/guzdial/mediasources/hello.wav
>>> lowerhello=shift(hello,0.75)
```

That will work really well. But what if the factor for sampling is *more* than 1.0?

```
>>> higherhello=shift(hello,1.5)
I wasn't able to do what you wanted.
The error java.lang.ArrayIndexOutOfBoundsException has
occurred
Please check line 7 of /Users/guzdial/shift-broken.py
```

Why? What's happening? Here's how you could see it: Print out the source-Index just before the setSampleValueAt. You'd see that the sourceIndex becomes *larger* than the source sound. Of course, that makes sense. If each time through the loop we increment the targetIndex by 1, but increment the sourceIndex by *more than 1*, we'll get past the end of the source sound before we reach the end of the target sound. But how do we avoid this?

Here's what we want to happen: If the sourceIndex ever gets larger than the length of the source, we want to reset the sourceIndex—probably back to 1. The key word there is *if*, or even if.

We *can* tell Python to make decisions based on a *test*. We use `if` as a statement to do something if a test is true. In our case, the test is `sourceIndex > getLength(source)`. We can test on <, >, == (for equality), != (for inequality, not-equals) and even <= and >=. An `if` statement takes a *block*, just as `def` and `for` do. The block defines the things to do if the *test* in the `if` statement is true. In this case, our block is simply `sourceIndex = 1`.

The next recipe generalizes this and allows you to specify how much to shift the samples by.

RECIPE 68: Shifting the frequency of a sound

```
def shift(filename,factor):
    source = makeSound(filename)
    target = makeSound(filename)

    sourceIndex = 1
    for targetIndex in range(1, getLength(target)+1):
        setSampleValueAt(target, targetIndex, getSampleValueAt
(source, int(sourceIndex)))
        sourceIndex = sourceIndex + factor
        if sourceIndex > getLength(source):
            sourceIndex = 1

    play(target)
    return target
```

We can actually set the factor so that we get whatever frequency we want. We call this factor the *sampling interval*. For a desired frequency f_0, the sampling interval should be:

$$samplingInterval = (sizeOfSourceSound)\frac{f_0}{samplingRate}$$

This is how a keyboard synthesizer works. It has recordings of pianos, voices, bells, drums, whatever. By *sampling* those sounds at different sampling intervals, it can shift the sound to the desired frequency.

The last recipe in this section plays a single sound at its original frequency, then at two times, three times, four times, and five times. We had to modify `shift()` slightly to use `blockingPlay`. Try it with the original `play` and you'll hear the sounds collide because they are being generated faster than the computer can play them.

RECIPE 69: Playing a sound in a range of frequencies

```
def playASequence(file):
    # Play the sound five times, increasing the frequency
    for factor in range(1,6):
        shift(file,factor)

def shift(filename,factor):
    source = makeSound(filename)
    target = makeSound(filename)
```

```
sourceIndex = 1
for targetIndex in range(1,getLength(target)+1):
  setSampleValueAt(target,targetIndex,getSampleValueAt
(source,int(sourceIndex)))
  sourceIndex = sourceIndex + factor
  if sourceIndex > getLength(source):
    sourceIndex = 1

blockingPlay(target)
return target
```

8.4.1 Sampling as an Algorithm

You should recognize a similarity between the halving recipe, Recipe 66 and the recipe for scaling a picture up (making it larger), Recipe 32. To halve the frequency, we take each sample twice by incrementing by 0.5 and using the int() function to get the integer part of that. To make the picture larger, we take each pixel twice, adding 0.5 to our index variables and using the int() function on them. These are using the same *algorithm*—the same basic process is being used in each. The details of pictures vs. sounds aren't critical. The point is that the same basic process is being used in each.

We have seen other algorithms that cross media boundaries. Obviously, our increasing-red and increasing-volume functions (and the decreasing versions) are essentially doing the same thing. The way we blend pictures or sounds is the same. We take the component color channels (pixels) or samples (sounds) and add them using percentages to determine the amount from each that we want in the final product. As long as the percentages total 100%, we'll get a reasonable output that reflects the input sounds or pictures at the correct percentages.

Identifying algorithms like these is useful for several reasons. If we understand the algorithm in general (e.g., when it's slow and when it's fast, what it works for and what it doesn't, what the limitations are), then the lessons learned apply in the specific picture or sound instances. Knowing the algorithms is also useful for designers. When you are designing a new program, keep the algorithms in mind so that you can use them when they apply.

When we double or halve the sound frequency, we are also shrinking or doubling the length of the sound. You might want a target sound whose length is *exactly* the length of the sound rather than have to clear out extra stuff from a longer sound. You can do that with makeEmptySound. makeEmptySound(10) returns a new empty sound of 10 seconds in length.

■ 8.5 Additive Synthesis

Additive synthesis creates sounds by adding sine waves together. We saw earlier that it's really pretty easy to add sounds together. With additive synthesis, you can shape the waves yourself, set their frequencies, and create "instruments" that have never existed.

8.5.1 Making Sine Waves

Let's figure out how to produce a set of samples to generate a sound at a given frequency and amplitude.

From trigonometry, we know that if we take the sine of the radians from 0 to 2π, we'll get a circle. Spread that over time, and you get a sine wave. In other words, if you took values from 0 to 2π, computed the sine of each value, and graphed the computed values, you'd get a sine wave. From your really early math courses, you know that there's an infinity of numbers between 0 and 1. Computers don't handle infinity very well, so we'll actually only take *some* values between 0 and 2π.

To create the graph shown below, I filled 20 rows (a totally arbitrary number) of a spreadsheet with values from 0 to 2π (about 6.28). I added about 0.314 (6.28/20) to each preceding row. In the next column, I took the sine of each value in the first column, then graphed it.

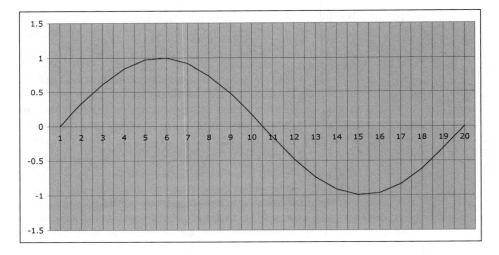

If we want to create a sound at a given frequency, say 440 Hz, we have to fit an entire cycle like the one in the graph into 1/440 of a second (440 cycles per second, meaning that each cycle fits into 1/440 second, or 0.00227 seconds). I made the graph using 20 values. Call it 20 *samples*. How many samples do I have to chop up the 440 Hz cycle into? That's the same as asking how many samples must go by in 0.00227 seconds. We know the sampling rate—that's the number of samples in one second. Let's say that it's 22,050 samples per second (our default sampling rate). Each sample is then (1/22050) 0.0000453 seconds. How many samples fit into 0.00227? That's 0.00227/0.0000453, or about 50. What we just did here mathematically is:

$$interval = 1/frequency$$

$$samplesPerCyle = \frac{interval}{1/samplingRate} = (samplingRate)(interval)$$

Now let's spell this out as Python. To get a waveform at a given frequency, say 440 Hz, we need 440 of these waves in a single second. Each one must fit into the interval of 1/*frequency*. The number of samples that needs to be produced during the interval is the sampling rate divided by the frequency, or interval $(1/f) * (sampling\ rate)$. Call that the *samplesPerCycle*.

At each entry of the sound *sampleIndex*, we want to:

■ Get the fraction of *sampleIndex* / *samplesPerCycle*.

■ Multiply that fraction by 2π. That's the number of radians we need. Take the *sine* of $(sampleIndex/samplesPerCycle) * 2\pi$.

■ Multiply the result by the desired amplitude and put it in the `sampleIndex`.

To build sounds, there are some *silent* sounds in the media sources. Our sine wave generator will use one second of silence to build a sine wave of one second. We'll provide an amplitude as input—that will be the *maximum* amplitude of the sound. (Since sine generates between −1 and 1, the range of amplitudes will be between −*amplitude* and *amplitude*.)

COMMON BUG: Set the media folder first!

If you're to use code that uses `getMediaPath`, you'll need to execute `setMediaPath` first.

RECIPE 70: Generate a sine wave at a given frequency and amplitude

```python
def sineWave(freq,amplitude):

    # Get a blank sound
    mySound = getMediaPath('sec1silence.wav')
    buildSin = makeSound(mySound)

    # Set sound constant
    sr = getSamplingRate(buildSin)          # sampling rate

    interval = 1.0/freq      # Make sure it's floating point
    samplesPerCycle = interval * sr    # samples per cycle
    maxCycle = 2 * pi

    for pos in range (1,getLength(buildSin)+1):
        rawSample = sin((pos / samplesPerCycle) * maxCycle)
        sampleVal = int(amplitude*rawSample)
        setSampleValueAt(buildSin,pos,sampleVal)

    return (buildSin)
```

Here we are building a sine wave of 880 Hz at an amplitude of 4,000.

```python
>>> f880=sineWave(880,4000)
>>> play(f880)
```

8.5.2 Adding Sine Waves Together

Now let's add sine waves together. As we said at the beginning of the chapter, that's pretty easy: Just add the samples at the same indices together. Here's a function that adds one sound into a second sound.

RECIPE 71: Add two sounds together

```
def addSounds(sound1,sound2):
    for index in range(1,getLength(sound1)+1):
        s1Sample = getSampleValueAt(sound1,index)
        s2Sample = getSampleValueAt(sound2,index)
        setSampleValueAt(sound2,index,s1Sample+s2Sample)
```

How are we going to use this function to add sine waves together? We need both of them at once. Turns out that it's easy:

MAKING IT WORK TIP: You can put more than one function in the same file!
It's perfectly okay to have more than one function in the same file. Just type them all in any order. Python will figure it out.

My file additive.py looks like this:

```
def sineWave(freq,amplitude):

    # Get a blank sound

    mySound =  getMediaPath('sec1silence.wav')
    buildSin = makeSound(mySound)

    # Set sound constant
    sr = getSamplingRate(buildSin)          # sampling rate

    interval = 1.0/freq            # make sure floating point
    samplesPerCycle =  interval * sr    # samples per cycle
    maxCycle = 2 * pi

    for pos in range (1,getLength(buildSin)+1):
        rawSample = sin((pos / samplesPerCycle)
* maxCycle)
        sampleVal = int(amplitude*rawSample)
        setSampleValueAt(buildSin,pos,sampleVal)

    return (buildSin)
def addSounds(sound1,sound2):
    for index in range(1,getLength(sound1)+1):
        s1Sample = getSampleValueAt(sound1,index)
        s2Sample = getSampleValueAt(sound2,index)
        setSampleValueAt(sound2,index,s1Sample+s2Sample)
```

Let's add together 440 Hz, 880 Hz (twice 440), and 1,320 Hz (880 + 440), but we'll have the amplitudes increase. We'll double the amplitude each time: 2,000, then 4,000, then 8,000. We'll add them all up into the name f440. At the end, I generate a 440 Hz sound so that I can listen to them both and compare.

```
>>> f440=sineWave(440,2000)
>>> f880=sineWave(880,4000)
>>> f1320=sineWave(1320,8000)
>>> addSounds(f880,f440)
>>> addSounds(f1320,f440)
>>> play(f440)
>>> just440=sineWave(440,2000)
>>> play(just440)
```

COMMON BUG: Beware of adding amplitudes past 32,767

When you add sounds, you add their amplitudes also. A maximum of 2,000 + 4,000 + 8,000 will never be greater than 32,767, but don't worry about that. Remember what happened when the amplitude got too high in the last chapter...

8.5.3 Checking Our Result

How do we know if we really got what we wanted? We can test our code by using the sound tools in the MediaTools. First, we save out a sample wave (just 400 Hz) and the combined wave.

```
>>> writeSoundTo(just440,"/Users/guzdial/mediasources/
just440.wav")
>>> writeSoundTo(f440,"/Users/guzdial/mediasources/
combined440.wav")
```

Open up each of these in turn in the sound editor. Right away, you'll notice that the wave forms look very different (Figure 8.2). That tells you that we did *something* to the sound, but what?

The way you can really check your additive synthesis is with an FFT. Generate the FFT for each signal. You'll see that the 440 Hz signal has a single spike (Figure 8.3). That's what you'd expect—it's supposed to be a single sine wave. Now look at the combined wave form's FFT (Figure 8.4). It's what it's supposed to be. You see three spikes there, and each succeeding one is double the height of the last one.

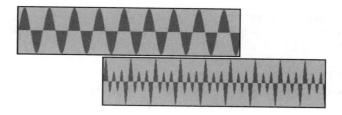

FIGURE 8.2: The raw 440 Hz signal on top, then the 440 + 880 + 1,320 Hz signal on the bottom.

FIGURE 8.3: FFT of the 440 Hz sound.

FIGURE 8.4: FFT of the combined sound.

8.5.4 Square Waves

We don't have to just add sine waves. We can also add *square waves*. These are literally square-shaped waves, moving between +1 and −1. The FFT will look very different, and the *sound* will be very different. It can actually be a much richer sound.

Try swapping this recipe in for the sine wave generator and see what you think. Note the use of an if statement to swap between the positive and negative sides of the wave halfway through a cycle.

RECIPE 72: Square wave generator for given frequency and amplitude

```
def squareWave(freq,amplitude):

    # Get a blank sound
    mySound = getMediaPath("sec1silence.wav")
    square = makeSound(mySound)

    # Set music constants
    samplingRate = getSamplingRate(square)    # sampling rate
    seconds = 1   # play for 1 second

    # Build tools for this wave
    # seconds per cycle: make sure floating point
    interval = 1.0 * seconds / freq
```

```
# creates floating point since interval is fl point
samplesPerCycle = interval * samplingRate
# we need to switch every half-cycle
samplesPerHalfCycle = int(samplesPerCycle / 2)
sampleVal = amplitude
s = 1
i = 1

for s in range (1, getLength(square)+1):
  # if end of a half-cycle
  if (i > samplesPerHalfCycle):
    # reverse the amplitude every half-cycle
    sampleVal = sampleVal * -1
    # and reinitialize the half-cycle counter
    i = 0
  setSampleValueAt(square,s,sampleVal)
  i = i + 1

return(square)
```

Use it like this:

```
>>> sq440=squareWave(440,4000)
>>> play(sq440)
>>> sq880=squareWave(880,8000)
>>> sq1320=squareWave(1320,10000)
>>> writeSoundTo(sq440,getMediaPath("square440.wav"))
Note: There is no file at /Users/guzdial/mediasources/
square440.wav
>>> addSounds(sq880,sq440)
>>> addSounds(sq1320,sq440)
>>> play(sq440)
>>> writeSoundTo(sq440,getMediaPath("squarecombined440.
wav"))
Note: There is no file at /Users/guzdial/mediasources/
squarecombined440.wav
```

You'll find that the waves (in the wave editor of MediaTools) really do look square (Figure 8.5), but the most amazing thing is all the additional spikes in FFT (Figure 8.6). Square waves really do result in a much more complex sound.

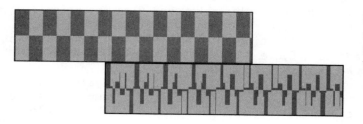

FIGURE 8.5: The 440 Hz square wave (*top*) and additive combination of square waves (*bottom*).

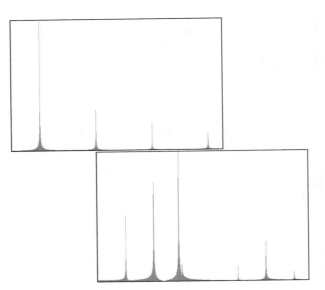

FIGURE 8.6: FFT's of the 440 Hz square wave (*top*) and additive combination of square waves (*bottom*).

8.5.5 Triangle Waves

Try triangle waves instead of square waves with this recipe.

RECIPE 73: Generate triangle waves

```
def triangleWav(freq):

    # Get a blank sound
    myFolder = setMediaPath()
    mySound = getMediaPath("sec1silence.wav")
    triangle = makeSound(mySound)

    # Set music constants
    # Loudness at 6000: could be any from 1 to 32768
    amplitude = 6000
    # sampling rate
    samplingRate = 22050
    # play for 1 second
    seconds = 1

    # Build tools for this wave
    # seconds per cycle: make sure floating point
    interval = 1.0 * seconds / freq
    # creates floating point since interval is fl point
    samplesPerCycle = interval * samplingRate
    # we need to switch every half-cycle
    samplesPerHalfCycle = int(samplesPerCycle / 2)
    # value to add for each subsequent sample; must be integer
    increment = int(amplitude / samplesPerHalfCycle)
```

```
# start at bottom and increment or decrement as needed
sampleVal = -amplitude
i = 1

# create 1 second sound
for s in range (1, samplingRate + 1):

  # if end of a half-cycle
  if (i > samplesPerHalfCycle):
    # reverse the increment every half-cycle
    increment = increment * -1
   # and reinit the half-cycle counter
    i = 0

  sampleVal = sampleVal + increment
  setSampleValueAt(triangle,s,sampleVal)
  i = i + 1

play(triangle)
```

■ 8.6 Modern Music Synthesis

Additive synthesis is how early music synthesizers worked. Nowadays, additive synthesis isn't too common because the sounds it generates are natural-sounding. Synthesizing from recorded sounds is quite common, but isn't pure synthesis in the sense of creating sounds out of nothing.

The most common synthesis technique today is probably *FM synthesis or frequency modulation synthesis*. In FM synthesis, an oscillator (a programmed object that generates a regular series of outputs) controls (modulates) frequencies with other frequencies. The result is a richer sound, less tinny or computer-sounding.

Another common technique is *subtractive synthesis*. In subtractive synthesis, *noise* is used as the input, and then *filters* are applied to remove unwanted frequencies. The result is, again, a richer sound, though typically not as rich as FM synthesis.

Why would we want to create sounds or music with computers anyway? What's the point when there are lots of great sounds, music, and musicians in the world? The point is that if you want to tell someone else *how* you got that sound, so that they could replicate the process or even modify the sound in some way (perhaps making it better), a program is the way to do it. A program succinctly captures and communicates a process—how a sound or a piece of music is generated.

8.6.1 MP3

Nowadays, the audio files on your computer are most commonly MP3 files (or perhaps MP4 or one of its related or descendant file types). MP3 files are sound (and video, in some cases) encodings based on the MPEG-3 standard. They are audio files, but compressed in special ways.

One way in which MP3 files are compressed is called *lossless compression*. As we know, there are techniques for storing data that use fewer bits. For example, we know that every sample is typically two bytes wide. What if we didn't store every sample, but instead stored the *difference* from the last sample to this sample? The difference between samples is usually much smaller than 32,767 to −32,768—it might be +/− 1000. That takes fewer bits to store.

But MP3 also uses *lossy compression*. It actually throws away some of the sound information. For example, if there's a really soft sound immediately after or simultaneous with a really loud sound, you won't be able to hear the soft sound. A digital recording keeps all those frequencies. MP3 throws away the ones you can't actually hear.

WAV files are compressed, but not as much as MP3, and they only use lossless techniques. MP3 files tend to be much smaller than the same sound in a WAV format. AIFF files are similar to WAV files.

8.6.2 MIDI

MIDI is the *Musical Instrument Digital Interface*. It's really a set of agreements between manufacturers of computer music devices (sequencers, synthesizers, drum machines, keyboards, etc.) for how their devices will work together. Using MIDI, you can control various synthesizers and drum machines from different keyboards.

MIDI is not used for encoding sound as much as encoding music. MIDI doesn't record what something sounds like but how it is played. Literally, MIDI encodes information like "Press the key down on synthesized instrument *X* at pitch *Y*," then later "Release the key *Y* on instrument *X*." The quality of MIDI sound depends entirely on the synthesizer, the device generating the synthesized instrument.

MIDI files tend to be very small. Instructions like "Play key #42 on track 7" are only some five bytes long. This makes MIDI attractive in comparison with large sound files. MIDI has been particularly popular for karaoke machines.

MIDI has an advantage over MP3 or WAV files in that it can specify a lot of music in very few bytes. But MIDI can't record sounds. For example, if you want to record a specific person's style of playing an instrument, or record *anyone* singing, you don't want to use MIDI. To capture actual sounds, you need to record the actual samples, so you'll need MP3 or WAV.

Most modern operating systems have pretty good synthesizers built into them. We can use them from Python. JES has built into it a function playNote that takes as input a MIDI note, a duration (how long to play the sound) in milliseconds, and an intensity (how hard to strike the key) from 0 to 127. playNote will always use a piano-sounding instrument. MIDI notes correspond to keys, not to frequencies. C in the first octave is 1, C# is 2. C in the fourth octave is 60, D is 62, and E is 64.

Here's a simple example of playing some MIDI notes from JES. We can use for loops to specify loops in the music.

RECIPE 74: Playing MIDI notes (example)

```
def song():
    playNote(60,200,127)
    playNote(62,500,127)
    playNote(64,800,127)
    playNote(60,600,127)
    for i in range(1,2):
        playNote(64,120,127)
        playNote(65,120,127)
        playNote(67,60,127)
```

Programming Summary

if	Allows Python to make decisions. if takes an expression to test for true or false (basically, anything that evaluates to 0 is false, and everything else is true). The block that follows is executed if it's true.
int	Returns the integer part of the input value.
setMediaPath	Lets you pick a folder where you can easily access media using getMediaPath.
getMediaPath	Takes an input of a base file name, then returns the complete path to that file (assuming it's in the media folder).

Problems

8.1 Rewrite the echo function (Recipe 63) to generate *two* echoes back, each delay samples previous. *Hint:* Start your index loop at 2*delay + 1, then access one echo sample at index-delay and another at index - 2*delay.

8.2 How long is a sound compared to the original when it's been frequency doubled (Recipe 65)?

8.3 Hip-hop DJ's move turntables so that sections of sound are moved forwards and backwards quickly. Try combining backwards play (Recipe 60) and frequency shifting (Recipe 65) to get the same effect. Play a second of a sound quickly forward, then quickly backward, two or three times. (You might have to move faster than just double the speed.)

8.4 Consider changing the if block in the frequency shift recipe (Recipe 68) to sourceIndex = sourceIndex - getLength(source). What's the difference from just setting the sourceIndex to 1? Is this better or worse? Why?

8.5 If you use the shifting recipe (Recipe 68) with a factor of 2.0 or 3.0, you'll get the sound repeated or even triplicated. Why? Can you fix it? Write shiftDur that takes a number of samples (or even seconds) to play the sound.

8.6 Change the shift function in Recipe 68 to shiftFreq, which takes a frequency instead of a factor, then plays the given sound at the desired frequency.

8.7 Using the sound tools, figure out the characteristic pattern of different instruments. For example, pianos tend to have a pattern the opposite of what we created—the amplitudes *decrease* as we get to higher sine waves. Try creating a variety of patterns and see how they sound and how they look.

8.8 When musicians work with additive synthesis, they will often wrap *envelopes* around the sounds, and even around each added sine wave. An envelope *changes* the amplitude over time—it might start out small, then grow (rapidly or slowly), then hold at a certain value during the sound, and then drop before the sound ends. That kind of pattern is sometimes called the *attack-sustain-decay (ASD) envelope*. Pianos tend to attack quickly, then decay quickly. Flutes tend to attack slowly and sustain as long as you want. Try implementing that for the sine and square wave generators.

To Dig Deeper

Good books on computer music say a lot about creating sounds from scratch, as in this chapter. One of my favorites for understandability is *Computer Music: Synthesis, Composition, and Performance* by Dodge and Jerse [10]. The "bible" of computer music is Curtis Roads's massive *The Computer Music Tutorial* [32].

One of the most powerful tools for playing with this level of computer music is *CSound*. It's a software music synthesis system, free, and totally cross-platform. The book by Richard Boulanger [6] has everything you need for playing with CSound.

CHAPTER 9

Design and Debugging

9.1 Designing Programs: How Do We Start?

9.2 Techniques of Debugging

9.3 Algorithms and Design

Chapter Learning Objectives

- *To know two different design strategies: top-down and bottom-up.*

- *To have several debugging strategies to use when figuring out their programming problems.*

Programming has been defined as "the art of debugging a blank sheet of paper."[1] The activity of programming and the activity of debugging are intricately connected. How do we do this? How do we make programs, and then make them actually *run*? That's what this chapter is about.

■ 9.1 Designing Programs: How Do We Start?

How do you start "debugging a blank sheet of paper"? There are many approaches, but the two most common are ***top-down*** and ***bottom-up***. In top-down design, you figure out what has to be done, refine the *requirements* until you know how to write the program, and then you create the solution program. In bottom-up design, you start with what you know and keep adding to it until you've got your program.

9.1.1 Top-down

Top-down design is how most engineering disciplines recommend designing. You start out by developing a list of *requirements*: what needs to be done, in English or math, that can be iteratively refined. Refining requirements means making them clearer and more specific. The goal of refining requirements in top-down design is to get to the point where the statements of the requirements can be directly implemented as program code.

The top-down process is preferred because it's understandable and you can plan for it—it's really what makes the business of software possible. Imagine working with a customer who wants you to program something. You are given a problem statement and then work with the customer to refine it to a set of

---

[1] `http://foldoc.doc.ic.ac.uk/foldoc/index.html`

requirements. You go build the program. If the customer is not happy with it, you can test to see if the software meets the requirements. If it does, and the customer agreed to the requirements, then you've met your agreement. If it doesn't, then you need to make it meet the requirements—but not necessarily meet the customer's changed needs.

In detail, the process looks something like this:

■ Start out with the problem statement. If you don't have one, write one. What are you trying to do?

■ Start refining the problem statement. Are there parts to the program? Perhaps you should use **hierarchical decomposition** to define subfunctions? Do you know that you have to open some pictures or set some constant values? And then are there some loops? How many do you need?

■ Keep refining the problem statement until you get to statements or commands or functions that you know. Write them down.

Let's try this on an example. Let's say that you have to *compute an hourly worker's pay*. That's our initial problem statement.

You know that there are taxes to be paid, social security, and benefits to deal with. This is part of the process of refinement—figuring out all of what the problem statement implies. Let's say, for now, that we only care about the taxes. We know that we have to compute a *gross pay* and a *net pay*, and we have a tax table that tells us how much tax to charge.

We can now make a more refined problem statement:

■ Write a function called pay that takes in as input a number of hours worked and the hourly rate to be paid. Compute the gross pay as the hours times the rate. Then compute a taxable amount.

■ If the pay is <100, charge a tax of 0.25. If the pay is $>= 100$ and <300, the tax rate is 0.35. If the pay is $>= 300$ and <400, the tax rate is 0.45. If the pay is $>= 400$, the tax rate is 0.50.

■ Print the gross pay and the net pay (gross-taxable amount).

This is clearly more refined, but still doesn't say *exactly* what has to be done in code. Let's try again.

1. Write a function called pay that takes in as input a number of hours worked and the hourly rate to be paid.

2. Compute the gross pay as the hours times the rate.

3. If the pay is <100, charge a tax of 0.25.

4. If the pay is $>= 100$ and <300, the tax rate is 0.35.

5. If the pay is $>= 300$ and <400, the tax rate is 0.45.

6. If the pay is $>= 400$, the tax rate is 0.50.

7. Compute a taxable amount as tax rate * gross.
8. Print the gross pay and the net pay (gross-taxable amount).

This is now really easy to translate into program code. Each of these statements can be translated into a line of code. The first step above suggests:

```
def pay(hours,rate):
```

Steps 1 through 3 suggest:

```
def pay(hours,rate):
  gross = hours * rate
  if gross < 100:
    tax = 0.25
```

And so on, until we get to:

```
def pay(hours,rate):
  gross = hours * rate
  if gross < 100:
    tax = 0.25
  if 100 <= gross < 300:
    tax = 0.35
  if 300 <= gross < 400:
    tax = 0.45
  if gross >= 400:
    tax = 0.50
  taxableAmount = gross * tax
  print Gross pay:,gross
  print Net pay:,gross-taxableAmount
```

If we followed this same process and defined functions (*procedures*) instead of lines of code, we would be using ***procedural abstraction***. In procedural abstraction, you define high-level functions that call lower-level functions. The lower-level functions are easy to write and test, and the higher-level functions become easy to read because they're simply calling lower-level functions. We'll see more procedural abstraction in actual practice in chapters to come.

9.1.2 Bottom-up

Bottom-up is a very different process. You start with some idea of what you want to do—you could call it a problem statement. But instead of refining the problem, you focus on building the solution program. You want to reuse code from other programs as much as possible.

The most important thing you do with bottom-up design is to *try* your program *very* often. Does it do what you want? Does it do what you *expect*? Does it make sense? If not, add print statements and explore the code until you understand what it's doing. If you don't know what it does, you can't change it into what you want.

Here's what the bottom-up process typically looks like, starting from a problem statement:

■ How much of the problem do you already know how to do? How much of it can you get from other programs that you've written?
Does the problem say that you have to manipulate sound? Try a couple of the sound recipes in the book to remember how to do that. Does it say that you have to change red levels? Can you find a recipe that does that and try it?

■ Now, can you add some of these pieces (that you can write or can steal from other programs) together? Can you put together a couple of recipes that do *part* of what you want?

■ Keep growing the program. Is it closer to what you need? What else do you need to add?

■ Run your program *often*. Make sure it works, and that you understand what you have so far.

■ Repeat until you're satisfied with the result.

The way we did background subtraction and chromakey is a good example of a bottom-up process. We started out with the idea of removing the background of someone and putting them in a new picture. Where do we start?

We can imagine that part of the problem is finding all the pixels that are part of the person or part of the background. We've done things like that before, as when we found all the brown in Barbara's hair in order to turn it red (Recipe 33). That tells us that we're going to want to check if there's a large enough distance between a person color and a background color, and if so, we want to bring in a new background's pixel's color—the pixel at the same point. We've done things like that, too, as when we copied pictures into the canvas.

At this point, we could probably write something like:

```
if distance(personColor,bgColor) < someThresholdValue:
  bgColor = getColor(getPixel(newBackground,x,y))
  setColor(getPixel(personPicture,x,y),bgColor)
```

That's the guts of the background subtraction recipe. The rest of it is simply setting up the variables (Recipe 42). But then, when we tried it, we found that it didn't work very well, for a variety of reasons. That's what led us to chromakey (Recipe 43). Chromakey is a better way of figuring out which pixels are part of the background and which are part of the foreground, but the basic process is the same as swapping the background—so most of the program is reusable in the new context.

The key process here is to take ideas (or even lines of code) from other projects, and combine them, testing what you're doing all the time. Bottom-up programming is quite close to "debugging a blank sheet of paper." Debugging is a really critical skill in bottom-up design or programming.

■ 9.2 Techniques of Debugging

How do you figure out what your program is doing if it runs but isn't doing what you want? This is the process of *debugging*. Debugging is figuring out what your program is doing, how that differs from what you *want* it to be doing, and how to get the program from where it is to where you need it to be.

Getting an error message is the *easiest* kind of debugging. You have some indication from Python about what the error is, and you have some idea (a line number) about where the error is. That tells you where to look to fix the problem and make the error go away.

The much harder kind of debugging is where the program works but doesn't do what you want. Now you have to figure out what the program is doing, and what you want it to be doing.

The first step is *always* to **Figure out what the program is doing**. Whether you have explicit error messages or not, this is always the first thing to do. If you get an error, the important question is why the program worked up to there, and what variable values were present at that point such that the error occurred.

COMPUTER SCIENCE IDEA: Learn to trace code!
The most important thing you can do when debugging your programs is to be able to trace your code. Think about your program the way the computer does. Walk each line and figure out what it does.

Start out debugging by walking the code, at least the lines around where the error is occurring. What does the error say? What might be causing the error? What are the values of the variables before and after that point? The interesting question is why the error occurred *now*. Why didn't it happen earlier in the program?

If you can, run the program. It's always easier to have the computer *tell* you what's happening instead of having to figure it out yourself. That said, simply executing your functions won't give you the answer. Add print statements to your code to show you what values the variables have.

DEBUGGING TIP: Print statements are your friends!
Print out what's going on in your programs. Print variables when you can't figure out what's going on from tracing the program. Print out the values of equations that are too complex. Print out simple statements like "I'm in this function now!" to let you know that you are reaching the functions you think you're calling. Let the computer *tell* you what it's doing.

Sometimes, especially in a loop, you'll want to use a function called printNow. printNow takes a string as input then prints it to the Command Area *as soon as it occurs*. print, in contrast, doesn't display anything to the Command Area until the function is done running, which makes it less useful for debugging—you don't get to see what's happening *when* it's happening.

DEBUGGING TIP: Don't be afraid to change the program

Save a new copy of your program, then edit out all the parts you're confused about. Can you get the rest to run? Now start adding pieces back in (copy-paste) from the original copy of your program. Changing the program so that you're only running part of it at a time is a great way to come to know what's going on.

9.2.1 Testing the End Conditions

Professional programmers test every program extensively to make sure that it works the way they expect. They focus on testing *end conditions*. What's the smallest input that the program should work with? What's the largest input that the program should work with? Make sure that the program can work with both the smallest and largest possible inputs—that's testing the end conditions.

You can also use this strategy for debugging your programs. Let's say that your picture-manipulation program fails (generates an error, or doesn't seem to stop) with a particular picture, and you've tried to trace the program but can't figure out why it's failing. Try it with a different picture. Does it work with a smaller picture? How about with an empty (all white or all black) picture? Maybe you'll find that your program works but is just so slow that you didn't think it was working with the larger picture.

Sometimes functions that manipulate indices (e.g., scaling programs) may fail on programs of one size but not another. For example, mirroring programs may work with odd-number indices but not even-number indices. Try inputs with different kinds of sizes to see which trigger your error.

9.2.2 Finding Which Statement to Worry About

The bugs that I find hardest to figure out are the ones that *look* just fine. Spacing errors and mismatched parentheses fall into this category. These are particularly hard to find in large programs, where the error just says that there's a problem "somewhere" around a given line, but Python isn't exactly sure where.

If I can't figure it out, I use a time-honored strategy: Get rid of all the statements that you're sure about. Simply put a "#" in front of the statements that you think are okay. If you comment out an if or for, make sure that you also comment out the block after the statement. Now try again.

If the error goes away, then you were wrong—you actually commented out the statements where the problem is. Uncomment a few and try again. When the error message comes back, the error is in one of the lines that you just uncommented.

If the error is still there, you now have only a few statements to check—the ones that are still uncommented. Eventually the error goes away or you have a single line that's uncommented. Either way, you then know which lines are suspect.

9.2.3 Seeing the Variables

Besides printing, there are other tools built into JES to help you figure out what your programs are doing. The showVars function will show you all the variables and their values at the point when it's executed (Figure 9.1). It will show you both the variables in the current *context* and the variables in the *global* context (accessible even from the Command Area). You can use showVars() in the Command Area to see the variables you've created there—perhaps you'd forgotten their names, or wanted to see what the values were in several variables at once.

The other powerful tool in JES is the *Watcher*. The Watcher allows you see which lines are being executed *as* they are executed. Figure 9.2 shows the Watcher running the code given below—the makeSunset() function from Recipe 12. We simply open the Watcher (from the debug menu or from the WATCHER button), then use the Command Area as normal. Whenever we execute our own functions, the Watcher will run.

```
def makeSunset(picture):
  reduceBlue(picture)
  reduceGreen(picture)

def reduceBlue(picture):
  for p in getPixels(picture):
    value=getBlue(p)
    setBlue(p,value*0.7)

def reduceGreen(picture):
  for p in getPixels(picture):
    value=getGreen(p)
    setGreen(p,value*0.7)
```

We can PAUSE execution, then STEP through it from there. We can also STOP execution, go FULL SPEED, or even set a speed from slow to fast. When you have

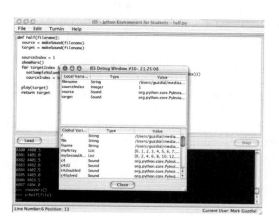

FIGURE 9.1: Seeing the variables using showVars().

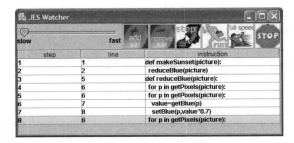

FIGURE 9.2: Stepping through the makeSunset() function with the Watcher.

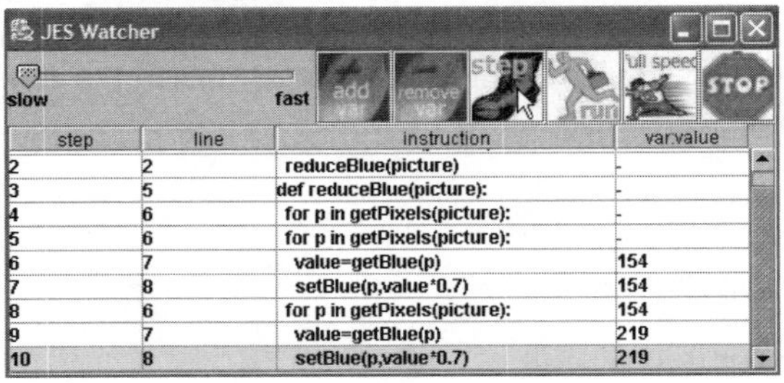

FIGURE 9.3: Watching the variable value in the makeSunset() function with the Watcher.

the Watcher open, the program *will* run more slowly. The faster the program runs, the less information will be displayed (i.e., not every line executed will show up in the Watcher).

Besides stepping through execution and seeing which statements get executed when, you can also observe particular variables. After clicking ADD VARIABLE, you will be prompted for the name of the variable. Then, when the Watcher runs, the value of the variable will be displayed along with the line. When the variable doesn't have a value yet, you'll see that too (Figure 9.3).

■ 9.3 Algorithms and Design

Algorithms are general descriptions of processes that can be implemented in any specific programming language. Knowledge of algorithms is one of the tools in professional programmers' toolboxes. We've seen several algorithms so far:

■ The *sampling algorithm* is a process that can be used to shift a sound's frequency up or down or to scale a picture smaller or larger. We don't have to talk about loops or incrementing source or target indices to describe the sampling algorithm. The sampling algorithm works by changing how we copy samples or pixels from a source to a target—instead of taking every sample or pixel, we can take every other sample/pixel, or every sample/pixel twice, or some other pattern of sampling.

■ We've also seen how we copy pixels or samples from a source to a target. It's a similar process all the time.

■ We've seen that blending is essentially the same for both pixels and samples. We apply a weighting to each of the pixels or samples being summed, then add the weighted values to create a blended sound or a blended picture.

The role of algorithms in design is to allow us to *abstract* a description of the program to be designed, above the basic program code. Professional programmers know lots of algorithms, and this allows them to think through program design problems at high levels. We can talk about negating pictures and mirroring the negated pictures *without* talking about loops or source and target indices. We can focus on more abstract names like "mirroring" without focusing on code.

Programmers also know a lot *about* the algorithms they know. They know how to make the algorithms efficient, and when they're not useful, and what the hitches about them might be. For example, we know that when scaling sound, we have to be careful not to go beyond the bounds of the sound. There are better and worse algorithms, in terms of how quickly they execute and how much memory they require. We will say more about speed of algorithms in Chapter 13.

Programming Summary

`printNow`	Prints the input to the function *immediately*, while the program is still running. This allows you to see what's going on while it's running.
`showVars`	Displays all the existing variables and their values.

Problems

9.1 Consider this program:

```
def testme(p,q,r):
  if q > 50:
    print r
  value = 10
  for i in range(1,p):
    print "Hello"
    value = value - 1
  print value
  print r
```

If we execute testme(5,51,"Hello back to you!"), what will print?

9.2

```
def newFunction(a, b, c):
    print a
    list1 = range(1,5)
    value = 0
    for x in list1:
        print b
        value = value +1
    print c
    print value
```

If you call the preceding function by typing
newFunction("I", "you", "walrus")
what will the computer print?

PART 4

TEXT, FILES, NETWORKS, DATABASES, AND UNIMEDIA

CHAPTER 10

Creating and Modifying Text

10.1 Text as Unimedia
10.2 Strings: Making and Manipulating Strings
10.3 Files: Places to Put Your Strings and Other Stuff
10.4 Extending Our Language Capabilities Using Modules
10.5 Networks: Getting Our Text from the Web
10.6 Using Text to Shift Between Media

Chapter Learning Objectives

The media learning goals for this chapter are:

- *To generate text in a form-letter style.*

- *To manipulate structured text, such as phone and address listings.*

- *To write programs to directly access and use text information from the Internet.*

- *To generate random structured text.*

- *To use text to change encodings of information (e.g., creating visualizations of sounds)*

The computer science goals for this chapter are:

- *To access object components using dot notation.*

- *To manipulate strings.*

- *To read and write files.*

- *To understand file structures like trees.*

- *To write programs that manipulate programs, which leads to powerful ideas like interpreters and compilers.*

- *To use modules, such as the random and os utilities.*

- *To use iteration with a while loop.*

- *To access the Internet by program.*

■10.1 Text as Unimedia

Nicholas Negroponte, founder of the MIT Media Lab, said that what makes computer-based multimedia possible is the fact that the computer is actually **unimedia**. The computer really only understands one thing: zeros and ones. We can use the computer for multimedia because any medium can be encoded as zeros and ones.

But he might as well have been talking about *text* as the unimedia. We can encode any medium to text; and, what's even better than the zeros and ones, we can *read* the text! Later in this chapter, we map sounds to text and then back to sounds, and we do the same with pictures. But once we're in text, we don't have to go back to the original medium: We can map sounds to text and then to pictures, and thus create *visualizations* of sounds.

The World Wide Web is primarily text. Visit any Web page, then go to the menu of your Web browser and choose to "View the source." What you will see is text. Every Web page is actually text. The text references the pictures, sounds, and animations that appear when you view the page, but the page itself is defined as text. The words in the text are in a notation called *HyperText Markup Language (HTML)*.

Until now, we've been able to get by with a relatively few programming-language ideas. JES was designed so that we can do all our sound and picture work using only assignment, `for`, `if`, `print`, `return`, and functions. But programming languages have more features and capabilities than just these. In this chapter, we start to show you what's under the hood of JES to give you more capability in your programming.

■10.2 Strings: Making and Manipulating Strings

Text is typically manipulated as **strings**. A string is a sequence of characters. Strings are stored in memory as an array, just like sounds. Strings are a contiguous sequence of our memory mailboxes—the mailboxes right next to one another. The string "Hello" would be stored in five mailboxes right next to one another: one mailbox holding the binary code representing "H", the next one holding "e", the next one holding "l", and so on.

Strings are defined with sequences of characters inside quote marks. Python is unusual in that it allows several different kinds of quoting. We can use single quotes, double quotes, or even triple quotes. We can *nest* quotes. If we start a string with double quotes, then we can use single quotes inside the string because the string isn't ended until the next set of double quotes. If you start a string with single quotes, you can put all the double quotes you want inside the string, because Python is waiting for the single quotes to end.

```
>>> print 'This is a single-quoted string'
This is a single-quoted string
>>> print "This is a double-quoted string"
This is a double-quoted string
>>> print """This is a triple-quoted string"""
This is a triple-quoted string
```

Why triple quote? Because it allows us to embed new lines and spaces and tabs in our strings. We can't use it easily from the Command Area, but we can in the Program Area.

```
def sillystring():
    print """This is using triple quotes.  Why?



Because we can do this."""

>>> sillystring()
This is using triple quotes.  Why?



Because we can do this.
```

The value of having so many different kinds of quotes is to make it easy to put quotes *inside* of strings. For example, HTML uses double quotes as part of its notation. If you want to write a Python function that creates HTML pages (a common use for Python), then you will need strings that contain quotes. Since any of these quotes work, you can embed double quotes by simply using single quotes.

```
>>> print " " "
Your code contains at least one syntax error, meaning it
is not legal jython.
>>> print ' " '
 "
```

A string can be thought of as an array or sequence of characters. It really is a sequence—you can use for to walk along all the characters.

```
>>> for i in "Hello":
...     print i
...
H
e
l
l
o
```

In memory, a string is a series of consecutive mailboxes (to continue our metaphor of memory as a mailroom), each containing the binary code for the corresponding character. The function ord() gives us the ASCII (American Standard Code for Information Interchange) encoding for each character. Thus, we find that the string "Hello" is five mailboxes, the first containing 72, and then 101, and then 108, and so on.

```
>>> str = "Hello"
>>> for char in str:
...        print ord(char)
...
72
101
108
108
111
```

In JES, that's a slight simplification. The version of Python we're using, Jython, is built on Java, which is actually *not* using ASCII to encode its strings. It's using *Unicode* which is an encoding for characters where two bytes are used for each character. Two bytes gives us 65,536 possible combinations. All those extra possible codes allow us to go beyond a simple Latin alphabet, numbers, and punctuation. We can represent Hiragana, Katakana, and other *glyph* (graphic depictions of characters) systems.

What this should tell you is that there are many more possible characters than can be typed at the keyboard. Not only are there special symbols, but there are invisible characters like tabs and pressing the return/enter key. We type these in Python strings (and in many other languages, such as Java and C) using *backslash escapes*. Backslash escapes are the backslash key \ followed by a character.

■ \t is the same as typing the tab key.

■ \b is the same as typing the backspace key (which is not a particularly useful character to put in a string, but you can). When you print \b, it shows up as a box on most systems—it's not actually printable (see below).

■ \n is the same as typing the enter/return key.

■ \uXXXX where XXXX is a code made up of 0–9 and A–F (known as a *hexadecimal* number) represents the Unicode character with that code. You can look up the codes at http://www.unicode.org/charts.

(Given below is an image, in order make the unicode glyphs appear.)

```
>>> print "hello\tthere.\nMark"
hello    there.
Mark
>>> print u"\uFEED"
٬
>>> print u"\u03F0"
ϰ
>>> print "This\bis\na\btest"
This␢ is
a␢ test
```

Remember that we used an 'r' at the start of a filename string earlier in this book for example,

```
r"C:\Documents and Settings\Mark Guzdial\My Documents"
```

An 'r' tells Python to read the string in *raw mode*. All the backslash escapes are ignored. That's important in Windows paths because Windows uses backslashes as *delimiters*. If your filename begins with a 'b,' for example, Python would view that \b as a backspace character, not as a delimiter-b.

We can easily add strings together using + (also called **concatenation** of strings) and get strings' lengths using the function len().

```
>>> hello = "Hello"
>>> print len(hello)
5
>>> mark = ", Mark"
>>> print len(mark)
6
>>> print hello+mark
Hello, Mark
>>> print len(hello+mark)
11
```

We use the square bracket notation ([]) to reference parts of strings.

■ string[n] returns the *n*th character in the string, where the first character in the string is zero.

■ string[n:m] returns a *slice* of the string starting at the *n*th character and preceding up to *but not including* the *m*th (similar to how the range() function works). You can optionally leave out *n* or *m*. If *n* is missing, it's assumed to be zero (start of the string). If *m* is missing, it's assumed to be the end of the string. We can also use negative numbers at either end to trim off that much from that side.

We can think about the characters of the string as being in boxes, each with its own index number.

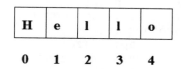

```
>>> hello = "Hello"
>>> print hello[1]
e
>>> print hello[0]
H
>>> print hello[2:4]
ll
```

```
>>> print hello
Hello
>>> print hello[:3]
Hel
>>> print hello[3:]
lo
>>> print hello[:]
Hello
>>> print hello[-1:]
o
>>> print hello[:-1]
Hell
```

10.2.1 String Methods: Introducing Objects and Dot Notation

Everything in Python is actually more than just a value—it's an *object*. An object combines data (like a number or a string or a list) with the *methods* that can act upon that object. Methods are like functions, except that they're not globally accessible. You can't execute a method the way you can execute pickAFile() or makeSound(). A method is a function that can only be accessed *through* an object.

Strings in Python are objects. They are not only sequences of characters—they also have methods that are not globally accessible but are known only to strings. To execute a method of a string, you use *dot notation*. You type object.method().

An example method known only to strings is capitalize(). It capitalizes the string it's called upon. It will not work on a function or on a number.

```
>>> test="this is a test."
>>> print test.capitalize
<builtin method 'capitalize'>
>>> print test.capitalize()
This is a test.
>>> print capitalize(test)
A local or global name could not be found. You need to
define the function or variable before you try to use it
in any way.
NameError: capitalize
>>> print 'this is another test'.capitalize()
This is another test
>>> print 12.capitalize()
Your code contains at least one syntax error, meaning
it is not legal jython.
```

There are *many* useful string methods.

■ startswith(prefix) returns true if the string starts with the given suffix. Remember that true in Python is anything 1 or greater, and false is zero.

```
>>> letter = "Mr. Mark Guzdial requests the pleasure of
your company..."
>>> print letter.startswith("Mr.")
```

```
1
>>> print letter.startswith("Mrs.")
0
```

■ endswith(suffix) returns true if the string ends with the given suffix. endswith is particularly useful for checking whether a filename is the right kind for a program.

```
>>> filename="barbara.jpg"
>>> if filename.endswith(".jpg"):
...        print "It's a picture"
...
It's a picture
```

■ find(findstring) and find(findstring,start) and find(find-string,start,end) all find the findstring in the object string and return the index number where the string starts. In the optional forms, you can tell it what index number to start from, and even where to stop looking.

This is very important: The find() method returns -1 if it fails. Why -1? Because any value 0 to whatever *could* be a valid index where a search string might be found.

```
>>> print letter
Mr. Mark Guzdial requests the pleasure of your company...
>>> print letter.find("Mark")
4
>>> print letter.find("Guzdial")
9
>>> print len("Guzdial")
7
>>> print letter[4:9+7]
Mark Guzdial
>>> print letter.find("fred")
-1
```

There also exists rfind(findstring) (and the same variations with optional parameters) that search from the end of the string toward the front.

■ upper() translates the string to uppercase.

■ lower() translates the string to lowercase.

■ swapcase() makes all uppercase into lowercase, and vice versa.

■ title() makes just the first characters uppercase and the rest lower.

These methods can be *cascaded*—one modifying the result of another.

```
>>> string="This is a test of Something."
>>> print string.swapcase()
tHIS IS A TEST OF sOMETHING.
>>> print string.title().swapcase()
tHIS iS a tEST oF sOMETHING.
```

■ isalpha() returns true if the string is not empty and is all letters—no numbers and no punctuation.

■ isdigit() returns true if the string is not empty and all numbers. You might use this if you were checking the results of some search you were doing. Say that you were writing a program to look for stick prices. You want to parse out a current *price*, not a stock name. If you get it wrong, maybe your program might make buys or sells that you don't want. You could use isdigit() to check your result automatically.

■ replace(search,replace) searches for the search string and replaces it with the replace string. It returns the result but doesn't change the original string.

```
>>> print letter
Mr. Mark Guzdial requests the pleasure of your company...
>>> letter.replace("a","!")
'Mr. M!rk Guzdi!l requests the ple!sure of your comp!ny...'
>>> print letter
Mr. Mark Guzdial requests the pleasure of your company...
```

10.2.2 Lists: Powerful, Structured Text

Lists are very powerful structures that we can think about as a kind of *structured text*. Lists are defined with square brackets with commas between their elements, but they can contain just about anything—including sublists. Like strings, you can reference parts with square bracket notations, and you can add them together with +. Lists are also sequences, so you can use a for loop on them to walk through their pieces.

```
>>> mylist = ["This","is","a", 12]
>>> print mylist
['This', 'is', 'a', 12]
>>> print mylist[0]
This
>>> for i in mylist:
...        print i
...
This
is
a
12
>>> print mylist + ["Really!"]
['This', 'is', 'a', 12, 'Really!']
>>> anotherlist=["this","has",["a",["sub","list"]]]
>>> print anotherlist
['this', 'has', ['a', ['sub', 'list']]]
>>> print anotherlist[0]
this
>>> print anotherlist[2]
['a', ['sub', 'list']]
>>> print anotherlist[2][1]
['sub', 'list']
```

```
>>> print anotherlist[2][1][0]
sub
>>> print anotherlist[2][1][0][2]
b
```

Lists have a set of methods that they understand but strings do not.

- append(something) puts something in the list at the end.
- remove(something) removes something from the list if its there.
- sort() puts the list in alphabetical order.
- reverse() reverses the list.
- count(something) tells you the number of times that something is in the list.
- max() and min() are functions we've seen before that take a list as input and give you the maximum and minimum values in the list.

```
>>> list = ["bear","apple","cat","elephant","dog","apple"]
>>> list.sort()
>>> print list
['apple', 'apple', 'bear', 'cat', 'dog', 'elephant']
>>> list.reverse()
>>> print list
['elephant', 'dog', 'cat', 'bear', 'apple', 'apple']
>>> print list.count('apple')
2
```

One of the most important string methods, split(delimiter), converts a string into a list of substrings, separating on a delimiter string that you provide. This allows us to convert strings into lists.

```
>>> print letter.split(" ")
['Mr.', 'Mark', 'Guzdial', 'requests', 'the', 'pleasure',
'of', 'your', 'company...']
```

Using split() we can process *formatted text*—text where the separation between parts is a well-defined character, like *tab-delimited text* or *comma-delimited text* from a spreadsheet. Here's an example using structured text to store a phone book. The phone book has lines separated by newlines, and parts separated by colons. We can split on the newlines, then the colons, to get a list of sublists. Searches through this can be made with a simple for loop.

RECIPE 75: A simple phone book application

```
def phonebook():
    return """
Mary:893-0234:Realtor:
Fred:897-2033:Boulder crusher:
Barney:234-2342:Professional bowler:"""
```

```
def phones():
  phones = phonebook()
  phonelist = phones.split('\n')
  newphonelist = []
  for list in phonelist:
    newphonelist = newphonelist + [list.split(":")]
  return newphonelist

def findPhone(person):
  for people in phones():
    if people[0] == person:
      print "Phone number for",person,"is",people[1]
```

How it works: There are three functions here: one to provide the phone text, the other to create the phone list, and the third to look up a phone number.

■ The first function, phonebook, creates the structured text and returns it, using triple quotes so that the lines can be formatted with newline characters. The format is name, colon, phone number, colon, and job, then colon and end of the line.

```
>>> print phonebook()

Mary:893-0234:Realtor:
Fred:897-2033:Boulder crusher:
Barney:234-2342:Professional bowler:
```

■ The second function, phones, returns a list of all the phones. It accesses the phone list through phonebook, then splits it into lines. The result of split is a list comprising a string with colons in it. The loop in phones then chops up each list using split on the colons. What phones returns, then, is a list of lists.

```
>>> print phones()
[[''], ['Mary', '893-0234', 'Realtor', ''], ['Fred',
'897-2033', 'Boulder crusher', ''], ['Barney', '234-2342',
'Professional bowler', '']]
```

■ Finally, the third function, findPhone, takes a name as input and finds the corresponding phone number. It loops over all the sublists that phones returns and finds the one where the first item in the sublist (index number 0) is the input name. It then prints the result

```
>>> findPhone('Fred')
Phone number for Fred is 897-2033
```

10.2.3 Strings Have No Font

Strings have no *font* (characteristic look of the letters) or *style* (typically the boldface, italics, underline, and other effects applied to the string) associated with them. Font and style information is added to strings using word-processors and other programs. Typically, these are encoded as *style runs*.

A style run is a separate representation of the font and style information with indices into the string to show where the changes should take place. For example, **The old** *brown* fox runs might be encoded as [[bold 0 6][italics 8 12]].

Think about strings with style runs. What do you call this combination of related information? It's clearly not a single value. Could we encode the string with the style runs in a complex list? Sure—we can do just about *anything* with lists!

Most software that manages formatted text will encode strings with style runs as an **object**. Objects have data associated with them, perhaps in several parts (like strings and style runs). Objects know how to act upon their data, using *methods* that may be known only to objects of that type. If the same method name is known to multiple objects, it probably does the same thing, but probably not in the same way.

This is foreshadowing. Objects will be discussed later.

■10.3 Files: Places to Put Your Strings and Other Stuff

Files are large named collections of bytes on your hard disk. Files typically have a **base name** and a **file suffix**. The file barbara.jpg has the base name of "barbara" and a file suffix of "jpg" that tells you that the file is a JPEG picture.

Files are clustered into **directories** (sometimes called **folders**). Directories can contain other directories as well as files. There is a base directory on your computer which is referred to as the **root directory**. On a computer using the Windows operating system, the base directory will be something like C:\. A complete description of what directories to visit to get to a particular file from the base directory is called a **path**.

```
>>> file=pickAFile()
>>> print file
C:\Documents and Settings\Mark Guzdial\My
Documents\mediasources\640x480.jpg
```

The path that is printed tells us how to go from the root directory to the file 640x480.jpg in my mediasources directory. We start at C:\, choose the directory Documents and Settings, then the directory Mark Guzdial, then the directory My Documents, then the directory mediasources.

We call this structure a **tree** (Figure 10.1). We call C:\ the **root** of the tree. The tree has **branches** where there are subdirectories. Any directory can contain more directories (branches) or files, which are referred to as **leaves**. Except for the root, each **node** of the tree (branch or leaf) has a single **parent** branch node, though a parent can have multiple **children** branches and leaves.

We need to know about directories and files if we're going to manipulate files, and especially lots of files. If you're dealing with a big Web site, you are going to be working with a lot of files. If you are going to be dealing with video, you will have about 30 files (individual frames) for each second of video. You don't really want to write a line of code to open each frame. You want to write programs that will walk directory structures to process Web or video files.

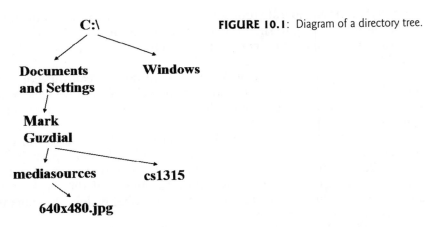

FIGURE 10.1: Diagram of a directory tree.

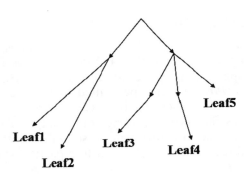

FIGURE 10.2: Diagram for the tree described in the list.

We can also represent trees in lists. Because lists can contain sublists, just as directories can contain subdirectories, it's a pretty easy encoding. The important point is that lists allow us to represent complex, hierarchical relationships, like trees (Figure 10.2).

```
>>> tree = [["Leaf1","Leaf2"],[["Leaf3"],["Leaf4"],
"Leaf5"]]
>>> print tree
[['Leaf1', 'Leaf2'], [['Leaf3'], ['Leaf4'], 'Leaf5']]
>>> print tree[0]
['Leaf1', 'Leaf2']
>>> print tree[1]
[['Leaf3'], ['Leaf4'], 'Leaf5']
>>> print tree[1][0]
['Leaf3']
>>> print tree[1][1]
['Leaf4']
>>> print tree[1][2]
Leaf5
```

10.3.1 Opening and Manipulating Files

We open files in order to read or write them. We use a function named (not surprisingly) open(filename,how). The filename can be a complete path or just a base filename and suffix. If you don't provide a path, the file will be opened in the current JES directory.

The how input is a string describing what you want to do with the file.

■ "rt" means "read the file as text—translate the bytes into characters for me."

■ "wt" means "write the file as text."

■ "rb" and "wb" mean "read and write bytes" (respectively). You use these if you are going to manipulate *binary files* (like JPEG, WAV, Word, or Excel files).

The function open() returns a file object that you then use to manipulate the file. The file object understands a set of methods.

■ file.read() reads the whole file as a giant string. (If you opened the file for writing, don't try to read from it.)

■ file.readlines() reads the whole file into a list where each element is a single line. You can only use read() or readlines() once per file opening.

■ file.write(somestring) writes somestring to the file. (If you opened the file for reading, don't try to write to it.)

■ file.close() closes the file. If you were writing to the file, closing to it makes sure that all the data gets written out on the disk. If you were reading from the file, it releases the memory that's used for manipulating the file. In either case, it's a good idea to close your files when you're done with them. Once you close a file, you can't read or write the file again until you reopen it.

Here are examples of opening a program file that we wrote earlier and of reading it in as a string and as a list of strings.

```
>>> program=pickAFile()
>>> print program
C:\Documents and Settings\Mark Guzdial\My
Documents\py-programs\littlepicture.py
>>> file=open(program,"rt")
>>> contents=file.read()
>>> print contents
def littlepicture():
  canvas=makePicture(getMediaPath("640x480.jpg"))
  addText(canvas,10,50,"This is not a picture")
  addLine(canvas,10,20,300,50)
  addRectFilled(canvas,0,200,300,500,yellow)
  addRect(canvas,10,210,290,490)
  return canvas
>>> file.close()
>>> file=open(program,"rt")
>>> lines=file.readlines()
```

```
>>> print lines
['def littlepicture():\n', '
canvas=makePicture(getMediaPath("640x480.jpg"))\n', '
addText(canvas,10,50,"This is not a picture")\n', '
addLine(canvas,10,20,300,50)\n', '
addRectFilled(canvas,0,200,300,500,yellow)\n', '
addRect(canvas,10,210,290,490)\n', '   return canvas']
>>> file.close()
```

Here's an example of writing a silly file. The \n creates the new lines in the file.

```
>>> writefile = open("myfile.txt","wt")
>>> writefile.write("Here is some text.")
>>> writefile.write("Here is some more.\n")
>>> writefile.write("And now we're done.\n\nTHE END.")
>>> writefile.close()
>>> writefile=open("myfile.txt","rt")
>>> print writefile.read()
Here is some text.Here is some more.
And now we're done.

THE END.
>>> writefile.close()
```

10.3.2 Generating Form Letters

Not only can we write programs to take apart structured text, we can write programs that *assemble* structured text. One of the classic structured texts that we're all too familiar with is spam or form letters. The really good spam writers (if that's not a contradiction in terms) fill in details that actually refer to *you* in the message. How do they do this? It's pretty easy—they have a function that takes in the relevant input and plugs it into the right places.

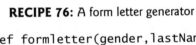

RECIPE 76: A form letter generator

```
def formletter(gender,lastName,city,eyeColor):
    file = open("formletter.txt","wt")
    file.write("Dear ")
    if gender=="F":
        file.write("Ms. "+lastName+":\n")
    if gender=="M":
        file.write("Mr. "+lastName+":\n")
    file.write("I am writing to remind you of the offer ")
    file.write("that we sent to you last week. Everyone in ")
    file.write(city+" knows what an exceptional offer this
is!")
    file.write("(Especially those with lovely eyes of
"+eyeColor+"!)")
    file.write("We hope to hear from you soon.\n")
```

```
file.write("Sincerely,\n")
file.write("I.M. Acrook, Attorney at Law")
file.close()
```

How it works: This function takes a gender, a last name (family name), city, and eye color as input. It opens a `formletter.txt` file, then writes out an opening, tuned to the gender of the recipient. It writes out a bunch of text, inserting the input into the right places. Then closes the file.

When this is executed with `formletter("M","Guzdial","Decatur", "brown")`, it generates:

```
Dear Mr. Guzdial:
I am writing to remind you of the offer that we
sent to you last week. Everyone in Decatur knows what an
exceptional offer this is!(Especially those with lovely
eyes of brown!)We hope to hear from you soon.
Sincerely,
I.M. Acrook,
Attorney at Law
```

10.3.3 Writing Out Programs

Now let's start *using* files. Our first program will do something pretty interesting—let's write a program to *change* another program. We'll read the `littlepicture.py` file, and change the text string that's inserted into the picture. We'll `find()` the `addText()` function, then search for each of the double quotes. Then we'll write out a new file with everything from `littlepicture.py` up to the first double quote, insert our new string, and put in the rest of the file from the second double quote to the end.

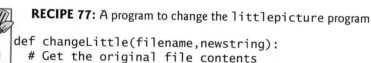

RECIPE 77: A program to change the `littlepicture` program

```
def changeLittle(filename,newstring):
  # Get the original file contents
  programfile="littlepicture.py"
  file = open(programfile,"rt")
  contents = file.read()
  file.close()
  # Now, find the right place to put our new string
  addtext = contents.find("addText")
  #Double quote after addText
  firstquote = contents.find('"',addtext)
  #Double quote after firstquote
  endquote = contents.find('"',firstquote+1)
  # Make our new file
  newfile = open(filename,"wt")
  newfile.write(contents[:firstquote+1]) # Include the quote
  newfile.write(newstring)
  newfile.write(contents[endquote:])
  newfile.close()
```

How it works: This program opens up the file *littlepicture.py* (the name assumes that it's in the JES directory, since no path is provided). It reads the whole thing in as a big string, then closes the file. Using the `find` method, it finds where the `addText` is, where the first double quote is, and where the last double quote is. It then opens up a new file (for writable text: "wt") and writes out all of the little program up to the first double quote. Then it writes out the input string. Then it writes out the rest of the little program from the last double quote on. Thus, it replaces the string that's added. Finally, it closes the new file.

When we run this with `changeLittle("sample.py","Here is a sample of changing a program")`, we get in `sample.py`:

```
def littlepicture():
  canvas=makePicture(getMediaPath("640x480.jpg"))
  addText(canvas,10,50,"Here is a sample of changing a
program")
  addLine(canvas,10,20,300,50)
  addRectFilled(canvas,0,200,300,500,yellow)
  addRect(canvas,10,210,290,490)
  return canvas
```

This is how vector-based drawing programs work. When you change a line in AutoCAD or Flash or Illustrator, you're actually changing the underlying representation of the picture—in a real sense, a little program whose execution results in the picture you're working with. When you change the line, you're actually changing the program, which is then re-executed to show you the updated picture. Is this process slow? Thank God for Moore's Law! Computers are fast enough that we just don't notice.

Being able to manipulate text is quite important for gathering data on the Internet. Most of the Internet is just text. Go to your favorite Web page, then use the VIEW SOURCE option in the menu. That's the text that defines the page you're seeing in the browser. Later, we'll learn how to download pages directly from the Internet, but for now, let's assume that you've saved (*downloaded*) pages or files from the Internet onto your disk, and then we'll do searches from there.

For example, there are places on the Internet where you can grab sequences of nucleotides associated with things like parasites. I found a file of this type that looks like this:

```
>Schisto unique AA825099
gcttagatgtcagattgagcacgatgatcgattgaccgtgagatcgacga
gatgcgcagatcgagatctgcatacagatgatgaccatagtgtacg
>Schisto unique mancons0736
ttctcgctcacactagaagcaagacaatttacactattattattattatt
accattattattattattactattattattattactattattta
ctacgtcgctttttcactccctttattctcaaattgtgtatccttccttt
```

Let's say that we had a subsequence (like "ttgtgta") and wanted to know which parasite it was part of. If we read in this file into a string, we could search for the subsequence. If it's there (i.e., the `find` result is not equal <> to −1), we search *backwards* from there to find the " >" that starts each parasite name, then *forward* to the end of line (newline character) to get the name of the file. If we don't find the subsequence (find() returns a −1), the subsequence isn't there.

RECIPE 78: Finding a subsequence in parasite nucleotide sequences

```
def findSequence(seq):
  sequencesFile = getMediaPath("parasites.txt")
  file = open(sequencesFile,"rt")
  sequences = file.read()
  file.close()
  # Find the sequence
  seqloc = sequences.find(seq)
  #print "Found at:",seqloc
  if seqloc <> -1:
    # Now, find the ">" with the name of the sequence
    nameloc = sequences.rfind(">",0,seqloc)
    #print "Name at:",nameloc
    endline = sequences.find("\n",nameloc)
    print "Found in ",sequences[nameloc:endline]
  if seqloc == -1:
    print "Not found"
```

How it works: The function findSequence takes a part of a sequence as an input. It opens the parasites.txt file (in the media folder specified with setMediaPath) and reads the whole thing into the string sequences. We look for the sequence in the string sequences using find. If it's found (i.e., the result isn't −1), then we look *backwards* from where we found the sequence (seqloc) to the beginning of the string (0) to find the " >" which starts the sequence. We then search forward from the greater-than sign to the end of the line ("\n"). This gives us where in the original sequences string we can find the name of the parasite that our input subsequence is from.

There are programs that wander the Internet, gathering information from Web pages. For example, Google's news page (http://news.google.com) isn't written by reporters. Google has programs that go out and snag headlines out of *other* news sites. How do these programs work? They simply download pages from the Internet and chop out the desired pieces.

For example, let's say that you wanted to write a function that would give you the current temperature by reading it off a local weather page. In Atlanta, a good weather page is http://www.ajc.com/weather—the weather page of the *Atlanta Journal-Constitution*. By viewing the source, we can find where the current temperature appears on the page, and what the key features of the text are around it to grab just the temperature. Here's the relevant part of the page that I found one day:

```
<td ><img src="/shared-local/weather/images/ps.gif"
width="48" height="48" border="0"><font size=-2><br></font>
<font size="-1"
```

```
face="Arial, Helvetica, sans-serif"><b>Currently</b><br>
Partly sunny<br> <font size="+2">54<b>&deg;</b></font>
<font face="Arial, Helvetica, sans-serif" size="+1">
F</font></font></td> </tr>
```

You can see the word Currently in there, then the temperature just before the characters <b>°. We can write a program to chop out those pieces and return the temperature, given that the weather page is saved in a file named ajc-weather.html. Now this program won't *always* work with the current AJC weather page. The page format may change, and the key text we're looking for might move or disappear. But as long as the format is the same, this recipe will work.

RECIPE 79: Get the temperature off a weather page

```
def findTemperature():
    weatherFile = getMediaPath("ajc-weather.html")
    file = open(weatherFile,"rt")
    weather = file.read()
    file.close()
    # Find the Temperature
    curloc = weather.find("Currently")
    if curloc <> -1:
        # Now, find the "<b>&deg;" following the temp
        temploc = weather.find("<b>&deg;",curloc)
        tempstart = weather.rfind(">",0,temploc)
        print "Current temperature:",weather[tempstart+1:temploc]
    if curloc == -1:
        print "They must have changed the page format -- can't
    find the temp"
```

How it works: This function assumes that the file ajc-weather.html is stored in the media folder specified with setMediaPath. The function findTemperature opens and reads the file as text, then closes it. We look for the word "Currently." If we find it (the result is not -1), we look for the degree marker after the "Currently" (stored in curloc). We then search backwards for the end of the previous tag, " >." The temperature is between these points. If curloc is −1, we give up because we couldn't find the word "Currently."

■10.4 Extending Our Language Capabilities Using Modules

In every programming language, there's a way of extending the basic functions of the language with new ones. In Python, this functionality is referred to as *importing a module*. A *module* is simply a Python file with new capabilities defined in it. When you import a module, it's as if you typed that Python file in at that point and all the objects, functions, and variables in it become defined at once. Python comes with an extensive library of modules that you can use to do a wide range of things, such as accessing the Internet, generating random numbers, and accessing files in a directory—a useful thing to do when developing Web pages or working with video.

Let's use that as our first example. The module we'll use is the os module. The function in the os module that knows how to list the files in a directory is listdir(). We access the piece of the module using dot notation.

```
>>> import os
>>> print os.listdir("C:\Documents and Settings\Mark Guzdial
\My Documents\mediasources\pics")
['students1.jpg', 'students2.jpg', 'students5.jpg',
'students6.jpg', 'students7.jpg', 'students8.jpg']
```

We can use os.listdir() to title pictures in a directory or to insert a statement, such as a copyright claim. Now listdir() just returns the base filename and suffix. That's enough to make sure that we have pictures and not sounds or something else. But it doesn't give us complete paths for makePicture. To get a complete path, we can combine the input directory with the base filename from listdir()—but we need a path delimiter between the two pieces. Python has a standard that if a filename has a "//" in it, that will be replaced with whatever the right path delimiter is for the operating system you're using.

RECIPE 80: Title a set of pictures in a directory

```
import os

def titleDirectory(dir):
    for file in os.listdir(dir):
        print "Processing:",dir+"//"+file
        if file.endswith(".jpg"):
            picture = makePicture(dir+"//"+file)
            addText(picture,10,10,"Property of CS1315 at Georgia
Tech")
            writePictureTo(picture,dir+"//"+"titled-"+file)
```

How it works: The function titleDirectory takes a directory (path name, as a string) as input. It then walks through each filename file in the directory. If the filename ends with ".jpg," it's probably a picture. So we make the picture from the file in the given dir directory. We add text to the picture, then write the picture back out as "titled-" plus the filename, in the given dir directory.

10.4.1 More on Import and Your Own Modules

There are actually several forms of the import statement. The one we're using here, import module, makes all of the module available through dot notation. These are several other options:

■ We can import just a few things from a module, but then access them without using dot notation. This form is from module import.

```
>>> from os import listdir
>>> print listdir(r"C:\Documents and Settings")
['Default User', 'All Users', 'NetworkService', 'LocalService',
'Administrator', 'Driver', 'Mark Guzdial']
```

We can use the form `from module import *` to import *everything* from the module and access it without using dot notation at all.

■ We can `import module as newname` if we'd like to import a module but then use `newname` to reference the module. We'll use this in Chapter 15 to make it easier to access Java modules.

A module is just a Python file. You can import your own code as a module. If you have the function `findTemperature` in the file `findTemperatureFile.py` in the JES directory, you can simply execute `import findTemperature from findTemperatureFile` and then use `findTemperature` as if it were typed into your Program Area.

10.4.2 Another Fun Module: Random

Another fun and sometimes useful module is `random`. The base function `random.random()` generates random numbers (evenly distributed) between 0 and 1.

```
>>> import random
>>> for i in range(1,10):
...         print random.random()
...
0.8211369314193928
0.6354266779703246
0.9460060163520159
0.904615696559684
0.33500464463254187
0.08124982126940594
0.0711481376807015
0.7255217307346048
0.2920541211845866
```

Random numbers can be fun when they're applied to tasks like picking random words from a list. `random.choose()` does that.

```
>>> for i in range(1,5):
...         print random.choice(["Here", "is", "a", "list",
"of", "words", "in", "random", "order"])
...
list
a
Here
list
```

From there, we can generate random sentences by randomly picking nouns, verbs, and phrases from lists.

RECIPE 81: Randomly generate language

```
import random

def sentence():
  nouns = ["Mark", "Adam", "Angela", "Larry", "Jose",
"Matt", "Jim"]
  verbs = ["runs", "skips", "sings", "leaps", "jumps",
"climbs", "argues", "giggles"]
  phrases = ["in a tree", "over a log", "very loudly",
"around the bush", "while reading the newspaper"]
  phrases = phrases + ["very badly", "while skipping",
"instead of grading", "while typing on the CoWeb."]
  print random.choice(nouns), random.choice(verbs),
random.choice(phrases)
```

How it works: We simply create lists for nouns, verbs, and phrases—taking care that all the combinations make sense in terms of number. The print statement defines the desired structure: a random noun, then a random verb, then a random phrase.

```
>>> sentence()
Jose leaps while reading the newspaper
>>> sentence()
Jim skips while typing on the CoWeb.
>>> sentence()
Matt sings very loudly
>>> sentence()
Adam sings in a tree
>>> sentence()
Adam sings around the bush
>>> sentence()
Angela runs while typing on the CoWeb.
>>> sentence()
Angela sings around the bush
>>> sentence()
Jose runs very badly
```

The basic process here is common in simulation programs. What we have is a structure defined in the program: a definition of what counts as a noun, a verb, and a phrase, and a statement that what we want is a noun, then a verb, then a phrase. The structure gets filled in with random choices. The interesting question is how much can be simulated with a structure and randomness. Could we simulate intelligence this way? And what's the difference between a *simulation* of intelligence and a really thinking computer?

Imagine a program that reads input from the user and then generates a random sentence. Maybe there are a few *rules* in the program that search for keywords and respond to them, like:

```
if input.find(mother) <> -1:
    print "Tell me more about your mother"
```

Joseph Weizenbaum wrote a program like this many years ago, called *Doctor* (later known as `Eliza`). His program would act like a Rogerian psychotherapist, echoing back whatever you said, with some randomness, but searching for keywords so that it would seem to really be "listening." The program was meant as a joke, not a real effort to create a simulation of intelligence. To Weizenbaum's dismay, people took it seriously. They started treating it like a therapist. Weizenbaum changed his research direction from *artificial intelligence* to concern over the ethical use of technology and how easily people can be fooled by technology.

■10.5 Networks: Getting Our Text from the Web

A *network* is formed whenever computers communicate with one another. Rarely does the communication take place with voltages over wires, the way that a computer encodes 0's and 1's internally. It's too hard to maintain specific voltages over distances. Instead, 0's and 1's are encoded in some other way. For example, a **modem** (literally *modulator-demodulator*) maps 0's and 1's to different audio frequencies. When we hear these different tones, it sounds like a bunch of buzzing bees to us, but to modems, it's pure binary.

Like onions and ogres, networks have layers. At the bottom level is the physical substrate. How are the signals being passed? Higher levels define how data is encoded. What makes up a zero? A one? Do we send one bit at a time? A **packet** of bytes at a time? Even higher levels define the **protocol** for communication. How does my computer tell your computer that it wants to talk and what it wants to talk about? How do I address your computer at all? By thinking about these distinct layers, and keeping them distinct, we can easily swap out one part without changing the others. For example, most people with a direct connection to a network use a wired connection to an **Ethernet** network, but Ethernet is actually a mid-level protocol that works over wireless networks.

Humans also have protocols. If I walk up to you, hold out my hand, and say, "Hi, my name is Mark," you will most certainly hold out your hand and say something like "My name is Gene" (assuming that your name is Gene—if it wasn't, that would be pretty funny). There's an unwritten protocol for humans about how to greet one another. Computer protocols are about the same things, but they're written down to communicate the process exactly. What's said isn't too different. One computer may send the message 'HELO' to another to start a conversation (I don't know why the protocol writers couldn't spare the extra 'L' to spell it right), and a computer may send 'BYE' to end the conversation. (We even sometimes call the start of a computer protocol the "*handshake*.") It's all about establishing a connection and making sure that both sides understand what's going on.

The *Internet* is a network of networks. If you have a device in your home so that your computers can talk to one another (e.g., a *router*), then you have a network. With just that, you can probably copy files around between computers and print. When you connect your network to the wider Internet (through an *Internet Service Provider (ISP)*), your network becomes part of the Internet.

The Internet is based on a set of agreements about a whole bunch of things:

■ *How computers will be addressed:* Currently, each computer on the Internet has a 32-bit number associated with it—four byte values that are usually written like this separated by periods "101.132.64.15." These are called *IP addresses* (for Internet Protocol addresses).

There is a system of *domain names* by which people can refer to specific computers without knowing their IP addresses. For example, when you access http://www.cnn.com, you are actually accessing http://64.236.24.20. (Go ahead and try it! It works.) There is a network of *domain name servers* that keep track of names like "www.cnn.com" and map them to addresses like "64.236.24.20." You can be connected to the Internet and still not be able to get to your favorite Web sites if your domain name server is broken—but you might be able to get to it if you type in the IP address directly.

■ *How computers will communicate*: Data will be placed in *packets* that have a well-defined structure, including the sender's IP address, the receiver's IP address, and a number of bytes per packet.

■ *How packets are routed around the Internet:* The Internet was designed in the time of the *Cold War*. It was designed to withstand a nuclear attack. If a section of the Internet is destroyed (or damaged, or blocked as a form of censorship), the packet-routing mechanism of the Internet will simply find a route around the damage.

But the topmost layers of the network define what the data being passed around *means*. One of the first applications placed on top of the Internet was electronic mail. Over the years, the mail protocols have evolved to standards today like *POP* (Post Office Protocol) and *SMTP* (Simple Mail Transfer Protocol). Another old and important protocol is *FTP* (File Transfer Protocol).

These protocols aren't super-complicated. When the communication ends, one computer will probably say 'BYE' or 'QUIT' to the other. When one computer tells another computer to accept a file via FTP, it literally says "STO filename" (again, early computer developers didn't want to spare the two more bytes to say "STORE.")

The *World Wide Web* is yet another set of agreements, developed mostly by Tim Berners-Lee. The Web is based on top of the Internet, simply adding more protocols on top of the existing ones.

■ *How to refer to things on the Web:* Resources on the Web are referenced using *URLs*, *Uniform Resource Locators*. A URL specifies the protocol to use to address the resource, the domain name of the *server* that can provide the resource, and the *path* to the resource on that server. For example, a URL like `http://www.cc.gatech.edu/index.html` says "Use the HTTP protocol to talk to the computer at `www.cc.gatech.edu` and ask it for the resource index.html."

Not every file on every computer attached to the Internet is accessible via a URL. There are some preconditions before a file is accessible via a URL. First, an Internet-accessible computer has to be running a piece of software that understands a protocol that Web browsers understand, typically HTTP or FTP. We call a computer that is running such a piece of software a *server*. A browser that accesses a server is called a **client**. Second, a server typically has a *server directory* accessible via that server. Only files in the directory, or subdirectories within the directory, are available.

■ *How to serve documents:* The most common protocol on the Web is **HTTP**, **HyperText Transfer Protocol**. It defines how resources are served on the Web. HTTP is really simple—your browser literally says to a server things like "GET index.html" (just those letters!).

■ *How documents will be formatted:* Documents on the Web are formatted using **HTML**, **HyperText Markup Language**.

You'll notice the term **HyperText** showing up frequently in reference to the Web. HyperText is literally nonlinear text. It's a term invented by Ted Nelson to describe the kind of reading that we all do on the Web, but that didn't exist before computers: Read a little on one page, then click a link and read a little over there, then click BACK and continue reading where you left off. The basic idea of HyperText dates back to Vannevar Bush, who was one of President Franklin Roosevelt's science advisers, but it wasn't until the computer came along that we could envision implementing Bush's model of a *Memex*—a device for capturing flows of thought. Tim Berners-Lee invented the Web and its protocols as a way of supporting rapid publication of research findings with connections between documents. The Web is certainly not the penultimate HyperText system. Systems like the ones that Ted Nelson worked on wouldn't allow "dead links" (links that are no longer accessible). But for all its warts, the Web *works*.

A browser (e.g., Internet Explorer, Netscape Navigator, Mozilla, Opera) understands a lot about the Internet. It usually knows several protocols, such as HTTP, FTP, *gopher* (an early HyperText protocol), or *mailto* (SMTP). It knows HTML, how to format it, and how to grab resources referenced within the HTML, like JPEG pictures. It is also possible to access the Internet without nearly that much overhead. Mail clients (e.g., Outlook and Eudora) know some of these protocols without knowing all of them. Even JES understands a little bit about SMTP and HTTP to support turnin of assignments.

Python, like other modern languages, provides modules to support access to the Internet without all the overhead of a browser. Basically, you can write small programs that are clients. Python's module `urllib` allows you to open URLs and read them as if they were files.

```
>>> import urllib
>>> connection = urllib.urlopen("http://www.ajc.com/
```

```
weather")
>>> weather = connection.read()
>>> connection.close()
```

Using this example, we can fix our temperature-reading program (Recipe 79) to read the weather page directly from the Internet.

RECIPE 82: Get the temperature from a live weather page

```
def findTemperatureLive():
    # Get the weather page
    import urllib #Could go above, too
    connection=urllib.urlopen("http://www.ajc.com/weather")
    weather = connection.read()
    connection.close()
    #weatherFile = getMediaPath("ajc-weather.html")
    #file = open(weatherFile,"rt")
    #weather = file.read()
    #file.close()
    # Find the Temperature
    curloc = weather.find("Currently")
    if curloc <> -1:
        # Now, find the "<b>&deg;" following the temp
        temploc = weather.find("<b>&deg;",curloc)
        tempstart = weather.rfind(">",0,temploc)
        print "Current temperature:",weather[tempstart+1:temploc]
    if curloc == -1:
        print "They must have changed the page format -- can't
find the temp"
```

How it works: The function findTemperatureLive is nearly identical to the last one, except that we're reading the string weather from the AJC Web site *live*. We use the module urllib to gain the ability to read the Web page as a string, and then search the string in the same way that we did the file previously.

We can use FTP via the ftplib in Python.

```
>>> import ftplib
>>> connect = ftplib.FTP("cleon.cc.gatech.edu")
>>> connect.login("guzdial","mypassword")
'230 User guzdial logged in.'
>>> connect.storbinary("STOR barbara.jpg",
open(getMediaPath("barbara.jpg")))
'226 Transfer complete.'
>>> connect.storlines("STOR JESintro.txt",
open("JESintro.txt"))
'226 Transfer complete.'
>>> connect.close()
```

To create interaction on the Web, we need programs that actually generate HTML. For example, when you type a phrase into a text area and then click the SEARCH button, you are actually causing a program to execute on the server

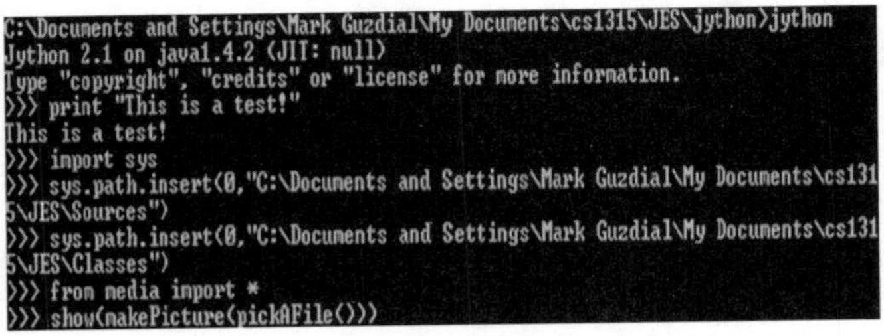

```
C:\Documents and Settings\Mark Guzdial\My Documents\cs1315\JES\jython>jython
Jython 2.1 on java1.4.2 (JIT: null)
Type "copyright", "credits" or "license" for more information.
>>> print "This is a test!"
This is a test!
>>> import sys
>>> sys.path.insert(0,"C:\Documents and Settings\Mark Guzdial\My Documents\cs131
5\JES\Sources")
>>> sys.path.insert(0,"C:\Documents and Settings\Mark Guzdial\My Documents\cs131
5\JES\Classes")
>>> from media import *
>>> show(makePicture(pickAFile()))
```

FIGURE 10.3: Using Jython outside of JES, even to do media.

that executes your search and then *generates* the HTML (Web page) that you see in response. Python is a common language for this kind of programming. Its modules, ease of quoting, and ease of writing make it excellent for writing interactive Web programs.

What you are learning here is *directly* usable in Python (or Jython). Commands like for and print work as-is in both Python and Jython. The modules ftplib and urllib are exactly the same in Python and Jython. The media work we're doing works in Jython with only a few extra commands (Figure 10.3). You literally are learning a language used for creating the interactive Web.

Let's talk a little about what's needed to use the media capabilities in Jython without using JES.

■ To find modules to import, Python uses a variable called sys.path to list all the directories where it should look for modules. If you want to use the JES modules in Jython, you need to put the location of those module files in your sys.path. You need to import sys to get access to the sys.path variable, then use the method insert to put the JES Sources and Classes directories (for Windows) in your path (see Figure 10.3). On the Macintosh, you will need to reference the Java and Jython code inside the JES application, typing something like sys.path.insert(0,"/users/guzdial/JES.app/Contents/Resources/ Java").

■ You then use from media import * to make things like pickAFile and makePicture available in Jython.

In case you were wondering, yes, the statement from media import * is actually inserted (invisibly to you the programmer) into your Program Area each time you press the LOAD button. That's how the special media features of JES are made available to your programs.

■10.6 Using Text to Shift Between Media

As we said at the beginning of this chapter, we can think about text as *unimedia*. We can map from sound to text and back again, and the same with pictures. And more interestingly, we can go from sound to text … to pictures.

Why would we want to do any of this? Why should we care about transforming media in this way? For the same reasons that we care about digitizing media at all. Digital media transformed into text can be more easily transmitted from place to place, checked for errors, and even corrected for errors. It turns out that very often when you are attaching binary files to an e-mail message, your binary file is actually converted to text first. In general, *choosing a new representation allows you to do new things.*

Mapping sound to text is easy. Sound is just a series of samples (numbers). We can easily write these out to a file.

RECIPE 83: Write a sound to a file as text numbers

```
def soundToText(sound,filename):
    file = open(filename,"wt")
    for s in getSamples(sound):
        file.write(str(getSample(s))+"\n")
    file.close()
```

How it works: We're taking an input sound and a filename as input, then opening the filename for writable text. We then loop though each sample and write it to the file. We're using the function `str()` here to convert a number into its string representation so that we can add a newline to it and write it to a file.

What do we do with sound as text? Manipulate it as a series of numbers, as with Excel (Figure 10.4). We can quite easily do modifications, such as multiplying each sample by 2.0 here. We can even graph the numbers, and see the same kind of sound graph as we've seen in MediaTools (Figure 10.5). (You will get an error, though—Excel doesn't like to graph more than 32,000 points, and at 22,000 samples per second, 32,000 samples is not a long sound.)

How do we convert a series of numbers back into a sound? Say that you do some modification to the numbers in Excel, and now you want to hear the result. How do you do it? The mechanics of Excel are easy: Simply copy the column you want into a new worksheet, save it as text, then get the pathname of the text file to use in Python.

The program itself is a little more complicated. When going from sound to text, we knew that we could use `getSamples` to write out all the samples. But how do we know how many lines are in the file? We can't really use

FIGURE 10.4: Sound-as-text file read into Excel.

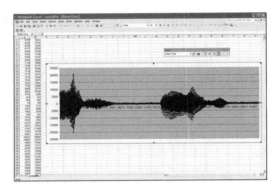

FIGURE 10.5: Sound-as-text file graphed in Excel.

getLines—it doesn't exist. We have to watch out for two problems: (a) having more lines in the file than we can fit into the sound that we're using to read into, and (b) running out of lines before we reach the end of the sound.

To do this, we're going to use a new programming-language construct called a while loop. A while loop, like an if, takes an expression and executes its block if the expression proves to be true. It differs from an if because *After* executing the block, a while loop *retests* the expression. If it's still true, the whole block is executed again. Eventually, you hope that the expression will become false, and then the line after the while's block will execute. If it doesn't, you get something called an *infinite loop*.

```
while 1==1:
    print "This will keep printing until the computer is
turned off."
```

For our text-to-sound example, we want to keep reading samples from the file and storing them into the sound *as long as* we have numbers in the file *and as long as* there is still room in the sound. We use the function float() to convert the string number into a real number. (int would work, too, but this gives us the chance to introduce float.)

```
>>> print 2*"123"
123123
>>> print 2 * float("123")
246.0
```

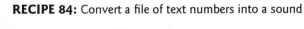

RECIPE 84: Convert a file of text numbers into a sound

```
def textToSound(filename):
    #Set up the sound
    sound = makeSound(getMediaPath("sec3silence.wav"))
    soundIndex = 1
    #Set up the file
    file = open(filename,"rt")
    contents=file.readlines()
    file.close()
```

```
fileIndex = 0
# Keep going until run out of sound space or run out of
file contents
   while (soundIndex < getLength(sound)) and (fileIndex
< len(contents)):
   sample=float(contents[fileIndex])  #Get the file line
   setSampleValueAt(sound,soundIndex,sample)
   fileIndex = fileIndex + 1
   soundIndex = soundIndex + 1
   return sound
```

How it works: The function textToSound takes a filename as input that contains the samples as numbers. We open up a silent three-second sound to hold the sound. soundIndex stands for the next sample to read, and fileIndex stands for the next number to read for the file list contents. The while loop says to keep going until *either* the soundIndex goes past the length of the sound *or* the fileIndex goes past the end of the file (in the list contents). In a loop we convert the next string in the list to a float, set the sample value to that, then increment both fileIndex and soundIndex. When we're done (by either condition in the while), we return the input sound.

But we don't *have* to map from sounds to text and back to sounds. We could decide to go to a picture instead. The program below takes a sound and maps each sample to a pixel. All we have to do is to define our mapping, how we want to represent the samples. I chose a very simple one: If the sample is greater than 1,000, the pixel is red; if less than −1,000 it is blue, and everything else is green (Figure 10.6).

We now have to deal with the case where we run out of samples before we run out of pixels. To do this, we use yet another new programming construct: a break. A break statement stops our current loop and goes to the line below it. In this example, if we run out of samples, we stop the for loop that is processing the pixels.

RECIPE 85: Visualizing sound

```
def soundToPicture(sound):
   picture = makePicture(getMediaPath("640x480.jpg"))
   soundIndex = 1
   for p in getPixels(picture):
     if soundIndex > getLength(sound):
       break
     sample = getSampleValueAt(sound,soundIndex)
     if sample > 1000:
       setColor(p,red)
     if sample < -1000:
       setColor(p,blue)
     if sample <= 1000 and sample >= -1000:
       setColor(p,green)
     soundIndex = soundIndex + 1
   return picture
```

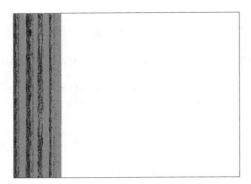

FIGURE 10.6: A visualization of the sound "This is a test".

How it works: In soundToPicture, we open up a 640 × 480 blank picture and take a sound as input. For each of the pixels in the picture, we get a sample value at soundIndex and figure out a mapping to a color, then set the pixel p to that color. We then increment the soundIndex. If the soundIndex ever goes past the end of the sound, we simply break and bail out of the loop. We return the created picture at the end.

Think about how WinAmp does its visualizations, or how Excel or Media-Tools graph, or how this program does its visualization. Each is just deciding a different way of mapping from samples to colors and space. It's just a mapping. It's all just bits.

COMPUTER SCIENCE IDEA: It's all just bits.

Sound, pictures, and text are all just "bits." They're just information. We can map from one to the other any way we wish. We merely have to define our representation.

10.6.1 Using Lists as Structured Text for Media Representations

Lists, as we have already said, are very powerful. It's pretty easy to go from sound to lists.

RECIPE 86: Map sounds to lists

```
def soundToList(sound):
    list = []
    for s in getSamples(sound):
        list = list + [getSample(s)]
    return list

>>> list = soundToList(sound)
>>> print list[0]
6757
>>> print list[1]
6852
>>> print list[0:100]
```

```
[6757, 6852, 6678, 6371, 6084, 5879, 6066, 6600, 7104,
7588, 7643, 7710, 7737, 7214, 7435, 7827, 7749, 6888, 5052,
2793, 406, -346, 80, 1356, 2347, 1609, 266, -1933, -3518,
-4233, -5023, -5744, -7394, -9255, -10421, -10605, -9692,
-8786, -8198, -8133, -8679, -9092, -9278, -9291, -9502,
-9680, -9348, -8394, -6552, -4137, -1878, -101, 866, 1540,
2459, 3340, 4343, 4821, 4676, 4211, 3731, 4359, 5653, 7176,
8411, 8569, 8131, 7167, 6150, 5204, 3951, 2482, 818, -394,
-901, -784, -541, -764, -1342, -2491, -3569, -4255, -4971,
-5892, -7306, -8691, -9534, -9429, -8289, -6811, -5386,
-4454, -4079, -3841, -3603, -3353, -3296, -3323, -3099,
-2360]
```

Going from pictures to lists is similarly easy—we simply have to define our representation. How about mapping each pixel as its X and Y positions, then its red, green, and blue channels? We have to use double square brackets because we want these five values as sublists inside the big list.

RECIPE 87: Map pictures to lists

```
def pictureToList(picture):
    list = []
    for p in getPixels(picture):
        list = list + [[getX(p),getY(p),getRed(p),getGreen(p),
getBlue(p)]]
    return list
```

```
>>> picture = makePicture(pickAFile())
>>> piclist = pictureToList(picture)
>>> print piclist[0:5]
[[1, 1, 168, 131, 105], [1, 2, 168, 131, 105], [1, 3, 169,
132, 106], [1, 4, 169, 132, 106], [1, 5, 170, 133, 107]]
```

Going back again is also easy. We simply have to make sure that our X and Y positions are within the bounds of our canvas.

RECIPE 88: Map lists to pictures

```
def listToPicture(list):
    picture = makePicture(getMediaPath("640x480.jpg"))
    for p in list:
        if p[0] <= getWidth(picture) and p[1]
<= getHeight(picture):
            setColor(getPixel(picture,p[0],p[1]),makeColor(p[2],
p[3],p[4]))
    return picture
```

We can figure out that this will work because we can see how the mapping works both ways and then consider just the mapping from lists to pictures. The numbers don't *have* to have come from a picture. We could just as easily have mapped from weather data or stock ticker data or just about anything into a list of numbers that we then visualize. It's all bits ...

All we're really doing here is changing the encoding. We're not changing the base information at all. Different encodings offer us different capabilities.

A really smart mathematician, Kurt Gödel, used the notion of encodings to come up with one of the most brilliant proofs of the 20th century. He proved the *Incompleteness theorem*, thereby demonstrating that any powerful mathematical system cannot prove all mathematical truths. He figured out a mapping from mathematical statements of truth to numbers. This was long before we had ASCII, where such mappings are commonplace. Once these statements were numbers, he was able to show that there are numbers representing true statements that could not be derived from the mathematical system. In this way, he showed that no system of logic can prove all true statements. By changing his encoding, he gained new capabilities, and thus was able to prove something that no one knew before.

Programming Summary

General program pieces

`while`	Creates a loop. Executes the body iteratively as long as the provided logical expression is true (i.e., not zero)
`break`	Breaks a loop immediately—jumps to the end of the `for` or `while`.
`urllib`, `ftplib`	Module for using URLs or FTP access.
`random`	Module for generating random numbers or making random choices.
`os`, `sys`	Module for manipulating operating system or Python system.
`str`	Converts numbers (or other objects) to their string representations.
`float`	Converts a number or string to its floating-point equivalent representation.

String functions, functions, and pieces

`string[n]`, `string[n:m]`	Returns the character in the string at position n (`[n]`), or the substring from n to $m - 1$. Remember that these start at index 0.
`startswith`	Returns true if the string starts with the input string.
`endswith`	Returns true if the string ends with the input string.
`find`	Returns the index if the input string is found in the string; -1 otherwise.
`upper`, `lower`	Converts the whole string to the specified case.
`isalpha`, `isdigit`	Returns true if the whole string is alphabetic or numeric (digits), respectively.

replace	Takes two input substrings—replaces all instances of the first with the second in the given string.
split	Bursts a string into a list of substrings using the input string as the delimiter.

List functions and pieces

append	Appends the input to the end of the list.
remove	Removes the input from the list.
sort	Sorts the list.
reverse	Reverses the list.
count	Counts the number of times the input appears in the list.
max, min	Given a list of numbers as input, returns the maximum or minimum (respectively) value in the list.

Problems

10.1 Go to a page with a lot of text in it, like http://www.cnn.com and use your browser's menus to SAVE the file as something like mypage.html. Edit the file using JES or even an editor like Windows Notepad. Find some text in the page that you can see when you view the page, like a headline or article text. *Change it!* Instead of "protesters" rioting, make it "College students" or even "kindergarteners." Now OPEN that file in your browser. You've just rewritten the news!

10.2 Match the letter of the definition next to the appropriate phrase below. *(Yes, you will have one unused definition.)*

___ **Domain Name Server** ___ **Web Server** ___ HTTP ___ HTML
___ **Client** ___ **IP Address** ___ FTP ___ URL

(a) A computer that matches names like *www.cnn.com* to their addresses on the Internet.

(b) A protocol used to move files between computers (e.g., from your personal computer to a larger computer that acts as a Web server).

(c) A string that explains how (what protocol) and on what machine (domain name) and where on the machine (path) a particular file can be found on the Internet.

(d) A computer that offers files through HTTP.

(e) The protocol on which most of the Web is built, a very simple form aimed at rapid transmission of small bits of information.

(f) What a browser (like Internet Explorer) is when contacting a server like *yahoo.com*

(g) The tags that go into Web pages to identify parts of the page and how they should be formatted.

(h) A protocol used for transmitting electronic mail between computers.

(i) The numeric identifier of a computer on the Internet—four numbers between 0 and 255, like *120.32.189.12*

10.3 Write short essay responses to these questions.

(a) Give me one example of a task for which you would not write a program, and give me another example of a task for which you would write a program.

(b) What's the difference between an array, a matrix, and a tree? Give an example where we have used each to represent some data of interest to us.

(c) What is dot notation and when do you use it?

(d) Why is red a bad color to use for chromakey?

(e) What's the difference between a function and a method?

(f) Why is a tree a better representation than an array for files on a disk? Why do you have many directories on your disk, and not just one gigantic one?

(g) What are some advantages that vector-based graphics have over bitmap graphical representations (like JPEG, BMP, GIF)?

10.4 For each of the following, see if you can figure out the representation in terms of bits and bytes.

(a) Internet addresses are four numbers, each between 0 and 255. How many bits are in an Internet address?

(b) In the programming language Basic, lines can be numbered, each one between 0 and 65535. How many bits are needed to represent a line number?

(c) Each pixel's color has three components, red, green, and blue, each of which can be between 0 and 255. How many bits are needed to represent a pixel's color?

(d) A string in some systems can only be up to 1,024 characters. How many bits are needed to represent the length of a string?

10.5 Respond to the following Internet-related questions:

(a) What is a domain name server? What does it do?

(b) What are FTP, SMTP, and HTTP? What are they each used for?

(c) What is HyperText?

(d) What is the difference between a client and a server?

(e) How does knowing how to manipulate text help you in gathering and creating information on the Internet?

(f) What is the Internet?

(g) What is an ISP? Can you give an example of one?

10.6 You've seen code to mirror pictures in Recipe 19, and you've seen code to mirror sounds in Recipe 61. It should be pretty easy to use the same algorithm to mirror *text*. Write a function to take a string, then return the mirrored string with the front half copied over the second half.

10.7 Extend the form letter recipe to take an input of a pet's name and type, and reference the pet in the form letter. `"Your pet "+petType+","+petName+" will love our offer!"` might generate `"Your pet poodle, Fifi, will love our offer!"`.

10.8 Imagine that you have a list of the genders (as single characters) of all the students in your class, in order of their last name. The list will look something like "MFFMMMFFMFMMFFFM" where M is male and F is female. Write a function (below) percentageGenders(string) to accept a string that represents the genders. You are to count all of the M's and F's in the string, and print out the ratio (as a decimal) of the each gender. For example, if the input string were "MFFF," then the function should print something like "There are 0.25 males, 0.75 females" (*Hint:* Better multiply something by 1.0 to make sure that you get floats not integers.)

10.9 You worked late into the night on an assignment and didn't realize that you wrote a huge section of your term paper with your fingers on the wrong home keys.

Where you meant to type: "This is an unruly mob." You actually typed: "Ty8s 8s ah 7hr7o6 j9b."

Basically you swapped: 7 for U, 8 for I, 9 for O, 0 for P, U for J, I for K, O for L, H for N, and J for M. (Those were the only keystrokes you got wrong—you caught yourself before you got much further.) You also never touched the shift key, so it's only lowercase letters that you care about.

Knowing Python as you do, you decide to write a quick program to fix your text. Write a function fixItUp that takes a string as input and returns a string with the characters put the way that they ought to have been.

*10.10 Write a function doGraphics that will take a list as input. The function doGraphics will start by creating a canvas from the 640x480.jpg file in the MediaSources folder. You will draw on the canvas according to the commands in the input list. Each element of the list will be a string. There will be two kinds of strings in the list:

- "b 200 120" means to draw a black dot at x position 200 and y position 120–(200,120). The numbers, of course, will change, but the command will always be a "b". You can assume that the input numbers will always have three digits.
- "l 000 010 100 200" means to draw a line from position (0, 10) to position (100,200)

So an input list might look like: ["b 100 200","b 101 200","b 102 200","l 102 200 102 300"] (but have any number of elements).

To Dig Deeper

The book that I use for making my way through the Python modules is Frederik Lundh's *Python Standard Library* [27].

CHAPTER 11

Making Text for the Web

11.1 HTML: The Notation of the Web
11.2 Writing Programs to Generate HTML
11.3 Databases: A Place to Store Our Text

Chapter Learning Objectives

The media learning goals for this chapter are:

- *To gain some basic skill with HTML.*
- *To automatically generate HTML for input data, like an index page for a directory of images.*
- *To use databases to generate Web content.*

The computer science goals for this chapter are:

- *To use another number base, hexadecimal, for specifying RGB colors.*
- *To distinguish between XML and HTML.*
- *To explain what SQL is and what it has to do with relational databases.*
- *To create and use subfunctions (utility functions).*
- *To know one use for hash tables (dictionaries).*

■11.1 HTML: The Notation of the Web

The World Wide Web is mostly text, and most of the text is in the specification language *HTML* (HyperText Markup Language). HTML is based on *SGML* (Structured General Markup Language), which is a way of adding additional text to one's text to identify logical parts of the document: "This here is the title," "This here is a heading," and "This is just a plain ole paragraph." Originally, HTML (like SGML) was supposed to just identify logical parts of a document—how it *looked* was up to the browser. Documents were *expected* to look different from one browser to another. But as the Web evolved, two separate goals developed: being able to specify *lots* of logical parts (e.g., prices, part numbers, stocker ticker codes, temperatures), and being able to control formatting very carefully.

248

For the first goal, *XML* (eXtensible Markup Language) evolved. This allows you to define new tags like `<partnumber>7834JK</partnumber>`. For the second goal, things like *cascading style sheets* were developed. Yet another markup language was developed *XHTML*, which is HTML in terms of XML.

For most of this chapter, we'll be introducing XHTML, but we're not going to distinguish it from the original HTML. We'll just talk about it as HTML.

We're not going to have a complete tutorial for HTML here. There are many of these available, both in print and on the Web, and many are high-quality. Enter "HTML tutorial" into your favorite search engine and take your pick. Instead, we'll talk here about some general notions of HTML, and mention the tags that you should really know.

A markup language means that text is inserted into the original text to identify the parts. In HTML, the inserted text, called *tags*, is delimited with angle brackets: less-than and greater-than signs. For example, `<p>` starts a paragraph, and `</p>` ends a paragraph.

Web pages have several parts, and the parts nest within each other. The first is a *doctype* right at the top of the page that announces the *kind* of page this is (i.e., whether the browser should try to interpret it as HTML, XHTML, CSS, or something else). Following the doctype comes a heading (`<head>...</head>`) and a body (`<body>...</body>`). The heading can contain information like the title *nested* within it—the ending of the title comes before the ending of the head. The body has many pieces nested within it, such as headings (h1 starts and ends before the body ends) and paragraphs. All of the body and head nests within an `<html>...</html>` set of tags. Figure 11.1 shows a simple Web page's source, and Figure 11.2 shows how the page appears in Internet Explorer. Try this yourself. Simply type it in with JES, save it with an `html` file suffix, and then open it in a Web browser. The only difference between this file and any Web page is that this file lives on your disk. If it were on a Web server, it would be a Web page.

COMMON BUG: Browsers are forgiving but usually wrong.

Browsers are very forgiving. If you forget the DOCTYPE or make mistakes in the HTML, a browser will literally guess at what you meant and then try to show it. Murphy's Law, though, says that it will guess *wrong*. If you want your Web page to look just the way you want, get the HTML right.

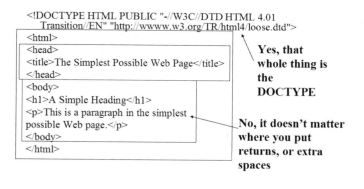

```
<!DOCTYPE HTML PUBLIC "-//W3C//DTD HTML 4.01
   Transition//EN" "http://wwww.w3.org/TR/html4/loose.dtd">
<html>
<head>
<title>The Simplest Possible Web Page</title>
</head>
<body>
<h1>A Simple Heading</h1>
<p>This is a paragraph in the simplest
possible Web page.</p>
</body>
</html>
```

Yes, that whole thing is the DOCTYPE

No, it doesn't matter where you put returns, or extra spaces

FIGURE 11.1: Simple HTML page source.

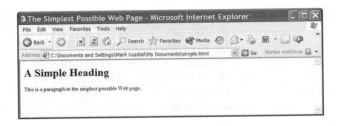

FIGURE 11.2: Simple HTML page open in Internet Explorer.

Here are some of the tags that you should know well:

■ The <body> tag can take parameters to set the background, text, and link colors. These colors can be simple color names like "red" or "green," or they can be specific RGB colors.

You specify colors in ***hexadecimal***. Hexadecimal is a number system, whereas the decimal number system is base 10, hexadecimal is base 16. The decimal numbers 1 to 20 translate to hexadecimal 1, 2, 3, 4, 5, 6, 7, 8, 9, A, B, C, D, E, F, 10, 11, 12, 13, and 14. Think of hexadecimal "14" and one 16 plus 4, to give 20.

The advantage of hexadecimal is that each digit corresponds to four bits. Two hexadecimal digits correspond to a byte. Thus, the three bytes of RGB colors are six hexadecimal digits, in RGB order. Hexadecimal FF0000 is red—255 (FF) for red, 0 for green, and 0 for blue. 0000FF is blue. 000000 is black, and FFFFFF is white.

■ Headings are specified using tags <h1>...</h1> through <h6>...</h6>. Smaller numbers are more prominent.

■ There are lots of tags for different kinds of styles: emphasis ..., italics <i>...</i>, boldface ..., bigger <big>...</big> and smaller <small>...</small> fonts, typewriter font <tt>...</tt>, preformatted text <pre>...</pre>, block quotes <blockquote>...</blockquote>, and subscripts _{...} and superscripts ^{...} (Figure 11.3). You can also control things like font and color using the <font>...</font> tags.

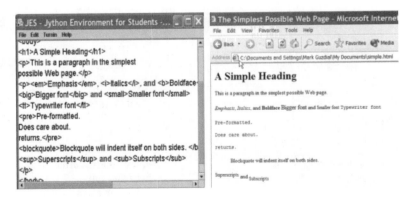

FIGURE 11.3: HTML styles.

```
<!DOCTYPE HTML PUBLIC "-
  //W3C//DTD HTML 4.01
  Transition//EN"
  "http://wwww.w3.org/TR/html4/loose.d
  td">
<html>
<head>
<title>The Simplest Possible Web
    Page</title>
</head>
<body>
<h1>A Simple Heading</h1>
<p>This is a paragraph in the simplest
    <br /> possible Web page.</p>
<image src="mediasources/flower1.jpg" />
</body>
</html>
```

FIGURE 11.4: Inserting an image into an HTML page.

■ You can insert breaks without new paragraphs using `<br />`.

■ You use the `<image src="image.jpg"/>` tag to insert images (Figure 11.4). The `image` tag takes an image as an `src=` parameter. What comes after that is an image specification, in one of several forms.

    ■ If it's just a filename (like `"flower1.jpg"`), then it's assumed to be an image in the same directory as the HTML file referencing it.

    ■ If it's a path, it's assumed to be a path *from the same directory as the HTML page* to that image. So if I had an HTML page in `"My Documents"` that referenced an image in my `mediasources` directory, I might have a reference to `"mediasources/flower1.jpg"`. You can use UNIX conventions here (e.g., `".."` references the parent directory, so `"../images/flower1.jpg"` would say to go to the parent directory, then down to `images` to grab image `flower1.jpg`).

    ■ It can also be a complete URL—you can reference images entirely on other servers.

You can also manipulate the width and height of images with options to the image tag (e.g., `<image height="100" src="flower.jpg">` to limit the height to 100 pixels) and adjust the width so that the picture keeps its height: width ratio. Using the option `alt` you can specify text to be displayed if the image can't be displayed (e.g., for audio or Braille browsers).

■ You use the *anchor tag* `<a href="someplace.html">anchor text</a>` to create links from anchor text somewhere else. In this example, `someplace.html` is the *target* for the anchor—it's where you go when you click on the *anchor*. The *anchor* is what you click on. It can be text, like `anchor text`, or it can be an image. As seen in Figure 11.5, the target can also be a complete URL.

Note, too, in Figure 11.5 that line breaks in the source file don't show up in the browser. We can even have line breaks in the middle of an anchor tag, and they don't affect the view. The breaks that *matter* (i.e., that show up in the browser view) are generated by tags like `<br />` and `<p>`.

```
<body>
<h1>A Simple Heading</h1>
<p>This is a paragraph in the simplest
<br />
possible Web page.</p>
<image src="mediasources/flower1.jpg"
    alt="A Flower" />
<p>Here is a link to
<a href=
"http://www.cc.gatech.edu/~mark.guzdial/"
    >Mark Guzdial</a>

</body>
```

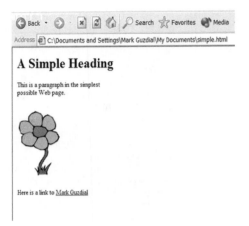

FIGURE 11.5: An HTML page with a link in it.

```
<table border="5">
<tr><td>Column
   1</td><td>Column
   2</td></tr>
<tr><td>Element in column
   1</td><td>Element in
   column 2</td></tr>
</table>
```

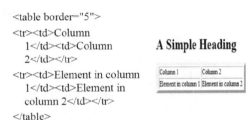

FIGURE 11.6: Inserting a table into an HTML page.

■ You create bullet lists (*unordered lists*) and numbered lists (*ordered lists*) using the `<ul>...</ul>` and `<ol>...</ol>` tags, respectively. Individual items are specified using tags `<li>...</li>`.

■ Tables are created using `<table>...</table>` tags. Tables are constructed out of table rows using `<tr>...</tr>` tags, and each row consists of several table data items identified with `<td>...</td>` tags (Figure 11.6). Table rows next within tables, and table data items next within table rows.

There is *lots* more to HTML, such as frames (having subwindows within one's HTML page window), divisions (`<div />`), horizontal rules (`<hr />`), and applets and JavaScript. The items listed above are the most critical for understanding the rest of this chapter.

■11.2 Writing Programs to Generate HTML

HTML itself is not a programming language. HTML can't specify loops, conditionals, variables, data types, or anything else we've learned about specifying process. HTML is used to describe structure, not process.

That said, we can easily write programs to generate HTML. Python's multiple ways of quoting strings come in *really* handy here!

RECIPE 89: Generating a simple HTML page

```
def makePage():
    file=open("generated.html","wt")
    file.write("""<!DOCTYPE HTML PUBLIC "-//W3C//DTD HTML 4.01
Transition//EN" "http://wwww.w3.org/TR/html4/loose.dtd">

<html>
<head> <title>The Simplest Possible Web Page</title>
</head>
<body>
<h1>A Simple Heading</h1>
<p>Some simple text.</p>
</body>
</html>""")
    file.close()
```

This works, but it's really boring. Why would you write a program to write what you can do with a text editor? You write programs for replicability, communicating process, and tailoring. Let's make a home page creator.

RECIPE 90: Initial home page creator

```
def makeHomePage(name, interest):
    file=open("homepage.html","wt")
    file.write("""<!DOCTYPE HTML PUBLIC "-//W3C//DTD HTML 4.01
Transition//EN" "http://wwww.w3.org/TR/html4/loose.dtd">
<html>
<head>
<title>"""+name+"""'s Home Page</title>
</head>
<body>
<h1>Welcome to """+name+"""'s Home Page</h1>
<p>Hi!  I am """+name+""".  This is my home page!
I am interested in """+interest+"""</p>
</body>
</html>""")
    file.close()
```

Thus, executing makeHomePage("Mark","reading") will create:

```
<!DOCTYPE HTML PUBLIC "-//W3C//DTD HTML 4.01
Transition//EN" "http://wwww.w3.org/TR/html4/loose.dtd">
<html>
<head>
<title>Mark's Home Page</title>
</head>
<body>
<h1>Welcome to Mark's Home Page</h1>
```

```
<p>Hi!  I am Mark.  This is my home page!
I am interested in reading</p>
</body>
</html>
```

DEBUGGING TIP: Write the HTML first

Programs to generate HTML can be confusing. Before you start trying to write one, write the HTML. Make up a sample of what you want the HTML to look like. Make sure that it works in your browser. *Then* write the Python function that generates that kind of HTML.

Modifying this program is painful, though. There is so much detail in the HTML, and all that quoting is hard to get around. We're better off using *subfunctions* to break up the program into pieces that are easier to manipulate. This is, again, an example of using **procedural abstraction**. Here's a version of the recipe where we confine the parts that we'll change most often to the top.

RECIPE 91: Improved home page creator

```
def makeHomePage(name, interest):
    file=open("homepage.html","wt")
    file.write(doctype())
    file.write(title(name+"'s Home Page"))
    file.write(body("""
<h1>Welcome to """+name+"""'s Home Page</h1> <p>Hi!  I am
"""+name+""".  This is my home page! I am interested in
"""+interest+"""</p>"""))
    file.close()

def doctype():
    return '<!DOCTYPE HTML PUBLIC "-//W3C//DTD HTML 4.01
Transition//EN" "http://wwww.w3.org/TR/html4/loose.dtd">'

def title(titlestring):
    return "<html><head><title>"+titlestring+"</title></head>"

def body(bodystring):
    return "<body>"+bodystring+"</body></html>"
```

We can grab content for our Web pages from anywhere we want. Here is a recipe that can pull information out of a directory provided as input and generates an index page of those images (Figure 11.7). We're not going to list the doctype() and other *utility functions* here—we'll just focus on the part we care about. And that is how we should think about it—just the part we care about; we write doctype() once, then forget about it!

```
<!DOCTYPE HTML PUBLIC "-//W3C//DTD
    HTML 4.01 Transition//EN"
    "http://wwww.w3.org/TR/html4/loose.dtd"
    ><html><head><title>Samples from
    C:\Documents and Settings\Mark
    Guzdial\My
    Documents\mediasources\pics</title></hea
    d><body><h1>Samples from
    C:\Documents and Settings\Mark
    Guzdial\My Documents\mediasources\pics
    </h1>
<p>Filename: students1.jpg<image
    src="students1.jpg" height="100" /></p>
<p>Filename: students2.jpg<image
    src="students2.jpg" height="100" /></p>
<p>Filename: students5.jpg<image
    src="students5.jpg" height="100" /></p>
<p>Filename: students6.jpg<image
    src="students6.jpg" height="100" /></p>
<p>Filename: students7.jpg<image
    src="students7.jpg" height="100" /></p>
<p>Filename: students8.jpg<image
    src="students8.jpg" height="100" /></p>
```

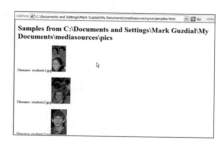

FIGURE 11.7: Creating a thumbnail page.

RECIPE 92: Generate a thumbnail page

```
import os

def makeSamplePage(directory):
  samplesfile=open(directory+"//samples.html","wt")
  samplesfile.write(doctype())
  samplesfile.write(title("Samples from "+directory))
  # Now, let's make up the string that will be the body.
  samples="<h1>Samples from "+directory+" </h1>"
  for file in os.listdir(directory):
    if file.endswith(".jpg"):
      samples=samples+"<p>Filename: "+file
      samples=samples+'<image src="'+file+'" height="100"
/></p>'
  samplesfile.write(body(samples))
  samplesfile.close()
```

We can pull information off the Web to create new Web content. That's how sites like *Google News* work.[1] Here's a version of our home page creator that gathers the temperature live (designed especially for Atlanta).

RECIPE 93: Generate home page with temperature information

```
import urllib

def makeHomePage(name, interest):
  file=open("homepage.html","wt")
  file.write(doctype())
```

---

[1] http://news.google.com

```
  file.write(title(name+"'s Home Page"))
  file.write(body("""
<h1>Welcome to """+name+"""'s Home Page</h1> <p>Hi!  I am
"""+name+""".  This is my home page! I am interested in
"""+interest+"""</p> <p>Right here and right now it's
"""+findTemperatureLive()+""" degrees. (If you're in
the North, nyah-nyah!)"""))
  file.close()

def findTemperatureLive():
  # Get the weather page
  import urllib
  connection=urllib.urlopen("http://www.ajc.com/weather")
  weather = connection.read()
  connection.close()
  #weatherFile = getMediaPath("ajc-weather.html")
  #file = open(weatherFile,"rt")
  #weather = file.read()
  #file.close()
  # Find the Temperature
  curloc = weather.find("Currently")
  if curloc <> -1:
    # Now, find the "<b>&deg;" following the temp
    temploc = weather.find("<b>&deg;",curloc)
    tempstart = weather.rfind(">",0,temploc)
    return weather[tempstart+1:temploc]
  if curloc == -1:
    return "They must have changed the page format -- can't
find the temp"
```

Remember the random sentence generator? We can add that, too.

RECIPE 94: Home page generator with random sentences

```
import urllib
import random

def makeHomePage(name, interest):
  file=open("homepage.html","wt")
  file.write(doctype())
  file.write(title(name+"'s Home Page"))
  file.write(body("""
<h1>Welcome to """+name+"""'s Home Page</h1> <p>Hi!  I am
"""+name+""".  This is my home page! I am interested in
"""+interest+"""</p> <p>Right here and right now it's
"""+findTemperatureLive()+""" degrees. (If you're in the
North, nyah-nyah!).</p> <p>Random thought for the day:
"""+sentence()+"""</p>"""))
  file.close()
```

```
def sentence():
  nouns = ["Mark", "Adam", "Angela", "Larry", "Jose",
"Matt", "Jim"]
  verbs = ["runs", "skips", "sings", "leaps", "jumps",
"climbs", "argues", "giggles"]
  phrases = ["in a tree", "over a log", "very loudly",
"around the bush", "while reading the news"]
  phrases = phrases + ["very badly", "while skipping",
"instead of grading", "while typing on the CoWeb."]
  return random.choice(nouns)+" "+random.choice(verbs)+"
"+random.choice(phrases)+"."

def findTemperatureLive():
  # Get the weather page
  import urllib
  connection=urllib.urlopen("http://www.ajc.com/weather")
  weather = connection.read()
  connection.close()
  #weatherFile = getMediaPath("ajc-weather.html")
  #file = open(weatherFile,"rt")
  #weather = file.read()
  #file.close()
  # Find the Temperature
  curloc = weather.find("Currently")
  if curloc <> -1:
    # Now, find the "<b>&deg;" following the temp
    temploc = weather.find("<b>&deg;",curloc)
    tempstart = weather.rfind(">",0,temploc)
    return weather[tempstart+1:temploc]
  if curloc == -1:
    return "They must have changed the page format -- can't
find the temp"
```

How it works: Let's walk through the whole large example.

■ We are going to need both urllib and random in this function, so we import both of them at the top of our Program Area.

■ Our main function is makeHomePage. We call it with a name and an interest to mention.

■ At the top of makeHomePage, we open the HTML file we're writing, then write out the doctype using the utility function (it's not listed here, but would have to be in the Program Area). We write out the title (using the title function) with the input name inserted, and then the body (using the body function).

■ The input to the body function is a long string, whose construction is where we're actually invoking findTemperatureLive() and sentence(). We use triple-quoting so that we can put in returns wherever we want them. We write out the name and the interest by concatenating them into the middle of the HTML string.

■ We call `findTemperatureLive()` midway through the body string. Note that this version is somewhat different from the one we built last chapter. Here we `return` the result strings rather than simply use `print`. By returning them, we can use the result and insert it into our HTML body string.

■ We call `sentence()` as our `"Random thought for the day:"`. Again, `sentence()` is slightly different in that it is using `return` instead of `print` so that we can use the output in our HTML body string.

■ Finally, back at `makeHomePage`, we close the HTML file, and we're done.

Where do you think large Web sites get all their information? There are *so* many pages in those Web sites. Where do they get it all? Where do they store it all?

■11.3　Databases: A Place to Store Our Text

Large Web sites use **databases** to store their text and other information in. Sites like EBay.com, Amazon.com, and CNN.com have large databases with lots of information in them. The pages at these sites aren't generated by somebody typing in information. Instead, programs walk over the database gathering all the information and generating HTML pages. They may do this on a timed basis, to keep updating the page. (See the "last generated" information at CNN.com or Google News.)

Why databases rather than simple text files? There are four reasons:

■ Databases are fast. Databases store *indices* that keep track of where key information (like last name or ID number) is in a file, so that you can find "Guzdial" right away. Files are indexed on filename, but not on the content *in* the file.

■ Databases are standardized. You can access the Microsoft Access, Informix, Oracle, Sybase, and MySQL databases from any number of tools or languages.

■ Databases can be **distributed**. A great many users, on different computers across a network, can put information into a database and pull information out of it.

■ Databases store **relations**. When we used lists to represent pixels, we had to keep in our heads which number meant what. Databases store names for *fields* of data. When a database knows which fields are important (e.g., which ones you're going to search on most often), it can be indexed on those fields.

Python has built-in support for several different databases, and provides a general support for any kind of database called anydbm (Figure 11.8). **Keys** go in square brackets, and those are the fields that you get the fastest access through. Both keys and values can only be strings using anydbm. Here's an example of retrieving information from anydbm.

```
>>> db = anydbm.open("mydbm","r")
>>> print db.keys()
['barney', 'fred']
```

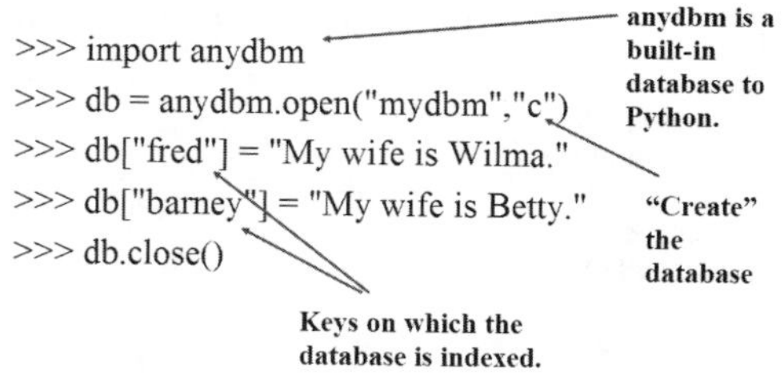

```
>>> import anydbm
>>> db = anydbm.open("mydbm","c")
>>> db["fred"] = "My wife is Wilma."
>>> db["barney"] = "My wife is Betty."
>>> db.close()
```

anydbm is a built-in database to Python.

"Create" the database

Keys on which the database is indexed.

FIGURE 11.8: Using the simple database.

```
>>> print db['barney']
My wife is Betty.
>>> for k in db.keys():
...        print db[k]
...
My wife is Betty.
My wife is Wilma.
>>> db.close()
```

Another Python database, shelve, allows you to put strings, lists, numbers, or just about anything in the value.

```
>>> import shelve
>>> db=shelve.open("myshelf","c")
>>> db["one"]=["This is",["a","list"]]
>>> db["two"]=12
>>> db.close()
>>> db=shelve.open("myshelf","r")
>>> print db.keys()
['two', 'one']
>>> print db['one']
['This is', ['a', 'list']]
>>> print db['two']
12
```

11.3.1 Relational Databases

Most modern databases are relational databases. In relational databases, information is stored in tables (Figure 11.9). Columns in a relational table are named, and rows of data are assumed to be related.

Complex relationships are stored across multiple tables. Let's say that you have a bunch of pictures of students, and you want to keep track of which students are in which pictures—where there is more than one student in a given picture. You might record a structure like that in a collection of tables for recording students and student IDs, pictures and picture IDs, then the mapping between studentIDs and pictureIDs, as in Figure 11.10.

How would you use tables like the one in Figure 11.10 to figure out which picture Brittany is in? You start up by looking up Brittany's ID in the student table, then look up the picture ID in the picture-student table, then look up the

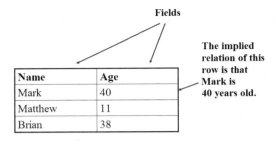

FIGURE 11.9: An example relational table.

Name	Age
Mark	40
Matthew	11
Brian	38

Picture	PictureID
Class1.jpg	P1
Class2.jpg	P2

StudentName	StudentID
Katie	S1
Brittany	S2
Carrie	S3

PictureID	StudentID
P1	S1
P1	S2
P2	S3

FIGURE 11.10: Representing more complex relationships across multiple tables.

picture name in the picture table, to result in Class1.jpg. How about figuring out who's in that picture? You look up the ID in the picture table, then look up which student IDs are related to that picture ID, and then look up the student names.

This use of multiple tables to answer a *query* (a request for information from a database) is called a *join*. Database joins work best if the tables are kept simple, with only a single relation per row.

We can use a structure called a *hash table* or *dictionary* (other languages sometimes call them *associative arrays*) to create rows for database relational tables using shelve. Hash tables allow us to relate keys and values, like databases, but only in memory.

```
>>> row='StudentName':'Katie','StudentID':'S1'
>>> print row
{'StudentID': 'S1', 'StudentName': 'Katie'}
>>> print row['StudentID']
S1
>>> print row['StudentName']
Attempt to access a key that is not in a dictionary.
>>> print row['StudentName']
Katie
```

Besides defining all of the hash table at once, we can fill in the hash table in pieces.

```
>>> picturerow = {}
>>> picturerow['Picture']='Class1.jpg'
```

```
>>> picturerow['PictureID']='P1'
>>> print picturerow
{'Picture': 'Class1.jpg', 'PictureID': 'P1'}
>>> print picturerow['Picture']
Class1.jpg
```

Now we can create a relational database by storing each table in a separate shelve database and representing each row as a hash table.

RECIPE 95: Creating a relational database using shelve

```
import shelve
def createDatabases():
    #Create Student Database
    students=shelve.open("students.db","c")
    row = {'StudentName':'Katie','StudentID':'S1'}
    students['S1']=row
    row = {'StudentName':'Brittany','StudentID':'S2'}
    students['S2']=row
    row = {'StudentName':'Carrie','StudentID':'S3'}
    students['S3']=row
    students.close()
    #Create Picture Database
    pictures=shelve.open("pictures.db","c")
    row = {'Picture':'Class1.jpg','PictureID':'P1'}
    pictures['P1']=row
    row = {'Picture':'Class2.jpg','PictureID':'P2'}
    pictures['P2']=row
    pictures.close()
    #Create Picture-Student Database
    pictures=shelve.open("pict-students.db","c")
    row = {'PictureID':'P1','StudentID':'S1'}
    pictures['P1S1']=row
    row = {'PictureID':'P1','StudentID':'S2'}
    pictures['P1S2']=row
    row = {'PictureID':'P2','StudentID':'S3'}
    pictures['P2S3']=row
    pictures.close()
```

How it works: The function createDatabases actually creates three different database tables.

■ The first one is students.db. We create dictionaries (hash tables) representing Katie, who is "S1," then store that in the database students using the student ID "S1" as the index. We do the same for Brittany and Carrie—it's okay to use the same row variable for each of them, because we simply create the hash table and then store it to the database.

■ Next we create the pictures.db database. We set up the relationship between the "Picture" Class1.jpg and its ID "P1." Then we store that in the pictures database. We repeat the process for the picture Class2.jpg. Could we have used a variable database for each database? Since we only open one at a time, then close it before the next one, we certainly could have. But it would have been less readable.

■ Finally, we open and fill the pict-students.db database. We create rows relating the picture IDs to the student IDs, store them in the database, then close the database.

Using the databases we just created, we can do a *join*. Obviously, the idea is that we would be doing this lookup sometime after creating the database, and maybe after adding lots more entries to it. (If we only had two pictures and three students in the database, this would be a pretty silly exercise in programming.) We have to loop through the data to find the values we need to match across databases.

RECIPE 96: Doing a join with our shelve database

```
def whoInClass1():
  # Get the pictureID
  pictures=shelve.open("pictures.db","r")
  for key in pictures.keys():
    row = pictures[key]
    if row['Picture'] == 'Class1.jpg':
      id = row['PictureID']
  pictures.close()
  # Get the students' IDs
  studentslist=[]
  pictures=shelve.open("pict-students.db","c")
  for key in pictures.keys():
    row = pictures[key]
    if row['PictureID']==id:
      studentslist.append(row['StudentID'])
  pictures.close()
  print "We're looking for:",studentslist
  # Get the students' names
  students = shelve.open("students.db","r")
  for key in students.keys():
    row = students[key]
    if row['StudentID'] in studentslist:
      print row['StudentName'],"is in the picture"
  students.close()
```

How it works: Each of the parts of the join requires a different loop through our database.

■ First, we open pictures.db and name it pictures. We loop through all the keys, getting each row (hash table), and checking if the 'Picture' entry is Class1.jpg. When we find it, we store the picture ID in id. We close the database because we're done with it.

■ Next, we open `pict-students.db` in `pictures` (it's okay to reuse the name). We know that there may be more than one student in a picture, so we create a list to store all the student IDs that we find, `studentslist`. For each key in `pictures`, we look for `'PictureID'` entries in the hash table that match our `id`. When we find one, we append the `'StudentID'` part of the hash table onto our `studentslist`.

■ Finally, we open the `students.db` database in `students`. We loop through all the `keys` and get the hash table `row`. We use a neat feature of lists that we haven't seen previously: We can ask whether a string is `in` the list `studentslist`. If the given `'StudentID'` is one of those that we're looking for (in `studentslist`), then we print the corresponding `'StudentName'` from the `row` hash table. Finally, we close the `students` database to clean up.

Running this looks like this:

```
>>> whoInClass1()
We're looking for: ['S2', 'S1']
Brittany is in the picture
Katie is in the picture
```

11.3.2 Working with SQL

Real databases don't make you do loops to do joins. Instead, you typically use **SQL (Structured Query Language)** to manipulate and query databases. There are actually several languages in the SQL database language family, but we're not going to make distinctions here. SQL is a large and complex programming language, and we're not going to even attempt to go over all of it. But we are going to touch on enough of it to give you a sense of what SQL is like and how it's used.

SQL can be used with many different databases, including Microsoft Access. Python can talk to virtually all of them in the way that we'll be using it here. There are also freely available databases like **MySQL** that use SQL and can be controlled from Python. If you want to play with the examples we'll be doing here, you can install *MySQL* from `http://www.mysql.com` into JES. You need to set up MySQL, and you need to download the *JAR file* that allows Java to access MySQL and put that in your `jython Lib` folder.

To manipulate a MySQL database from JES, you need to create a *connection* that will provide you with a *cursor* to manipulate via SQL. I use MySQL from JES with a function like this, so that I can execute `con = getConnection()`.

RECIPE 97: Getting a MySQL connection from Jython
I find all these details hard to remember, so I hide them in a function and just say `con = getConnection()` with this in my Program Area:

```
com.ziclix.python.sql import zxJDBC def getConnection():
    db =zxJDBC.connect("jdbc:mysql://localhost/test", "root",
None, "com.mysql.jdbc.Driver")
    con = db.cursor()
    return con
```

To execute SQL commands from here, we use an `execute` method on the connection like this:

```
con.execute("create table Person (name VARCHAR(50),
age INT)")
```

Here's a very brief taste of SQL:

- To create a table in SQL, we use `create table tablename (columnname datatype,...)`. So in the example above, we're creating *Person* table with two columns: a name with a variable number of characters up to 50, and an integer age. Other datatypes include numeric, float, date, time, year, and text.

- We insert data into SQL using `insert into tablename values (column-value1, columnvalue2,...)`. Here's where our multiple kinds of quotes come in handy.

```
con.execute('insert into Person values ("Mark",40)')
```

- Think about selecting data in a database as literally selecting, as you would in a word-processor or a spreadsheet, the rows that you want in the table. Some examples of selection commands in SQL are:

```
Select * from Person
Select name,age from Person
Select * from Person where age>40
Select name,age from Person where age>40
```

We can do all of this from Python. Our connection has an ***instance variable*** (like a method, but known only to objects of that type), `rowcount`, that tells you the number of rows selected. The method `fetchone()` gives you the next selected row, as a ***tuple*** (think of this as a special kind of list—we can use it just like a list for most purposes).

```
>>> con.execute("select name,age from Person")
>>> print con.rowcount
3
>>> print con.fetchone()
('Mark', 40)
>>> print con.fetchone()
('Barb', 41)
>>> print con.fetchone()
('Brian', 36)
```

We can also select using a condition.

RECIPE 98: Selecting and showing data with a conditional select

```
def showSomePersons(con, condition):
    con.execute("select name, age from Person "+condition)
    for i in range(0,con.rowcount):
        results=con.fetchone()
        print results[0]+" is "+str(results[1])+" years old"
```

How it works: The function showSomePersons takes the input of a database connection con and a condition, which is meant to be a string containing an SQL where clause. We then ask the connection to execute a select SQL command. We concatenate the condition onto the end of our select command. We then have a loop for each of the rows returned from the selection (using con.rowcount to get that number of rows). We use fetchone to get each response and print it. Note the use of normal list indexing on the returned tuple.

Here's an example of using showSomePersons:

```
>>> showSomePersons(con,"where age >= 40")
Mark is 40 years old
Barb is 41 years old
```

We can now think about doing one of our joins using a conditional select. The next code snippet says "Return a picture and student name, from these three tables, where the student name is 'Brittany', where the students' ID is the same as the student ID in the student-picture IDs table, and the picture ID from the IDs table is the same as the ID in the picture table."

```
Select
    p.picture,
    s.studentName
From
    Students as s,
    IDs as i,
    Pictures as p
Where
    (s.studentName="Brittany") and
    (s.studentID=i.studentID) and
    (i.pictureID=p.pictureID)
```

11.3.3 Using a Database to Build Web Pages

Now let's get back to our Web page creator. We can store information in our database, retrieve it, then put it in our Web page—just like Amazon, CNN, and eBay.

```
>>> import anydbm
>>> db=anydbm.open("news","c")
>>> db["headline"]="Katie turns 8!"
>>> db["story"]="""My daughter, Katie, turned 8 years old
yesterday. She had a great birthday. Grandma and Grandpa
came over. The previous weekend, she had three of her
friends over for a sleepover then a morning run to
Dave and Buster's."""
>>> db.close()
```

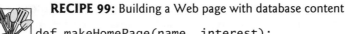

RECIPE 99: Building a Web page with database content

```
def makeHomePage(name, interest):
    file=open("homepage.html","wt")
    file.write(doctype())
    file.write(title(name+"'s Home Page"))
    # Import the database content
    db=anydbm.open("news","r")
    file.write(body("""
<h1>Welcome to """+name+"""'s Home Page</h1> <p>Hi!  I am
"""+name+""".  This is my home page! I am interested in
"""+interest+"""
</p> <p>Right here and right now it's
"""+findTemperatureLive()+""" degrees. (If you're in the
North, nyah-nyah!).</p>
<p>Random thought for the day:
"""+sentence()+"""</p>
<h2>Latest news:
"""+db["headline"]+"""</h2>
<p>"""+db["story"]+"</p>"))
    file.close()
    db.close()

#Rest, like findTemperatureLive(), from previous examples
```

Now we can think about how a large Web site like CNN.com works. Reporters enter stories into a database that are distributed all over the world. Editors (also distributed or all in one place) retrieve stories from the database, update them, then store them back. On a regular basis (perhaps more often when a hot story emerges) the Web page generation program runs, gathers up the stories, and generates the HTML. "POOF! You have a large Web site!" Databases are really critical to how large Web sites run.

Problems

11.1 Your father calls you. "My tech support people are saying that the company Web site is down because the database program is broken. What does the database have to do with our company Web site?" You explain to him how databases can be integral to running large Web sites. Explain both (a) how the Web site comes to be authored through the database, and (b) how the HTML is actually created.

11.2 You have a new computer that seems to connect to the Internet, but when you try to go to http://www.cnn.com you get a "Server Not Found" error. You call tech support, and they tell you to try to go to http://64.236.24.20. That works. Now both you and the tech know what's wrong with your computer's settings. What isn't working properly, since you can get to a site via the Internet but can't get the domain name www.cnn.com to be recognized?

11.3   Given a folder with images in it, create an index HTML page with links to each image. Write a function that takes a string which is the path to a directory. You will create a page in the folder named `index.html` that should be an HTML page containing a link to every JPEG file in the directory.

You will also generate a thumbnail (half the size) copy of each image. Use `makeEmptyPicture` to create a blank picture of the right size, then scale down the original picture into the blank picture. Name the new image "half-" + the original file name (e.g., if the original file name was "fred.jpg", save the half-size image as "half-fred.jpg"). The anchor in the link to each full-size picture should be the half-size image.

11.4   You're thinking about adding something to your HTML home page generator that will make random, relevant comments about the weather depending on the temperature.

- If it's going to be less than 32, you want to insert either "Watch out for ice!" or "Is it going to snow?"
- If it's going to be between 32 and 50, you want to insert either "I can't wait for winter to be over!" or "Come on, Spring!"
- If it's over 50 but less than 80, you want to insert either "It's getting warmer!" or "Light jacket weather."
- If it's over 80, you want to insert either "FINALLY! Summer!" or "Time to go swimming!"

Write a function named `weathercomment` that will take a temperature as input and return one of the phrases randomly. In other words, you want to use the temperature to decide which are the relevant phrases, then pick one randomly from there.

To Dig Deeper

There are several good books on using Python and Jython for Web development and programming. I particularly recommend the books by Gupta [17] and Hightower [22] for their discussions of the use of Java in database contexts.

PART 5

MOVIES

## CHAPTER 12

Creating and Modifying Movies

12.1 Generating Animations
12.2 Working with Video Source

Chapter Learning Objectives

The media learning goals for this chapter are:

- *To understand how a series of still images can be perceived as motion.*
- *To create animations with different motions and effects.*
- *To use video sources for animations and processing.*

The computer science goals for this chapter are:

- *To use subfunctions to make coding easier.*

Movies (video) are actually very simple to manipulate. They are arrays of pictures (*frames*). You need to be concerned with the *frame rate* (the number of frames per second), but it's mostly just things you've seen before. We're going to use the term *movies* to refer generically to *animations* (motion generated entirely by graphical drawings) and *video* (motion generated by some kind of photographic process).

What makes movies work is a feature of our visual system called *persistence of vision*. We do not see every change that happens in the world. For example, you don't typically see your eyes blink, even though they do it quite often (typically 20 times a minute). But each time that we blink we don't panic and think, "Where'd the world go?" Instead, our eyes retain an image for a short time and keep telling the brain that the same image is there.

If we see one *related* picture after another fast enough, our eye retains the image and our brain sees continuous motion. "Fast enough" is about 16 frames per second—we see the 16 related pictures within a second, we think continuous motion. If the pictures aren't related, our brain reports a *montage*, a collection of disparate (though perhaps thematically connected) images. We refer to this 16 *frames per second* (*fps*) as the lower bound for the sensation of motion.

Early silent pictures were 16 fps. Motion pictures standardized on 24 fps to make sound smoother—16 frames per second didn't provide enough physical space on the film to encode enough sound data. (Ever wonder why silent pictures often look fast and jerky? Think about what happens when you scale up a picture or sound—that's exactly what happens if you play a 16 fps movie at 24 fps.) Digital video (e.g., video cameras) captures at 30 fps. How high is useful? There are some U.S. Air Force experiments suggesting that pilots can recognize a blurb of light in the shape of an aircraft (and figure out what kind it is) in 1/200 of a second. Video game players say that they can discern a difference between 30 fps video and 60 fps video.

Movies are challenging to work with because of the amount and speed of the data involved. ***Real-time processing*** of video (e.g., doing some modification to each frame as it comes in or goes out) is hard because whatever processing you do has to fit into 1/30 of a second. Let's do the math for how many bytes are needed to record video:

■ One second of 640 × 480 frame size images at 30 fps means 30(*frames*) * 640 * 480(*pixels*) = 9,216,000 pixels.

■ At 24-bit color (one byte for each of R, G, and B), that's 27,648,000 bytes, or 27 megabytes *per second*.

■ For a 90-minute feature film, that's 90 * 60 * 27,648,000 = 149,299,200,000 bytes—149 gigabytes.

Digital movies are almost always stored in a compressed format. A DVD only stores 6.47 gigabytes, so even on a DVD the movie is compressed. Movie format standards like *MPEG*, *QuickTime*, and *AVI* are all compressed movie formats. They don't record every frame—they record *key frames* and then record the differences between one frame and the next. The *JMV* format is slightly different—it's a file of JPEG images, so every frame is there, but every frame is compressed.

Movies can use some different compression techniques than pictures or sounds. Think about watching someone walk across a frame of a camera. Between two successive frames, only a little bit changes—where the person just was, and where they now are. If we recorded only those differences, and not all the pixels for the whole frame, then we save a lot of space.

An MPEG movie is really just an MPEG image sequence merged with an MPEG (like MP3) audio file. We're going to follow that lead and *not* deal with sound here. The tools described in the next section *can* create movies with sound, but the real trick of processing movies is handling all the images. That's what we're going to focus on here.

■12.1 Generating Animations

To make movies, we're going to create a series of JPEG frames and then reassemble them. There is a tool on the CD called *MovieMaker* that can take a series of JPEG images and turn them into a QuickTime movie (Figure 12.1). The MediaTools application on the CD can let you watch a movie as a

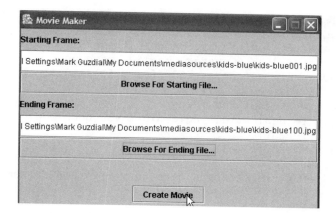

FIGURE 12.1: Running the MovieMaker application on CD.

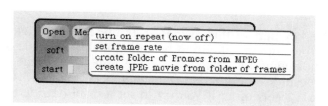

FIGURE 12.2: Create a JPEG Movie (Menu button in Video Tools) in MediaTools Application to see movie.

series of JPEG images. You can see the frames by reassembling the JPEG frames into a JPEG movie (JMV) (Figure 12.2)—you can also open and play JMV movies from the MediaTools application. You can get external tools such as Apple's QuickTime Pro (http://www.apple.com/quicktime) or ImageMagick (http://www.imagemagick.org/) which can create QuickTime, MPEG, or AVI movies from individual frames (or go in reverse and burst a movie into a bunch of frames).

Once you create a movie, you can play it from within JES using open-Movie() by using a statement like openMovie(pickAFile()) in the Command Area. openMovie() can open MPEG, AVI, or QuickTime movies, and it requires QuickTime (the free version) to be installed on your computer along with *Java for QuickTime* (which is an option on the QuickTime installer for Windows computers).

As we do our movie programs, we'll place all of our frames in a single directory, and number them so that the tools know how to reassemble them into a movie in the right order. We'll literally name our files frame01.jpg, frame02.jpg, and so on. It's important to include the leading zeroes, so that the files are in numeric order when placed in alphabetical order.

Here's our first movie-generating program, which simply moves a red rectangle down the screen (Figure 12.3).

RECIPE 100: Simple motion of a rectangle in a line

```
def movingRectangle(directory):
    for frame in range(1,100): #99 frames
        canvas = makePicture(getMediaPath("640x480.jpg"))
```

```
      if frame < 50: #Less than 50, move down
        # Generate new positions each frame number
        addRectFilled(canvas,frame*10,frame*5, 50,50,red)
      if frame >= 50: #Greater than 50, move up
        addRectFilled(canvas,(50-(frame-50))*10,(50-(frame
  -50))*5, 50,50,red)
        # Now, write out the frame
        # Have to deal with single digit vs. double digit frame
  numbers differently
      framenum=str(frame)
      if frame < 10:
        writePictureTo(canvas,directory+"//frame0"+framenum+
  ".jpg")
        if frame >= 10:
          writePictureTo(canvas,directory+"//frame"+framenum+
  ".jpg")
```

How it works: The key part of this recipe are the lines right after makePic-
ture(). We have to compute a different position for the rectangle depending
on the current frame number. The equations in the addRectFilled() functions
compute different positions for different frame numbers (Figure 12.4).

While setPixel() gets upset if you try to set a pixel outside the bounds
of the picture, the graphics functions like addText() and addRect() don't
generate errors for going beyond the borders. They'll simply *clip* the image for
the picture (show only what they can), so you can create simple code to make
animations and not worry about going out of bounds. This makes creating a
tickertape movie really pretty easy (Figure 12.5).

frame01.jpg   frame02.jpg   frame50.jpg

FIGURE 12.3: A few frames from the first
movie: Moving a rectangle down and up.

When frame==1	We're actually drawing addRectFilled(canvas,10,5,50,50,red)
When frame==2	We're actually drawing addRectFilled(canvas,20,10,50,50,red)
When frame==49	We're actually drawing addRectFilled(canvas,490,285,50,50,red)
When frame==50	Because $50 - (50 - 50) = 50$, we'er actually drawing addRectFilled(canvas,500,250,50,50,red)
When frame==50	Because $50 - (51 - 50) = 50 - 1 = 49$, we'er actually drawing addRectFilled(canvas,490,285,50,50,red)– just where we were at frame==49
When frame==99	Because $50 - (51 - 99) = 50 - 49 = 1$, we'er actually drawing addRectFilled(canvas,10,5,50,50,red)– just where we started out

FIGURE 12.4:   Tracing the computation of position.

FIGURE 12.5: From execution of tickertape function.

RECIPE 101: Generate a tickertape movie

```
def tickertape(directory,string):
  for frame in range(1,100): #99 frames
    canvas = makePicture(getMediaPath("640x480.jpg"))
    #Start at right, and move left
    addText(canvas,600-(frame*10),100,string)
    # Now, write out the frame
    # Have to deal with single digit vs. double digit frame
numbers differently
    framenum=str(frame)
    if frame < 10:
      writePictureTo(canvas,directory+"//frame0"+framenum+
".jpg")
    if frame >= 10:
      writePictureTo(canvas,directory+"//frame"+framenum+
".jpg")
```

How it works: The function `tickertape` takes a directory in which the frames of the movie will be stored and a string to write out. For each of 99 frames (from 1 to 100, but not including 100), we make an empty frame from 640x480.jpg and put the string into it as text. The y position is always at 100 (same position vertically), and the x position (horizontally) is at 600-(`frame*10`). As the frame number increases, this equation gets smaller. So each frame has the string drawn closer to the left side (smaller x values) of the frame. We convert the `frame` number to a string `framenum` and use that to make a filename with the right number of leading zeroes.

Can we move more than one thing at once? Sure! Our drawing code just gets a little more complicated because we're drawing more than one thing at once. We could just move to things with linear motion like all the examples up until now, but let's try something different. Here's a recipe that uses *sine* and *cosine* to create circular motion to match our linear motion of Recipe 100 (Figure 12.6).

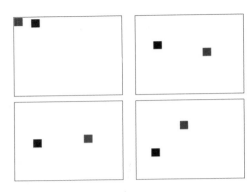

FIGURE 12.6: Moving two rectangles at once.

RECIPE 102: Move two objects at once

```
def movingRectangle2(directory):
  for frame in range(1,100): #99 frames
    canvas = makePicture(getMediaPath("640x480.jpg"))
    if frame < 50: #Less than 50, move down
      # Generate new positions each frame number
      addRectFilled(canvas,frame*10,frame*5, 50,50,red)
    if frame >= 50: #Greater than 50, move up
      addRectFilled(canvas,(50-(frame-50))*10,(50-(frame
  -50))*5, 50,50,red)
      # Let's have one just moving around
      bluex = 100+ int(10 * sin(frame))
      bluey = 4*frame+int(10* cos(frame))
      addRectFilled(canvas,bluex,bluey,50,50,blue)
      # Now, write out the frame
      # Have to deal with single digit vs. double digit frame
  numbers differently
      framenum=str(frame)
      if frame < 10:
        writePictureTo(canvas,directory+"//frame0"+framenum+
  ".jpg")
        if frame >= 10:
          writePictureTo(canvas,directory+"//frame"+framenum+
  ".jpg")
```

How it works: We know that sin and cos generate values between −1 and 1. (You remember that, right?) The x position of the blue box is set by 100 + int(10 * sin(frame)). This means that the x position of the blue box will be around 100, plus or minus 10 pixels. It'll shift left to right and right to left as the values of sin change. The y position is determined by 4 * frame + int(10 * cos(frame)). The y position, then, is always increasing (the box is falling), but plus or minus 10, so there's a slight up-and-down motion while it's falling.

We don't have to create our animations only out of things that we can do with graphics primitives. We can use the same kinds of images we've used previously through setColor(). This kind of code runs pretty slowly.

DEBUGGING TIP: printNow() to print NOW

There is a JES function called printNow() that takes a string and prints it *immediately*—it doesn't wait until the function is done to print the line to the Command Area. That's useful when you want to know what frame number a function is on. You might want to go look at the first few frames from the operating system by double-clicking on them once they are generated.

The recipe below moves Barb's head around on the screen. This function took over a minute to complete on my fastest computer.

RECIPE 103: Move Barb's head

```
def moveahead(directory):
  barbf=getMediaPath("barbara.jpg")
  barb = makePicture(barbf)
  for frame in range(1,100): #99 frames
    printNow("Frame number: "+str(frame))
    canvas = makePicture(getMediaPath("640x480.jpg"))
    # Now, do the actual copying
    sourceX = 45
    for targetX in range(frame*3,frame*3+((200-45)/2)):
      sourceY = 25
      for targetY in range(frame*3,frame*3+((200-25)/2)):
        color = getColor(getPixel(barb,int(sourceX),
int(sourceY)))
        setColor(getPixel(canvas,targetX,targetY), color)
        sourceY = sourceY + 2
      sourceX = sourceX + 2
    # Now, write out the frame
    # Have to deal with single digit vs. double digit frame
numbers differently
    framenum=str(frame)
    if frame < 10:
      writePictureTo(canvas,directory+"//frame0"+framenum+
".jpg")
    if frame >= 10:
      writePictureTo(canvas,directory+"//frame"+framenum+
".jpg")
```

How it works: We're embedding the recipe for copying Barb's face into the middle of the frame loop. The range of the target index variables is determined by the frame number, so that we copy Barb's face into a different position (increasing for both x and y) in each frame.

Our movie programs are getting more complicated now. We might want to be able to write them in parts, with the frame-writing part kept separate. This means that we can focus in the main body of the function on what we want in the frame, not on creating the frame. This is an example of ***procedural abstraction***.

RECIPE 104: Move Barb's head, simplified

```
def moveahead(directory):
  barbf=getMediaPath("barbara.jpg")
```

```
barb = makePicture(barbf)
for frame in range(1,100): #99 frames
  printNow("Frame number: "+str(frame))
  canvas = makePicture(getMediaPath("640x480.jpg"))
  # Now, do the actual copying
  sourceX = 45
  for targetX in range(frame*3,frame*3+((200-45)/2)):
    sourceY = 25
    for targetY in range(frame*3,frame*3+((200-25)/2)):
      color = getColor(getPixel(barb,int(sourceX),
int(sourceY)))
        setColor(getPixel(canvas,targetX,targetY), color)
      sourceY = sourceY + 2
    sourceX = sourceX + 2
  # Now, write out the frame
  writeFrame(frame,directory,canvas)

def writeFrame(num,directory,framepict):
  # Have to deal with single digit vs. double digit frame
numbers differently
  framenum=str(num)
  if num < 10:
    writePictureTo(framepict,directory+"//frame0"
+framenum+".jpg")
  if num >= 10:
    writePictureTo(framepict,directory+"//frame"
+framenum+".jpg")
```

But this writeFrame() function assumes two-digit maximum frame numbers. We could want more frames. Here's a version that allows for three-digit frame numbers.

RECIPE 105: Writeframe() for over 100 frames

```
def writeFrame(num,directory,framepict):
  # Have to deal with single digit vs. double digit frame
numbers differently
  framenum=str(num)
  if num < 10:
    writePictureTo(framepict,directory+"//frame00"+framenum+
".jpg")
  if num >= 10 and num<100:
    writePictureTo(framepict,directory+"//frame0"+framenum+
".jpg")
  if num >= 100:
    writePictureTo(framepict,directory+"//frame"+framenum+
".jpg")
```

We can use the image manipulations that we created in Chapter 3 over multiple frames to create quite interesting movies. Remember the sunset-generating program Recipe 11? Let's modify it to *slowly* generate a sunset across many

FIGURE 12.7: Frames from the slow-sunset movie.

frames. We modify it so that the difference between each frame is only 1%. This version actually goes too far, and generates a super-nova, but the effect is still pretty interesting (Figure 12.7 and in color insert Figure I.12).

RECIPE 106: Make a slow-sunset movie

```
def slowsunset(directory):
    canvas = makePicture(getMediaPath("beach-smaller.jpg"))
    #outside the loop!
    for frame in range(1,100): #99 frames
        printNow("Frame number: "+str(frame))
        makeSunset(canvas)
        # Now, write out the frame
        writeFrame(frame,directory,canvas)

def makeSunset(picture):
    for p in getPixels(picture):
        value=getBlue(p)
        setBlue(p,value*0.99) #Just 1     value=getGreen(p)
        setGreen(p,value*0.99)
```

How it works: It's key to this movie that we create the canvas *before* the frame loop. Within the frame loop, we simply keep using the same base canvas. This means that each call to makeSunset increases the "sunsetness" (no, it's not a word) by 1%. (We're not going to show writeFrame() anymore, since we assume that you'll include it in your Program Area and file.)

FIGURE 12.8: Frames from the slow-fade-out movie.

The swapbg() recipe that we made a while ago can also be used to good effect for generating movies. We modify the function in Recipe 42 to take a threshold as input, then we pass in the frame number as the threshold. The effect is a slow fade into the background image (Figure 12.8 and in color insert Figure I.13).

RECIPE 107: Fade out slowly

```
def slowfadeout(directory):
  bg = makePicture(getMediaPath("wall.jpg"))
  jungle = makePicture(getMediaPath("jungle2.jpg"))
  for frame in range(1,100): #99 frames
    canvas = makePicture(getMediaPath("wall-two-people.jpg"))
  #inside the loop!
    printNow("Frame number: "+str(frame))
    swapbg(canvas,bg,jungle,frame)
    # Now, write out the frame
    writeFrame(frame,directory,canvas)

def swapbg(person, bg, newbg,threshold):
  for x in range(1,getWidth(person)):
    for y in range(1,getHeight(person)):
```

```
personPixel = getPixel(person,x,y)
bgpx = getPixel(bg,x,y)
personColor= getColor(personPixel)
bgColor = getColor(bgpx)
if distance(personColor,bgColor) < threshold:
  bgcolor = getColor(getPixel(newbg,x,y))
    setColor(personPixel, bgcolor)
```

How it works: The frame number here is the threshold value for when we decide to swap in the new background instead of keeping the original pixels. As the threshold increases, we replace more and more of the pixels of the original picture with new background pixels. As the frame number increases, then, we end up having more new background and less of both the old background and the old foreground. Note that here we open the canvas *inside* the frame loop. We want the effect to be new for each frame, with the frame differences computed in swapbg with the changing threshold.

■12.2 Working with Video Source

As we said earlier, dealing with real video, in real-time, is very hard. We're going to cheat by saving the video as a sequence of JPEG images, manipulate the JPEG images, then convert back into a movie. This lets us use video as a source (e.g., for background images).

To manipulate movies that already exist, we have to break them into frames. The MediaTools application can do this for you for MPEG movies (Figure 12.9). The MENU button in the MediaTools application lets you save any MPEG movie as a series of JPEG frame pictures. Tools like Apple's QuickTime Pro can do the same for QuickTime and AVI movies.

12.2.1 Video Manipulating Examples

On your CD is a brief movie of my daughter Katie dancing around. Let's create a movie of Mommy (Barb) watching her daughter—we'll simply composite Barb's head onto the frames of Katie dancing (Figure 12.10 and in color insert Figure I.14).

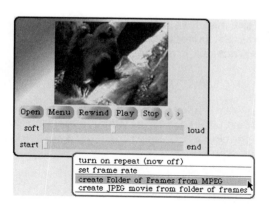

FIGURE 12.9: Saving MPEG movie as a series of frames in MediaTools application.

FIGURE 12.10: Frames from the Mommy watching Katie movie.

RECIPE 108: Make movie of Mommy watching Katie

```
import os

def mommywatching(directory):
    kiddir=r"C://kid-in-bg-seq"
    barbf=getMediaPath("barbara.jpg")
    barb = makePicture(barbf)
    frame = 0
    for file in os.listdir(kiddir):
      if file.endswith(".jpg"):
        frame = frame + 1
        printNow("Frame number: "+str(frame))
        framepic = makePicture(kiddir+"//"+file)
        # Now, do the actual copying
        sourceX = 45
        for targetX in range(frame*3, frame*3+((200-45)/2)):
         sourceY = 25
           for targetY in range(frame*3, frame*3+((200-25)/2)):
            color = getColor(getPixel(barb,sourceX,sourceY))
            setColor(getPixel(framepic,targetX,targetY),color)
            sourceY = sourceY + 2
         sourceX = sourceX + 2
        # Now, write out the frame
        writeFrame(frame,directory,framepic)
```

How it works: The directory where I have the video source images is `C:/kid-in-bg-seq`). I put that in a variable and get Barb's picture. The `frame` number is incremented in the loop, because we're actually going to read each frame individually as a video source via `os.listdir` on the `kiddir` (directory where the kid video frames are). We're lucky that `os.listdir` returns the frames in alphabetical order, which (with leading zeroes) is also numeric order. We read the file, make sure it's one of our JPEG frames, then open it and composite Barb's head into it. We then write out the frame using `writeFrame`.

We can certainly do more sophisticated image processing than simple composing or sunsets. For example, we can do *chromakey* on movie frames. That's how many computer-generated effects in real movies are made. To try this out, I took a simple video of my three children (Matthew, Katie, and Jenny) crawling in front of a blue screen (Figure 12.11 and in color insert Figure I.17). I didn't do the lighting right, so the background turned out to be black instead of blue. That turned out to be a critical error. As a result, the chromakey also modified Matthew's pants, Katie's hair, and Jenny's eyes, so that you can see the moon right through them (Figure 12.12 and in color insert Figure I.18). Like red, black is a color that one should *not* use for the background when doing chromakey.

FIGURE 12.11: Frames from the original kids crawling in front of a blue screen.

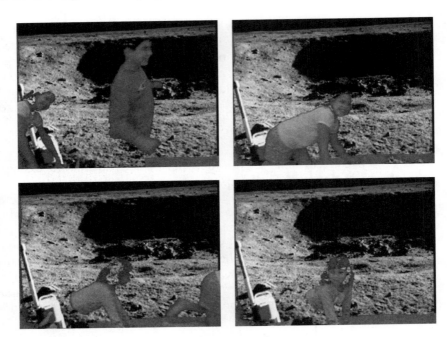

FIGURE 12.12: Frames from the kids on the moon movie.

RECIPE 109: Using chromakey to put kids on the moon

```
import os
def kidsOnMoon(directory):
    kids="C://kids-blue"
    moon=getMediaPath("moon-surface.jpg")
    bg=makePicture(moon)
    framenum = 0
    for framefile in os.listdir(kids):
        framenum = framenum + 1
        printNow("Frame: "+str(framenum))
        if framefile.endswith(".jpg"):
            frame=makePicture(kids+"//"+framefile)
            for p in getPixels(frame):
                if distance(getColor(p),black) <= 100:
                    setColor(p,getColor(getPixel(bg,getX(p),getY(p))))
            writeFrame(framenum,directory,frame)
```

I took video of a puppet show that was performed in black light. I found that it was very hard to see the puppets (Figure 12.13 and in color insert Figure I.15). Our eyes can detect luminance differences that media can't.

I tried to fix the movie with a program. I first tried lightening every pixel in every frame. That didn't work. It made all the black more white, but didn't improve the contrast. I then looked at the frames with the MediaTools. I found that the black parts are *really* black, and the light parts have really low RGB values.

FIGURE 12.13:   Frames from the original too-dark movie.

The program that works pretty well, I think, looks for pixels that are less black than pure black (with a threshold of only eight), and then makes it a lighter color by a couple of times (Figure 12.14 and in color insert Figure I.16). This program took a *long* time to run. On my 500-Mhz PowerPC G4 (a reasonable computer as of this writing), it took over a minute per frame to process, 160 frames total. The next chapter will help us to understand why programs take a long time to run.

RECIPE 110: Lightening dark frames

```
import os

def lightenFish(directory):
  framenum = 0
  for framefile in os.listdir(getMediaPath("dark-fish2")):
    framenum = framenum + 1
    printNow("Frame: "+str(framenum))
    if framefile.endswith(".jpg"):
      frame=makePicture(getMediaPath("dark-fish2")+"//"
+framefile)
      for p in getPixels(frame):
        color = getColor(p)
        if distance(color,black)>8:
          color=makeLighter(color)
```

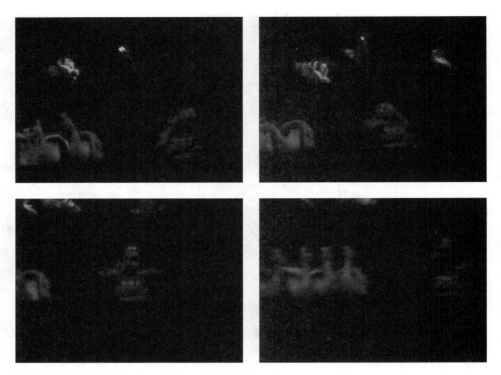

FIGURE 12.14:   Frames from the new lightened movie.

```
color=makeLighter(color)
setColor(p,color)
writeFrame(framenum,directory,frame)
```

Problems

12.1   Build an animation of at least three seconds in duration (30 frames at 10 fps, or 75 frames at 25 fps). You must have at least three things in motion during this sequence. You must use at least one composited image (a JPEG image that you scale (if necessary) and copy into the image) and one drawn image (a rectangle or line or text or oval or arc—anything that you draw). For at least one of the things in motion, change its *velocity* part-way through the animation—change the direction or the speed.

12.2   http://abcnews.go.com is a popular news site. Let's make a movie of it. Write a function that will input a directory as a string. Then:
   ■ Visit http://abcnews.go.com and pick out the top three news story headlines. (*Hint*: The anchors for the news story headlines all have <a href="/wire/ before them. Find that tag, then search for the beginning of the anchor <a href="/wire/, then you can find the anchor text, which is the headline.)

■ Create a ticker tape movie on the 640×480 canvas of all three news stories. Have one come across at $y = 100$, another at $y = 200$, and the third at $y = 300$. Generate 100 frames, and don't have the ticker tapes move more than 5 pixels per frame. (In 100 frames, you won't make it all the way across the screen—that's fine.) Store the frames to files in the input directory.

12.3   Change the movie of two people fading out (Recipe 107). Instead of fading in the jungle, fade in the original blank wall. The effect should be of two people disappearing.

12.4   Remember the blending of pictures in Recipe 41? Try blending one picture into another as a movie, slowly increasing the percentage of the second (incoming) image while decreasing the percentage of the original (outgoing) image.

PART 6

TOPICS IN COMPUTER SCIENCE

CHAPTER 13

Speed

13.1 Focusing on Computer Science
13.2 What Makes Programs Fast?
13.3 What Makes a Computer Fast?

Chapter Learning Objectives

- *To choose between compiled and interpreted programming languages, based on an understanding of machine language and how computers work.*
- *To know the categories of algorithms based on their complexity, and to avoid intractable algorithms.*
- *To consider processor choice based on an understanding of clock rates.*
- *To make decisions about computer storage options when aiming for optimizing speed.*

■13.1 Focusing on Computer Science

At this point, you probably have a lot of questions about what you've been doing in this book. You may be asking, for instance:

- Why is Photoshop so much faster than anything we do in JES?
- How fast can we get our programs to go?
- Does it always take this long to write programs? Can I write smaller programs to do the same things? Can I write programs more easily than this?
- What does programming look like in other programming languages?

The answers to most of these questions are known or are studied in *computer science*. This part of the book is an introduction to some of those topics as a signpost to get you started in exploring computer science further.

■13.2 What Makes Programs Fast?

Where does the speed go? You buy a really fast computer, and Photoshop seems really fast on it. Colors change as quickly as you change the slider. But then you run programs in JES and they just take *forever* (or 30 seconds, whichever comes first). Why?

13.2.1 What Computers Really Understand

In reality, computers do not understand Python, or Java, or any other language. The basic computer only understands one kind of language—*machine language*. Machine-language instructions are just values in the bytes in memory, and they tell the computer to do very low-level activities. In a real sense, the computer doesn't even "understand" machine language. The computer is just a machine with lots of switches that make data flow this way or that. Machine language is just a bunch of switch settings that make other switches in the computer change. We *interpret* these data switchings as addition, subtraction, loading data, and storing data.

Each kind of computer has its own machine language. Apple computers and computers that run Windows can't run one another's programs, not because of any philosophical or marketing differences, but because each kind of computer has its own *processor* (the core of the computer that actually executes the machine language). They *literally* don't understand one another. That's why an .exe program from Windows won't run on a Macintosh, and a Macintosh application won't run on a Windows computer. Executable files are (almost always) machine-language programs.

Machine language looks like a bunch of numbers—it's not particularly user-friendly. *Assembler language* is a set of human-readable words (or near-words) that corresponds one-to-one with machine language. Machine language instructions tell the computer to do things like store numbers into particular memory locations or into special locations (variables or registers) in the computer, test numbers for equality or comparison, or add numbers together or subtract them.

An assembler program to add two numbers together and store them somewhere (and the corresponding machine language generated by an *assembler*) might look like this:

```
LOAD #10,R0      ; Load special variable R0 with 10
LOAD #12,R1      ; Load special variable R1 with 12
SUM R0,R1        ; Add special variables R0 and R1
STOR R1,#45      ; Store the result into memory location #45

01 00 10
01 01 12
02 00 01
03 01 45
```

An assembler program that can make a decision could look like this:

```
LOAD R1,#65536   ; Get a character from keyboard
TEST R1,#13      ; Is it an ASCII 13 (Enter)?
JUMPTRUE #32768  ; If true, go to another part of the
                   program
CALL #16384      ; If false, call func. to process the new
                   line
```

```
Machine Language:
05 01 255 255
10 01 13
20 127 255
122 63 255
```

Input and output devices are often just memory locations to the computer. Maybe, when you store a 255 to location 65,542, the red component of the pixel at (101, 345) is suddenly set to maximum intensity. Maybe each time the computer reads from memory location 897,784, it's a new sample just read from the microphone. In this way, these simple loads and stores can also handle multimedia.

Machine language is executed very quickly. I am typing this on a computer with a 900-megahertz (Mhz) processor. What that means *exactly* is hard to define, but roughly it means that this computer processes 900 *million* machine-language instructions *per second*. A 2-gigahertz (Ghz) processor handles 2 *billion* instructions per second. A 12-byte machine-language program that corresponds to something like a = b + c executes on my mid-range computer in something like 12/900,000,000 of a second.

13.2.2 Compilers and Interpreters

Applications like Adobe Photoshop and Microsoft Word are typically **compiled**. This means that they were written in a computer language like C or C++ and then *translated* into machine language using a program called a **compiler**. The programs then execute at the speed of the base processor.

However, programming languages like Python, Java, Scheme, Squeak, Director, and Flash are actually (in most cases) *interpreted*. They execute at a slower speed. It's the difference between *translating* and then doing instructions versus simply doing the instructions.

A detailed example might help. Consider this exercise:

> Write a function doGraphics that will take a list as input. The function doGraphics will start by creating a canvas from the 640x480.jpg file in the mediasources folder. You will draw on the canvas according to the commands in the input list.
>
> Each element of the list will be a string. There will be two kinds of strings in the list:
>
> ■ "b 200 120" means to draw a black dot at x position 200 y position 120. The numbers, of course, will change, but the command will always be a "b". You can assume that the input numbers will always have three digits.
>
> ■ "l 000 010 100 200" means to draw a line from position (0, 10) to position (100, 200)
>
> So an input list might look like ["b 100 200","b 101 200","b 102 200","l 102 200 102 300"] (but have any number of elements).

```
>>> canvas=doGraphics(["b 100
    200","b 101 200","b 102
    200","l 102 200 102 300","l
    102 300 200 300"])
Drawing pixel at  100 : 200
Drawing pixel at  101 : 200
Drawing pixel at  102 : 200
Drawing line at 102 200 102 300
Drawing line at 102 300 200 300
>>> show(canvas)
```

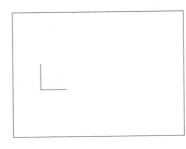

FIGURE 13.1: Running the doGraphics interpreter.

Here's a solution to the exercise. We look at each string in the list, compare the first character as a "black pixel" command or a "list" command, then chop out the right coordinates (converting them to numbers with int()), and doing the appropriate graphics command. This solution works—see Figure 13.1.

RECIPE 111: Interpret graphics commands in a list

```
def doGraphics(mylist):
    canvas = makePicture(getMediaPath("640x480.jpg"))
    for command in mylist:
        if command[0] == "b":
            x = int(command[2:5])
            y = int(command[6:9])
            print "Drawing pixel at ",x,":",y
            setColor(getPixel(canvas, x,y),black)
        if command[0] =="l":
            x1 = int(command[2:5])
            y1 = int(command[6:9])
            x2 = int(command[10:13])
            y2 = int(command[14:17])
            print "Drawing line at",x1,y1,x2,y2
            addLine(canvas, x1, y1, x2, y2)
    return canvas
```

How it works: We accept the list of graphics commands as input in mylist. We open a blank 640x480.jpg canvas for drawing on. For each string command in the input list, we check the first character (command[0]) to figure out what type of command it is. If it's a "b" (black pixel), we chop out the x and y coordinates from the string (since they're always the numbers of the same length, we know exactly where they'll be), then draw the pixel on the canvas. If it's an "l" (line), we get the four coordinates and draw the line. At the end, we return the canvas.

What we've just done is implement a new language for graphics. We have even created an *interpreter* that reads the instructions for our new language and creates the picture that goes along with it. In principle, this is just what Postscript, PDF, Flash, and AutoCAD are doing. Their file formats specify pictures in just the way that our graphics language does. When they draw (*render*) the image to the screen, they are *interpreting* the commands in that file.

While we probably can't tell from such a small example, this is a relatively slow language. Consider the program shown below—would it run faster than reading the list of commands and interpreting them? Both this program and the list in Figure 13.1 generate the exact same picture.

```
def doGraphics():
  canvas = makePicture(getMediaPath("640x480.jpg"))
  setColor(getPixel(canvas, 100,200),black)
  setColor(getPixel(canvas, 101,200),black)
  setColor(getPixel(canvas, 102,200),black)
  addLine(canvas, 102,200,102,300)
  addLine(canvas, 102,300,200,300)
  show(canvas)
  return canvas
```

In general, we'd probably guess (correctly) that the direct instructions given above will run faster than reading the list and interpreting it. Here's an analogy that might help. I took French in college, but I'm really bad at it. Let's say that someone gave me a list of instructions in French. I could meticulously look up each word, figure out the instructions, and do them. What if I am asked to do the instructions again? Go look up each word again. Ten times? Ten lookups. Now let's imagine that I wrote down the English (my native language) translation of the French instructions. I can very quickly repeat doing the list of instructions as often as you like. It takes me no time to look up any word (though it probably depends on what I'm being asked to do—brain surgery is *out*). In general, figuring out the language takes up some time that is just overhead—simply *doing* the instructions (or drawing the graphics) will always be faster.

Here's an idea: Could we *generate* the above program? Could we write a program that takes as input the list graphics language we invented, then writes a Python program that draws the same pictures? Turns out not to be that hard. This is a ***compiler*** for the graphics language.

RECIPE 112: Compiler for new graphics language

```
def makeGraphics(mylist):
  file = open("graphics.py","wt")
  file.write('def doGraphics():\n')
  file.write('  canvas = makePicture(getMediaPath
("640x480.jpg"))\n');
  for i in mylist:
    if i[0] == "b":
      x = int(i[2:5])
      y = int(i[6:9])
      print "Drawing pixel at ",x,":",y
      file.write('  setColor(getPixel(canvas, '+str(x)+',
'+str(y)+'),black)\n')
    if i[0] =="l":
      x1 = int(i[2:5])
      y1 = int(i[6:9])
```

```
        x2 = int(i[10:13])
        y2 = int(i[14:17])
        print "Drawing line at",x1,y1,x2,y2
        file.write('  addLine(canvas, '+str(x1)+','+str(y1)+',
'+ str(x2)+','+str(y2)+')\n')
    file.write('  show(canvas)\n')
    file.write('  return canvas\n')
    file.close()
```

How it works: The compiler accepts the *same* input as the interpreter, but instead of opening a `canvas` to write to, we open a `file`. We write to the file the start of a `doGraphics` function–the `def` and the code to create a `canvas` (indented two spaces so that it's inside the block of the `doGraphics` function). Note that we're not really *making* the `canvas` here—we're simply writing out the command to make the canvas, which will be executed *later* when `doGraphics` is executed. Then, just like the interpreter, we figure out which graphics command it is ("b" or "l") and we figure out the coordinates from the input string. Then we write out to the file the commands to do the drawing. At the end, we write out commands to `show` and `return` the `canvas`, and finally we `close` the file.

Now the compiler has a lot of overhead. We still have to look up what the commands mean. If we only have a small graphics program to run, and we only need it once, we might as well just run the interpreter. But what if we needed to run the picture 10 times, or 100 times? Then we pay the overhead of compiling the program *once*, and the next 9 or 99 times, we run it as fast as we possibly can. That will almost certainly be faster than doing the interpretation overhead 100 times.

This is what compilers are all about. Applications like Photoshop and Word are written in languages like C or C++ and are then *compiled* to *equivalent* machine-language programs. The machine-language program does the same thing that the C language says to do, just as the graphics programs created from our compiler do the same things as our graphics language says to do. But the machine-language program runs *much* faster than we could interpret the C or C++.

Jython programs are actually *interpreted*, and not once but *twice*. Jython is written in Java, and Java programs don't typically compile to machine language. (Java *can* be compiled to machine language—it's just not the normal thing that people do with Java.) Java programs compile to a machine language for a *make-believe processor*—a **virtual machine**. The *Java Virtual Machine* doesn't really exist as a physical processor. It's a definition of a processor. What good is that? It turns out that since machine language is *very* simple, building a machine-language *interpreter* is pretty easy to write.

The result is that a Java Virtual Machine interpreter can be very easily made to run on just about any processor. This means that a program in Java is compiled *once* and then runs *everywhere*. Devices as small as wristwatches can run the same Java programs that run on large computers.

When you run a program in JES, it's actually compiled to Java—an equivalent Java program is written for you. Then the Java is compiled for the Java

Virtual Machine. Finally, the Java Virtual Machine interpreter runs the Java machine language of your program. All of which will always be slower than running a compiled form of the same thing.

That's the first part of the answer to the question "Why is Photoshop always faster than JES?" JES is interpreted *twice*, which will always be slower than Photoshop running in machine language.

Then why have an interpreter at all? There are many good reasons. Here are three:

■ Do you like the Command Area? Did you even once ever type in some example code just to *try* it? That kind of interactive, exploratory, trying-things-out programming is only available with interpreters. Compilers don't let you try things out line by line and print the results. Interpreters are good for learners.

■ Once a program is compiled to Java machine language, it can be used *anywhere*, as-is, from huge computers to programmable toaster ovens. That's a big savings for software developers. They only ship one program, and it runs on anything.

■ Virtual machines are safer than machine language. A program running in machine language might do all kinds of nonsecure things. A virtual machine can carefully keep track of the programs it is interpreting to make sure that they only do safe things.

13.2.3 How Fast Can We Really Go?

The raw power of compiled as compared to interpreted programs is only part of the answer of why Photoshop is faster. The deeper part, and one that can actually lead to interpreted programs being *faster* than compiled programs, is in the design of the *algorithms*. There's a temptation to think, "Oh, it's okay if it's slow now. Wait 18 months, we'll get double the processor speed, and then it will be fine." There are some algorithms that are *so* slow they will never end in your lifetime, and others that can't be written at all. Rewriting the algorithm to be *smarter* about what we ask the computer to do can have a dramatic impact on performance.

An ***algorithm*** is a description of the way a computer must behave to solve a problem. A program (functions in Python) consists of executable interpretations of algorithms. The same algorithm can be implemented in many different languages. There is always more than one algorithm to solve the same problem—some computer scientists study algorithms and come up with ways to compare them and state which are better than others.

We've seen several algorithms that appear in different ways but are really doing the same things:

■ Sampling to scale a picture up or down or to lower or raise the frequency of a sound.

■ Blending to merge two pictures or two sounds.

■ Mirroring of sounds and pictures.

We can compare algorithms based on several criteria. One is how much *space* the algorithm needs to run. How much memory does the algorithm require? This can become a significant issue for media computation because so much memory is required to hold all that data. Think about how bad an algorithm would be that needed to hold *all* the frames of a movie in a list in memory at the same time.

The most common criterion used to compare algorithms is *time*. How much time does the algorithm take? We don't mean clock time, but how many steps the algorithm requires. Computer scientists use **Big-Oh notation**, or $O(\ )$ to refer to the magnitude of the running time of an algorithm. The idea of Big-Oh is to express how much slower the program gets as the input data get larger. It tries to ignore differences between languages, even between compiled versus interpreted, and focus on the number of *steps* to be executed.

Think about our basic picture- and sound-processing functions like `increaseRed()` or `increaseVolume()`. Some of the complexity of these functions is hidden in functions like `getPixels()` and `getSamples()`. In general, though, we refer to these as being $O(n)$. The amount of time the program takes to run is proportional linearly to the input data. If the picture or sound doubled in size, we'd expect the program to take twice as long to run.

When we figure out Big-Oh, we typically clump the body of the loop into one step. We think about these functions as processing each sample or pixel once, so the real-time sink in these functions is the loop, and it doesn't really matter how many statements are in the loop.

Unless there is another loop in the loop body, that is. Loops are multiplicative in terms of time. Nested loops multiply the amount of time needed to run the body. Think about this toy program:

```
def loops():
  count = 0
  for x in range(1,5):
    for y in range(1,3):
      count = count + 1
      print x,y,"--Ran it ",count,"times"
```

When we run it, we see that it actually executes eight times—four for the x's, two for the y's, and $4 * 2 = 8$.

```
>>> loops()
1 1 --Ran it  1 times
1 2 --Ran it  2 times
2 1 --Ran it  3 times
2 2 --Ran it  4 times
3 1 --Ran it  5 times
3 2 --Ran it  6 times
4 1 --Ran it  7 times
4 2 --Ran it  8 times
```

How about movie code? Since it takes so long to process, is it actually a more complex algorithm? No, not really. Movie code is just processing each pixel once, so it's still $O(n)$. It's just that the n is really, *really* big!

Not all algorithms are $O(n)$. There is a group of algorithms called **sorting algorithms** that are used to order data in alphabetical or numerical order. The simplest of these algorithms (like the **bubble sort**) has complexity $O(n^2)$. If a list has 100 elements, it'll take on the order of 10,000 steps to sort the 100 elements with this kind of sort. However, there are smarter algorithms (like the **quicksort**) that have complexity $O(nlogn)$. The same list of 100 elements would only take 460 steps to process. These kinds of differences start to have huge clock-time differences when you're talking about processing 10,000 customers to put them in order for reports.

13.2.4 Making Searching Faster

Consider how you might look up a word in the dictionary. One way is to check the first page, then the next page, then the next page, and so on. That's called a *linear search*, and it's $O(n)$. It's not very efficient. The *best case* (the fastest the algorithm could possibly be) is that the problem is solved in one step—the word is on the first page. The *worst case* is n steps where n is the number of pages—the word could be on the last page. The *average case* is $n/2$ steps—the word is halfway through.

We can implement this as searching in a list.

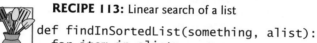

RECIPE 113: Linear search of a list

```
def findInSortedList(something, alist):
    for item in alist:
        if item == something:
            return "Found it!"
    return "Not found"
```

```
>>> findInSortedList ("bear",["apple","bear","cat","dog",
"elephant"])
'Found it!'
>>> findInSortedList ("giraffe",["apple","bear","cat",
"dog", "elephant"])
'Not found'
```

But let's use the fact that dictionaries are already in sorted order. We can be smarter about how we search for a word, and do it in $O(log(n))$ time ($log(n) = x$ where $2^x = n$). Split the dictionary in the middle. Is the word before or after the page you're looking at? If after, look from the middle to the end (e.g., again split the book, but from the middle to end). If before, look from the start to the middle (split halfway between start and middle). Keep repeating until you find the word or it couldn't possibly be there. This is a more efficient algorithm. In the best case, the word is in the first place you look. In the average and worst case, it's $log(n)$ steps—keep dividing the n pages in half, and you'll have at most $log(n)$ splits.

Here's a simple (i.e., not the best possible, but illustrative) implementation of this kind of a search, called a ***binary search***.

RECIPE 114: Simple binary search

```
def findInSortedList(something, alist):
    start = 0
    end = len(alist) - 1
    while (start + 1) < end: #While there are more to search
        checkpoint = int((start+end)/2.0)
        if checkpoint < 0 or checkpoint > len(alist):
            break
        if alist[checkpoint]==something:
            return "Found it!"
        if alist[checkpoint]<something:
            start=checkpoint
        if alist[checkpoint]>something:
            end=checkpoint
    return "Not found"
```

How it works: We start with the low-end marker `start` at the beginning of the list (0 since we're using Python indexing here), and `end` at the end of the list (length of the list minus 1, for the same zero-based reason). As long as there is *something* between `start` and `end`, we continue to search. We compute `checkpoint` as halfway between `start` and `end`. If the `checkpoint` ever goes too low or too high, we didn't find the thing we're looking for, so we `break`. We then check to see if we found it. If so, we're done and we `return`. If not, we figure out whether we have to move `start` up to `checkpoint` or `end` down to `checkpoint`. And we continue searching. If we ever get through the whole loop, we didn't take the "Found it!" `return`, so we `return` that we didn't find.

To test this, I stuck in a line after the break that said:

```
printNow("Checking at: "+str(checkpoint)+
"Start:"+str(start)+"End:"+str(end))

>>> print
findInSortedList("giraffe",["apple","bear","cat",
"dog","elephant"])
Checking at: 2 Start:0 End:4
Checking at: 3 Start:2 End:4
Not found
>>> print
findInSortedList("bear",["apple","bear","cat",
"dog","elephant"])
Checking at: 2 Start:0 End:4
Checking at: 1 Start:0 End:2
Found it!
>>> print
findInSortedList("bob",["apple","bear","cat",
```

```
"dog","elephant"])
Checking at: 2 Start:0 End:4
Checking at: 1 Start:0 End:2
Not found
>>> print
findInSortedList("apple",["apple","bear","cat",
"dog","elephant"])
Checking at: 2 Start:0 End:4
Checking at: 1 Start:0 End:2
Not found
```

13.2.5 Algorithms That Never Finish or Can't Be Written

Here's a thought experiment: Imagine that you want to write a program that will generate hit songs for you. Your program will recombine bits of sounds that are some of the best riffs you've ever heard on various instruments—some 60 of them. You want to generate every combination of these 60 bits (some in, some out; some earlier in the song, some later). You want to find the combination that is less than 2 minutes 30 seconds (for optimal radio play time) and has the right amount of high and low volume combinations (and you've got a checkSound() function to do that).

How many combinations are there? Let's ignore order for right now. Let's say that you've got three sounds: *a*, *b*, and *c*. Your possible songs are *a*, *b*, *c*, *bc*, *ac*, *ab*, and *abc*. Try it with two sounds or four sounds, and you'll see that the pattern is the same as what we saw earlier with bits: For *n* things, every combination of include-or-exclude is 2^n. (If we ignore the fact that there is an empty song, it's $2^n - 1$.)

Therefore, our 60 sounds will result in 2^{60} combinations to run through our length and sound checks. That's 1, 152, 921, 504, 606, 846, 976 combinations. Let's imagine that we can do the checks in only a single instruction (unbelievable, of course, but we're pretending). On a 1.5-gigahertz computer, we can handle that many combinations in 768, 614, 336 seconds. Spell that out: That's 12, 810, 238 minutes, which is 213, 504 hours, which is 8, 896 days. That's 24 *years* to run the program. Now, since Moore's Law doubles process rates every 18 months, we will soon be able to run the program in much less time. Only *12 years!* If we cared about order, too (e.g., *abc* vs. *cba* vs. *bac*), the number of combinations has 63 zeroes in it.

Finding the absolutely optimal combination of just about anything is always time expensive. $O(2^n)$ like this is not an uncommon running time for these kinds of algorithms. But there are other problems that seem as if they should be do-able in a reasonable time, but aren't.

One of these is the famous *Traveling Salesman Problem*. Imagine that you're a salesperson, and you're responsible for many different clients—let's say 30, half the size of the optimization problem. To be efficient, you want to find the shortest path on the map that will let you visit each client exactly once, and not more than once.

The best-known algorithm that gives an optimal solution for the Traveling Salesman Problem is $O(n!)$. That's n factorial. There are algorithms that take less time to run that give close but not guaranteed shortest paths. For 30 cities, the number of steps to execute with one of these $O(n!)$ algorithms is 30!, or $265, 252, 859, 812, 191, 058, 636, 308, 480, 000, 000$. Go ahead and run that on a 1.5-gigahertz processor—it won't get done in your lifetime.

The really aggravating part is that the Traveling Salesman Problem isn't a made-up, toy problem. There really are people who have to plan the shortest routes in the world. There are similar problems that are basically the same algorithmically, like planning the route of a robot on a factory floor. This is a big, hard problem.

Computer scientists classify problems into three piles:

■ Many problems, like sorting, can be solved with an algorithm whose running time has a complexity that's a polynomial, like $O(n^2)$. We call these *class P* (P for polynomial) problems.

■ Other problems, like optimization, have known algorithms, but the solutions are so hard and big that we know we can't solve them in a reasonable time even for reasonable amounts of data. We call these problems *intractable*.

■ Still other problems, like the Traveling Salesman, *seem* intractable, but maybe there's a solution in class P that we just haven't found yet. We call these *class NP*.

One of the biggest unsolved problems in theoretical computer science is proving either that class NP and class P are completely distinct (i.e., we'll never solve the Traveling Salesman optimally in polynomial time), or that class NP is within class P.

You may be wondering whether *anything* can be proved about algorithms. There are so many different languages, and different ways of writing the same algorithm. How can we positively *prove* that something is doable or not doable? We can, it turns out. In fact, Alan Turing proved that there are even algorithms that *can't be written*.

The most famous algorithm that can't be written is the solution to the *Halting Problem*. We've already written programs that can read other programs and write out other programs. We can imagine a program that can read one program and tell us things about it (e.g., how many `print` statements are in it). Can we write a program that will input another program (e.g., from a file), then tell us whether the program will ever *stop*? Think about the input program having some complex `while` loops where it's hard to tell whether the expression in the `while` loop is ever `false`. Now imagine a bunch of these, all nested within one another.

Alan Turing proved that such a program could never be written. He used proof by absurdity. He showed that if such a program (call it H) could be written, you could try feeding that program to itself as input. Now H takes input, a program, right? What if you modified H (call it H2) so that if H said, "This one halts!" H2 would loop forever (e.g., `while 1:`). Turing showed that such a setup would announce that the program would halt only if it loops forever, and would halt only if it announces that it would loop forever.

The really amazing thing is that Turing came up with this proof in 1936—almost 10 years before the first computers were built. He defined a mathematical concept of a computer called a *Turing machine* and was able to make such proofs before physical computers even came into existence.

Here's another thought experiment: Is human intelligence computable? Our brains are executing a process that enables us to think, right? Can we write down that process as an algorithm? And if a computer executes that algorithm, is it thinking? Is a human reducible to a computer? This is one of the big questions in the field of *artificial intelligence*.

13.2.6 Why Is Photoshop Faster Than JES?

We can now answer the question of why Photoshop is faster than JES. First, Photoshop is compiled, so it runs at raw machine-language speeds.

But the other part is that Photoshop has algorithms that are smarter than what we're doing. For example, think about the programs where we searched for colors, like in Chromakey or in making Barb's hair red. We know that the background color and the hair color were clumped next to one another. What if, instead of linearly searching all the pixels, you just searched from where the color was what you were looking for until you didn't find that color anymore. Finding the boundary this way would be a smarter search. That's the kind of thing that Photoshop does.

∎13.3 What Makes a Computer Fast?

Computers are getting faster all the time—Moore's Law promises us that. But knowing this doesn't help us to compare computers that all belong to the same Moore's Law generation. How do you compare ads in the paper and figure out which of the listed computers is *really* the fastest?

Simply being fast is only one criterion for picking a computer, of course. There are issues of cost, how much disk space you need, what kind of expansion features you need, and so on. But in this section we'll explicitly deal with what the various factors in computer ads mean in terms of computer speed (see Figure 13.2 for some examples).

13.3.1 Clock Rates and Actual Computation

When computer ads state that they have a "Some-brand Processor 2.8 Ghz" or "Other-brand Processor 3.0 Ghz," what they're talking about is the *clock rate*. The processor is the smarts of your computer—it's the part that makes

- AMD Athlon™ XP Processor 3000+ with QuantiSpeed™ Architecture
- 400MHz Front Side Bus
- 512KB L2 Cache
- DVD-ROM Drive
- CD-RW Drive
- 512MB DDR SDRAM
- 120.0GB Hard Drive

- Intel® Celeron® Processor 2.7GHz
- CD-RW Drive
- 400MHz Front Side Bus
- 128KB L2 Cache
- 256MB DDR SDRAM
- 40.0GB Hard Drive

FIGURE 13.2: A couple of sample computer advertisements.

decisions and does computation. It does all this computing work at a certain *pace*. Imagine a drill sergeant shouting, "Go! Go! Go! Go!" That's what the clock rate is—it tells you how fast the drill sergeant shouts "Go!" A clock rate of 2.8 Ghz means that the clock *pulses* (the drill sergeant shouts "Go!") 2.8 *billion* times per second.

This doesn't mean that the processor actually does something useful with every "Go!" Some computations have several steps, so it may take several pulses of the clock to complete a single useful computation. But *in general* a faster clock rate implies faster computation. Certainly, for the same *kind* of processor, a faster clock rate implies faster computation.

Is there really any difference between 2.8 Ghz and 3.0 Ghz? Or is 1.0 Ghz with processor X about the same as 2.0 Ghz with processor Y? These are much tougher questions. It's not really that much different from arguing over Dodge versus Ford trucks. Most processors have their advocates and their critics. Some will argue that Processor X can do a certain search in very few clock pulses because of how well it's designed, so it's clearly faster even at a slower clock rate. Others will say that Processor Y is still faster overall because its average number of clock pulses per computation is so low—and how common is the type of search that X does so fast, anyway? It's almost like arguing about whose religion is better.

The real answer is to try some realistic work on the computer that you're considering. Does it feel fast enough? Check reviews in computer magazines—they often use realistic tasks (like sorting in Excel and scrolling in Word) to test the speed of computers.

13.3.2 Storage: What Makes a Computer Slow?

The speed of your processor is only one factor in what makes a computer fast or slow. Probably a bigger factor is where the processor goes to get the data it works with. Where are your pictures when your computer goes to work on them? That's a much more complex question.

You can think about your storage as being in a hierarchy, from the fastest to the slowest.

■ Your fastest storage is your *cache memory*. Cache is memory that is physically located on the same silicon chip as your processor (or very, very close to it). Your processor takes care of putting as much as possible in the cache and leaving it there as long as it's needed. Cache is accessed far faster than anything else on your computer. The more cache memory you have, the more things the computer can access very quickly. But cache (of course) is also your most expensive storage.

■ Your *RAM* storage (whether it's called **SDRAM** or any other kind of **RAM**) is your computer's main *memory*. RAM (an acronym for **Random Access Memory**) of 256 Mb (megabytes) means 256 *million* bytes of information. It's where your programs reside when they're executing, and it's where the data that your computer is directly acting upon is located. Things are in your RAM storage before they're loaded into the cache. RAM is less expensive than cache memory, and is probably your best investment in terms of making your computer faster.

■ Your *hard disk* is where you store all your *files*. Your program that you're executing now in RAM started out as an .exe (executable) file on your hard disk. All your digital pictures, digital music, word-processing files, spreadsheet files, and so on, are stored on your hard disk. Your hard disk is your *slowest* storage, but it's also your largest. A hard disk of 40 Gb means that you can store 40 *billion* bytes on it. That's a *lot* of space—and it's pretty small these days.

Movement between levels in the hierarchy means a huge speed difference. I've heard it said that if the speed of access of cache memory is like reaching for a paper clip on your desk, then getting something off the hard disk means traveling to Alpha Centauri—four light years away from Earth. Obviously, we *do* get things off our disk at reasonable speeds (which really implies that cache memory is phenomenally fast!), but the analogy does emphasize how very different the levels of the hierarchy are in respect to speed. The bottom line is that the more you have of the faster memory, the faster your processor can get the information you want and the faster your overall processing will be.

You'll see advertisements occasionally mentioning the *system bus*. The system bus is how signals are sent around your computer—from video or network to hard disk, from RAM to the printer. A faster system bus clearly implies a faster overall system, but a faster system bus may not influence (for example) the speed of your experience with JES or Photoshop. First, even the fastest bus is much slower than the processor—400 million pulses per second versus 4 billion pulses per second. Second, the system bus doesn't usually influence the access to cache or memory, and that's where most of the speed is won or lost anyway.

There are things that you can do to make your hard disk as fast as possible for your computation. The speed of the disk isn't that significant for processing time—even the fastest disks are still far slower than the slowest RAM. Leaving enough free space on your disk for *swapping* is important. When your computer doesn't have enough RAM for what you're asking it to do, it stores some of the data that it isn't currently using from RAM on your hard disk. Moving data to and from your hard disk is a slow process (relatively speaking, compared to access to RAM). Having a fast disk with enough free space that the computer doesn't have to search around for *swap space* helps with processing speed.

How about the network? In terms of speed, the network doesn't really help you. The network is magnitudes slower than your hard disk. There are differences in network speeds that do influence your overall experience, but not necessarily the speed of processing of your computer. Wired Ethernet connections tend to be faster than wireless Ethernet connections. Modem connections are slower.

13.3.3 Display

How about the display? Does the speed of your display really affect the speed of your computer? No, not really. Computers are really, *really* fast. The computer can repaint everything even on really large displays faster than you can perceive.

The only application where the display speed may matter is really high-end computer gaming. Some computer gamers claim that they can perceive a difference between 50 frames per second and 60 frames per second updates of the screen. If your display was really large and everything had to be repainted with every update, then *maybe* a faster processor would make a difference you could perceive. But I think most modern computers update so quickly that you just wouldn't notice a difference.

Problems

13.1 You've now seen some examples of Class P problems (e.g., sorting and searching), intractable problems (optimization of the song elements), and Class NP problems (e.g., the Traveling Salesman Problem). Search the Web and find at least one more example of each class of problem.

13.2 Try something that takes a while in JES (e.g., chromakey on a large image) so that you can time it on a stopwatch. Now time the same JES task on several different computers with different amounts of memory and different clock rates (and different amounts of cache, if you can). See what difference the different factors make in terms of the time it takes to complete the task in JES.

To Dig Deeper

To learn more about what makes a program work *well*, I recommend reading *Structure and Interpretation of Computer Programs* [2]. It's not about gigahertz and cache memories, but it tells a lot about how you should think about your programs to make them work well.

CHAPTER 14

Styles of Programming

14.1 Using Functions to Make Programming Easier
14.2 Functional Programming: Programming in Very Few Lines
14.3 Object-Oriented Programming

Chapter Learning Objectives

- *To write programs more easily with more functions.*

- *To use functional programming to make powerful programs very quickly.*

- *To use object-oriented programming to make programs easier to develop in teams, more robust, and easier to debug.*

- *To understand such features of object-oriented programs as polymorphism, encapsulation, and aggregation.*

- *To be able to choose between different styles of programming for different purposes.*

■14.1 Using Functions to Make Programming Easier

Why do we use functions? How can we use them to make programming easier?

Functions are for managing complexity. Can we write all our programs as one large function? Sure, but it gets *hard*. As programs grow in size, they grow in complexity. We use functions—

- To hide away details so that we only focus on what we care about.

- To find the right place to make changes as you need to in a program—finding the right function is easier than finding a single line in few thousand lines of code.

- To make it easier to test and debug our programs.

If we break a program into smaller pieces, we can test them separately. Think about our HTML programs. We can test functions like doctype(), title(), and body() separately from the Command Area, rather than always having to test the whole thing as a whole. This way, you can deal with the smaller functions and smaller problems until they are solved—then you can ignore them and focus on the bigger problems.

```
>>> print doctype()
<!DOCTYPE HTML PUBLIC "-//W3C//DTD HTML 4.01
Transition//EN" "http://www.w3.org/TR/html4/loose.dtd">
>>> print title("My title string")
<html><head><title>My title string</title></head>
>>> print body("<h1>My heading</h1><p>My paragraph</p>")
<body><h1>My heading</h1><p>My paragraph</p></body></html>
```

Being able to test functions as shown above is more than simply making it easier to debug. It also enables you to *trust* your functions. Try them in different ways. Convince yourself that the function always performs the task you're asking it to do. Once you have this trust, you can ask the function to do its task without thinking about it—then you can do some amazingly powerful things (see the next section).

Adding additional functions makes the whole program easier if the functions are chosen well. If we have subfunctions that do smaller pieces of the overall task, we talk about changing the **granularity** of the functions. If the granularity gets too small, it swaps one kind of complexity for another. But at the right level, it makes the overall program easier to understand and to change.

Think about the home page program like this, with much smaller granularity than what we were doing before:

RECIPE 115: Smaller granularity home page generator

```
def makeHomePage(name, interest):
    file=open("homepage.html","wt")
    file.write(doctype())
    file.write(startHTML())
    file.write(startHead())
    file.write(title(name+"'s Home Page"))
    file.write(endHead())
    file.write(startBody())
    file.write(heading(1, "Welcome to " + name + "'s Home
Page") )
    myparagraph = paragraph( "Hi!  I am " + name + ".  This is
my home page! I am interested in " + interest + "</p>" )
    file.write(myparagraph)
    file.write(endBody())
    file.write(endHTML())
    file.close()

def doctype():
    return '<!DOCTYPE HTML PUBLIC "-//W3C//DTD HTML 4.01
Transition//EN" "http://wwww.w3.org/TR/html4/loose.dtd">'

def startHTML():
    return '<html>'
```

```
def startHead():
  return '<head>'

def endHead():
  return '</head>'

def heading(level,string):
  return "<h"+str(level)+">"+string+"</h"+str(level)+">"

def startBody():
  return "<body>"

def paragraph(string):
  return "<p>"+string+"</p>"

def title(titlestring):
  return "<title>"+titlestring+"</title>"

def endBody():
  return "</body>"

def endHTML():
  return "</html>"
```

This version is even easier to test, but now there's the new complexity of remembering all those function names you just made up!

MAKING IT WORK TIP: Use subfunctions for the hard parts

Whenever you have a hard part in a program, break it into subfunctions so that you can debug and fix each of them separately.

Think about the HTML program to generate a samples page. The loop was the hard part of the program, so let's break it into a separate subfunction. This makes it easier to change how links are formatted—it's all down in the subfunction.

RECIPE 116: Samples page creator with a subfunction

```
def makeSamplePage(directory):
  samplesfile=open(directory+"//samples.html","wt")
  samplesfile.write(doctype())
  samplesfile.write(title("Samples from "+directory))
  # Now, let's make up the string that will be the body.
  samples="<h1>Samples from "+directory+" </h1>"
  for file in os.listdir(directory):
    if file.endswith(".jpg"):
      samples = samples + fileEntry(file)
  samplesfile.write(body(samples))
  samplesfile.close()
```

```
def fileEntry(file):
  samples="<p>Filename: "+file+"<br />"
  samples=samples+'<img src="'+file+'" height="100"
width="100"/></p>'
  return samples
```

Breaking out the pieces like this is part of ***procedural abstraction***. Procedural abstraction is:

- State the problem. Figure out what you want to do.
- Break the problem into subproblems.
- Keep breaking the subproblems into smaller problems until you know how to write the program that solves the smaller problem.
- Your goal is for the main function to basically tell all the subfunctions what to do. Each subfunction should do *one and only one* logical task.

We can think about procedural abstraction as filling in a *tree* of functions (see Figure 14.1). Making modifications is a matter of changing *one* node (function) on this tree, and making additions is a matter of adding a node. For example, adding in the functionality to handle WAV files in our samples page only requires changing the function `fileEntry`, when it's broken down like this (Figure 14.2).

■14.2 Functional Programming: Programming in Very Few Lines

If you're willing to *trust* your functions, you can write fewer lines of code and get the same programs written. When you really understand functions, and trust that your functions do what you meant them to do, you can do

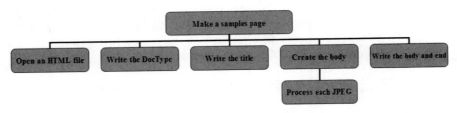

FIGURE 14.1: A hierarchy of functions for creating a samples page.

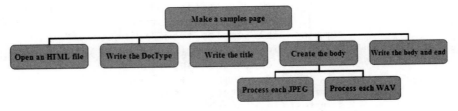

FIGURE 14.2: Changing the program is only a slight change to the hierarchy.

amazing things in a very few lines of code. We can write functions that apply functions to data, and even have functions call themselves in a process called **recursion**.

Functions are just names that are associated with values that are pieces of code, rather than lists or sequences or numbers or strings. We invoke or call a function by stating its name followed by inputs in parentheses. Without parentheses, the name of the function still has a value—it's the function's code. Functions can also be *data*—they can be passed as inputs to *other* functions!

```
>>> print makeSamplePage
<function makeSamplePage at 4222078>
>>> print fileEntry
<function fileEntry at 10206598>
```

apply() is a function that takes as input another function and the inputs (as a sequence or list) to that function. Literally, apply() applies the function to the input.

```
def hello(someone):
  print "Hello,",someone
>>> hello("Mark")
Hello, Mark
>>> apply(hello,["Mark"])
Hello, Mark
>>> apply(hello,["Betty"])
Hello, Betty
```

A more useful function that takes functions as input is map(). It's a function that takes a function and a sequence as input. But map applies the function to *each* input in the sequence, and returns whatever the function returns for each input.

```
>>> map(hello, ["Mark","Betty","Matthew","Jenny"])
Hello, Mark
Hello, Betty
Hello, Matthew
Hello, Jenny
[None, None, None, None]
```

filter() also takes a function and a sequence as input. It applies the function to each element of the sequence. If the *return value* of the function on that element is true (1), then the filter returns that element. If the return is false (0), then the filter skips that element. We can use filter() to quickly pull out data of interest to us.

```
def rname(somename):
  if somename.find("r") == -1:
    return 0
```

```
    if somename.find("r") != -1:
      return 1
```

```
>>> rname("January")
1
>>> rname("July")
0
>>> filter(rname, ["Mark","Betty","Matthew","Jenny"])
['Mark']
```

We can rewrite rname() above (a function that returns true if the input word contains an 'r') in a much shorter form. Expressions actually do evaluate to 1 or 0 (true or false). We can perform operations on these *logical values*. One of these **logical operators** is not—it returns the opposite of its input value. So here's rname() written using logical operators.

```
def rname2(somename):
  return not(somename.find("r") == -1)
```

```
>>> filter(rname2, ["Mark","Betty","Matthew","Jenny"])
['Mark']
```

reduce() also takes a function and a sequence, but reduce *combines* the results. Below is an example where we total all the numbers: 1 + 2, then (1 + 2) + 3, then (1 + 2 + 3) + 4, and finally (1 + 2 + 3 + 4) + 5. The total so far is passed in as the a input.

```
def add(a,b):
  return a+b
```

```
>>> reduce(add,[1,2,3,4,5])
15
```

Let's look at the example again: Doesn't it seem like a waste to have to create that add function when it's so small and does so little? It turns out that we don't have to give a function a name in order be able to use it. A nameless function is called a lambda. This is a very old term in computer science, one that dates back to one of the original programming languages, Lisp. Wherever you would otherwise use a function name, you can just stick in a lambda. The syntax of a lamda is the word lambda followed by input variables separated by commas, then a colon, then the body of the function. Here are some examples, including the above reduce example recreated with lambda. As you can see, we can define functions that are virtually identical to the ones typed in the Program Area by assigning a name to a lambda.

```
>>> reduce(lambda a,b:a+b, [1,2,3,4,5])
15
>>> (lambda a:"Hello,"+a)("Mark")
'Hello,Mark'
```

```
>>> f=lambda a:"Hello, "+a
>>> f
<function <lambda> at 27525947>
>>> f("Mark")
'Hello, Mark'
```

Using reduce and lambda, we can do real computation. Here's a function that computes *factorial*. Remember that the factorial of n is $n * n - 1 * n - 2... * 1$.

RECIPE 117: Factorial using lambda and reduce

```
def factorial(a):
    return reduce(lambda a,b:a*b, range(1,a+1))
```

How it works: It's easiest to read this program right to left. The first thing we do is to create a list of all the numbers from 1 to a with range(1,a+1). We then use reduce to apply a function (the lambda) that multiplies all the numbers in the input list one by the next, by the next, and on until finished.

```
>>> factorial(2)
2
>>> factorial(3)
6
>>> factorial(4)
24
>>> factorial(10)
3628800
```

You might be thinking at this point, "Okay, map, filter, and reduce look like they might be useful. *Might*. Sometimes. But why in the world would anyone want to use apply? That's the same as just typing the function call ourselves, isn't it?" That's true, but we can actually *make* map, filter, and reduce using apply. We can literally make any version of these that we might want ourselves using apply.

```
def mymap(function,list):
    for i in list:
        apply(function,[i])
```

```
>>> mymap(hello, ["Fred","Barney","Wilma","Betty"])
Hello, Fred Hello, Barney Hello, Wilma Hello, Betty
```

This style of programming is called *functional programming*. What we've been doing is defining procedures, so it's called *procedural programming*. Focusing on functions as data and on functions that use functions as input are the key ideas in functional programming.

Functional programming is amazingly powerful. You apply layers upon layers of functions to other functions, and you end up doing a lot in a few lines of program code. Functional programming is used a lot in building artificial intelligence systems and in building prototypes. These are areas where the problems are hard and ill-defined, so you want to be able to do a lot with only a few lines of program code—even if those few lines are pretty hard to read for most people.

Remember the function to turn Barb's hair red—Recipe 33? Here it is again:

```
def turnRed():
  brown = makeColor(57,16,8)
  file="/Users/guzdial/mediasources/barbara.jpg"
  picture=makePicture(file)
  for px in getPixels(picture):
    color = getColor(px)
    if distance(color,brown)<50.0:
      redness=int(getRed(px)*1.5)
      blueness=getBlue(px)
      greenness=getGreen(px)
      setColor(px,makeColor(redness,blueness,greenness))
  show(picture)
  return(picture)
```

We can write it as only a *single line* of program code. We need two utility functions—one that will check a single pixel for whether we want to turn the pixel red and another that will actually do it. Our single line of program code filters out the pixels that match our criteria for changing, then maps the change function to those pixels. In functional programming, you don't write functions with big loops. Instead, you write small functions and apply them to the data. It's like we're bringing the function to the data, rather than making the function go get all the data.

RECIPE 118: Turn hair red, functionally

```
def turnHairRed(pic):
  map(turnRed,filter(checkPixel,getPixels(pic)))

def checkPixel(apixel):
  brown = makeColor(57,16,8)
  return distance (getColor(apixel),brown)<100.0

def turnRed(apixel):
  setRed(apixel,getRed(apixel)*1.5)
```

How it works: The function turnRed takes a single pixel and increases its redness by 50%. The function checkPixel returns true or false if an input pixel is close enough to brown. The function turnHairRed takes a picture as input, then applies checkPixel using filter to all the pixels in the input picture (using getPixels). If the pixel is brown enough, filter returns it. We then use map to apply turnRed to all the pixels that filter returns.

Here's how we use it:

```
>>> pic=makePicture(getMediaPath("barbara.jpg"))
>>> map(turnRed, filter(checkPixel, getPixels(pic)))
```

14.2.1 Recursion: A Powerful Idea

Recursion is writing functions that call *themselves*. Instead of writing loops, you write a function that loops by calling itself again and again and again. When you write a recursive function, you always have at least two pieces:

■ What to do when you're done (e.g., when you're processing the very last item in the data), and

■ What to do when the data are larger, which usually involves processing one element of the data, then recalling the function to deal with the rest.

We can think about functions like decreaseRed() like this.

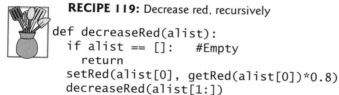

RECIPE 119: Decrease red, recursively

```
def decreaseRed(alist):
    if alist == []:    #Empty
        return
    setRed(alist[0], getRed(alist[0])*0.8)
    decreaseRed(alist[1:])
```

How it works: If the input list of pixels is empty, then we stop (return). Otherwise, we take the first pixel in the list (alist[0]) and decrease its red by 20% (multiply by 0.8). Then we call decreaseRed on the *rest* of the list (alist[1:]).

We'd call this version like this: decreaseRed(getPixels(pic)). *Warning:* it actually won't work even for reasonable-size pictures. Python (and the Java underlying Jython) don't expect recursion of this amount of depth, so they run out of memory. It does work with *really* small pictures.

Let's take a smaller function to explore:

```
>>> downUp("Hello")
Hello
ello
llo
lo
o
lo
llo
ello
Hello
```

Recursion can be hard to get your head around. It really relies on you *trusting* your functions. Does the function do what it's supposed to do? Then just call it, and it'll do the right thing.

We're going to talk about recursion in three ways to help you understand it. The first way is ***procedural abstraction***—breaking the problem down into the smallest pieces that we can write down easily as functions, and reusing as much as possible.

Let's think about downUp for one-character words. That's easy:

```
def downUp1(word):
    print word
```

```
>>> downUp1("I")
I
```

Now let's do downUp for two-character words. We'll reuse downUp1 because we have it already.

```
def downUp2(word):
    print word
    downUp1(word[1:])
    print word
>>> downUp2("it")
it
t
it
>>> downUp2("me")
me
e
me
```

Now for three-character words:

```
def downUp3(word):
    print word
    downUp2(word[1:])
    print word
```

```
>>> downUp3("pop")
pop
op
p
op
pop
>>> downUp3("top")
top
op
p
op
top
```

Are we seeing a pattern yet? Let's try it:

```
def downUpTest(word):
  print word
  downUpTest(word[1:])
  print word

>>> downUpTest("hello")
hello
ello
llo
lo
o
I wasn't able to do what you wanted.
The error java.lang.StackOverflowError has occurred
```

What happened? When we got down to one character, we just kept recalling downUpTest until we ran out of memory in an area called the *Stack*. We need to be able to tell our function "If we're down to only a single character, just print it and do *not* call yourself again!" The function shown below works.

RECIPE 120: downUp recursively

```
def downUp(word):
  if len(word)==1:
    print word
    return
  print word
  downUp(word[1:])
  print word
```

Here's our second way of thinking about recursion: good old tracing! I'll insert comments indented.

```
>>> downUp("Hello")
```

	The len(word) is not 1, so we print the word
Hello	
	Now we call downUp("ello") Still not one character, so print it
ello	
	Now we call downUp("llo") Still not one character, so print it

---

llo

> Now we call downUp("lo")
> Still not one character, so print it

---

lo

> Now call downUp(o")
> *Thats one character!* Print it, and return

---

o

> downUp("lo") now continues from its call to downUp("o")
> It prints again and ends.

---

lo

> downUp("llo") now continues (back from downUp("lo"))
> It prints and ends.

---

llo

> downUp("ello") now continues.
> It prints and ends.

---

ello

> Finally, the last line of the original downUp("Hello") can run.

Hello

===

A third way of thinking about this is to imagine a *function invocation* as an *elf*—a little person inside the computer who's going to do what you say.

Here are the downUp instructions to the elves:

1. Accept a word as input.
2. If your word has only one character, write it on the screen and you're done. Stop and sit down.
3. Write your word down on the screen.
4. Hire another elf to do the same instructions and give the new elf your word minus the first character.
5. Wait until the elf you hired is done.
6. Write your word down on the screen again. You're done.

I suggest trying this in your own class—it's fun and helps recursion make sense. It works something like this:

■ We start out hiring our first elf with the input "Hello."

(Think of this as an abstraction of an elf.)

■ The elf carrying "Hello" follows the instructions. He accepts the word as input, sees that it has more than character, and writes it on the screen: `Hello`. It then hires a new elf and gives it the input "ello."

■ The "ello"-carrying elf accepts the input, sees that it has more than one character, and writes it on the screen (`ello`, right under `Hello`). She then hires a new elf and hands it the input "llo."

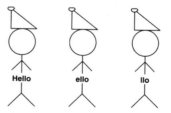

■ At this point, we can make a few observations. Each elf is only aware of the elf to his left—the one he hired. He has to wait for that elf to finish before he can finish. When the elves start finishing, the first ones to finish will be the ones to the right, who were the last ones to be hired. We call this a *stack*—the elves "stack up" left to right, and the *last* one up is the *first* one out.

If the original input was a really big word (e.g., "antidisestablishmentarianism"), you could imagine not having enough room for all the elves to stack up. We'd call that *stack overflow*—that's literally the error that Python gives you if the recursion gets too deep (i.e., too many elves).

■ Imagine that we continue the simulation. We hire elves for "lo" and "o." The "o" elf writes down her o, then sits down.

■ The "lo" elf now finishes up. She writes lo on the screen—which is below the o which is below the lo. And the "lo" elf sits down. That leaves us with three more elves awaiting their turns.

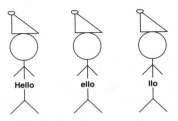

■ The "llo" elf writes llo and sits down.

■ The "ello" elf has been waiting for the "llo" elf to finish. He writes ello on the screen and sits down.

■ Finally, the "Hello" elf writes down Hello for the second time and sits down. The stack is now empty.

Why use functional programming and recursion? Because it lets you do a lot in a very few lines of code. It's a very useful technique for dealing with hard problems. Any kind of loop can be implemented with recursion, so it's the most flexible and powerful form of looping.

■14.3 Object-Oriented Programming

The most common style of programming today is ***object-oriented programming***. We're going to define it in contrast with the procedural programming that we've been doing up until now.

Back in the 1960s and 1970s, procedural programming was the dominant form of programming. People used *procedural abstraction* and defined lots of functions at high and low levels, and reused their functions wherever possible. This worked reasonably well—up to a point. As programs got really large and complex, with many programmers working on them at the same time, procedural programming started to break down.

Programmers ran into problems with procedure conflicts. People would write programs that modified data in ways that other people didn't expect. They would use the same names for functions and find that their code couldn't be integrated into one large program.

There were also problems in *thinking* about programs and the tasks the programs were supposed to perform. Procedures are about *verbs*—tell the computer to do this, tell the computer to do that. But it's not clear whether that's the way people think best about problems.

Object-oriented programming is *noun-oriented programming*. Someone building an object-oriented program starts by thinking about what the nouns are in the *domain* of the problem—what are the people and things that are part of this problem and its solution? The process of identifying the objects, what each of them knows about (with respect to the problem), and what each of them has to do is called ***object-oriented analysis***.

Programming in an object-oriented way means that you define variables (called ***instance variables***) *for the objects* and you define functions (called ***methods***) *for the objects*. You have very few or even *no* global functions or variables—things that are accessible everywhere. Instead, objects talk to one another by asking each other to do things via their methods. Adele Goldberg, one of the pioneers of object-oriented programming, calls this "Ask, don't touch." You can't just "touch" data and do whatever you want with it—instead, you "ask" objects to manipulate their data through their methods.

The term "object-oriented programming" was invented by Alan Kay. Kay is a brilliant multidisciplinary character—he holds undergraduate degrees in mathematics and biology, a Ph.D. in computer science, and has been a professional jazz guitarist. In 2004 he was awarded the ACM Turing Award, the Nobel Prize of computing. Kay saw object-oriented programming as a way of developing software that could truly scale to large systems. He described objects as being like biological *cells* that work together in well-defined ways to make the whole organism work. Like cells, objects would—

■ Help manage *complexity* by distributing responsibility for tasks across many objects rather than one big program.

■ Support *robustness* by making the objects work relatively independently.

■ Support *reuse* because each object would provide *services* to other objects (tasks that the object would do for other objects, accessible through its methods), just as real-world objects do.

The notion of starting from nouns is part of Kay's vision. *Software*, he said, is actually a *simulation* of the world. By making software *model* the world, it becomes clearer how to make software. You look at the world and how it works, then copy that into software. Things in the world *know* things—these become *instance variables*. Things in the world can *do* things—these become *methods*.

14.3.1 An Object-Oriented Slide Show

Let's use object-oriented techniques to build a slide show program. Let's say that we want to show a picture, then play a corresponding sound and wait until the sound is done before going on to the next picture. We'll use the function (mentioned many chapters ago) *blockingPlay()*.

RECIPE 121: Slide show as one big function

```
def playslideshow():
    pic = makePicture(getMediaPath("barbara.jpg"))
    snd = makeSound(getMediaPath("bassoon-c4.wav"))
    show(pic)
    blockingPlay(snd)
    pic = makePicture(getMediaPath("beach.jpg"))
    snd = makeSound(getMediaPath("bassoon-e4.wav"))
    show(pic)
    blockingPlay(snd)
    pic = makePicture(getMediaPath("santa.jpg"))
    snd = makeSound(getMediaPath("bassoon-g4.wav"))
    show(pic)
    blockingPlay(snd)
    pic = makePicture(getMediaPath("jungle2.jpg"))
    snd = makeSound(getMediaPath("bassoon-c4.wav"))
    show(pic)
    blockingPlay(snd)
```

This isn't a very good program from any perspective. From a procedural programming perspective, there's an awful lot of duplicated code here. It would be nice to get rid of it. From an object-oriented programming perspective, we should have an *object*: a slide.

As we mentioned, objects have two parts. Objects *know* things—these become *instance variables*. Objects can *do* things—these become *methods*. We're going to access both of these using dot notation.

So what does a slide know? It knows its *picture* and its *sound*. What can a slide do? It can *show* itself, by showing its picture and (block) playing its sound.

To define a slide object in Python (and many other object-oriented programming languages, including Java and C++), we must define a slide *class*. A class defines the instance variables and methods for a set of objects—that is, what each object of that class knows and can do. Each object of the class is called an *instance* of the class. We'll make multiple slides by making multiple instances of the slide class—just as our bodies might make multiple kidney cells or multiple heart cells, each of which knows how to do certain kinds of tasks.

To create a class in Python, we start with:

```
class slide:
```

What comes after this, indented, are the methods for creating new slides and playing slides. Let's add a *show()* method to our slide class.

```
class slide:
  def show(self):
    show(self.picture)
    blockingPlay(self.sound)
```

To create new instances, we call the class name like a function. We can define new instance variables by simply assigning them. So here is how to create a slide and give it a picture and sound.

```
>>> slide1=slide()
>>> slide1.picture = makePicture(getMediaPath
  ("barbara.jpg"))
>>> slide1.sound = makeSound(getMediaPath
  ("bassoon-c4.wav"))
```

We can now show our slide by saying `slide1.show()`.

What's this `self` stuff? When we execute `object.method()`, Python finds the method in the object's class, then calls it, using the instance object as an *input*. It's Python style to name this input variable `self` (because it is the object itself). Since we have the object in the variable `self`, we can then access its picture and sound by saying `self.picture` and `self.sound`.

But this is still pretty hard to use if we have to set up all the variables from the Command Area. How could we make it easier? What if we could pass in the sound and picture for the slides as *inputs* to the `slide` class, as if the class were a real function? We can do this by defining something called a **constructor**.

To create new instances with some inputs, we must define a function named `__init__`. That's "underscore-underscore-i-n-i-t-underscore-underscore." It's the predefined name in Python for a method that *initializes* new objects. Our `__init__` method needs three inputs: the instance itself (because all methods get that), a picture, and a sound.

RECIPE 122: A Slide Class

```
class slide:
  def __init__(self, pictureFile,soundFile):
    self.picture = makePicture(pictureFile)
    self.sound = makeSound(soundFile)

  def show(self):
    show(self.picture)
    blockingPlay(self.sound)
```

We can use our slide class to define a slide show like this.

RECIPE 123: A slide show, using our `Slide` class

```
def playslideshow():
    slide1 = slide(getMediaPath("barbara.jpg"), getMediaPath
("bassoon-c4.wav"))
    slide2 = slide(getMediaPath("beach.jpg"),getMediaPath
("bassoon-e4.wav"))
    slide3 = slide(getMediaPath("santa.jpg"),getMediaPath
("bassoon-g4.wav"))
    slide4 = slide(getMediaPath("jungle2.jpg"),getMediaPath
("bassoon-c4.wav"))
    slide1.show()
    slide2.show()
    slide3.show()
    slide4.show()
```

One of the features of Python that make it so powerful is that we can mix object-oriented and functional programming styles. Slides are now objects that can easily be stored in lists, like any other kind of Python object. Here's an example of the same slide show where we use map to show the slide show.

RECIPE 124: Slide show, in objects and functions

```
def showSlide(aslide):
    aslide.show()

def playslideshow():
    slide1 = slide(getMediaPath("barbara.jpg"), getMediaPath
("bassoon-c4.wav"))
    slide2 = slide(getMediaPath("beach.jpg"),getMediaPath
("bassoon-e4.wav"))
    slide3 = slide(getMediaPath("santa.jpg"),getMediaPath
("bassoon-g4.wav"))
    slide4 = slide(getMediaPath("jungle2.jpg"),getMediaPath
("bassoon-c4.wav"))
    map(showSlide,[slide1,slide2,slide3,slide4])
```

Is the object-oriented version of the slide show easier to write? It certainly has less replication of code. It features *encapsulation* in that the data and behavior of the object are defined in one and only one place, so that any change to one is easily changed in the other. Being able to use lots of objects (like lists of objects) is called *aggregation*. This is a very powerful idea. We don't always have to define new classes—we can often use the powerful structures we know, like lists with existing objects, to great impact.

14.3.2 Joe the Box

The earliest example used to teach object-oriented programming was developed by Adele Goldberg and Alan Kay—it's called *Joe the Box*. Imagine that you have a class Box like the one below:

```
class Box:
  def __init__(self):
    self.setDefaultColor()
    self.size=10
    self.position=(10,10)
  def setDefaultColor(self):
    self.color = red
  def draw(self,canvas):
    addRectFilled(canvas, self.position[0],
 self.position[1], self.size, self.size, self.color)
```

What will you see if you execute the following code?

```
>>> canvas = makeEmptyPicture(400,200)
>>> joe = Box()
>>> joe.draw(canvas)
>>> show(canvas)
```

Let's trace it out.

■ Obviously, the first line just creates a black canvas that is 400 pixels wide and 200 pixels high.

■ When we create joe, the __init__ method is called. The method setDefault-Color is called on joe, so he gets a default color of red. When self.color=red is executed, the *instance variable* color is created for joe and gets a value of red. We return to __init__, where joe is given a size of 10 and a position of (10,10) (size and position both become new instance variables).

■ When joe is asked to draw himself on the canvas, he's drawn as a red, filled rectangle (addRectFilled), at *x* position 10 and *y* position 10, with a size of 10 pixels on each side.

We could add a method to Box that allows us to make joe change his size.

```
class Box:
  def __init__(self):
    self.setDefaultColor()
    self.size=10
    self.position=(10,10)
  def setDefaultColor(self):
    self.color = red
  def draw(self,canvas):
    addRectFilled(canvas, self.position[0],
 self.position[1], self.size, self.size, self.color)
  def grow(self,size):
    self.size=self.size+size
```

Now we can tell joe to grow. A negative number like -2 will cause joe to shrink. A positive number will cause joe to grow—though we'd have to add a move method if we wanted him to grow much and still fit on the canvas.

Now consider the following code added to the same Program Area.

```
class SadBox(Box):
    def setDefaultColor(self):
        self.color=blue
```

Note that SadBox lists Box as a *superclass*. This means that SadBox *inherits* all the methods of Box. What will you see if you execute the code below?

```
>>> jane = SadBox()
>>> jane.draw(canvas)
>>> repaint(canvas)
```

Let's trace it out:

■ When jane is created as a SadBox, the method __init__ is executed in class Box.

■ The first thing that happens in __init__ is that we call setDefaultColor *on the input object* self. That object is now jane. So we call jane's setDefaultColor. We say that SadBox's setDefaultColor *overrides* Box's.

■ The setDefaultColor for jane sets the color to blue.

■ We then return to executing the rest of Box's __init__. We set jane's size to 10 and position to (10,10).

■ When we tell jane to draw, she appears as a 10 × 10 blue square at position (10,10). If we hadn't moved or grown joe, he would disappear as jane is drawn on top of him.

Note that joe and jane are each a different *kind* of Box. They have the same instance variables (but different *values* for the same variables) and mostly know the same things. Because both understand draw, for example, we say that draw is *polymorphic*. Different objects of different classes do the same kind of thing when told to execute the method. A SadBox (jane) is slightly different in how it behaves when it created, so it knows some things differently. Joe and Jane highlight some of the basic ideas of object-oriented programming: inheritance, specialization in subclasses, and shared instance variables while having different instance variable values.

14.3.3 Object-Oriented Media

Of course, we've been using objects already. Pictures, sounds, samples, and colors are all objects. Our lists of pixels and samples are certainly examples of aggregation. The functions we've been using are actually just covering up the underlying methods. We certainly can just call the objects' methods directly.

```
>>> pic=makePicture(getMediaPath("barbara.jpg"))
>>> pic.show()
```

Here's how the *function* show() is defined. You can ignore raise and __class__. The key point is that the function is simply executing the existing method.

```
def show(picture):
    if not picture.__class__ == Picture:
        print "show(picture): Input is not a picture"
        raise ValueError
    picture.show()
```

Did you notice that we defined the method show() for slides, the same name that we have for showing pictures? First of all, we can clearly do that—objects can have their own methods with names that other objects also use. Much more powerful is that each of these methods with the same name can achieve the same *goal*, but in different ways. For both slides and pictures, the method show() says, "Show the object." But what's really happening is different in each case: Pictures just show themselves, but slides show their pictures and play their sounds.

COMPUTER SCIENCE IDEA: Polymorphism

When the same name can be used to invoke different methods that achieve the same goal, we call that *polymorphism*. It's very powerful for the programmer. You simply tell an object show()—you don't have to care exactly what method is being executed, and you don't even know exactly what object it is that you're telling the object to show. You the programmer simply specify your *goal*, to show the object. The object-oriented program handles the rest.

There are several examples of polymorphism built into the methods that we're using in JES.[1] For example, both pixels and colors understand the methods setRed, getRed, setBlue, getBlue, setGreen, and getGreen. This allows us to manipulate the colors of the pixels without pulling out the color objects separately. We could have defined the functions to take both kinds of inputs or to provide different functions for each kind of input, but both of those options get confusing. It's easy to do with methods.

```
>>> pic=makePicture(getMediaPath("barbara.jpg"))
>>> pic.show()
>>> pixel = getPixel(pic,100,200)
>>> print pixel.getRed()
73
>>> color = pixel.getColor()
>>> print color.getRed()
73
```

---

[1] Recall that JES is an environment for programming in Jython, which is a specific kind of Python. The media supports are part of what JES provides—they're not part of the core of Python.

Another example is the method `writeTo()`. The method `writeTo(filename)` is defined for both pictures and sounds. Did you ever confuse `writePictureTo()` and `writeSoundTo()`? Isn't it easier to just always write `writeTo(filename)`? That's why that method is named the same in both classes, and why polymorphism is so powerful. (You may be wondering why we didn't introduce this in the first place. Were you ready in Chapter 2 to talk about dot notation and polymorphic methods? Didn't think so.)

Overall, there are actually many more methods defined in JES than functions. More specifically, there are a bunch of methods for drawing onto pictures that aren't available as functions.

■ As you would expect, pictures understand `pic.addRect(color,x,y,width,height)`, `pic.addRectFilled(color,x,y,width,height)`, `pic.addOval(color,x,y,width,height)`, and `pic.addOvalFilled(color,x,y,width,height)`.

See Figure 14.3 for examples of rectangle methods drawn from the following example.

```
>>> pic=makePicture (getMediaPath("640x480.jpg"))
>>> pic.addRectFilled (orange,10,10,100,100)
>>> pic.addRect (blue,200,200,50,50)
>>> pic.show()
>>> pic.writeTo("newrects.jpg")
```

See Figure 14.4 for examples of ovals drawn from the following example.

```
>>> pic=makePicture (getMediaPath("640x480.jpg"))
>>> pic.addOval (green,200,200,50,50)
>>> pic.addOvalFilled (magenta,10,10,100,100)
>>> pic.show()
>>> pic.writeTo("ovals.jpg")
```

■ Pictures also understand *arcs*. Arcs are literally parts of a circle. The two methods are `pic.addArc(color,x,y,width,height,startangle,arcangle)` and `pic.addArcFilled(color,x,y,width,height,startangle,arcangle)`. They draw arcs for `arcangle` degrees, where `startangle` is the

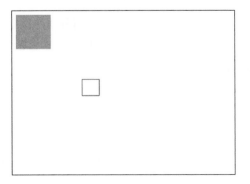

FIGURE 14.3: Examples of rectangle methods.

FIGURE 14.4: Examples of oval methods.

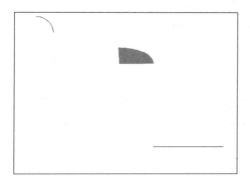

FIGURE 14.5: Examples of arc methods.

starting point. 0 degrees is at 3 o'clock on the clock face. A positive arc is counter-clockwise, and negative is clockwise. The center of the circle is the middle of the rectangle defined by (x, y) with the given `width` and `height`.

■ We can also now draw colored lines, using `pic.addLine(color,x1,y1, x2,y2)`.

See Figure 14.5 for examples of arcs and lines drawn from the following example.

```
>>> pic=makePicture (getMediaPath("640x480.jpg"))
>>> pic.addArc(red,10,10,100,100,5,45)
>>> pic.show()
>>> pic.addArcFilled (green,200,100,200,100,1,90)
>>> pic.repaint()
>>> pic.addLine(blue,400,400,600,400)
>>> pic.repaint()
>>> pic.writeTo("arcs-lines.jpg")
```

■ Text in Java can have styles, but these are limited to make sure that all platforms can replicate them. `pic.addText(color,x,y,string)` is the one we would expect to see. There is also `pic.addTextWithStyle(color,x,y, string,style)`, which takes a style created from `makeStyle(font,emphasis,`

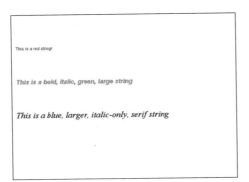

FIGURE 14.6: Examples of text methods.

size). The font is sansSerif, serif or mono. The emphasis is italic, bold, or plain, or sum them to get combinations (e.g., italic+bold. size is a point size).

See Figure 14.6 for examples of text drawn from the following example.

```
>>> pic=makePicture (getMediaPath("640x480.jpg"))
>>> pic.addText(red,10,100,"This is a red  string!")
>>> pic.addTextWithStyle (green,10,200,"This is a bold,
 italic, green, large string", makeStyle(sansSerif,
 bold+italic,18))
>>> pic.addTextWithStyle (blue,10,300,"This is a blue,
 larger, italic-only, serif string", makeStyle(serif,
 italic,24))
>>> pic.writeTo("text.jpg")
```

The older media functions that we wrote can be rewritten in method form.

RECIPE 125: Making a sunset using methods

```
def makeSunset(picture):
    for p in getPixels(picture):
        p.setBlue(p.getBlue()*0.7)
        p.setGreen(p.getGreen()*0.7)
```

The methods for accessing samples are getSampleValue and getSampleObjectAt.

RECIPE 126: Turn a sound backwards using methods

```
def backwards(filename):
    source = makeSound(filename)
    target = makeSound(filename)

    sourceIndex = source.getLength()
    for targetIndex in range(1,target.getLength()+1): .
        # The method is getSampleValue, not getSampleValueAt
```

```
sourceValue =source.getSampleValue(sourceIndex)
# The method is setSampleValue, not setSampleValueAt
target.setSampleValue(targetIndex,sourceValue)
sourceIndex = sourceIndex - 1

return target
```

14.3.4 Why Objects?

One role for objects is to reduce the number of names that you have to remember. Through polymorphism, you only have to remember the name and the goal, not all the various global functions.

More important, though, objects encapsulate data and behavior. Imagine that you wanted to change the name of an instance variable and then all the methods that use the variable. That's alot to change. What if you miss one? Changing them all in one place, together, is useful.

Aggregation is also a significant benefit of object systems. You can have lots of objects doing useful things. Want more? Just create them!

Python's objects are similar to the objects of many languages. One significant difference is in access to instance variables, though. In Python, any object can access and manipulate any other object's instance variables. That's not true in languages like Java, C++, or Smalltalk. In these other languages, access to instance variables from other objects is limited and can even be eliminated entirely—then you can only access objects' instance variables through methods called *getters* and *setters* (to get and set the instance variable).

Another big part of object systems that we haven't addressed is *inheritance*. We can declare one class (*parent class*) to be *inherited* by another class (*child class*). Inheritance provides for instant polymorphism—the instances of the child automatically have all the data and behavior of the parent class. The child can then add more behavior and data to what the parent class had. This is called making the child a *specialization* of the parent class. For example, a 3-D rectangle instance might know and do everything that a rectangle instance does by saying `class rectangle3D(rectangle)`.

Inheritance gets a lot of press in the object-oriented world, but it's a trade-off. It reduces even further the duplication of code. But in actual practice, inheritance isn't used all *that* much, and it can be confusing. Whose method is being executed when I type this?

```
mybox = rectangle3D()
mybox.draw()
```

So when should you use objects? You should define your own object classes when you have data in groups (e.g., pictures and sounds) and behavior that you want to define for all instances of the group. You should use existing objects *all the time*. They're very powerful. If you're not comfortable with dot notation and the ideas of objects, you can stick with functions—they work just fine. Objects just give you a leg up on more complex systems.

Programming Summary

Some of the functions and programming pieces that we met in this chapter.

Functional Programming

`apply`	Inputs a function and a list as input to the function, where the list has as many elements as the function takes as input. Calls the function on the input.
`map`	Inputs a function and a list of several inputs to the function. Calls the function on each of the inputs and returns a list of the outputs (`return` values).
`filter`	Inputs a function and a list of several inputs to the function. Calls the function on each of the list elements and returns the *input element* if the function returns true (non-zero) for that element.
`reduce`	Inputs a function that takes two inputs and a list of several inputs to the function. The function is applied to the first two list elements, then the result of that is used as input with the next list element, then the result of that is used as input with the *next* list element, and so on. The overall result is returned at the end.

Object-Oriented Programming

`class`	Lets you define a class. The keyword `class` takes a class name and an optional superclass in parentheses, ending with a colon. Methods for the class follow, indented within the class block.
`__init__`	The name of the method called on an object when it's first created. It's not required to have one.

Graphics methods

`addRect, addRect-Filled`	The *methods* in the `Picture` class for drawing rectangles and filled rectangles.
`addOval, addOval-Filled`	The methods in the `Picture` class for drawing ovals and filled ovals.
`addArc, addArc-Filled`	The methods in the `Picture` class for drawing arcs and filled arcs.
`addText, addTextWithStyle`	The methods in the `Picture` class for drawing text and text with style elements (like boldface or sans-serif).

addLine	The method in the Picture class for drawing a line.
getRed, getGreen, getBlue	The methods for both Pixel and Color objects for getting the red, green, and blue color components.
setRed, setGreen, setBlue	The methods for both Pixel and Color objects for setting the red, green, and blue color components.

Problems

14.1 Here's a puzzle. You have six blocks. One of them weighs more than the other. You have a scale, but you can only use it twice. Find the heaviest one. (a) Write down your process as an algorithm. (b) What searching method is this like?

14.2 Change the functional turnHairRed() in Recipe 118 into *only* a single line by recoding the utility functions as lambda functions.

14.3 Try writing upDown():

```
>>> upDown("Hello")
Hello
Hell
Hel
He
H
He
Hel
Hell
Hello
```

Try to write it *both* recursively and without recursion. Which is easier? Why?

14.4 Try writing more of our sound and picture examples from the earlier chapters using methods instead of JES functions.

14.5 Try writing some of our sound and picture examples from the earlier chapters *functionally*, using things like filter and map.

14.6 Some object-oriented questions:

■ What is the difference between an instance and a class?

■ How are functions and methods different?

■ How is object-oriented programming different from procedural programming and functional programming?

■ What is polymorphism?

■ What is encapsulation?

■ What is aggregation?

■ How did biological cells influence the development of the idea of objects?

14.7 Make some modifications to Joe the Box.

■ Add a method to Box named setColor that takes a color as input, then makes the input color the new color for the box. (Maybe setDefaultColor should call setColor?)

■ Add a method to Box named setSize that takes a number as input, then makes the input number the new size for the box.

■ Add a method to Box named setPosition that takes a list or tuple as argument, then makes that input the new position for the box.

■ Change __init__ so that it uses setSize and setPosition rather than simply setting the instance variables.

*14.8 Finish the Joe the Box example.

(a) Implement grow and move. The method move takes as input a relative distance like (-10,15) to move 10 pixels up (x position) and 15 pixels to the right (y position).

(b) Draw patterns by creating joe and jane, then move a little and draw, grow a little and draw, then repaint the new canvas.

To Dig Deeper

There is lots more to do with Python in exploring procedural, functional, and object-oriented programming styles. I recommend the books by Mark Lutz (especially [28]) and Richard Hightower [22] as nice introductions to the deeper realms of Python. You might also explore some of the tutorials at the Python Web site (http://www.python.org).

CHAPTER 15

Creating Graphical User Interfaces

15.1 Where Do Graphical User Interfaces Come From?
15.2 Creating a Basic Graphical User Interface
15.3 Callbacks and Layout Managers
15.4 Using Scrolling Lists

Chapter Learning Objectives

- *To make graphical user interfaces out of components such as windows, text fields, buttons, and scrolling lists.*

- *To use callbacks to handle user interface events.*

- *To use trees for conceptualizing user interface structure.*

■15.1 Where Do Graphical User Interfaces Come From?

The first computers were incredibly painful and tedious to work with. You "programmed" them by literally rewiring them. There was no screen, so you couldn't have a "graphical" user interface at all. Our common experience of using a keyboard to interact with the computer didn't come until much later.

In the late 1960s, the dominant mode of interaction with the computer was through *punched cards*. Using a keyboard on a card punch machine, you prepared your instructions for the computer on pieces of cardboard that were then ordered in the right sequence and loaded into the computer. Heaven help the person who dropped a stack of cards and had to reorder the hundreds of cards that made up a large program. The typical output from the computer back to the programmer consisted of large piles of paper printouts, though there was some starting work with computer music and computer graphics (on expensive specialized monitors).

In the 1960s and 1970s, computer scientists began envisioning a new role for the computer in its interaction with humans. Douglas Engelbart had the idea that a computer might *augment* human intelligence by reminding us of things, helping us to visualize ideas, and helping us collaborate, even with audio and video conferencing (which he demonstrated for the first time in 1968 with features that even tools like NetMeeting don't have today). Those were really radical ideas. Alan Kay went a step further and suggested the idea of *personal computers* that you might interact with to learn through creating and exploring multimedia—a goal for the computer that he called a *Dynabook*. This was an amazing vision, given where human–computer interaction was at that time.

It was hard to imagine interacting "creatively" with a computer in multimedia when all the interaction took place through cardboard cards. In the early 1970s, Kay and his team (Adele Goldberg, Dan Ingalls, Ted Kaehler, and others) at the Xerox PARC (Palo Alto Research Center) set out to invent the user interface for the Dynabook. Engelbart's group had already invented the *mouse*. Others had come up with the idea of *windows*, but Kay's group made the analogy of a window being like a piece of paper that could overlap on your *desktop*. They invented *menus* that would pop up and then go away. In sum, they invented the *WIMP interface* (overlapping Windows, Icons, Menus, and mouse Pointer), also called the *desktop interface* (because the interface was meant to resemble a physical working desk). That's where the *graphical user interface* as we know it today (also known as a *GUI* and pronounced "gooey") was born.

■15.2 Creating a Basic Graphical User Interface

In JES, we have the advantage of programming in Jython (as opposed to Python) and its special relationship with Java. Java has a very nice set of user interface objects and methods called *Swing*. We can use all of Swing from within JES without doing anything special.

We're going to build our first GUI from the Command Area. It won't do much, but it will help us see the basic components and how to use them. The problem we're going to work toward solving is having a new way to browse files. Rather than always using a pickAFile file dialog, we'll have a window that will let us explore the contents of files—viewing pictures in JPEG files and listening to sounds in WAV files.

The first thing we need to do is to make Swing available to us in JES. As with any other set of capabilities that go beyond the base language, we need to use an import statement.

```
>>> import javax.swing as swing
```

The name javax.swing is the formal name that Java uses for identifying the Swing user interface toolkit. That's a lot to type in dot notation whenever we use it, so we ask Jython to let us use an *alias* for it: swing.

Now we can create our first window. A window in Swing is called a JFrame. We create an instance of JFrame just as we would create any instance of a class in Jython.

```
>>> win = swing.JFrame("File Contents Viewer",
    size=(200,200))
```

Let's talk about what's in this function call.

■ The first part is the title of the window: "File Contents Viewer".

■ The next part specifies the default size of the window. We'll be able to make it bigger later, but 200 pixels wide by 200 pixels high is how we'll first see the window.

We're using a different kind of function call here that we haven't used up until now. Rather than simply associating input values with input variables by *position* (e.g., the first value goes to first input variable), it's possible to do it by name explicitly. Here we're seemingly setting the input variable size by assignment in the function call. User interface tools tend to have many options, so making the input variable settings explicit makes the code a bit more readable.

We can now make our window become *visible* by explicitly setting visible to true (Figure 15.1).

```
>>> win.visible = 1
```

While it's nice to get a window up on the screen, it is not particularly useful. The window doesn't *do* anything yet because there's nothing in it. The window will resize if you drag a corner or a side, and it will close (but don't close it yet). Let's next put something in our window.

Let's add a *text field* to our window. This will allow us to display text. The class we use is JTextField.

```
>>> field=swing.JTextField(preferredSize=(200,20))
```

In this example, we're creating a JTextField with a default size of 200 pixels across and 20 pixels top-to-bottom. We're naming it field. Let's put some text into this field. A JTextField instance has an instance variable named text. When we set this instance variable, we're setting the contents of the field.

```
>>> field.text = "Welcome to Swing!"
```

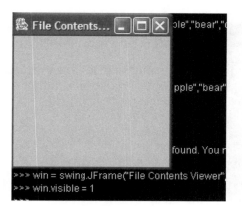

FIGURE 15.1: Opening our first JFrame (window).

Great—we now have an *invisible* text field. Not the most useful thing in the world. To make it visible, we need to put it in a window—we can't have a text field floating in space. But in order to do this, we need to say something about how user interfaces are constructed in memory.

User interfaces are constructed as a **tree**. There are components inside components. Our win window (instance of JFrame) actually has a lot of components to it, such as the title bar, the close box, and so on. The big (currently empty) part where we would expect to see pieces like text fields and buttons is called the **content pane**. In order to get the text field into our window, we need to add it to the content pane—we call this **composing** the text field within the window. When we do this, Jython responds with all the details of what's inside the field—a *big* long list.

```
>>> win.contentPane.add(field)
javax.swing.JTextField[, 0, 0, 0x0, invalid,
layout=javax.swing.plaf.basic.BasicTextUI$UpdateHandler,
alignmentX=null, alignmentY=null,
border=javax.swing.plaf.BorderUIResource$CompoundBorderUI
  Resource@518924,
flags=296, maximumSize=, minimumSize=,
preferredSize=java.awt.Dimension[width=200, height=20],
caretColor=javax.swing.plaf.ColorUIResource[r=0, g=0, b=0],
disabledTextColor=javax.swing.plaf.ColorUIResource[r=153,
  g=153, b=153], editable=true,
margin=javax.swing.plaf.InsetsUIResource[top=0, left=0,
  bottom=0, right=0], selectedTextColor=javax.swing.plaf.
  ColorUIResource[r=0, g=0, b=0], selectionColor=javax.
  swing.plaf.ColorUIResource [r=204, g=204, b=255],
  columns=0, columnWidth=0, command=,
  horizontalAlignment=LEADING]
```

Our window is still empty. To see our text field, we have to remind the window to be visible (much as we have to tell a Picture to repaint). Then we can see our window and our text field (Figure 15.2).

FIGURE 15.2: Our *JFrame* window with a *JTextField* text area composed.

Now let's add a ***button*** to our user interface. A button is a graphical object that users can click on to generate events. The class that we use for buttons in Swing is called JButton.

```
>>> button=swing.JButton("View Contents",preferredSize=
(200,20))
```

In this example, we're creating an instance of JButton with a label of "View Contents" and naming it button. Again, we're giving it a default size of 200 pixels across and 20 pixels top-to-bottom. To make it appear in the window, we add it to the content pane (with a *long* response), then remind the window to be visible (Figure 15.3).

```
>>> win.contentPane.add(button)
javax.swing.JButton[, 0, 0, 0x0, invalid,
layout=javax.swing.OverlayLayout, alignmentX=0.0,
 alignmentY=0.5, border=javax.swing.plaf.BorderUIResource
 $CompoundBorderUIResource@9165fa,
flags=296, maximumSize=, minimumSize=,
preferredSize=java.awt.Dimension[width=200, height=20],
defaultIcon=, disabledIcon=, disabledSelectedIcon=,
margin=javax.swing.plaf.InsetsUIResource[top=2, left=14,
 bottom=2, right=14], paintBorder=true, paintFocus=true,
 pressedIcon=, rolloverEnabled=false, rolloverIcon=,
 rolloverSelectedIcon=, selectedIcon=, text=View
 Contents,defaultCapable=true]
>>> win.visible=1
```

Our user interface at this point is wholly unsatisfactory. Neither our button nor our text area is legible. Clicking on the button makes nothing at all happen. Fixing up these problems is the point of the next section, but let's set the stage a bit here.

Think about the internal structure of our user interface. We have a window (JFrame) containing a content pane which itself contains a text area (JTextField) and a button (JButton). What we have is a *tree* (Figure 15.4).

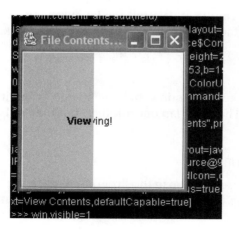

FIGURE 15.3: Our *JFrame* window with text and button composed.

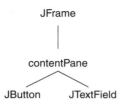

JFrame

contentPane

JButton   JTextField

FIGURE 15.4: Representing the internal structure of our user interface as a tree.

FIGURE 15.5: Our first window after packing and growing.

What our tree doesn't show us is how things should be laid out within the components. We will use a *layout manager* to structure how the tree is rendered.

There is a default layout manager when one isn't specified. The layout isn't very good as a default, but we can try it. We tell the layout manager to take a shot at rendering the user interface tree by telling the window to pack.

```
>>> win.pack()
>>> win.visible=1
```

The initial result of this is a teeny window, but when you expand it, you can see that both pieces are there. They overlap one another, but they're both there (Figure 15.5).

■15.3 Callbacks and Layout Managers

Let's start over again and create a program in the Program Area. User interfaces are much easier to manage with object-oriented programming. You may recall reading about Alan Kay in the chapter on object-oriented programming. Modern

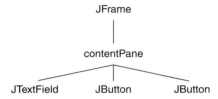

FIGURE 15.6: Representing the internal structure of the *File Contents Viewer* GUI.

object-oriented programming and graphical user interfaces were developed at the same time by the same people, so they fit together. Objects make GUIs easier.

In order to make our buttons do anything, we have to use ***callbacks***. We have to tell them what code to execute (to "call back" to) when a ***user interface event*** of interest (like clicking on a button, or tabbing out a field, or double-clicking on an item in a list) occurs. It's easiest to use methods for callbacks because this avoids the issue of ***scope***. At the time the button is clicked, which functions and variables will be available and in the current context? That's a hard question to answer. But if the user interface is associated with an instance of a class, we can expect that all the methods and instance variables associated with that instance will be available.

Here's a recipe that actually builds our file contents viewer, with a slightly more extended user interface structure than what we described earlier (Figure 15.6). The idea is to have a JTextField that holds a filename in the current media path. When you click the JButton "View Contents," the named file is shown (if it's a picture) or played (if it's a sound). The second JButton "Set Folder" lets you change the default media folder.

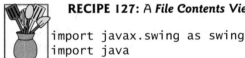

RECIPE 127: A *File Contents Viewer* with text field and buttons

```
import javax.swing as swing
import java

class FileContentsViewer(swing.JFrame):
  def __init__(self):
    swing.JFrame.__init__(self, title="File Contents
Viewer", size=(200,200))
    self.contentPane.layout=java.awt.FlowLayout()

    self.field=swing.JTextField(size=(200,60))
    self.field.text="barbara.jpg"
    self.contentPane.add(self.field)

    fileView = swing.JButton("View Contents", size=(65,30),
actionPerformed=self.checkContents)
    self.contentPane.add(fileView)

    setFolder = swing.JButton("Set Folder", size=(65,30),
actionPerformed=self.setFolder)
```

```
        self.contentPane.add(setFolder)
        self.visible = 1

    def checkContents(self,event):
      if self.field.text.endswith(".jpg"):
        pic = makePicture(getMediaPath(self.field.text))
        show(pic)
      if self.field.text.endswith(".wav"):
        snd=makeSound(getMediaPath(self.field.text))
        play(snd)

    def setFolder(self,event):
      setMediaPath()
```

To use this recipe we create an instance of the class, like `fcv = FileContentsViewer()`. We make it visible in `__init__`, so that it shows up right away (Figure 15.7).

How it works: This is a fairly complex example, so let's walk through it piece by piece.

■ We start out importing `swing` and also the general `java` libraries.

We create the class `FileContentsViewer` as a subclass of `JFrame`. This means that creating an instance of `FileContentsViewer` is actually creating a window. But this makes it a little trickier to create the basic window—how do we pass on to `JFrame` all those settings like the window title and default size?

At the start of the `__init__` method, we explicitly call `JFrame`'s `__init__` method. That's where we set the `title` and the `size`. We call it by saying `self.JFrame.__init__`, which is saying, "I want to call one of my parent class's `__init__` method, but call it through me, `self`, so that all references to `self` in the method are references to me." This makes sure that *this* window is the one whose `title` and `size` are set.

FIGURE 15.7: *File Contents Viewer* with text field and buttons.

■ Next comes a piece of code that we haven't seen yet: `self.contentPane.layout = java.awt.FlowLayout()`. `java.awt.FlowLayout` is a class that is one of those layout managers we mentioned earlier. To make an instance of `FlowLayout` be the layout manager for our window, we tell our `contentPane` to make its `layout` be an instance of `FlowLayout`. `FlowLayout` is not a particularly sophisticated layout manager—it simply puts one thing right after the other. (That is, at least, better than the default layout manager, which allowed things to *overlap* one another.)

The name is a little complex to understand. The name `java.awt.FlowLayout` means, "In the `java` module, find the `awt` module (a windowing toolkit—the original UI tools in Java before Swing was introduced), and use the `FlowLayout` class there." It is possible to have modules (or *libraries* or *packages*, which are other names for similar ideas) within other modules.

■ The lines of code that create the text field are similar to the ones that we saw before. We create the text file with a default size of 200 pixels wide and 60 pixels high. We put some text into it as a default value. Then we add the text field to the window's `contentPane`. Note that the `JTextField` is stored in the object's instance variable `field`. This allows methods of `FileContentsViewer` to access the field through `self.field`, and the text in the field as `self.field.text`.

■ Our first `JButton` is the one to view the content of whatever filename is typed into the field. Note that we do *not* store the button in an instance variable. We don't need to. None of the methods in `FileContentsViewer` will need to access the button after it's created. We use the normal variable `fileView` to name the button while we're setting it up, then let the variable disappear when the method ends and its context (scope) ends.

The button is named "View Contents," and has a size of 65 pixels across and 30 pixels high. (I tried others and decided that I liked this size best—do feel free to try different ones and see what you like.) The important part for us is the `actionPerformed`.

The `actionPerformed` identifies what method will be used for a *callback*. The expression `actionPerformed=self.checkContents` means "When this button is clicked, call the method on me `checkContents`." The clicking on the button (mouse down and mouse up, with the mouse pointer over the button) is referred to as a ***user interface event*** or just an ***event***. Setting up the `actionPerformed` callback sets up the linkage between the user interface event and the specific method (which appears a bit later in the program).

■ The second `JButton` that we create is to change the media folder, if you want. If you click on it, it called `self.setFolder`.

■ Finally, in the `__init__` method, we make the window visible.

■ Next comes the method `checkContents`, which is used as the callback for the "View Contents" button. *The inputs to a callback method **must** be `self,event`.* The input `self` has to be there, because this is a method. The `event` is an event object that gets passed to all the callback methods. We really don't have much control over how the callback method gets called. A callback method, by its nature, is one that we don't call from the Command Area—it's only called by Swing itself in response to a user interface event.

The event object has details about what kind of user interface event occurred. Was the mouse pressed down (called a *mouse down event*), or released after being pressed down (called a *mouse up event*)? In this example, we know that the method is being called as a callback on a button, but you could imagine the same method being used as a callback for several different buttons or other event-generating GUI elements. Then the method might need to look at the event object to figure out which event it was.

■ The checkContents method is like much of the code that we saw in the earlier chapters. We check whether the filename in the field.text ends in ".jpg" or ".wav," then we make the picture or sound and show or play it.

■ The method setFolder is the callback for the "Set Folder" method. It takes the same inputs as checkContents, because that's how callbacks are set up. But then we just execute setMediaPath.

DEBUGGING TIP: Add more fields for debugging

The fact that callbacks are only called from within the user interface makes them difficult to debug. You can't print from within them. If there's a bug in them, no errors are displayed anywhere. If there are any problems with the callback, clicking the button just does nothing. So you have to be more innovative in your debugging. What I've sometimes done is to insert an extra text field for debugging and "print" things to it as a way of checking values in the running program.

■15.4 Using Scrolling Lists

The FileContentsViewer is a pretty lousy user interface. We have to remember the file names—if we mistype them, it simply won't work. It only works with the current media folder. What if you want to look at files in several different folders? It would be nice to be able to open several file viewers at once.

We are going to build one more version of the FileContentsViewer trying to make it a little more usable. We'll open up this FileContentsViewer on a given directory, like this one: fcv = FileContentsViewer("/Users/guzdial/mediasources") This way, you can open several at once on different directories. Instead of the text field, we'll have a scrolling list of all the files in the input directory so that you can point-and-click on the filename instead of typing it in (Figure 15.8).

RECIPE 128: *File Contents Viewer* with scrolling list

```
import javax.swing as swing
import os
import java
```

FIGURE 15.8: *File Contents Viewer* with a scrolling list.

```
class FileContentsViewer(swing.JFrame):
  def __init__(self,directory):
    swing.JFrame.__init__(self, title="File Contents
Viewer", size=(210,250))
    self.contentPane.layout = java.awt.BorderLayout()

    self.currentDirectory = directory
    self.files=swing.JList(os.listdir(self.
currentDirectory))
    pane = swing.JScrollPane(self.files)
    self.contentPane.add(pane,java.awt.BorderLayout.CENTER)

    fileView = swing.JButton("View Contents", size=(65,30),
actionPerformed=self.fileView)
    self.contentPane.add(fileView, java.awt.BorderLayout.
SOUTH)
    self.pack()
    self.visible = 1

  def fileView(self,event):
    selected=self.files.getSelectedIndices()
    selectedFile = self.files.getModel( ).getElementAt
(selected[0])
    selectedFile = self.currentDirectory+ "//"+ selectedFile
    if selectedFile.endswith(".jpg"):
      pic = makePicture(selectedFile)
      show(pic)
    if selectedFile.endswith(".wav"):
      snd = makeSound(selectedFile)
      play(snd)
```

How it works: Most of this FileContentsViewer is very similar to the one in the preceding section. The difference is mainly in the scrolling pane and list that we use to show the files. The way we compose this structure is that the ***scrolling***

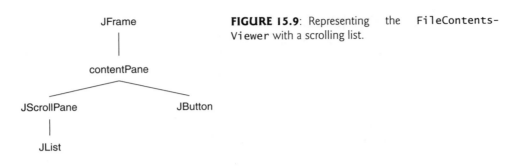

FIGURE 15.9: Representing the `FileContents-Viewer` with a scrolling list.

pane (`JScrollPane`) is added to the windows `contentPane` and the list (`JList`) is composed inside the scrolling pane (Figure 15.9). In case you want a list that does *not* scroll, Swing also gives you that option.

■ We use a different layout manager in this example. The layout manager `java.awt.BorderLayout` is smarter than the other layout managers we've seen and allows us to tell it where GUI elements should go in the window.

■ This version of `FileContentsViewer` takes in a `directory` as input. This directory is saved inside the object in an instance variable `self.directory`. We create the `JList` as `self.files`, using the list of file names from `os.listdir` on the `directory`. We create the scrolling pane `JScrollPane` as `pane` (we don't expect to ever need to access the scrolling pane after it's created), and take `self.files` (the list) as what the scrolling pane scrolls.

■ We add the scrolling pane to the window in the center (`java.awt.Border-Layout.CENTER`) of the window. `BorderLayouts` allow us to specify where we want something added.

■ We create the "View Contents" button much as we did before, but now we add it in at the bottom of the window (`java.awt.BorderLayout.SOUTH`).

■ When the button is pushed, the method `fileView` is used for callback. Now we have to figure out which button is clicked on.

  ■ We ask the list `self.files` to tell us which things are selected—`get-SelectedIndices()`. This gives a list of index numbers (zero-based). We don't really want to deal with many files selected at once, so we'll only use the first one.

  ■ We get the first index `selected[0]`, and get the element at this index, using the original list of file names that we put in the list. That original list of file names can be accessed through `getModel()` on the list.

  ■ The filename is no longer in `getMediaPath` as it was in the earlier `FileContentsViewer`. Fortunately, since we saved the input directory, we can create the whole path to the file using `self.currentDictionary + "//" + selectedFile`. Now we can make the media object and view it.

Programming Summary

Here are some of the pieces that we talked about using to program GUIs in JES.

JFrame	The class that creates windows in Java Swing. JFrame instances have contentPanes that contain their pieces and a visible flag. They know how to pack themselves using a layout manager.
JTextField	The class that creates text fields (places to show text) in Java Swing.
JButton	The class that creates buttons (things to click to generate action) in Java Swing.
JScrollPane	The class that handles scrolling for things like lists.
JList	The class that handles lists.

Problems

15.1 In our first FileContentsViewer, what do you think would happen if we did *not* provide a default value for the text? We used "barbara.jpg" in the recipe. Try making that the *empty string*, " (a string with no characters in it).

15.2 Create a file contents viewer that works by useful name rather than filename. Create a kind of FileContentsViewer where you construct a hash table associating a useful name ("Red Caterpillar on Green Leaf") with the actual path and file name. List the names in the scrolling list. When a user chooses a name, open up the corresponding file (to show or play).

15.3 Build a textual rock-scissors-paper player with a GUI. Create an RSP window with a button and a text area in it. When the user clicks the button, the computer randomly selects "rock," "scissors," or "paper" and displays that word in the text area.

15.4 Build an audio version of the rock-scissors-paper player. Record yourself saying "rock," "scissors," and "paper." Create a user interface with a single button in it. When the user clicks on the button, it randomly chooses one of the three sounds and then plays it.

To Dig Deeper

This is just the briefest overview of how to build user interfaces, and we haven't talked at all about how to do it *well*. It's fairly easy to put up a user interface. It's much harder to put up a user interface that is usable and useful. A good book on designing good user interfaces is *Human–Computer Interaction* [9]. A good book on the details of building user interfaces (and how toolkits like Swing work) is *Developing User Interfaces* [30].

CHAPTER 16

JavaScript: A Web Page Programming Language

16.1 JavaScript Syntax
16.2 JavaScript Inside of Web Pages
16.3 User Interfaces in JavaScript
16.4 Multimedia in JavaScript

Chapter Learning Objectives

■ *To see variables, iteration, and conditionals in another programming language—and to recognize them as understandable.*

■ *To be able to use a little JavaScript in Web pages.*

What do other programming languages look like? This question may be occurring to you now. You may also be champing at the bit to do some programming with things you've heard about, such as Web page programming. In this chapter, we do a little bit of each of these by introducing *JavaScript*, a programming language that can be embedded within Web pages to allow control of HTML and pieces of Web pages through programs.

■16.1 JavaScript Syntax

We call the *look* of a programming language its **syntax**. Python is a fairly traditional programming language in terms of its syntax. It doesn't look much different from Java or C++ or other languages. Languages like *Scheme* and *Smalltalk* look much more different. There are several things that you should expect to be different and that you'll need to explore when comparing the syntax (look) of different languages:

■ How do you define variables? In many languages, you must *declare* the variables and their *types* (e.g., floating point vs. integer vs. string vs. list) before you can assign them.

■ How is each line constructed? In languages like Java and C, each line must end with a semicolon.

- How are *blocks* defined? How do you group statements for loops, conditionals, and function bodies?
- How do you define functions, procedures, methods, classes, and so on?

JavaScript is meant to be a ***scripting language*** like Python. This means that it's meant to be used easily, by nonprofessional programmers, to solve relatively simple tasks. No one is going to use JavaScript to write the master calculation program for the IRS, or something that tracks all the accounts for holders of MasterCards. It's designed to *look* a lot like Java (and C), so as to make it easier to pick up for people familiar with those languages.

JavaScript can be used either to program the Web *server* or from within an HTML page. We're going to emphasize the latter. When JavaScript is inside an HTML page, it's actually executed by the browser—your browser contains a *JavaScript interpreter* (just as JES is a Python interpreter). We call this ***client-side JavaScript***.

In JavaScript, variables are supposed to be declared before use, but you don't have to specify their type. As in Python, the type will be determined based on how you use it. However, JavaScript isn't strict about this—you can simply say a = 12;. But it's more correct to *declare* the variable as something you'll be using by either typing something like var a = 12; or

```
var a;
...
a = 12;
```

JavaScript defines *blocks* using curly braces. You can use any indentation you want, but the block begins with a curly brace and ends with a close curly brace.

```
function test()
{
    document.writeln("This is a test");
}
```

We'll find many differences between Python and JavaScript when we get down to how we write individual lines.

- JavaScript ends each line with a semicolon (;). This can be a little annoying, but the trade-off is that you can now have returns in the middle of lines. You can break up lines so that they are readable to you, as long as they end with a semicolon.

```
var myvariable = (4 * x) +
                 (5 * y);
```

- JavaScript uses function instead of Python's def. Similarly, input variables are specified in parentheses after the function name. There is no colon at the end of the line.

■ JavaScript's `for` is mostly just used for numbers and has different parts to it. After the keyword `for` comes a parenthesized list of three expressions separated by semicolons. The first expression is evaluated *before* the `for` loop begins. The second expression is evaluated at the *end* of the `for` loop to see if we continue looping—if the expression is true, we keep looping. The third expression is what to do before repeating the loop. We'll see a `for` loop in Figure 16.3.

■ In JavaScript, we use `write` and `writeln` instead of Python's `print`, and instead of writing to a Command Area, we'll actually be writing to the HTML page itself.

But in a real sense, these are just details. The basic operation of JavaScript is not unlike Python. Statements are still executed one after the other, there are still variables, loops, and conditionals, and we'll still have functions and methods. All of what you knew before still applies.

JavaScript is *all* about objects. Just about every function is actually a method. There isn't a global `print`, and there's not even a global `write` or `writeln`. Instead, to write into the document, we'll use `document.write()` (or, to end the line with a newline, `document.writeln()`). The `document` here is the HTML document itself.

■16.2 JavaScript Inside of Web Pages

JavaScript sits inside of HTML pages—there is no Program Area, and no separate JavaScript files.[1] You use the tags `<script>...</script>` to embed the JavaScript into the HTML. `<script>` tags can go in two places in the HTML document. Inside the heading (`<head>...</head>`), `<script>` tags are generally used to *define* functions that will be used elsewhere. In the body of the HTML document, `<script>` tags are used to actually execute JavaScript.

Figure 16.1 shows our simple Web page from the HTML chapter with an embedded JavaScript function. The function is defined in `<script>` tags in the heading, and then is called down in the body (Figure 16.2). All this function does is insert the words "This is a test" into the document at the same place where the function call (`test()`) appears in the document just below the picture.

JavaScript functions don't have to just insert plain text. They can also insert HTML (Figure 16.3). The HTML, like the text, will be inserted where the JavaScript function is called. The interesting thing about this is that it means that the JavaScript function is called *before* the HTML is formatted. Thus it's possible to insert headings and other formatting commands into the document.

Of course, it's not too useful to simply insert text into the document that we could have simply typed ourselves. JavaScript, with extensions, can actually do database searches and insert the results into the Web page—this means that you can have Web pages that automatically get updated from a database when

---

[1] It is possible to have JavaScript in separate files, but we're not going to go into how to do that.

```
<!DOCTYPE HTML PUBLIC "-//W3C//DTD
    HTML 4.01 Transition//EN"
    "http://wwww.w3.org/TR/html4/loose.dtd">
<html>
<head>
<title>The Simplest Possible Web Page</title>
<script>
function test()
{
   document.writeln("This is a test");
}
</script>
</head>
<body>
<h1>A Simple Heading</h1>
<p>This is a very simple web page.</p>
<p><image src="mediasources/barbara.jpg" />
<script> test() </script></p>
</body>
</html>
```

FIGURE 16.1: Simple JavaScript function.

```
<script>
function test()
{
   document.writeln("This is a test");
}
</script>
</head>
<body>
<h1>A Simple Heading</h1>
<p>This is a very simple web page.</p>
<p><image src="mediasources/barbara.jpg" />
<script> test() </script></p>
```

Here's a function named "test" with no inputs, that only writes out a string.

Here we execute the function.

FIGURE 16.2: Showing the parts of the simple JavaScript function.

```
<script>
function insertHead()
{
   document.writeln("<h1>This is a test</h1>");
}
</script>
</head>
<body>
<h1>A Simple Heading</h1>
<p>This is a very simple web page.</p>
<p><image src="mediasources/barbara.jpg" />
</p>
<script> insertHead() </script>
</body>
</html>
```

FIGURE 16.3: Using JavaScript to insert HTML.

```
<html>
<head>
<title>The Simplest Possible Web Page</title>
<script>
function countToTen()
{
  document.write("<ul>");
  for (i=1; i<= 10; i++)
  {
    document.write("<li>Item number: ",i);
  }
  document.write("</ul>");
}
</script>
</head>
<body>
<h1>A Simple Heading</h1>
<p>This is a very simple web page.</p>
<p><image src="mediasources/barbara.jpg" />
</p>
<script> countToTen() </script>
</body>
</html>
```

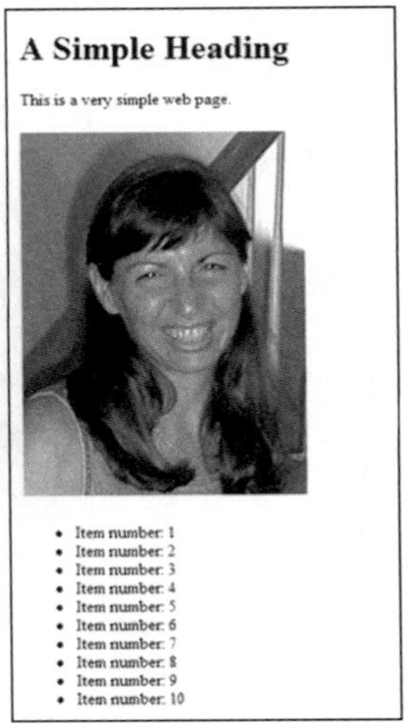

A Simple Heading

This is a very simple web page.

- Item number: 1
- Item number: 2
- Item number: 3
- Item number: 4
- Item number: 5
- Item number: 6
- Item number: 7
- Item number: 8
- Item number: 9
- Item number: 10

FIGURE 16.4: Using JavaScript to compute a loop.

```
function countToTen()
{
  document.write("<ul>");
  for (i=1; i<= 10; i++)
  {
    document.write("<li>Item number: ",i);
  }
  document.write("</ul>");
}
```

We can write out <ul> and </ul>

Creating an item for each value of i

FIGURE 16.5: Computing a list that counts to 10.

the page is served to the user (client). We can show a little bit of this flexibility here. Imagine that you had something computable that you wanted to put into a Web page, like a list from 1 to 10. Sure you could type it all in, but that would be somewhat tedious. Instead we could ask JavaScript to compute it for us (Figure 16.4).

Let's take apart this function in a little detail (Figure 16.5). The function countToTen() starts out by writing the unordered list opening <ul>, then each of the list items <li>, and then finally the list closing tag </ul>.

As we started to explain earlier, for loops in JavaScript take some explaining.

```
for (i=1; i<= 10; i++)
  {
    document.write("<li>Item number: ",i);
  }
```

for loops have three parts, separated by semicolons. The first part is what to do when the loop first starts. Here it's set the variable i to 1. Next comes how to decide when to stop. Here it's when i becomes greater than 10. Finally, there's what to do each time through the loop. Here it's

```
<p>This is a very simple web
    page.</p>
<p><image
    src="mediasources/barbara.jpg
    " />
</p>
<p>This is being served to you on
    <script>document.write(Date()
    );
</script></p>
```

FIGURE 16.6: Inserting the date and time into a Web page.

increment i by 1, using a special notation i++. This is a notation that was invented for the programming language C and has since been adopted by many other languages.

Most of the operators in JavaScript are the same ones you know from Python: +, -, *, /, <, >, >=, <=, ==, <>, != and even ! for logical not. (Like Python, + works in JavaScript to merge two strings together as well as for addition.)

You might be wondering at this point, "Okay, but can I insert anything *useful* with JavaScript?" Sure—anything you can compute. There are lots of built-in methods that give you all kinds of useful information. You don't even have to write a function—you can just list a script line in the middle of your HTML. In Figure 16.6 you can see a Web page that tells you the time when the page script was being executed.

■16.3 User Interfaces in JavaScript

JavaScript is also really useful for creating Web pages that interact with the user. Here's an example of a JavaScript function that puts up *dialogs*, little windows that interact with the user with prompts and simple buttons (Figure 16.7).

```
function check()

    var agree = false;
    agree = confirm('Do you enjoy CS?');
    if (agree)
        notes=prompt("Give me one good thing about CS:");
    if (! agree)
        notes=prompt("Why don't you like CS?");
    alert("You said:"+notes);


<script> check() </script>
</body>
</html>
```

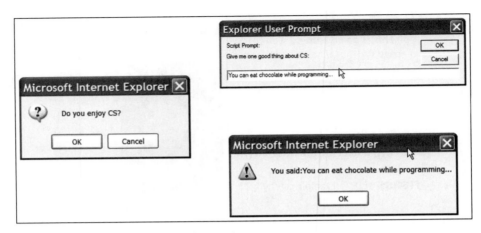

FIGURE 16.7:   Example JavaScript dialog windows.

This example uses three kinds of dialogs (exactly the same way that annoying Web pages put these up):

■ A confirm() dialog box displays a single line of text and returns true or false.

■ An alert() beeps and displays one line with an OK button. There is no return value.

■ A prompt() asks the user for one line of text, then returns that text.

This function runs when you first load the page into your browser. Is that what you really want to happen? The user goes to your page and suddenly, before any text appears, dialog boxes pop up. It's more natural to have these kinds of boxes pop up when the user clicks on something.

Events are the key to responding to users. Events are actions taken by the user that can be caught by your program in JavaScript. We say that an event *triggers* a JavaScript program. Events include the user typing a key, moving the mouse, or clicking the mouse. Example events include:

■ onKeyPress is triggered when the user presses a key and releases it.

■ onKeyDown and onKeyUp are triggered on either the downstroke or upstroke of pressing a key.

■ onClick and onDblClick are triggered on clicking or double clicking on something.

■ onMouseOver, onMouseOut, and onMouseMove are triggered when the mouse is over something, moves off of something, or moves at all when over something.

■ onMouseDown and onMouseUp are for pressing the mouse key down or back up.

■ onChange is triggered when a text field is changed.

```
<body>
<h1>A Simple Heading</h1>
<p>This is a very simple web
    page.</p>
<p><image
    src="mediasources/barbara.jpg
    " onClick='alert("You clicked
    me!")' />
</p>

</body>
```

FIGURE 16.8: Example catching the `onClick` event.

There are many more events defined in JavaScript, and some of them depend on the specific browser. Netscape Navigator has some slightly different events than Microsoft Internet Explorer, for example.

To catch an event, you assign the event to some JavaScript code in a string. Most events can be used with anchor or image tags. `onChange` can be used with text fields, as we'll see in just a few pages. Figure 16.8 is an example of catching a mouse click event on a picture, then putting up a dialog box in response.

We can use events to do all kinds of different things, including opening a window and going to a new URL in that window. We open windows in JavaScript with the `open()` function. The `open()` function takes three inputs: the URL to go to, the name of the window, and optionally, the properties of the window to change. Here's an example for opening up a separate window when an image is clicked upon (Figure 16.9).

```
<html>
<head>
<title>The Simplest Possible Web Page</title>
<script>
function goToHawaii()
{
    var win=open('http://www.cc.gatech.edu/~mark.guzdial/
 hawaii/','Hawaii');
}
</script>
</head>
<body>
<h1>A Simple Heading</h1>
<p>This is a very simple web page.</p>
<p><image src="mediasources/beach.jpg"
 onClick="goToHawaii()" />
This page was created on <script> document.write(Date());
</script></p>
</body>

</html>
```

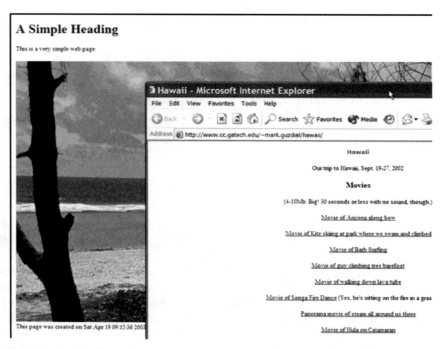

FIGURE 16.9:   Opening a JavaScript window.

Windows are objects in JavaScript. We manipulate their instance variables as ***properties***. Here's an example of changing the properties of the window as it opens (Figure 16.10).

```
<head>
<title>The Simplest Possible Web Page</title>
<script>
function goToHawaii()
{
   var
   win=open('http://www.cc.gatech.edu/~mark.guzdial/hawaii/
 ', 'Hawaii', "titlebar=no,width=200");
}
</script>
</head>
```

Windows aren't the only objects in JavaScript with useful properties to change. It turns out that even plain old list items have `style` properties, which in turn have `color` properties. We access these using *dot notation* (Figure 16.11). The current object in JavaScript is called `this`. In this example, list items start in one color, turn another when the mouse comes over them, and then another when the mouse leaves.

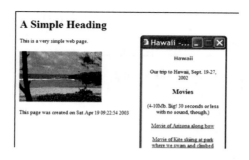

FIGURE 16.10: Changing the new JavaScript window.

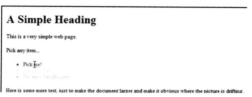

FIGURE 16.11: Changing color of list items.

```
<body> <h1>A Simple Heading</h1> <p>This is a very simple
web page.</p>
<p>Pick any item...</p>
<ul>
<li onmouseover="this.style.color='green'"
onmouseout="this.style.color='black'">Pick me!</li>
<li onmouseover="this.style.color='red'"
onmouseout="this.style.color='yellow'">No, pick me!</li>
<li onmouseover="this.style.color='magenta'"
onmouseout="this.style.color='pink'">No, no -- I'm the
one!</li>
</ul>
```

Most often, though, when we think about user interfaces, we probably think about having *fields* (places where users can type text) and *buttons* (graphical areas where the user can click). To create fields and buttons in HTML (for JavaScript to control and manipulate), we need a *form*. Forms are created with tags `<form>...</form>` (Figure 16.12). Some examples of things we can have in forms include:

■ `<input type="text" name="address1">` creates a single line text field named `address1`.

■ `<input type="button" value="Click me">` creates a button that appears on the page as `Click me`.

■ `type="textarea"` is for larger text fields with more than one line.

■ `type="radio"` is for radio buttons—those round buttons that usually appear in series where only one in a set can be selected.

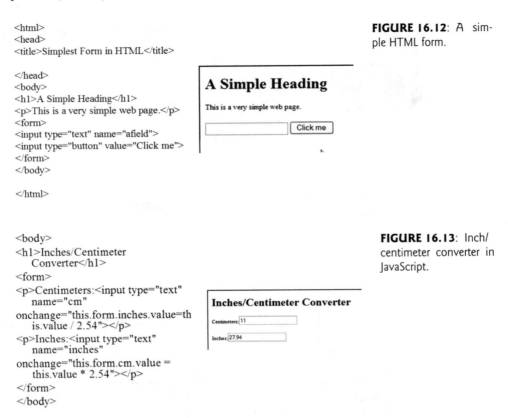

```
<html>
<head>
<title>Simplest Form in HTML</title>

</head>
<body>
<h1>A Simple Heading</h1>
<p>This is a very simple web page.</p>
<form>
<input type="text" name="afield">
<input type="button" value="Click me">
</form>
</body>

</html>
```

FIGURE 16.12: A simple HTML form.

```
<body>
<h1>Inches/Centimeter
   Converter</h1>
<form>
<p>Centimeters:<input type="text"
   name="cm"
onchange="this.form.inches.value=th
   is.value / 2.54"></p>
<p>Inches:<input type="text"
   name="inches"
onchange="this.form.cm.value =
   this.value * 2.54"></p>
</form>
</body>
```

FIGURE 16.13: Inch/centimeter converter in JavaScript.

Normally, forms are connected to URLs. Form URLs are often **_CGI scripts_**, little programs (often written in Python) that will process the form and then respond to the user with a new HTML page. Using JavaScript, we can actually do computation on forms completely from within the HTML page. Figure 16.13 is an inch-to-centimeter converter programmed in JavaScript that uses an HTML form for input. You'll notice several features of JavaScript here. The names of inputs in the form are actually properties of the form, as is the value of the text area, and all of these can be changed.

■16.4 Multimedia in JavaScript

It's possible to do multimedia programming in JavaScript, but not as we've been doing it here. There is really no way to manipulate samples or pixels from JavaScript—JavaScript deals with much higher levels of data. The most common way to deal with multimedia in JavaScript is through **_plug-ins_**. Plug-ins to browsers, like Apple QuickTime, RealVideo, and Netscape LiveAudio, can be manipulated from JavaScript.

We can do simple animations in JavaScript. There is a `setInterval()` function that can make a JavaScript function to run at regular intervals—as when we'd like an animation to update. Divisions (set up with `<div>...</div>`

tags) can be controlled with styles (note the tag at the top) that come from cascading style sheets, and they have positions. Given these two pieces, it's possible to move the picture of Barb slowly over time.

```
<html>
<head>
<title>The Simplest Possible Web Page</title>
<style>
#barb  position: absolute; left:0; top: 0;
</style>
<script>
function drift()
{
    var object = document.all.barb.style;
    object.pixelTop = object.pixelTop + 5;
    object.pixelLeft = object.pixelLeft + 5;
}
</script>
</head>
<body onLoad="setInterval('drift()',100)">
<h1>A Simple Heading</h1>
<p>This is a very simple web page.</p>
<div id="barb">
<p><image src="mediasources/barbara.jpg"  />
</p>
</div>
<p>Here is some more text, just to make the document larger
and make it obvious where the picture is drifting.
</body>

</html>
```

Okay, this is a pretty contorted example to show a pretty weak animation. JavaScript isn't really designed to do this level of programming. Rather, it's *glue* to make things work together that are already defined at a high level. It doesn't deal well with frames or pixels or samples, but it's great for telling QuickTime to play a movie or to increase the audio in RealAudio.

JavaScript is better than Python for the kind of high-level programming where you're combining things and controlling items on an HTML page. It's very powerful to be able to embed the programming inside the HTML page. But Python is a more full-featured programming language that allows you to do a wide range of things from programming servers to chromakey movies.

To Dig Deeper

There are a lot of good books on JavaScript. I recommend the ones by Danny Goodman, such as *JavaScript and DHTML Cookbook* [15].

APPENDIX A

Quick Reference to Python

■ A.1 Variables

Variables start with a letter and can be any word *except* one of the *reserved words*. These are: and, assert, break, class, continue, def, del, elif, else, except, exec, finally, for, from, global, if, import, in, is, lambda, not, or, pass, print, raise, return, try, while, yield.

We can use `print` to get a printable representation of an expression (e.g., a variable). If we simply type the variable without `print`, we get the internal representation—functions and objects tell us about where they are in memory, and strings appear with their quotes.

```
>>> x = 10
>>> print x
10
>>> x
10
>>> y='string'
>>> print y
string
>>> y
```

```
'string'
>>> p=makePicture(pickAFile())
>>> print p
Picture, filename C:\Documents and Settings\Mark Guzdial\My
Documents\mediasources\7inX95in.jpg height 684 width 504
>>> p
<media.Picture instance at 6436242>
>>> print sin(12)
-0.5365729180004349
>>> sin
<java function sin at 26510058>
```

■ A.2 Function Creation

We define functions with def. def x(a,b): defines a function named "x" that takes two input values which will be bound to variables "a" and "b." The body of the function comes after the def and is indented.

The function can return values using the return statement.

■ A.3 Loops and Conditionals

We create most of our loops using for, which takes an index variable and a list. The body of the loop is executed once for each element of the list.

```
>>> for p in [1,2,3]:
...         print p
...
1
2
3
```

The list in a for is often generated using a range function. range can take one, two, or three inputs. With one input, the range is from zero to the input. With two, the range starts at the first input and stops *before* the second. With three, the range starts at the first, takes steps of the third, and ends *before* the second.

```
>>> range(4)
[0, 1, 2, 3]
>>> range(1,4)
[1, 2, 3]
>>> range(1,4,2)
[1, 3]
```

The loop while takes a logical expression and executes its block as long as the logical expression is true.

```
>>> x = 1
>>> while x < 5:
...         print x
...         x = x + 1
...
1
```

```
2
3
4
```

A break immediately ends the current loop.

An if takes a logical expression and evaluates it. If it is true, the if's block is executed. If it is false, the else: clause is executed, if one exists.

```
>>> if a < b:
...         print "a is smaller"
... else:
...         print "b is smaller"
```

■ A.4 Operators and Representation Functions

+, -, *, /, **	Addition, subtraction, multiplication, division, and exponentiation. Order of precedence is algebraic.
<, >, ==, <=, >=	Logical operators less-than, greater-than, equal-to, less-than-or-equal, greater-than-or-equal.
< >, !=	Logical operators not-equal (both of them are equivalent).
and, or, not	Logical conjunctives and, or, and codenot.
int()	Returns the integer part of the input (floating-point number or string.)
float()	Returns a floating-point version of the input.
str()	Returns a string representation of the input.
ord()	Given an input character, returns the ASCII numeric representation.

■ A.5 Numeric Functions

abs()	Absolute value.
sin()	Sine.
cos()	Cosine.
max()	Maximum value of the inputs (including a list).
min()	Minimum value of the inputs (including a list).
len()	Returns the length of the input sequence.

■ A.6 Sequence Operations

Sequences (strings, lists, tuples) can be added together for concatenation (e.g., s1 + s2).

Elements of a sequence can be accessed using slices:

■ `seq[n]` accesses the *n*-th element of the list (the first element is zero).

■ `seq[n:m]` accesses the elements starting at the *n*-th up to *but not including* the *m*-th.

■ `seq[:m]` accesses elements from the start up to but not including the *m*-th.

■ `seq[n:]` accesses elements from the *n*-th to the end of the sequence.

■ A.7 String Escapes

`\t`	Tab character
`\b`	Backspace
`\n`	Newline
`\r`	Return
`\uXXXX`	Unicode character, hexadecimal XXXX

Precede a string with "r" as in `r"C:\mediasources"` to treat a string in raw mode, ignoring escapes.

■ A.8 Useful String Methods

■ `count(sub)`: returns the number of times `sub` appears in the string.

■ `find(sub)`: returns the index where `sub` appears in the string, or returns -1 if not found. `find` can take an optional starting point and an optional ending point. `rfind` takes the same inputs but works right to left.

■ `upper()`, `lower()`: convert the string to all upper or all lowercase.

■ `isalpha()`, `isdigit()`: return true if all the characters in the string are alphabetic or all numeric, respectively.

■ `replace(s,r)`: replaces all instances of "s" with "r" in the string.

■ `split(d)`: returns a list of sublists where the character d is the split point.

■ A.9 Files

Files are opened with **open** with two inputs: the filename and a file mode. The file mode is "r" for reading, "w" for writing, and "a" for appending, concatenated with a "t" for text or a "b" for binary.

File methods include:

■ `read()`: returns the whole file as a string.

■ `readlines()`: returns the whole file as a list of strings delimited by lines.

■ `write(s)`: writes the string s to the file.

■ **A.10** Lists

Lists are indexed like sequences using slides. They are concatenated using +.
List methods include:

- append(a): appends the item a to the list.
- remove(b): removes the item b from the list.
- sort(): sorts the list.
- reverse(): reverses the list.
- count(s): returns the number of times that the element s appears in the list.

■ **A.11** Dictionaries, Hash Tables, or Associative Arrays

Dictionaries are created with {}. They can be accessed by a key.

```
>>> d = {'cat':'Diana', 'dog':'Fido'}
>>> print d
{'cat': 'Diana', 'dog': 'Fido'}
>>> print d.keys()
['cat', 'dog']
>>> print d['cat']
Diana
```

■ **A.12** External Modules

Modules are accessed using import. They can also be input as an alias import javax.swing as swing). Specific pieces can be imported, without any need for dot notation to access them, using from module import n1, n2. All pieces of a module can be imported and accessed without dot notation using from module import *.

■ **A.13** Classes

Classes are created using the class keyword followed by the name of the class and, in parentheses, an optional superclass (one or more). Methods follow and are indented. The *constructor* method (one called when a new instance of the class is created) must be named __init__.

■ **A.14** Functional Methods

apply	Inputs a function and a list as input to the function, where the list has as many elements as the function takes as input. Calls the function on the input.
map	Inputs a function and a list of several inputs to the function. Calls the function on each of the inputs and returns a list of the outputs (**return** values).
filter	Inputs a function and a list of several inputs to the function. Calls the function on each of the list elements and returns *the input element* if the function returns true (non-zero) for that element.

reduce
Inputs a function that takes two inputs and a list of several inputs to the function. The function is applied to the first two list elements, the result of this is used as input with the next list element, then the result of this is used as input with the *next* list element, and so on. The overall result is returned at the end.

Bibliography

1. AAUW, *Tech-Savvy: Educating Girls in the New Computer Age*, American Association of University Women Education Foundation, New York, 2000.

2. HAROLD ABELSON, GERALD JAY SUSSMAN, and JULIE SUSSMAN, *Structure and Interpretation of Computer Programs*, 2d ed., MIT Press, Cambridge, MA, 1996.

3. KEN ABERNETHY and TOM ALLEN, *Exploring the Digital Domain: An Introduction to Computing with Multimedia and Networking*, PWS Publishing, Boston, 1998.

4. ACM/IEEE, *Computing Curriculum 2001*, `http://www.acm.org/sigcse/cc2001` (2001).

5. BETH ADELSON and ELLIOT SOLOWAY, "The Role of Domain Experience in Software Design," *IEEE Transactions on Software Engineering* **SE-11** (1985), no. 11, 1351–1360.

6. RICHARD BOULANGER (ed.), *The Csound Book: Perspectives in Synthesis, Sound Design, Signal Processing, and Programming*, MIT Press, Cambridge, MA, 2000.

7. AMY BRUCKMAN, "Situated Support for Learning: Storm's Weekend with Rachael," *Journal of the Learning Sciences* **9** (2000), no. 3, 329–372.

8. JOHN T. BRUER, *Schools for Thought: A Science of Learning in the Classroom*, MIT Press, Cambridge, MA, 1993.

9. ALAN J. DIX, JANET E. FINLAY, GREGORY D. ABOWD, and RUSSELL BEALE, *Human–Computer Interaction*, 2d ed., Prentice Hall, Upper Saddle River, NJ, 1998.

10. CHARLES DODGE and THOMAS A. JERSE, *Computer Music: Synthesis, Composition, and Performance*, Schimer-Thomason Learning, New York, 1997.

11. MATTHIAS FELLEISEN, ROBERT BRUCE FINDLER, MATTHEW FLATT, and SHRIRAM KRISHNA-MURTHI, *How to Design Programs: An Introduction to Programming and Computing*, MIT Press, Cambridge, MA, 2001.

12. ANN E. FLEURY, "Encapsulation and Reuse as Viewed by Java Students," *Proceedings of the 32nd SIGCSE Technical Symposium on Computer Science Education* (2001), 189–193.

13. JAMES D. FOLEY, ANDRIES VAN DAM, and STEVEN K. FEINER, *Introduction to Computer Graphics*, Addison Wesley, Reading, MA, 1993.

14. ANDREA FORTE and MARK GUZDIAL, *Computers for Communication, Not Calculation: Media as a Motivation and Context for Learning*, HICSS 2004, Big Island, HI IEEE Computer Society 2004.

15. DANNY GOODMAN, *JavaScript & DHTML Cookbook*, O'Reilly & Associates, Sebastapol, CA, 2003.

16. MARTIN GREENBERGER, "Computers and the World of the Future," Transcribed recordings of lectures at the Sloan School of Business Administration, April 1961, MIT Press, Cambridge, MA, 1962.

17. RASHI GUPTA, *Making Use of Python*, Wiley, New York, 2002.

18. MARK GUZDIAL, *Squeak: Object-Oriented Design with Multimedia Applications*, Prentice Hall, Englewood, NJ, 2001.

19. MARK GUZDIAL and KIM ROSE (eds.), *Squeak, Open Personal Computing for Multimedia*, Prentice Hall, Englewood, NJ, 2001.

20. IDIT HAREL and SEYMOUR PAPERT, "Software Design as a Learning Environment," *Interactive Learning Environments* **1** (1990), no. 1, 1–32.

21. BRIAN HARVEY, *Computer Science Logo Style*, 2d ed., vol. 1: *Symbolic Computing*, MIT Press, Cambridge, MA, 1997.

22. RICHARD HIGHTOWER, *Python Programming with the Java Class Libraries*, Addison-Wesley, Reading, MA, 2003.

23. DAN INGALLS, TED KAEHLER, JOHN MALONEY, SCOTT WALLACE, and ALAN KAY, "Back to the Future: The Story of Squeak, a Practical Smalltalk Written in Itself," *OOPSLA'97 Conference Proceedings*, ACM, Atlanta, 1997, pp. 318–326.

24. JANET KOLODNER, *Case-Based Reasoning*, Morgan Kaufmann, San Mateo, CA, 1993.

25. HEATHER PERRY, LAUREN RICH, and MARK GUZDIAL, *A CS1 Course Designed to Address Interests of Women*, pp. 190–194, ACM: New York ACM SIGCSE Conference 2004, Norfolk, VA, 2004.

26. MARGARET LIVINGSTONE, *Vision and Art: The Biology of Seeing*, Harry N. Abrams, New York, 2002.

27. FREDERIK LUNDH, *Python Standard Library*, O'Reilly and Associates, Sebastapol, CA, 2001.

28. MARK LUTZ and DAVID ASCHER, *Learning Python*, O'Reilly & Associates, Sebastopol, CA, 2003.

29. JANE MARGOLIS and ALLAN FISHER, *Unlocking the Clubhouse: Women in Computing*, MIT Press, Cambridge, MA, 2002.

30. DAN OLSEN, *Developing User Interfaces*, Morgan Kaufmann Publishers, San Mateo, CA, 1998.

31. M. RESNICK, *Turtles, Termites, and Traffic Jams: Explorations in Massively Parallel Microworlds*, MIT Press, Cambridge, MA, 1997.

32. CURTIS ROADS, *The Computer Music Tutorial*, MIT Press, Cambridge, MA, 1996.

Index